Understanding human well-being   2006

The UNU World Institute for Development Economics Research (UNU-WIDER) was established by the United Nations University as its first research and training centre and started work in Helsinki, Finland, in 1985. The purpose of the institute is to undertake applied research and policy analysis on structural changes affecting developing and transitional economies, to provide a forum for the advocacy of policies leading to robust, equitable and environmentally sustainable growth and to promote capacity-strengthening and training in the field of economic and social policy-making. Its work is carried out by staff researchers and visiting scholars in Helsinki and via networks of collaborating scholars and institutions around the world.

World Institute for Development Economics Research (UNU-WIDER)
Katajanokanlaituri 6 B, FIN-00160 Helsinki, Finland
www.wider.unu.edu

Understanding human well-being

Edited by Mark McGillivray and Matthew Clarke

TOKYO • NEW YORK • PARIS

© United Nations University, 2006

The views expressed in this publication are those of the authors and do not necessarily reflect the views of the United Nations University.

United Nations University Press
United Nations University, 53-70, Jingumae 5-chome,
Shibuya-ku, Tokyo 150-8925, Japan
Tel: +81-3-3499-2811 Fax: +81-3-3406-7345
E-mail: sales@hq.unu.edu general enquiries: press@hq.unu.edu
www.unu.edu

United Nations University Office at the United Nations, New York
2 United Nations Plaza, Room DC2-2062, New York, NY 10017, USA
Tel: +1-212-963-6387 Fax: +1-212-371-9454
E-mail: unuona@ony.unu.edu

United Nations University Press is the publishing division of the United Nations University.

Cover design by Mea Rhee

Printed in India

UNUP-1130

ISBN 92-808-1130-4

Library of Congress Cataloging-in-Publication Data

Understanding human well-being / edited by Mark McGillivray and Matthew Clarke.
   p. cm.
 Includes bibliographical references and index.
 ISBN 9280811304 (pbk.)
 1. Quality of life. 2. Social indicators. 3. Well-being. 4. Poverty. 5. Equality. I. McGillivray, Mark. II. Clarke, Matthew, Dr.
HN25.U53   2006
306.09′045—dc22   2006028858

Contents

List of figures viii

List of tables x

List of contributors xv

Foreword xix
    Anthony Shorrocks

Acknowledgements xxi

List of acronyms xxii

Introduction 1

1 Human well-being: Concepts and measures 3
    Mark McGillivray and Matthew Clarke

Part I: Human well-being concepts 17

2 Does it matter that we do not agree on the definition of poverty? A comparison of four approaches 19
    Caterina Ruggeri Laderchi, Ruhi Saith and Frances Stewart

3 Economic well-being and non-economic well-being 54
    Andrew Sumner

4 The four qualities of life: Ordering concepts and measures of
    the good life 74
    Ruut Veenhoven

5 Inequalities, agency and well-being: Conceptual linkages and
    measurement challenges in development 101
    Douglas A. Hicks

Part II: Well-being measures and applications 117

6 On the measurement of human well-being: Fuzzy-set theory
    and Sen's capability approach 119
    Mina Baliamoune-Lutz

7 Benchmarking sustainable development: A synthetic
    meta-index approach 139
    Laurens Cherchye and Timo Kuosmanen

8 Adjusting human well-being indices for gender disparity:
    Insightful empirically? 169
    Mark McGillivray and J. Ram Pillarisetti

9 Well-being and the complexity of poverty: A subjective
    well-being approach 182
    Mariano Rojas

10 International inequality in human development dimensions 207
    Mark McGillivray

11 Assessing well-being using hierarchical needs 217
    Matthew Clarke

12 Assessing poverty and inequality at a detailed regional level:
    New advances in spatial microsimulation 239
    Ann Harding, Rachel Lloyd, Anthea Bill and Anthony King

Part III: Well-being case studies 263

13 Longevity in Russia's regions: Do poverty and low public
    health spending kill? 265
    Oleksiy Ivaschenko

14 The medium- and long-term effects of an expansion of education on poverty in Côte d'Ivoire: A dynamic microsimulation study 298
   Michael Grimm

15 Dynamics of poverty in Ethiopia 326
   Arne Bigsten and Abebe Shimeles

16 Prospects for "pro-poor" growth in Africa 353
   Arne Bigsten and Abebe Shimeles

Index 377

List of figures

4.1	Four qualities of life	77
4.2	Fit with Brock's classification	83
4.3	Fit with McCall's classification	83
4.4	Meanings measured by Ware's SF-36 Health Survey	85
4.5	Meanings measured by Cummins's Comprehensive Quality of Life Scale	86
4.6	Meanings measured by Allardt's "Dimensions of Welfare"	87
4.7	Meanings measured by the UNDP's human development index	88
4.8	Inclusive measures for specific qualities of life	94
7.1	Cumulative distribution functions: Average, DEA and MISD	160
11.1	Comparison of FHNI, 1985–2000	226
11.2	Comparison of GDP per capita (1995 US$), 1985–2000	227
11.3	Comparison of HDI, 1985–2000	229
12.1	Estimated poverty rates by postcode before the policy change, Victoria and Queensland, 2001	249
12.2	Estimated change in poverty rates by postcode as a result of the policy change, Victoria and Queensland	251
12.3	Estimated number of people in poverty by postcode before the policy change, Victoria and Queensland, 2001	254
13.1	Life expectancy at birth in Russia, 1990–2000	266

13.2	Life expectancy at birth in selected regions of Russia, 1990–2000	267
13.3	Life expectancy in Russia's regions, 1998	269
13.4	Life expectancy in Russia's regions, 2000	270
13.5	Money income poverty (headcount index) in Russia's regions, 1998	278
13.6	Disposable resources poverty (headcount index) in Russia's regions, 1998	279
13.7	Public health spending per capita in Russia's regions, 1998	281
14.1	Level and inequality of household income per capita	319
14.2	Relative changes of mean household income per capita by percentiles (income in 2015 relative to REFSIM)	320
15.1	Vulnerability and chronic poverty in rural Ethiopia	349
15.2	Vulnerability and chronic poverty for urban Ethiopia	349
16.1	Per capita income and the Gini coefficient for selected African countries	355
16.2	Per capita income-inequality trade-off	362

List of tables

2.1	Nussbaum's list of features essential to full human life	32
2.2	A comparison of the four approaches to poverty	42
2.3	Monetary and capability poverty compared: Selected countries, percentage of population in poverty	45
2.4	Lack of overlaps between monetary and CA poverty	46
3.1	Evolution of the dominant meaning and measurement of well-being, 1950s–2000s	56
3.2	Most commonly used economic measures of well-being	61
3.3	Most commonly used non-economic measures of well-being	64
3.4	Commonly used composite indicators and their components	67
6.1	Parameters for computing degrees of membership	126
6.2	UNDP and fuzzy-set-based indices	128
6.3	HDI: Composite index and country ranking	130
6.4	Degrees of membership for selected human well-being components	132
7.1	Summary of selected ISDs	147
7.2	MISD rankings, high-income countries	152
7.3	MISD rankings, upper-middle-income countries	153
7.4	MISD rankings, lower-middle-income countries	154
7.5	MISD rankings, low-income countries	155
7.6	Summary statistics of MISD values, four income classes	156
7.7	Developed versus developing countries, by region	157

7.8	Summary statistics of the weights	159
7.9	Summary statistics: Average, DEA and MISD	160
7.10	MISD-ISD (Spearman rank) correlation matrix	162
8.1	Coefficients of statistical association between PPP GDP per capita and the HDI	175
8.2	Coefficients of statistical association between PPP GDP per capita, the HDI and GDI	176
8.3	Coefficients of statistical association between PPP GDP per capita, the HDI and GEM	177
8.4	Coefficients of statistical association between PPP GDP per capita, the HDI, GDI and GEM	178
9.1	Sample distribution across national deciles of income	188
9.2	Subjective well-being distribution	188
9.3	Subjective well-being and household income in percentages, simplified SWB scale	189
9.4	Subjective well-being and socio-economic position in percentages	190
9.5	Subjective well-being and access to public services in percentages	191
9.6	Correlation matrix – Socio-economic indicators and SWB	191
9.7	Regression analysis – Socio-economic indicators and SWB	192
9.8	Personal expenditure and poverty perception in percentages	193
9.9	Personal expenditure and perception of economic well-being in percentages	194
9.10	Personal expenditure and perception of degree of satisfaction of material needs in percentages	194
9.11	Satisfaction in the domains of life average and standard deviation on a 1–7 scale	196
9.12	Subjective well-being and domain satisfaction correlation coefficients	197
9.13	Socio-economic indicators and domain satisfaction regression coefficient: R^2	197
9.14	Conceptual referent for happiness sample distribution across referents	199
9.15	Subjective well-being by conceptual referent for happiness: Average and standard deviation on a 1–7 scale	200
10.1	International inequality in human development dimensions	211
10.2	International inequality in transformed human development dimensions	213

10.3	Correlations between the HDI and its component variables	214
11.1	Selected well-being outcomes and indicators that correspond to Maslow's categories of needs	221
11.2	Data	230
12.1	Estimated number in poverty and the poverty rate before and after the policy change, 2001	247
12.2	Characteristics of residents of poor households in selected postcode in NSW compared with national profile of poor and non-poor Australians (before policy change)	256
13.1	Summary statistics of the poverty data, 1994–2000	276
13.2	Summary statistics of the public health spending data, 1994–2000	280
13.3	Summary statistics of the life expectancy data, 1994–2000	282
13.4	Estimates from the life expectancy equation	282
13.5	Estimates from the life expectancy equation (with interaction term)	283
13.6	Estimates from the life expectancy equation (with a time trend)	285
13.7	Estimates from the life expectancy equation (with a time trend and alternative dependent variable)	287
13.8	Estimates from the life expectancy equation (treating explanatory variables as predetermined)	289
14.1	Illiteracy rates (population 15 years and older)	301
14.2	Enrolment ratios	301
14.3	Probit estimations of the probability of being enrolled in t conditional on the state in $t-1$ (children aged between 5 and 25 years)	304
14.4	Observed and simulated enrolment ratios in 1998	306
14.5	Activity choice and labour income model	309
14.6	Agricultural profit function	311
14.7	Summary of the policy experiments, in percentages	313
14.8	Illiteracy rate and average years of schooling (simulations 1993–2015)	315
14.9	Average years of schooling by birth cohort simulated for Côte d'Ivoire for 2015 and observed for some other countries and regions in the 1990s	316
14.10	Income, inequality and poverty (simulations 1993–2015): REFSIM in levels, other levels in percentage deviations from REFSIM and for growth rate in absolute deviations	318
15.1	Definition of variables used in the study	332
15.2	Percentage of households by poverty status, 1994–1997	333

15.3	Descriptive statistics for selected variables according to the number of years in poverty, rural households	334
15.4	Descriptive statistics for selected variables according to the number of years in poverty, urban households	334
15.5	Percentage of rural households based on permanent income and current income by region	335
15.6	Percentage of urban households based on permanent income and current income by town	336
15.7	Transition probabilities by poverty status	336
15.8	Transition probabilities by expenditure decile for rural households	337
15.9	Transition probabilities by expenditure decile for urban households	337
15.10	Exit and re-entry hazard ratios conditional on duration	338
15.11	Odds ratios for the probability of exiting poverty, rural households	338
15.12	Odds ratios of logit estimates for entering poverty, rural households	339
15.13	Odds ratios of exiting poverty, urban households	340
15.14	Odds ratios for entering poverty, urban households	341
15.15	Marginal effects for the probability of exiting poverty for rural households	342
15.16	Marginal effects for the probability of re-entering poverty for rural households	343
15.17	Odds ratio: Marginal effects for the probability of exiting poverty for urban households	344
15.18	Marginal effects of the probability of re-entry into poverty for urban households	345
15.19	Determinants of vulnerability in rural Ethiopia	346
15.20	Determinants of vulnerability in urban Ethiopia	347
15.21	Vulnerability by inter-temporal consumption expenditure decile	348
15.22	Vulnerability by inter-temporal consumption expenditure decile	348
15.23	Measures of vulnerability for rural and urban households by the status of chronic poverty	348
15.24	Logit estimate for the determinants of chronic poverty in rural Ethiopia	350
16.1	Median values of Gini coefficient by region	354
16.2	Average annual percentage change of quintile income shares and the Gini coefficient	355
16.3	Average annual growth of national and quintile per capita income	356

16.4	Pro-poor growth measure for selected African countries...	359
16.5	Ambiguity in the Kakwani-Pernia measure of pro-poor growth	361
16.6	Equity-growth "trade-off" for selected African countries	363
16.7	Simulation of the impact of pattern of growth on poverty in Ethiopia	366
16.8	Simulation of pattern of growth on poverty in Mozambique	367
16.9	Simulation of pattern of growth on poverty in Uganda	367
16.10	Simulation of growth pattern on poverty in South Africa	368

Contributors

Mina Baliamoune-Lutz is associate professor of economics at the University of North Florida. Her research focuses on human development and the effects of institutions and trade on African economies.

Arne Bigsten is professor of development economics at Göteborg University. His research has concerned income distribution, poverty and growth, trade and aid and economic policy, particularly in Africa. He has undertaken projects for, among others, the World Bank, United Nations, OECD, ILO, UNU-WIDER and SIDA.

Anthea Bill, when working on this volume, was a research officer at the University of Canberra National Centre for Social and Economic Modelling (NATSEM). She has been involved in a number of projects examining the spatial dimensions of inequality, and more specifically of labour market outcomes in Australia. She is currently completing her masters at the University of Newcastle, where she works as a research officer.

Laurens Cherchye is professor of economics at the University of Leuven, Belgium, and a post-doctoral fellow of the Fund for Scientific Research, Flanders (FWO-Vlaanderen). His research mainly deals with the non-parametric analysis of observed production and consumption behaviour. This also includes the development of methodological tools for constructing synthetic indicators of economic performance.

Matthew Clarke is the programme leader of the postgraduate International Development programme within the School of Global Studies, Social Science and Planning at RMIT University, Melbourne.

Michael Grimm is professor of economics at the University of Göttingen, Germany. He is also a research associate at the Development Economics Research Institute (DIAL) in Paris and the German Institute for Economic Research (DIW) in Berlin. He works mainly on problems related to income distribution and poverty with a regional focus on West Africa. He teaches development economics, econometrics and welfare economics.

Ann Harding is professor of applied economics and social policy at the University of Canberra and inaugural director of the University's National Centre for Social and Economic Modelling (NATSEM). Ann's key research interests are income inequality, the redistributive impacts of government programmes and microsimulation modelling.

Douglas A. Hicks is associate professor of leadership studies and religion at the Jepson School of Leadership Studies of the University of Richmond and director of the University's Bonner Center for Civic Engagement. He is author of two books, *Inequality and Christian Ethics* (2000) and *Religion and the Workplace* (2003), both published by Cambridge University Press. He is an editor, with J. Thomas Wren and Terry L. Price, of the three-volume reference work *The International Library of Leadership* (2004), published by Edward Elgar. He has written articles for journals including *Leadership Quarterly* and *World Development*.

Oleksiy Ivaschenko is an economist at the World Bank. He holds a PhD in development economics. His major areas of research include poverty and inequality analysis, geographical distribution of welfare outcomes, health economics and applied econometrics (with a particular focus on panel data analysis).

Anthony King, at the time of writing, was a principal research fellow with the University of Canberra National Centre for Social and Economic Modelling (NATSEM). His research experience has centred on the application of microsimulation modelling across a range of policy areas. He is currently manager of the Participation Modelling Project in the Australian Treasury.

Timo Kuosmanen is assistant professor in the Environmental Economics and Natural Resources Group, Wageningen University, the Netherlands, and docent at the Department of Business and Economics, University of Joensuu, Finland. He is also associate editor of the *Journal of Productivity Analysis*. His research interests focus on efficiency issues in the contexts of production, markets, environment and investment.

Rachel Lloyd is a principal research fellow at the University of Canberra National Centre for Social and Economic Modelling (NATSEM). Rachel has had a wide range of experience in microsimulation modelling and has led both the STINMOD and regional teams. Her research interests include financial disadvantage and its spatial distribution.

Mark McGillivray is a senior research fellow at UNU-WIDER in Helsinki, Finland, and an inaugural fellow of the Human Development and Capabilities Association. His research interests include the allocation and impact of development aid and human well-being achievement.

J. Ram Pillarisetti is currently a faculty member at the Department of Economics, Faculty of Business, Economics and Policy Studies, Universiti Brunei Darussalam, Bandar Seri Begawan, Brunei Darussalam and a research fellow at the Department of Economics, Faculty of Business and Economics, Monash University, Victoria, Australia. His areas of research are development and environmental economics, with a focus on sustainable development, inequality in well-being and public policy.

Mariano Rojas is professor of economics at Universidad de las Americas, Puebla, Mexico. His research focuses on well-being and conceptions of economic development, as well as on the relationship between economic variables and subjective well-being.

Caterina Ruggeri Laderchi is currently with the Africa region of the World Bank working on poverty, labour markets and internal migration with a focus on Ethiopia and Sudan. Her recent work has been published in *The Urban Poor in Latin America* and *Analyzing the Distributional Impact of Reform*.

Ruhi Saith is currently a consultant with the Rural Development Division of the Planning Commission, Government of India, and a research associate at the International Development Centre, Queen Elizabeth House, University of Oxford. Research interests include a multidimensional approach to poverty analysis, and social mobilization with self-help group formation as a model for poverty alleviation.

Abebe Shimeles is currently a PhD candidate at the Department of Economics, Göteborg University. His main research interest is poverty, income distribution and labour markets, focusing on Africa, mainly Ethiopia.

Frances Stewart is professor of development economics and director of the Centre for Research on Inequality, Human Security and Ethnicity (CRISE), Queen Elizabeth House, University of Oxford. She is a fellow of Somerville College. A former Council member of the United Nations University, she is currently a board member of the International Food Policy Research Institute and an overseer of the Thomas Watson Institute for International Studies, Brown University. Formerly director of the International Development Centre, Queen Elizabeth House, she has also been special adviser to UNICEF on adjustment (1985–1986) and one of the chief consultants for the *Human Development Report* since its inception.

Andrew Sumner is a senior lecturer at London South Bank University and a research fellow at the London School of Hygiene and Tropical Medicine. Previously he worked at the University of East London and the School of Oriental and African Studies and for NGOs in the UK and overseas. He is a council member of the Development Studies Association, UK.

Ruut Veenhoven studied sociology. He was professor of humanism at Utrecht University in the Netherlands and is currently professor of social conditions for human happiness at Erasmus University, Rotterdam, in the Netherlands. He is also director of the World Database of Happiness.

Foreword

Improving human well-being, especially the lives of the poor, lies at the heart of all the activities undertaken by academics, practitioners, community leaders and others working in the development field. But what exactly constitutes an improvement in well-being is often contentious, because the concept is ambiguous and conveys different messages to different audiences. For a long time human well-being was closely aligned to economic well-being and assessed solely in terms of income. More recently it has assumed multidimensional characteristics, perhaps best encapsulated by the attributes identified and targeted by the Millennium Development Goals.

This book is an outcome of a UNU-WIDER project on the concept and measurement of human well-being. The book contains a rigorous and comprehensive analysis of human well-being, covering both conceptual advances and empirical applications. Various aspects of well-being are considered, including conventional monetary concepts and measures; educational and health achievement; longevity; gender equality; and self-assessed and subjective well-being. Traditional indices of human well-being, such as the UNDP human development index, are examined alongside new approaches based on, for example, the fulfilment of a hierarchy of needs. Case studies are included from numerous countries and regions (both developed and developing), and many of the chapters contain explicit policy recommendations.

It is now generally accepted that improving well-being requires higher levels of income, access to education and health services, political and civil freedom and gender equality. The research in this book draws on this current broad consensus but also seeks to extend the analysis and offer new empirical results and insights. The book will be valuable reading for a wide audience, not least of all those who have devoted themselves to improving the well-being of the poor without ever being entirely sure of what this actually means.

Anthony Shorrocks
Director, UNU-WIDER

Acknowledgements

This volume originates from a UNU-WIDER research project entitled Measuring Human Well-being. The board of UNU-WIDER provided valuable suggestions during the early stages of the project. Tony Shorrocks, director of UNU-WIDER, provided considerable encouragement, advice and support throughout the life of the project. Incisive and detailed comments from anonymous referees on an earlier draft of the volume were extremely useful in shaping the final product.

Few projects can function without the considerable support of a team. The Measuring Human Well-being project is no exception, having been supported by many UNU-WIDER staff. Special thanks are due to Anne Ruohonen and Adam Swallow. Anne served as the project secretary, providing efficient and timely support and consistent good humour. Adam provided excellent and timely publications advice, handling invariably complex matters with skill and sound judgement. Thanks are also due to Barbara Fagerman, Lea Hallbäck, Maria Kauppinen, Ara Kazandjian, Bruck Tadesse and Ans Vehmaanperä.

UNU-WIDER acknowledges financial contributions to the research programme by the governments of Denmark (Royal Ministry of Foreign Affairs), Finland (Ministry for Foreign Affairs), Norway (Royal Ministry of Foreign Affairs), Sweden (Swedish International Development Cooperation Agency – SIDA) and the United Kingdom (Department for International Development – DFID).

Mark McGillivray and Matthew Clarke

Acronyms

ABS	Australian Bureau of Statistics
AIH	absolute income hypothesis
CA	capability approach
BCPs	basic community profiles
BCR	*Brundlandt Commission Report*
BEPC	Brevet d'Etudes du Premier Cycle
BN	basic needs
CCD	Census Collection District
CEPE	Certificat d'Etudes Primaires et Elementaire
CURFs	confidentialized unit record files
DEA	data envelopment analysis
DFID	Department for International Development (United Kingdom)
DNG	distribution-neutral growth
EDG	equally distributed growth
EF	ecological footprint
ENV	Enquête de Niveau de Vie
ESI	environmental sustainability index
EWI	ecosystem well-being index
FHNI	fulfilment of hierarchical needs index
FSU	former Soviet Union
FGT	Foster, Greer and Thorbecke
GEM	gender empowerment measure
GDI	gender-related development index
GDP	gross domestic product
GLS	generalized least square
GMM	generalized method of moments

GNI	gross national income
GPI	genuine progress indicator
HALE	health-adjusted life expectancy
HBS	household budget survey (Russia)
HDI	human development index
HDR	Human Development Report
HES	Household Expenditure Survey (Australia)
HIPC	highly indebted poor countries
HPI	human poverty index
HWI	human well-being index
HWB	human well-being
IAHDI	inequality-adjusted human development index
ICT	information and communication technology
INS	Institut National de la Statistique de la Côte d'Ivoire
ISD	index of sustainable development
LSMS	living standards measurement survey (Russia)
MDGs	Millennium Development Goals
MISD	meta-index of sustainable development
NATSEM	National Centre for Social and Economic Modelling (Australia)
NHS	National Health Survey (Australia)
OLS	ordinary least squares
PPA	participatory poverty assessment
PPP	purchasing power parity
PQLI	physical quality of life index
PRA	participatory rural appraisal
PRSP	poverty reduction strategy papers
QOL	quality of life
REFSIM	reference simulation
RLMS	Russian Longitudinal Monitoring Survey
SD	sustainable development
SE	social exclusion
SIHC	Survey of Income and Housing Costs (Australia)
SLA	sustainable livelihoods approach
SSA	sub-Saharan Africa
SYNAGI	Synthetic Australian Geo-demographic Information
SWB	subjective well-being
TFR	total fertility rate
UNDP	United Nations Development Programme
UNRISD	United Nations Research Institute for Social Development
VOP	Voices of the Poor
WDR	World Development Report
WEF	World Economic Forum
WHO	World Health Organization
WI	well-being index
WWF	World Wildlife Fund

Introduction

1
Human well-being: Concepts and measures

Mark McGillivray and Matthew Clarke

Introduction

Understanding human well-being is a core task for both researchers and policy-makers. Determining whether human well-being has improved over time is of crucial importance, particularly with more than 1 billion people living on less than $1 a day. It is the central challenge for monitoring progress towards the Millennium Development Goals (MDGs), adopted by the international community at the UN Millennium Summit in September 2000. Among the many MDGs are halving, between 1990 and 2015, the proportion of people living in conditions of extreme income poverty and ensuring by 2015 that all children will be able to complete a full course of primary education (UN Millennium Project Report, 2005).

Human well-being, however, is an ambiguous concept. It lacks a universally acceptable definition and has numerous, and often competing, interpretations. As human well-being cannot be directly observed, it cannot be directly measured. Further, terms such as quality of life, welfare, well-living, living standards, utility, life satisfaction, prosperity, needs fulfilment, development, empowerment, capability expansion, human development, poverty, human poverty, land and, more recently, happiness are often used interchangeably with well-being without explicit discussion as to their distinctiveness.

Conceptualization of human well-being has evolved over time. Its multidimensional nature is now commonplace in discussion, yet in only recent times human well-being was considered analogous with income and consumption levels. Much of this shift reflects Sen's (1985, 1987a, 1987b) work on capabilities and functionings, and other work such as Nussbaum's (1988, 1992, 2000) central human capabilities, Doyal and Gough's (1991) intermediate human needs and Narayan et al.'s (2000) axiological needs, among many others. Subsequently, approaches to measuring human well-being have widened to incorporate these non-economic aspects. Issues such as gender and sustainability have also become increasingly integrated within human well-being analysis.

Given this evolution, it would seem incongruous that the most common measure of human well-being is still income. Income allows individuals (and nations at the aggregate level) to increase consumption, and consumption increases utility. However, little agreement exists within the literature on how consumption might represent human well-being. Well-being has been defined as a direct function of consumption (McKenzie, 1983; Slesnick, 1998), particularly in areas of great poverty (Hueting, 1980), as a function of consumption and the environment (Islam, 1998), as a function of consumer surplus (Johnson, 1996), as a function of consumption weighted by probability of survival (Nordhaus, 1998) and as marginal propensity to consume (Islam, 2000). Yet the limitations of income-based (or consumption-based) measures of human well-being are well known, including limitations around equity, environment and its own construction (see Clarke and Islam, 2004, for a summary).

Despite these weaknesses. though, income "continues to be regarded as the 'quintessential' well-being indicator" (Dasgupta, 2001: 53). One suspects that a major reason for this is data availability and reliability. Composite indicators, such as the human development index (HDI) (UNDP, 1990) and its forerunner, the physical quality of life index (Morris, 1979), were designed to challenge the hegemony of income as the representative measure of human well-being and overcome these weaknesses. The HDI is a function of life expectancy, adult literacy, school enrolments and GDP per capita. Its purpose is to extend consideration of human development of well-being away from the economic-centric nature suggested when simply using income.

Existing largely in parallel with the aforementioned *objective* considerations of human well-being is research on *subjective* well-being (or happiness). Subjective well-being involves a multidimensional evaluation of life, including cognitive judgements of life satisfaction and affective evaluations of emotions and moods (Diener, 1984; Argyle, 1987; Diener and Larsen, 1993; Eid and Diener, 2003). Three decades ago Easterlin (1974) examined links between income and happiness and found that while individuals with higher incomes were happier than those with lower incomes at a particular point in time, the happiness of a particular cohort did not increase with income over time. Happiness levels actually remained constant despite large increases in income. Cummins (1998) has proposed a theory of subjective well-being homeostasis, in which happiness is actively controlled and maintained by a set of psychological devices that function under the control of personality. While good or bad events will cause a short-term change in subjective well-being, these psychological devices will return human well-being to previous levels. Such adaptation resulting in this stagnant trend line poses serious difficulties for public policy-makers interested in improving human well-being over time.

Integrating well-being and sustainability measures has long existed within the literature (Sametz, 1968; Nordhaus and Tobin, 1973; Zolotas, 1981). Anand and Sen (2000) view sustainability as a concern for inter-generational equity. One approach integrating sustainability measurement into human well-being measures is the genuine progress index (GPI) (Daly and Cobb, 1990). The GPI is a monetary-based index that has been designed to ascertain the impact of a growing economy on sustainable well-being. It comprises a large number of individual benefit and cost items that account for these wide-ranging impacts of economic growth, including social and environmental benefits of costs as well as the standard economic variety. Therefore, whilst the GPI embraces some national accounting values, its full calculation depends on a number of other values that normally escape market valuation. Such attempts to adjust well-being indices using sustainability measures are not without criticism (Neumayer, 1999).

Regardless of the measurement approach selected, gender must be an important consideration in both conceptualizing and measuring human well-being. Yet much of the work in the literature fails to include gender analysis explicitly. The major difficulty, though, is that gender-adjusted measures are subject to the same criticisms as the variables on which they are based (Klasen, 2004). Further, gender-adjusted indicators tend to be very highly rank-correlated with their non-specific or non-adjusted counterparts, and with other well-being indicators, including income per capita. This is not of course an argument against using gender-specific or gender-adjusted indicators, merely one for improving their accuracy and comparability.

Given such an array of conceptualizations and approaches to measurement, how can one adequately make sense of human well-being? Various data are now widely published, often for large country samples. The UNDP, in its *Human Development Report 2004*, publishes data on life expectancy, adult literacy and school enrolment ratios for 177 countries; the *World Development Indicators* (World Bank, 2005) contains around 800 indicators for over 150 countries; and the *World Happiness Database* (Veenhoven, 2004) contains 2,300 surveys in 112 nations, dating from

1946 to the present. Concerns remain, however, about the reliability and comparability of many of these indicators. Most of the widely used social indicators are based on information obtained from national censuses. Yet many countries, especially the poorest, do not have the resources to conduct accurate censuses. No country conducts a yearly national census and some countries conduct them at irregular intervals. Data for the intervening years have to be estimated. Given these and a number of methodological problems, the data tend to be incomparable both between countries at a given point in time and within given countries over time; data can therefore be difficult to interpret, especially if a number of indicators of human well-being (such as in the MDGs) are being considered. But the compelling need to understand human well-being requires the use of these indicators, despite these weaknesses, as well as continuously improving both the conceptualization and the empirical estimation of human well-being.

Volume orientation and contents

Despite all these clear and obvious difficulties in assessing human well-being, this task is crucial. Improving human well-being, especially of the poor, must be and remain a central task for all public policy-makers. Even if the concept can be directly observed and metrically measured, attempts to assess public policy against this test of improving well-being are required. We now know more about human well-being and the related concepts of poverty and inequality than ever before, as a result of conceptual and methodological advances and better data. Yet despite this progress, the vitality of underlying concepts and the quality of data are repeatedly challenged and there remains much to be desired, particularly with regard to the world's poorest countries.

This book looks at advances in underlying well-being concepts and corresponding empirical measures and highly various analytical approaches. Its orientation is largely consistent with the view that well-being is multidimensional. Identifying an exhaustive list of dimensions is no easy task. Getting general agreement on the list and the relative importance of each component would appear to be an impossible one. It follows that identifying an exhaustive list of measures that all could agree on is also an impossible task. But there would appear to be general agreement that this list would include measures of health, education and income. Income is the most contentious of these variables, and many will argue that it is the least important. But it would appear to be difficult to argue that it is irrelevant and that it should be ignored altogether in the assessment and analysis of achieved well-being. The international community certainly does not subscribe to this view, given that reducing income poverty has been included among the MDGs.

The book therefore examines traditional monetary concepts and measurements along with concepts and measures in non-income spheres, including educational achievement, longevity, health and self-assessed or subjective well-being. Among the measures examined are the indices produced by the UNDP, including the well-known HDI, one of many non-exclusively monetary measures that have done much to refocus attention on the importance of non-monetary measures of human well-being.

Some of the book's chapters are purely conceptual, some are empirical and others a mix of the two. Some chapters review pre-existing concepts and measures, with a view of future developments, while others propose new measures or adjustments to pre-existing ones. Others provide case-study material relating to a mix of developing, transitional or developed countries.

This book is divided into three parts. Part I contains four chapters, each focusing on human well-being concepts. The seven chapters in part II provide various measures and empirical applications of human well-being, while part III includes four human well-being case studies.

Chapter 2 by Caterina Ruggeri Laderchi, Ruhi Saith and Frances Stewart asks whether it is important for general agreement around definitions of poverty to exist within the literature. While there is worldwide agreement on poverty reduction as an overriding goal of development policy, there is little agreement on the definition of poverty. Four approaches to the definition and measurement of poverty are reviewed in this chapter: the monetary, capability, social exclusion and participatory approaches. The theoretical underpinnings of the various measures and problems of operationalizing them are pointed out. The authors argue that each is a construction of reality, involving numerous judgements which are often not transparent. The different methods have different implications for policy, and also, to the extent that they point to different people as being poor, for targeting.

Andrew Sumner discusses the measurement of poverty and well-being in chapter 3. He provides a historical overview of the last 50 years. This is followed by discussion of three groupings of indicators: those measures based primarily on economic well-being, those based on non-economic well-being and composite indicators. Sumner argues that the choice of indicator should reflect its purpose and that economic measures are best when quick, rough-and-ready, short-run, aggregate inferences are required. In contrast, non-economic measures are better when greater depth regarding medium- or longer-term trends and/or disaggregation are required.

Human well-being is conceptualized as four simultaneous qualities of life by Ruut Veenhoven in chapter 4. The terms "quality of life", "well-being" and "happiness" denote different meanings; sometimes they are used as an umbrella term for all of value, and at other times to denote special merits. This chapter is about the specific meanings of the terms. It proposes a classification based on two bi-partitions; between life "chances" and life "results", and between "outer" and "inner" qualities. Together these dichotomies imply four qualities of life: liveability of the environment, life-ability of the individual, external utility of life and inner appreciation of life. This fourfold matrix can be applied in three ways: first to place related notions and alternative classifications, second to explore substantive meanings in various measures for quality of life and third to find out whether quality of life can be measured comprehensively.

The final chapter in part I, by Douglas A. Hicks, is concerned with inequalities, agency and well-being. Sen's (1985, 1987a, 1987b) capabilities approach has emphasized that inequalities can be analysed in various dimensions of human functioning. Indicators of these inequalities can be incorporated into assessments of well-being. The capabilities approach also highlights the intrinsic importance of agency and demonstrates empirically that agency is instrumentally valuable for achieving various functionings. This chapter draws together these discussions to delineate the relationships among inequalities, agency and well-being of disadvantaged persons. Relative deprivation (e.g. being illiterate or being in ill health) negatively affects a person's well-being and contributes to a lack of agency. Conversely, some (but not all) expressions of agency by disadvantaged persons can help reduce inequalities. This model provides a complex understanding of the dynamics of deprivation – and its alleviation.

In the first chapter of part II, Mina Baliamoune-Lutz introduces a fuzzy-set theory approach to measurement of human well-being. Baliamoune-Lutz suggests that Sen's (1985, 1987a, 1987b) influential work on human development has led economists to explore new areas that have become increasingly important for human well-being. In particular, Sen emphasizes the importance of the "freedom to choose". Freedom, however, is not always an exact (crisp) outcome, and membership in the freedom space can take place gradually. This chapter proposes a framework that uses fuzzy-set theory to measure human well-being consistent with Sen's capability approach.

The need for monitoring countries' overall performance in sustainable development is discussed by Laurens Cherchye and Timo Kuosmanen in chapter 7. While the need for sustainable development is widely recognized, the methods for aggregating vast amounts of empirical data remain rather crude. This chapter examines the so-called "benefit-of-the-doubt" weighting method as a tool for identifying benchmarks without imposing strong normative judgement about sustainable development priorities. The weighting method involves linear optimization techniques, and allows countries to emphasize and prioritize those sustainable development aspects in which they perform relatively well. Using this method, Cherchye and Kuosmanen construct a meta-index of sustainable development (MISD), which combines 14 existing aggregate sustainable development indices (developed by well-established organizations and/or expert teams) into a single synthesizing overall sustainable development index. Within a sample of 154 countries, this index identifies 6 benchmark countries (3 high-income countries and 3 upper-middle-income countries), but also a number of seriously underperforming countries. They view this approach as a first step towards more systematic international comparisons aimed at facilitating diffusion of the best practices and policies from the benchmark countries to the less developed world.

Chapter 8, by Mark McGillivray and J. Ram Pillarisetti, looks at the issue of adjusting well-being indicators for gender disparities. It is specifically concerned with the gender-related development index (GDI) and gender empowerment measure (GEM), composite indicators initially proposed by the UNDP in its *Human Development Report 1995*. It considers the extent to which these indices provide insights, with respect to country rankings, which pre-existing, non-gender-specific development indicators cannot provide. The latter indicators are PPP GDP per capita and the HDI.

Chapter 9, by Mariano Rojas, investigates human well-being from a subjective well-being approach. Using a Mexican database, Rojas shows that there is a weak relationship between subjective well-being and indicators of well-being such as income and consumption. Therefore, subjective well-being provides additional useful information to study human well-being and, in consequence, poverty. Three reasons for the existence of a weak relationship are studied: first, the fact that a person is much more than a consumer; second, the role of heterogeneity in human perceptions; and third, the existence of heterogeneity in purposes of life. Rojas argues that understanding and reducing poverty would be better served by a concept of human well-being which incorporates subjective well-being indicators and is based on the wholeness and complexity of human beings.

International inequality in well-being is examined by Mark McGillivray in chapter 10. Inter-country inequality in per capita income has been extensively researched over many decades. The literature on this topic is vast. A smaller but steadily growing number of studies have examined inequality among countries in multidimensional well-being. Most of these studies have looked at inequality in the HDI. Chapter 10 contributes to this literature. It examines HDI inequality among more than 170 countries over the period 1997–2002 using a number of different inequality measures. Unlike previous studies, McGillivray also looks at inequality in each of the HDI's components and PPP GDP per capita, asking whether they tell more of a story with respect to inequality than the index as a whole.

Matthew Clarke applies a hierarchical approach to measuring human well-being to eight South-East Asian countries in chapter 11. This hierarchical approach is underpinned by a rigorous psychological theory of human motivation (Maslow, 1970). Hierarchical human needs are classified into five categories: basic, safety, belonging, self-esteem and self-actualization. Within this chapter well-being is defined as a function of the extent to which society facilitates the attainment or fulfilment of the ultimate hierarchical need: self-actualization. Clarke operationalizes this approach by identifying outcomes and indicators that represent or correspond to the four lower levels of needs upon which the achievement of self-actualization is predicated. Eight indicators have been chosen to reflect these four hierarchical categories. A composite indicator of these eight indicators is calculated using an approach similar to that of the HDI. Weights are also assigned to the different levels within this hierarchy to reflect the shift from minimally adequate standards to higher levels of well-being within nations. The countries surveyed for the period 1985–2000 are Cambodia, Indonesia, Lao PDR, Malaysia, the Philippines, Singapore, Thailand and Viet Nam. Results for Australia are also provided as a comparative benchmark.

The Australian experience is discussed in chapter 12 by Ann Harding, Rachel Lloyd, Anthea Bill and Anthony King. In recent years new spatial microsimulation techniques, involving the creation of synthetic data about the socio-economic characteristics of households at a detailed regional level, have been developed. The data are potentially available at any level of geographic aggregation, down to the level of the census collection district within Australia (about 200 households). This chapter describes the results of initial attempts to link the new database to an existing static microsimulation model of taxes and transfers in Australia, so that the spatial impact upon poverty and inequality of possible policy changes can be assessed. This chapter then outlines the new techniques used to create the synthetic household microdata and demonstrates how they can be used to analyse poverty rates, the spatial impact of possible policy change and the characteristics of the poor by geographic area.

Four case studies of human well-being are presented in part III. A number of these case studies look at income measures, in part due to reasons of data availability. In chapter 13 Oleksiy Ivaschenko discusses longevity in the regions of Russia, examining the impact of changes in poverty and public health spending on intertemporal variations in longevity using a unique regional-level dataset that covers 77 regions of Russia over the period 1994–2000. A dynamic panel data model is used as a tool for the empirical analysis. The model is estimated using the Arellano-Bond dynamic panel data estimator.

Michael Grimm uses a dynamic microsimulation model to analyse the distributional effects of an expansion of education in Côte d'Ivoire in the medium and long term in chapter 14. The simulations are performed in order to replicate several policies in force or subject to debate in this country. Various hypotheses concerning the evolution of returns to education and labour demand are tested. The direct effects between education and income as well as the different transmission channels, such as occupational choices, fertility and household composition, are analysed.

Chapter 15, by Arne Bigsten and Abebe Shimeles, addresses issues related to the dynamics of income poverty using unique household panel data for urban and rural areas of Ethiopia for the period 1994–1997. Household characteristics that are correlated with the incidence of chronic poverty as well as vulnerability to poverty are highlighted. In chapter 16 they discuss which poverty reduction strategies are appropriate in rural areas compared to urban areas. Bigsten and Shimeles also discuss prospects for "pro-poor" growth in Africa. They examine trends in income distribution and its linkages to economic growth and poverty reduction in order to understand the prospects for achieving poverty reduction in Africa. They then examine the levels and trends in income distribution in some African countries and calculate pro-poor growth indices. Different growth patterns are simulated for Ethiopia, Mozambique, South Africa and Uganda.

Key conclusions

The chapters in this book provide a number of insights which will be useful to both researchers and policy-makers. Within part I, Ruggeri Laderchi, Saith and Stewart conclude that the definition of poverty does matter for poverty eradication strategies. Sumner's review of the literature highlights that whilst conceptualization of human well-being is very rich, its empirical operationalization is still lagging behind. He notes this is largely a function of data and suggests that a suite of measures would be a better way of assessing improvements in human well-being. The conclusion reached by Veenhoven is that whilst it is better to distinguish four distinct life qualities rather than quality of life, it is not possible, nor does it makes sense, to try to aggregate these qualities in any numerical way. He finds that the best available summary indicator of human well-being is how long and happily a person lives. Hicks finds that improving the human well-being of the poor is best served by equipping these same people to be agents of their own development. This involves increasing the effectiveness of social structures, which will require addressing inequality across an array of dimensions.

In part II, in terms of applying measures of human well-being, Baliamoune-Lutz concludes that the HDI and human well-being, when measured using fuzzy sets, yield different country rankings with significantly different levels of well-being for some countries. Thus she finds it is important to bear in mind that preferences and choices underlying both objective and subjective indicators of human well-being are vague; and that such vagueness can have major implications for the outcome of social and economic policies.

Cherchye and Kuosmanen show that measures of sustainable development can be benchmarked and comparative analysis between countries is possible. McGillivray and Pillarisetti conclude that, depending on the test statistic under consideration, there is some evidence that the GDI and GEM are, in an empirical sense, genuinely insightful indicators.

Rojas's chapter on well-being and the complexity of poverty highlights that not only are subjective well-being and socio-economic well-being different concepts, but they are not strongly correlated either. He concludes that subjective well-being indicators are important as they provide new information, beyond what traditional socio-economic indicators can provide. In discussing international inequality, McGillivray finds that the HDI and its components exhibit remarkably similar levels of inequality among countries but, as expected, much lower inequality than income per capita.

Clarke concludes that whilst a general increase of well-being based on the attainment of hierarchical needs is recorded across 8 countries in South-East Asia over the past 16 years, these improvements are much less (and often stagnant) than increases in well-being measured by single-dimension indicators, such as GDP per capita. He argues that policy-makers must consider hierarchical human needs and motivation when seeking to improve well-being through economic and social development activities.

The chapter on modelling poverty and inequality in Australia by Harding et al. found that restoring the social security rate paid to recipient couples to the same level paid to pensioner couples would reduce overall poverty in Australia by 0.3 per cent and reduce child poverty by 0.5 per cent. They suggest that their new model is useful for policy-makers in order to understand the different characteristics of those in poverty in different geographic areas.

The breadth of geographical reach makes the results of part III particularly interesting. The empirical results of Ivaschenko's chapter for the regions of Russia indicate that while male life expectancy responds more strongly than female life expectancy to economic circumstances, the latter appears to be more predisposed to the influence of public health spending. The results support the idea that the (positive) effect of public health spending on life expectancy is larger for those regions that experience higher incidences of poverty. The chapter also finds that the financial crisis which hit Russia at the end of 1998 had a significant negative effect on longevity independently of the factors directly related to poverty and public health spending.

Grimm finds the effects of educational expansion on the growth of household incomes, their distribution and poverty in Cote d'Ivoire depend very crucially on the hypothesis made on the evolution of returns to education and labour demand. For example, if returns to education remain constant and the labour market segments, the effects will be very modest.

In their study of poverty in Ethiopia, Bigsten and Shimeles find that the percentage of households remaining in poverty was twice as large in urban areas as in rural areas. This suggests that income variability is a serious problem in rural areas, while persistence is a key feature of urban poverty. In Bigsten and Shimeles's second contribution, on the possibility of pro-poor growth in Africa, they find that the balance between policies aimed at growth and measures aimed at redistribution should depend on the elasticity of the growth-equity trade-off.

The topics covered in this book provide a good illustration of the range of current research on both the conceptualization and the empirical measurement of multidimensional human well-being. It is hoped that these chapters will stimulate further research along similar lines.

REFERENCES

Anand, S. and A. Sen (2000) "Human Development and Economic Sustainability", *World Development* 28(12): 2029–2049.
Argyle, M. (1987) *The Psychology of Happiness*, London: Routledge.
Clarke, M. and S. Islam (2004) *Economic Growth and Social Well-being: Operationalising Normative Social Choice Theory*, Amsterdam: North Holland.
Cummins, R. A. (1998) "The Second Approximation to an International Standard of Life Satisfaction", *Social Indicators Research* 43: 307–334.
Daly, H. and J. Cobb (1990) *For the Common Good*, Boston, Mass.: Beacon Press.
Dasgupta, P. (2001) *Human Well-being and the Natural Environment*, Oxford: Oxford University Press.

Diener, E. (1984) "Subjective Well-being", *Psychological Bulletin* 95: 542–575.

Diener, E. and R. J. Larsen (1993) "The Experience of Emotional Well-being", in M. Lewis and J. M. Haviland, eds, *Handbook of Emotions*, New York: Guilford.

Doyal, L. and I. Gough (1991) *A Theory of Need*, London: Macmillan.

Easterlin, R. A. (1974) "Does Economic Growth Improve the Human Lot? Some Empirical Evidence", in P. A. David and M. W. Reder, eds, *Nations and Households in Economic Growth. Essays in Honour of Moses Abramovitz*, New York: Academic Press.

Eid, M. and E. Diener (2003) "Global Judgements of Subjective Well-being: Situational Variability and Long-term Stability", *Social Indicators Research* 65: 245–277.

Hueting, R. (1980) *New Scarcity and Economic Growth* (translated by T. Preston), Amsterdam: North Holland.

Islam, S. (1998) "Ecology and Optimal Economic Growth", paper presented at the Fifth Biennial Meeting of the International Society for Ecological Economists, Santiago, 15–19 November, unpublished.

—— (2000) "Applied Welfare Economics: Measurement and Analysis of Social Welfare by Econometric Consumption Models", mimeo, CSES, Victoria University, Melbourne.

Johnson, D. (1996) *Poverty, Inequality and Social Welfare in Australia*, Heidelberg: Physica-Verleg.

Klasen, S. (2004) "Gender-related Indicators of Well-Being", paper presented at the Twenty-eighth General Conference of the International Association for Research in Income and Wealth, Cork, 22–28 August, unpublished.

Maslow, A. (1970) *The Farther Reaches of the Human Mind*, New York: Viking Press.

McKenzie, G. (1983) *Measuring Economic Welfare*, Cambridge: Cambridge University Press.

Morris, M. (1979) *Measuring the Condition of the World's Poor: The Physical Quality of Life Index*, New York: Pergamon.

Narayan, D., R. Chambers, M. K. Shah and P. Petesch (2000) *Voices of the Poor: Crying Out for Change*, New York: Oxford University Press for the World Bank.

Neumayer, E. (1999) "The ISEW: Not an Index of Sustainable Economic Welfare", *Social Indicators Research* 48: 77–101.

Nordhaus, W. (1998) *The Health of Nations: Irving Fisher and the Contribution of Improved Longevity to Living Standards*, Cowles Foundation Discussion Paper No. 1200, New Haven: Cowles Foundation for Research in Economics.

Nordhaus, W. and J. Tobin (1973) "Is Growth Obsolete?", in M. Moss, ed., *The Measurement of Economic and Social Performance*, NBER, Studies in Income and Wealth 38, New York: Columbia University Press.

Nussbaum, M. C. (1988) "Nature, Function and Capability", *Oxford Studies in Ancient Philosophy*, Supplement 1: 145–184.

—— (1992) "Human Functioning and Social Justice", *Political Theory* 20(2): 202–246.

—— (2000) *Women and Human Development: The Capabilities Approach*, Cambridge: Cambridge University Press.
Sametz, A. (1968) "Production of Goods and Services: The Measurements of Economic Growth", in E. Sheldon and W. Moore, eds, *Indicators of Social Change*, New York: Russell Sage Foundation.
Sen, A. (1985) *Commodities and Capabilities*, Amsterdam: North Holland.
—— (1987a) "The Standard of Living: Lecture I, Concepts and Critiques", in G. Hawthorn, ed., *The Standard of Living*, Cambridge: Cambridge University Press.
—— (1987b) "The Standard of Living: Lecture II, Lives and Capabilities", in G. Hawthorn, ed., *The Standard of Living*, Cambridge: Cambridge University Press.
Slesnick, D. (1998) "Empirical Approaches to the Measurement of Welfare", *Journal of Economic Literature*, 36(December): 2108–2165.
UNDP (1990) *Human Development Report*, New York: Oxford University Press.
—— (1995) *Human Development Report 1995*, New York: Oxford University Press.
—— (2004) *Human Development Report 2004*, New York: Oxford University Press.
UN Millennium Project Report (2005) *Investing in Development: A Practical Plan for Achieving the Millennium Development Goals*, New York: UNDP.
Veenhoven, R. (2004) *World Happiness Database*, available from www.eur.nl/fsw/research/ happiness.
World Bank (2005) *World Development Indicators 2005*, Washington, D.C.: World Bank.
Zolotas, X. (1981) *Economic Growth and Declining Social Welfare*, New York: New York University Press.

Part I
Human well-being concepts

2
Does it matter that we do not agree on the definition of poverty? A comparison of four approaches

Caterina Ruggeri Laderchi, Ruhi Saith and Frances Stewart

Introduction

The elimination of poverty is a key concern of all those interested in the development of poor countries, and now provides the main justification for promoting economic growth and development. The central objective of the Millennium Development Goals, agreed by 149 countries at the UN Millennium Summit in New York, is the halving of poverty by 2015. In official discourse, such as by the World Bank and major donors, almost every policy is currently assessed in relation to its impact on poverty, ranging from debt relief to macroeconomic stabilization. Ironically, while the objective of poverty reduction currently has overwhelming support, particularly among the donor community, there is increasing debate about what this objective means.

To devise policies to reduce poverty effectively, it is important to know at what we are aiming. The current approach to the identification of poverty and policy formulation is rather messy: on the one hand, there is acknowledgement of its multidimensionality, combined with a pick-and-choose approach in advocacy with little consistency across studies; on the other hand, in practice the monetary approach mostly retains its dominance in descriptions and analysis, both nationally and internationally. Clarification of how poverty is defined is extremely important, as different definitions imply the use of different indicators for measurement: they may lead to the identification of different individuals and groups as poor and require different policies for poverty reduction. This chapter illustrates this by presenting a theoretical and an empirical comparison of different approaches to poverty. It concentrates on four alternative understandings of poverty: the monetary approach, the capabilities approach, social exclusion as defining poverty and the participatory approach.

Different interpretations of reality translate into different poverty measures. These differences, in part, reflect different views of what constitutes a good society and good lives. The main purpose in this chapter is to explore these differences and their implications, rather than assessing their merit. It is the authors' view that clearer and more transparent definitions of poverty are essential prerequisites of any development policy that puts poverty reduction at its centre. Current policy discourse has embraced broad multinational conceptualizations of poverty (e.g. the *World Development Report 2000/01*). The chapter aims to show that there may be tensions between the different dimensions considered, and that clarity is needed in understanding where these tensions lie and how such multidimensionality can be translated into measurement. Some issues common to any approach to the definition and measurement of poverty are discussed in the next section. This is followed by a theoretical comparison of the four approaches. The fourth section briefly presents some empirical findings on the extent to which the differences matter in practice. The final section reflects on some implications of the findings.

Common problems encountered in defining and measuring poverty

A number of general questions about how to define and measure poverty apply to all approaches, many of which were already apparent in the pioneering work of Rowntree (1902) in the late-nineteenth and early-twentieth centuries. It is helpful to discuss these in general terms before giving a detailed discussion of different approaches.

Firstly, a fundamental issue – which underlies the differences in the approaches considered here – is the *space* in which deprivation or poverty is defined and how that space is captured by the indicators chosen. Different poverty definitions span different "spheres of concerns", not all of which may be easily measured. For example, should the definition of poverty be confined to material aspects of life, or include social, cultural and political aspects? Is poverty to be measured in the space of utility or resources (broadly adopted by different versions of the monetary approach) or in terms of the freedom to live the life one values (as in the capabilities approach)? And for any approach what type of indicators should be used? For example, should indicators capture what *may be* achieved, given the resources available and the prevailing environment – that is, the *ability* to be and do a variety of things – or what *is actually* achieved by individuals?

Secondly, there is the question of the *universality* of the definition of poverty. Should we expect definitions and measurement indicators applied in one type of society to be transferable to other societies without serious modifications, or even at all? Two of the approaches considered (the monetary approach and social exclusion) were initially devised for developed countries. In each there are problems in translating their application to developing countries: in the monetary approach, for example, this involves heroic imputations of values for subsistence production; in social exclusion, substantial differences in societal norms lead to major differences in the defining characteristics of social exclusion. In contrast, the capabilities approach and participatory methods were first devised with developing countries in mind, and the reverse question applies. Here again it is clear that the interpretation of the approaches will differ between societies with radically different characteristics – this is not just a matter of developed versus developing countries, but also other major societal differences (e.g. between socialist and capitalist societies). To some extent methods are context-specific, and may need to be reinterpreted for particular societies for operationalization, which can make comparisons across contexts problematic.

Thirdly, there is the question of whether methods are "objective" or "subjective". Most statements about poverty suggest objectivity, i.e. it is implied that there is a certain reality "out there" which poverty statistics capture. To the extent that value judgements affect measurement, the methods are not objective, and the question then is who is making the value judgements: are they made implicitly by the researchers or statisticians who are measuring poverty? Are they made explicitly, and subject to sensitivity analysis, so that the effects of those value judgements can readily be evaluated? To what extent are they understood and shared by other stakeholders; for example through the political process or through a participatory process involving the poor themselves?

Fourthly, a crucial question is how to discriminate the poor from the non-poor through the use of poverty lines. Two related issues arise: firstly, what is the justification for adopting any such line; and secondly, to what extent is the poverty line defined as relative to a given context or intended to reflect some absolute standards of deprivation?

At a theoretical level, the choice of a definition of poverty relies on the crucial assumption that there is some form of discontinuity between the poor and the non-poor that can be reflected in the poverty line. Such a break can pertain to the behaviour of the poor, or to some salient feature that identifies the poor and that either moral or political considerations suggest should be addressed. For example, one approach, justified on political or moral grounds, is to define the poverty line at a level at which people can realize a full or decent life. Essentially, rights-based approaches to poverty do this, and similar concerns animate the capability approaches (e.g. Nussbaum, 2000). Expenditure requirements to ensure minimal nutrition are generally taken to be the fundamental break in the monetary approach (see below). Other types of "natural" breaks can be found: for example, evidence on the importance of social networks for provision of informal insurance and support mechanisms, as well as from participatory research, suggests there is a "break" in levels of resources below which people are considered unworthy of community support as they would not be able to reciprocate their obligations if needed (see e.g. Howard and Millard, 1997).

Considerable attention has been devoted to the issue of whether the threshold between the poor and non-poor should be sensitive to the characteristics of the overall population. At one extreme, the poverty line between poor and non-poor is defined with reference to some summary measure of the overall wealth distribution (as in the case of the member states of the European Union, where the poverty line is set at 60 per cent of the median of "equivalized" income). At the other extreme, a poverty line is set in terms of minimal requirements in the dimension of interest identified in absolute terms – for example on the basis of some needs of the individual deemed as essential for survival.

In reality it is difficult, perhaps impossible, to identify such absolute needs irrespective of societal standards. For example, in the era before the advent of writing, literacy could not be identified as an absolute requirement, yet now any definition of capability poverty would include this dimension. Further, most apparently "absolute" indicators of poverty contain some relative element, reflecting the need to maintain the relevance of a given definition over time. For example, although he did not take an explicitly relative approach in his second study of York in the 1930s, Rowntree updated his minimum requirements for people to be non-poor to include having a bath and a garden. Sen has pointed out that even if requirements can be set as absolute in terms of needs anchored to some standards with intrinsic value, they would generally need to be interpreted as relative in terms of resources. For example, if poverty is defined in absolute terms in relation to nutritional requirements, it is likely to some extent to be relative in income terms, since in richer societies people generally need more money to acquire the same nutrition – as cheaper foods are not available, transport is needed to shop and so on.

A fifth issue concerns the *unit* over which poverty is defined – this is partly a question of whether poverty is defined at the level of the individual or the family, and also a matter of the geographical unit of analysis. While it is individuals who suffer or enjoy their lives, data, particularly of a monetary kind, normally pertain to households, and some resources (not only money income, but also sanitation and clean water) come via the household and it is difficult to ascertain the benefits they provide to the individual. The geographic unit matters in three ways: firstly, for identifying the society with respect to which the relative poverty lines are drawn; secondly, for defining the boundaries of the relevant market – for example, to obtain prices for valuations; and thirdly, in terms of targeting, since when geographic areas are used for targeting, how the areas are defined will affect the efficiency of targeting.

Sixthly, a pervasive question is how to deal with multidimensionality: considering that individual well-being (and lack of it) manifests itself in multiple dimensions, should an aggregate index be developed, and if so how? The issue can be bypassed in a monetary approach by assuming that the monetary metric either captures the essence of deprivation or proxies all other deprivations. The proxying role of the monetary measures is reinforced to the extent that relevant heterogeneity between individuals can be adjusted for, so monetary resources become comparable across individuals. The other approaches, however, incorporate what Sen labels the constitutive plurality of a welfare assessment and therefore do not present themselves in the form of a single index. These approaches raise two questions: how each constituent dimension is to be measured, and how they are to be aggregated. Any aggregation requires a decision on whether and how the severity of deprivation in each of the basic dimensions should be included. Aggregation is helpful to summarize societal deprivation. However, in general there is no right way of aggregating. By definition aggregation implies a loss of information, whose influence on the final results should be appropriately tested for.

Seventhly, the time horizon over which poverty is identified needs to be defined. This is commonly viewed as a technical issue concerning the period of time over which poverty should be measured, i.e. over a month, a year or a longer time. Many people move in and out of poverty over seasons and years, thus the longer the time perspective the less poverty will appear. Yet short-run fluctuations are of particular interest if they entail far-reaching consequences for the most vulnerable individuals (consider childhood poverty's consequences for future physical and cognitive development). If poor households are credit and insurance constrained, and therefore unable to adopt income and consumption smoothing strategies (Morduch, 1995), there is a case for shorter time periods that allow a greater differentiation between the chronic poor (variously defined as those always below a poverty line, or those on average below a poverty line; Hulme and Shepherd, 2003) and the transitory poor. These considerations, however, do not apply to all approaches equally, as some capability and social exclusion measures, though observed at one point in time, by their nature indicate long-term deprivation either because they have long-term consequences (e.g. child malnutrition as revealed by low height for age) or because they are structural (e.g. some correlate of social exclusion, such as race).

Another aspect of the time horizon chosen relates to the concept of *lifetime* poverty. This could be seen as a statistical question concerning which and how many individuals are chronically poor throughout their lives. But it could also be approached in terms of life decisions: what critical decisions or circumstances in a person's life – pre-birth, in their early childhood, in their school years or as an adult, for example – led to lifetime poverty (or avoided it). This approach could be useful for causal and policy analysis.

Finally, there is a general question about the extent to which a definition of poverty offers (or should offer) a causal explanation for poverty, pointing to policies towards its alleviation. Some of the approaches are built on causal analysis, while others aim only at providing a description. The authors believe, however, that even such descriptive exercises influence the broad thrust of policy-making. This issue will be revisited in the concluding section.

An overview of the four approaches

The monetary approach

As noted, the monetary approach to the identification and measurement of poverty is the most commonly used. It identifies poverty with a shortfall in consumption (or income) from some poverty line, all measured in monetary values. The valuation of the different components of income or consumption is done at market prices, which requires identification of the relevant market and the imputation of monetary values for those items that are not valued through the market, such as subsistence production and, in principle, public goods (Grosh and Glewwe, 2000). The assumptions needed for such imputation are generally somewhat heroic. The key assumption of this way of proceeding is that, with appropriately devised tools, uniform monetary metrics can take into account all the relevant heterogeneity across individuals and their situations.

For economists, the appeal of the monetary approach lies in its being compatible with the utility-maximizing behaviour assumption that underpins microeconomics, i.e. that the objective of consumers is to maximize utility and that expenditures reflect the marginal value or utility people place on commodities. Welfare can then be measured as the total consumption enjoyed, proxied by either expenditure or income data, and poverty is defined as a shortfall below some minimum level of resources, which is termed the poverty line.

The validity of the approach then depends in part on:
- whether utility is an adequate definition of well-being
- whether monetary expenditure is a satisfactory measure of utility
- whether a shortfall in utility encompasses all we mean by poverty
- the justification for a particular poverty line.

The use of a monetary approach to poverty can, however, be justified in two quite different ways. First is the minimum-rights approach, where a certain basic income is regarded as a right without reference to utility but rather for the freedom of choice it provides (Atkinson, 1989; van Parijs, 1992). This view has not gained much following and faces many of the same problems as the welfare-based view, for example in determining the level of basic income to be chosen as a universal right. Secondly, the use of a monetary indicator is often invoked *not* because monetary resources measure utility, but because it is assumed it can appropriately proxy other aspects of welfare and poverty. In this view, while lack of resources does not exhaust the definition of poverty, monetary indicators represent a convenient short-cut method, based on data that are widely available, to identify those who are poor in many fundamental dimensions, not only in lack of resources but also nutrition, health, etc. Empirical investigations are needed to explore the validity of this assumption (see the next section).

Some outstanding issues concerning definition and measurement of monetary poverty

The modern monetary approach contains many elements already present in early analyses, especially Rowntree's method of identifying the poverty line (Booth, 1887; Rowntree, 1902). None the less, there have been many methodological advances in the development and standardization of this approach to measurement (e.g. Grosh and Glewwe, 2000), although some issues remain contentious, leading to theoretical and methodological choices that undermine the claims to objectivity of this approach.

The welfare indicator

Monetary poverty is arguably better measured by consumption data as these approximate welfare more closely than income (Deaton, 1997). Consumption also comes closer to a measure of long-term income, avoiding some of the short-term fluctuations in income and access to resources – under the assumption, of course, that individuals have access to credit and saving instruments. On the basis of a minimum-rights perspective, however, a case has been made for the use of income (Atkinson, 1989). It is theoretically possible to incorporate measures of non-marketed goods and services in estimates of either consumption (which is approximated by expenditure data, sometimes with adjustments for the use of services from durables) or income. In practice, however, these measures almost invariably include only *private* resources, and omit *social* income (i.e. a variety of goods and services provided publicly, e.g. schools, clinics, the environment). This can lead to a bias in the identification of the poor for targeting purposes towards those lacking private income, and an implicit bias in policy choices in favour of the generation of private income as against public goods provision.

The monetary poverty line
A key issue, noted earlier, is how to differentiate the poor and non-poor, and whether there is an objective way of doing so. In the case of the monetary approach, various technical solutions have been suggested for this differentiation, notwithstanding the fuzziness of the theoretical framework that underlies it. At a fundamental level, in fact, problems in identifying a poverty line stem from the fact that there is no theory of poverty that would clearly differentiate the poor from the non-poor.

Relative poverty lines can be determined by political consensus. In fact, in many developed countries a pragmatic way of determining the poverty line is to define those deprived as those who receive support from public sources. Atkinson (1989, 1998) has written extensively against this practice in the UK, pointing out that considering the poor as those who are entitled to social security benefits leaves this identification at the mercy of budgetary decisions.

Attempts to find an objective basis for an absolute poverty line aim at identifying behavioural breaks between the poor and non-poor. Issues of the nutritional needs for survival, and/or efficiency wages, provide the most common basis for such a break. An efficiency-wage argument has been made by Dasgupta (1993) and others (see Lewis and Ulph, 1998). Yet there are considerable ambiguities about what constitutes an efficiency wage and questions about whether this should be applied to those outside the workforce (e.g. the old or disabled), and the approach also raises the moral question of the appropriateness of defining poverty in such an instrumental way.

Ravallion (1998) has suggested that the poverty line should be defined as the "minimum cost of the poverty level of utility". Yet this does not get one much further, as the concept of a "minimum level of utility" is itself not well defined. More emphasis is given to the methodological (rather than the theoretical) issue of how to calculate this minimum. Ravallion suggests two methods for approaching this issue: one is the food energy intake method, which essentially amounts to a nutritionally based poverty line; the other is a "cost of basic needs" line, either starting with food and adding a non-food component (a method similar to Rowntree's), or starting with a list of basic needs (which of course themselves need to be defined) and costing them.

For the most part, nutritional requirements form the fundamental justification of, and practical basis for, defining the poverty line in the monetary approach. Yet there are problems about nutritionally based poverty lines. Differing metabolic rates, activities, size, gender and age among people mean that what is adequate varies among them (Sukhatme, 1982, 1989; Dasgupta, 1993; Payne, 1993). Then differing tastes, food availability and prices affect how much money income is needed to secure any particular level of nutrition. Moreover, poverty lines are often drawn up at the level of the household, yet the way resources are distributed within the household affects the nutrition levels of individuals within it (see later). All this suggests that it is not possible to draw up a unique poverty line based on nutritional requirements, but rather a range of income, from a minimum line below which everyone is certainly in poverty to a line above which no one would be in poverty, in nutritional terms. Such a practice is akin to the fairly common approach of adopting two poverty lines, identifying "poverty" and "extreme poverty". Lipton (1988), for example, has argued that there is a natural break in behaviour justifying a distinction between what he calls the "poor" and the "ultra-poor", defining the latter as households spending at least 80 per cent of their income on food, yet receiving less than 80 per cent of their calorie requirements. He argues that empirical work identifies 80 per cent as a maximum that people can spend on food because of other essential needs. However, some have questioned whether the 80/80 lines hold, and whether there is such a natural break that is universally valid (Anand, Harris and Linton, 1993). Others have used household perceptions to differentiate poverty and core poverty (see Clark and Qizilbash, 2002).

Individuals versus households
Economists' approach to welfare is essentially individualistic: welfare pertains to individuals, hence poverty (as a welfare shortfall) is a characteristic of individuals too. Income and consumption data, however, are normally collected by household, so that some adjustment is needed in translating household resources into individual poverty. Such an adjustment has three aspects: one is to estimate the needs of different individ-

uals; the second is to estimate the extent of economies of scale enjoyed; and the third is to consider how household resources are allocated to the different individuals within the household.

The issue of estimating individual resource needs involves both theoretical and practical problems. If a minimum-rights perspective is adopted and all individuals have the same rights, then it would be wrong to weight individual needs differently. However, if those rights are seen as relating not to resources but to outcomes (e.g. the right to a certain standard of living, or the right to certain achievements in terms of nutrition), or alternatively one adopts a utility-based perspective, adjustments that take different individual characteristics into account are justified.

In order to take into account both differences in needs and economies of scale in consumption, equivalence scales (defined as the "ratio of the cost [to a household] of achieving some particular standard of living, given its demographic composition, to the cost of a 'reference' household achieving that same standard of living") can be used (Banks and Johnson, 1993). Though this definition of equivalence scales assumes that they can be calculated by reference to observed behaviour, in practice there are considerable variations in the estimates, which are sensitive to the specific methods adopted. It should be noted that equivalence scale calculations are typically based on patterns of consumption of the "average" household, and do not fully take into account power or bargaining considerations which appear to play a role in the way resources are allocated within the household.

The importance of various adjustments for the empirical estimation of poverty has recently been illustrated powerfully by Szekely et al. (2000), who have shown that the poverty rate varies between 13 and 66 per cent of the population in 17 Latin American countries according to the methods adopted towards calculating equivalence scales, assumptions about the existence of economies of scale in household consumption, methods for treating missing or zero incomes and adjustments to handle misreporting. Given the magnitude of this variance, adopting stochastic dominance techniques (Atkinson and Bourguignon, 1987) to test the robustness of poverty estimates to varying assumptions on where the poverty line is set or how differences in needs are taken into account, as suggested by Lipton and Ravallion (1993), would indicate that many monetary estimates of poverty are not robust.

Aggregation issues
The issue of how to translate the identification of poverty at an individual level into an aggregate value is linked closely to the literature on social valuation. Following Sen's (1976) pioneering contribution, which applied a similar approach to poverty measurement to that used in the measure-

ment of inequality, the literature generally adopts an axiomatic approach to setting the desirable properties of a poverty index. Foster, Greer and Thorbecke (1984) made a fundamental contribution (FGT) offering a general formulation, including a valuation parameter of choice, alpha, which incorporates some of the most widely used indices.

It has become standard practice to compute FGT indices for values of alpha ranging from 0 to 2 in order to test the sensitivity of the poverty assessment to the distribution of resources among the poor.

Some conclusions on the monetary approach

At a theoretical level it has been shown that different theoretical interpretations underpin this approach. All of them have their weaknesses. The welfarist view, for example, assumes that all relevant heterogeneity between individuals can be controlled for, but this requires rather strong assumptions. Further, this approach disregards social resources that are of great importance in determining individual achievements in some fundamental dimensions of human well-being, such as health and nutrition. The alternative rights-based approach also fails to capture effective achievements in terms of human lives.

While the monetary approach has benefited from significant methodological developments in terms of measurement, these technical adjustments require numerous value judgements. Despite their apparent "scientificity", the estimates of poverty the approach provides are thus open to question – an example is the recent debate on the $1 a day poverty line (Reddy and Pogge, 2002; Ravallion, 2002). It should be noted that while many of the methodological elements which are part of a monetary poverty assessment are derived from economic theory (e.g. the literature on equivalence scales), poverty in itself is *not* an economic category. Though efforts have been made to identify natural breaks between poor and non-poor based on some behavioural characteristics, none is fully satisfactory in pointing to a unique poverty line.

It has also been emphasized that this approach is fundamentally addressed to *individual* achievements; social interactions and interdependencies are considered only from the mechanical point of view of appropriately scaling household resources to take into account different household structures.

The value judgements that form an intrinsic aspect of much of the methodology – for example, about what should constitute an essential consumption basket – like many other aspects of the methodology, are generally performed "externally", i.e. without the involvement of poor people themselves.

The three other approaches to deprivation reviewed in this chapter address some of the perceived defects of the monetary approach.

The capability approach

According to Sen (1985, 1997, 1999), who pioneered this approach, development should be seen as the expansion of human capabilities, not the maximization of utility or its proxy, money income. The capability approach (CA) rejects monetary income as its measure of well-being, and instead focuses on indicators of the freedom to live a "valued" life. In this framework, poverty is defined as deprivation in the space of capabilities, or failure to achieve certain minimal or basic capabilities, where "basic capabilities" are "the ability to satisfy certain crucially important functionings up to certain minimally adequate levels" (Sen, 1993: 41).

The CA constitutes an alternative way of conceptualizing individual behaviour, assessing well-being and identifying policy objectives, based on the rejection of utilitarianism as the measure of welfare and of utility maximization as a behavioural assumption (Sen, 1993). It is rooted in a critique of the ethical foundations of utilitarianism. It is argued that the only defensible basis for a utilitarian approach is to ground it in a concept of utility interpreted as "desire fulfilment". This implies letting individuals' mental disposition play a critical role in social evaluation while neglecting aspects such as their physical condition which influence their quality of life. As a result, people can be "satisfied" with what is a very deprived state (e.g. ill health, termed "physical condition neglect"), while their desires are constrained by what seems possible (described as "valuation neglect"). Furthermore, choices are affected by the social context not only in terms of its influence on expectations but also through strategic interactions, making observed behaviour in the market of dubious value for social valuation (Sen, 1985).

In the CA well-being is seen as the freedom of individuals to live lives that are valued (termed the capabilities of the individual), i.e. the realization of human potential. This emphasis on the "outcomes" characterizing the quality of life of individuals implies a shift away from monetary indicators (which at best can represent indirect measures of those outcomes) and a focus on non-monetary indicators for evaluating well-being or deprivation. Monetary resources are considered only as a means of enhancing well-being, rather than as the outcome of interest. Monetary resources may not be a reliable indicator of capability outcomes because of differences individuals face in transforming resources into valuable achievements (*functionings*), differences which depend on individual characteristics (e.g. differences between individuals in terms of metabolic rates; differences between able-bodied and handicapped individuals) or differences in the contexts individuals live in (e.g. differences between living in areas where basic public services are provided and areas where such services are absent). If the emphasis is on final outcomes, poverty (and more generally well-being) assessments should take into account the fact that some people need more resources than others to obtain the same achievements. The emphasis is therefore put on the idea of *adequacy* of monetary and other resources for the achievement of certain capabilities rather than their *sufficiency*, and the roles of externalities and social goods are brought into the picture as other influences over capabilities.

With their income individuals acquire commodities, and the utilization of these commodities' characteristics and those of publicly provided goods and services allows individuals to achieve certain functionings. Besides private monetary income and publicly provided goods and services, an individual's own personal characteristics (including age, gender and physical capacities) and the general environmental context help determine the capability set of the individual and the use made of this set, or the individual's functionings. Monetary resources, therefore, remain instrumentally related to the achievement of well-being (or, conversely, poverty), but do not exhaust the causal chain.

Operational issues in measuring poverty as capability failure

Translating the CA into an operational framework for poverty evaluation requires one to deal with several issues. Most fundamental is the definition of basic capabilities and of the levels of achievement that are to be considered essential.

Defining basic capabilities

In his work Sen does not provide a specific list of minimally essential capabilities (though he suggests that basic concerns such as being well-nourished, avoiding preventable morbidity, etc. should be part of such a list) nor guidelines for drawing up a universal list. Alkire (2002) has argued that the lack of specification was deliberate in order to allow room for choice across societies and ensure the relevance of the approach to different persons and cultures.

The problem of identification of basic capabilities is similar to that of the identification of basic needs (BN). Doyal and Gough (1991) attempted to define an objective and non-culturally sensitive list of BN using avoiding serious harm as a fundamental criterion. They include physical health and autonomy (which covers a person's level of understanding, mental health and a range of opportunities) as BN. Satisfiers to achieve these needs, or the actual goods and services required, are argued to vary across societies. Several attempts have been made specifically to define basic capabilities. The most influential is Nussbaum, who has argued that there is an "overlapping consensus" between different societies on the conception of a human being and what is needed to be fully human.

Table 2.1 Nussbaum's list of features essential to full human life

---
Life: normal length of life
Health: good health, adequate nutrition and shelter
Bodily integrity: movement; choice in reproduction
Senses: imagination and thought, informed by education
Emotions: attachments
Practical reasons: critical reflection and planning life
Affiliation: social interaction; protection against discrimination
Other species: respect for and living with other species
Play
Control over one's environment, politically (choice) and materially (property)

Source: Nussbaum (2000).

She hopes to arrive at a theory that is not "the mere projection of local preferences but is fully international and a basis for cross-cultural attunement" (Nussbaum, 2000: 74).

As can be seen from table 2.1, Nussbaum's list represents a Western late-twentieth-century conception of the "good life", raising doubts over its ability to reflect a genuine "overlapping consensus". Moreover, Nussbaum's list defines characteristics of a full human life at a very general level, and does not specify cut-off points for defining deprivation. Other attempts to define the essential capabilities have been conducted by Alkire (2002), Desai (1995) and Qizilbash (1998). Each arrives at similar lists. These lists and practical applications of the CA, e.g. by Drèze and Sen (1995), generally interpret the minimal essential capabilities as being constituted by health, nutrition and education – broadly the same as the list of basic needs identified in BN approaches (see e.g. Stewart, 1985; Streeten et al., 1981); Stewart (1995) further explores the differences between BN and the CA.

Measurement of capabilities

A second issue in making a CA to poverty operational is the translation of the concept of capabilities (i.e. all the possible achievements an individual may have, which together constitute the capability set) into something measurable. The crucial issue is, of course, that capabilities represent a set of *potential* outcomes and as such are difficult to identify empirically. Arguably, however, if the capabilities considered are basic enough individuals will not be willing to forgo them, so assessing their actual achievements, or functionings, should reveal the constraints they face. The identification of the capability set with the set of achieved functionings can be conceptualized as performing the evaluation of a set through one of its elements, in much the same way as economists value budget sets by considering the bundle of goods chosen (Sen and Foster,

1997); but this risks losing the key insight of the CA, which is its emphasis on freedom. In practice there has been a strong tendency to measure functionings rather than capabilities (i.e. life expectancy, morbidity, literacy, nutrition levels) in both micro and macro assessments. Using functionings makes the approach virtually identical to the BN approach in the measurement of poverty.

The poverty line
As in the other approaches, there is a need to identify breaks in the distribution of capabilities to differentiate the poor and non-poor. The choice of such breaks – which is necessary for each capability separately – appears to be context-dependent and somewhat arbitrary. The human poverty index developed by the UNDP can be taken as an example, since the concept of "human poverty" was primarily derived from the CA. The UNDP defined human poverty as "deprivation in three essential elements of human life – longevity, knowledge and decent standard of living" (UNDP, 1997: 18). The indicators adopted in the 2001 *Human Development Report* for the three elements were having less than 40 years' life expectancy at birth; adult illiteracy; and an average of not using improved water sources and under-five mortality (UNDP, 2001). It is clear that both choice of dimensions and cut-off standards are arbitrary and are likely to be revised according to the general standards attained in the world, the region or the country where poverty assessments are being made. This is exemplified by the fact that the UNDP adopted a different human poverty index for developed countries that includes life expectancy of below 60, lack of functional literacy among adults, the long-term unemployment rate and the population below an income poverty line of 50 per cent of median disposable household income in the country being assessed. Whether a universal conception of poverty from a CA perspective can be reconciled with changing measures has not been much discussed (Ruggeri Laderchi, 2001a).

Aggregation
The multidimensional emphasis of the capability framework makes the issue of aggregation particularly pertinent. It is arguable that since each of the different capabilities is intrinsically valuable, no trade-offs between achievements in one or other dimensions should be introduced. This severely limits the type of aggregative strategies that can be adopted. Yet aggregation can be desirable for political purposes and to reduce a large amount of information to manageable proportions (e.g. for inter-country comparisons). For policy purposes, fully aggregative strategies (i.e. those which arrive at full orderings by providing explicit trade-offs in terms of achievement in each dimension) are likely to be more useful than strat-

egies that arrive at only partial orderings (consider the case of having to identify regions to be given priority for poverty alleviation expenditure). Such fully aggregative strategies include, for example, the use of factor analysis to obtain data-driven weights in aggregating deprivations, fuzzy-sets applications, Borda rankings or the more familiar averages (popularized by the work done by the UNDP in constructing its human development and human poverty indices), to quote those methods that have been commonly used in a CA context. Using the concepts of union (a comprehensive approach by which an individual deprived in any dimension is considered poor) or intersection (an overlapping approach by which only individuals deprived in *all* dimensions are considered to be poor) is also a possible approach to aggregation.

A further issue is whether and how the severity of deprivation in each of the basic dimensions should form part of the aggregation procedures. Bourguignon and Chakravarty (2003), for example, provide a formula that allows for varying rates of trade-off across dimensions. Individuals' deprivations in each dimension can be weighted by the *distance* from each cut-off line, for example, differentiating and giving more weight to the extremely malnourished as against the malnourished.

Some conclusions on the capability approach

The CA represents a major contribution to poverty analysis because it provides a coherent framework for defining poverty in the context of the lives people live and the freedoms they enjoy. This approach draws attention to a much wider range of causes of poverty and options for policies than the monetary approach. The shift from the private resources to which individuals have access to the type of life they can lead addresses the neglect of social goods in the monetary approach and its narrow vision of human well-being. Yet, like the monetary approach, arriving at operational measures poses a number of methodological choices. Though decisions on these are also somewhat arbitrary, the choices made are arguably more visible, and therefore more easily subject to scrutiny, than in the monetary approach.

There are some features common to the CA and the monetary approach. Firstly, in principle both approaches take an individualistic perspective since both utility deprivation and capability failure are characteristics of individuals, even though, in both cases, communities and households are important determinants of achievements, especially for children and the old. Secondly, both typically represent external assessments, though in principle, as will be suggested later, both could be adapted to include more internal inputs. Thirdly, neither approach captures fundamental causes or dynamics of poverty. Fourthly, they aim to describe the situation at a point in time, providing data for, but not themselves directly involving, fundamental analysis of the causes of poverty, although some studies, of course, do follow up measurement with investigations of the causes of, or processes leading to, monetary and/or capability poverty (Dhatt and Ravallion, 1998; Baker, 1997). Both social exclusion and participatory approaches differ from the monetary and capability approaches in each of these respects.

Social exclusion

The concept of social exclusion (SE) was developed in industrialized countries to describe the processes of marginalization and deprivation that can arise even in rich countries with comprehensive welfare provisions. It was a reminder of the multiple faces of deprivation in an affluent society. The concept now forms a central aspect of EU social policy; several European Council decisions (starting with one at the Lisbon Council of March 2000) have adopted strategic goals and political processes aimed at countering the risk of poverty and SE. The concept of SE has been gradually extended to developing countries through the activities of various UN agencies (especially the International Labour Institute) and the Social Summit (Clert, 1999).

The European Union defines SE as a "process through which individuals or groups are wholly or partially excluded from full participation in the society in which they live" (European Foundation, 1995). This echoes the earlier work of Townsend, who defined deprivation as referring to people who "are *in effect excluded* from ordinary living patterns, customs and activities" (Townsend, 1979: 31, emphasis added). More precisely, Burchardt, Le Grand and Piachaud (1999) defined SE as occurring when a person is resident in society; but for reasons beyond his/her control cannot participate in normal activities of citizens in that society; and would like to do so. Others have argued that a person is excluded if the first two conditions hold, whether or not they actually desire to participate (Barry, 1998).

Atkinson (1998) identified three main characteristics of SE: *relativity* (i.e. exclusion is relative to a particular society); *agency* (i.e. people are excluded as a result of the action of an agent or agents); and *dynamics* (meaning that future prospects are relevant as well as current circumstances) (Micklewright, 2002). Room (1999) concurs with the relational and dynamic aspects and adds three others: the multidimensionality of SE; a neighbourhood dimension (i.e. that communal facilities are deficient or absent); and that major discontinuities are involved.

The dynamic focus and an emphasis on the processes that engender deprivation are distinguishing features of this approach compared to those reviewed earlier. It has been noted, for example, that SE is "a dynamic process, best described as descending levels: some disadvantages lead to some exclusion, which in turn leads to more disadvantages and more exclusion and ends up with persistent multiple (deprivation) disadvantages" (Eurostat Taskforce, 1998: 25). While the other approaches can study causes and interconnections between different elements of deprivation, such investigation is not part of the process of identifying the poor. In contrast, the *definition* of SE typically includes the process of becoming poor as well as some outcomes of deprivation.

SE also contrasts with the two previous approaches in making a social perspective central – that is to say SE is socially defined, and is often a characteristic of groups (e.g. aged, handicapped, racial or ethnic categories) rather than pertaining to individuals. This relational emphasis opens up a different policy agenda from the individualistic approaches: policies addressed to groups, such as eliminating discrimination and various forms of affirmative action. While other approaches can be extended to include these considerations, such as studies of vulnerability in a monetary perspective, SE is the only approach where these considerations play a constitutive role.

Multidimensionality is an intrinsic feature of SE. Indeed, being deprived in more than one, and perhaps many, dimensions is a key feature of SE, which raises aggregation issues similar to those of the CA. Furthermore, empirical work points to causal connections between different dimensions of exclusion, such as between employment and income; housing and employment; and formal sector employment and insurance. SE generally is found to have a strong connection with monetary poverty. For example, lack of monetary income is both an outcome of SE (arising from lack of employment) and a cause (e.g. of social isolation and low wealth).

In order to apply SE empirically to particular societies, these general statements about SE need to be interpreted more specifically. The precise characteristics of SE tend to be society-specific, since they identify exclusion from *normal* activities. The concept of SE thus necessarily involves a *relative* approach to the definition of poverty. In industrial countries the indicators adopted in empirical work normally include unemployment, access to housing, minimal income and social contacts and lack of citizenship or democratic rights.

The application of the concept of exclusion to developing countries raises difficult issues. Characteristics of SE here are likely to be different from those in developed countries. On the one hand, the defining features noted by Atkinson (1998) and Room (1999) are clearly highly relevant. On the other hand, it is difficult to identify appropriate norms to provide the benchmarks of exclusion, since exclusion from formal sector employment and social insurance coverage tends to apply to the majority of the population. Lack of these therefore does not imply exclusion from normal social patterns or relationships. To the extent that the normal may not be desirable, what is "normal" may not be satisfactory in defining the benchmarks of exclusion. Consequently there is a serious problem in deciding what would be appropriate SE characteristics. A further complication is that exclusion, as with the caste system, is part of the social system in some societies. Various solutions to the interpretation of SE in particular societies are possible: one is to take norms from *outside* the society, say from developed countries. Some work on the marginalization of societies in the process of globalization implicitly does just that (Room, 1999). Another is to derive the characteristics through consultation in participatory approaches. A third approach is to derive the characteristics empirically, by exploring what structural characteristics of a population (such as race, caste or region) are empirically correlated with multiple deprivations identified in other approaches. Empirical work in developing countries has adopted a variety of approaches to the definition of SE. It mostly takes definitions that seem relevant to the reality being studied, without providing much justification for their particular choice and rarely making any explicit reference to what is actually normal in the society (see e.g. Appasamy, Guhan and Hema, 1996; Cartaya, Magallanes and Dominiquez, 1997; Rodgers, Gore and Figueiredo, 1995).

Some conclusions on SE

SE is perhaps the least well defined and most difficult to interpret of the concepts of deprivation under review. Indeed, according to Micklewright (2002: 7), "exclusion is a concept that defies clear definition and measurement". Problems of definition are especially great in applying the concept to developing countries because "normality" is particularly difficult to define in multipolar societies, and because there can be a conflict between what is normal and what is desirable. The question of whether there exist relevant discontinuities also arises in a particularly difficult form, since the characteristics defining SE are society-specific and researchers in each country need to devise their own methods for identifying dimensions and appropriate breaks.

None the less, the approach is the only one that focuses intrinsically, rather than as an add-on, on the processes and dynamics that allow deprivation to arise and persist. Moreover, the analysis of exclusion lends itself to the study of structural characteristics of society and the situation of groups (e.g. ethnic minorities or the landless) that can generate and characterize exclusion, whereas the two individualistic approaches (monetary and CA) tend rather to focus on individual characteristics and circumstances. SE also leads to a focus on distributional issues – the situation of those deprived relative to the norm generally *cannot* improve without some redistribution of opportunities and outcomes – whereas monetary poverty (defined in absolute terms) and capability poverty can be reduced through growth without redistribution. The agency aspect of SE, noted by Atkinson (1998), also points to *excluders* as well as the *excluded*, with the main responsibility for improving the situation being on the former – again a contrast to the monetary and capability approaches that describe a world without analysing or attributing responsibility.

Participatory methods

Conventional poverty estimates, including both monetary and capability estimates, have been criticized for being *externally* imposed, and for not taking into account the views of poor people themselves. The participatory approach – pioneered by Chambers (1994, 1997) – aims to change this and get people themselves to participate in decisions about what it means to be poor and the magnitude of poverty. The practice of participatory poverty assessments (PPAs) evolved from participatory rural appraisal (PRA), defined as "a growing family of approaches and methods to enable local people to share, enhance and analyze their knowledge of life and conditions, to plan and to act" (Chambers 1994: 57).

Initially intended for small projects, PPAs were scaled up by the World Bank as a complement to their poverty assessments. An extensive multi-country exercise (23 countries) was carried out as background to the World Bank's 2000/01 *World Development Report* and published as *Voices of the Poor* (Narayan-Parker and Patel, 2000). Poverty reduction strategy papers (PRSPs) of the World Bank and the IMF, which form an important element in World Bank and IMF lending to poor countries, have further institutionalized the use of participatory methods.

Cornwall (2000) differentiates three types of PPA:
- those associated with self-determination and empowerment
- those associated with increasing the efficiency of programmes
- those emphasizing mutual learning.

The use of participatory exercises by the World Bank, especially in its poverty assessments, has tended to be instrumental, adopting PPAs primarily so that the poor would cooperate with programmes rather than to change the nature of the programmes themselves (type 2), while *Voices of the Poor* emphasizes type 3. There is little of self-determination and empowerment in most of this work.

Methods and tools

Contextual methods of analysis are involved – data collection methods that "attempt to understand poverty dimensions within the social, cultural, economic and political environment of a locality" (Booth et al., 1998: 52). The methods derive from and emphasize poor people's ability to understand and analyse their own reality.

A range of tools has been devised, including the use of participatory mapping and modelling, seasonal calendars and wealth and well-being ranking. The large variety of methods can be used flexibly. This contrasts with the other approaches, where a more rigid framework and methodology are involved.

Some challenges in truly operationalizing PPAs

In principle people themselves conduct PPAs, but inevitably it is nearly always outsiders who conduct the assessments and interpret the results. For example, *Voices of the Poor* identified five types of well-being – material, physical, security, freedom of choice and action and social well-being – a classification which emerged at least partly from subsequent rationalization of the materials gathered in the various studies. An evaluation of PPAs in Africa noted that certain themes were not emphasized in the analysis, and many were omitted altogether. There was obvious "selectivity" due to pressures to highlight what were considered to be policy-relevant conclusions (Booth et al., 1998).

Although the participatory methods are intended to determine the nature of projects and elicit the views of poor people to shape plans and contribute to development strategies, in practice their impact on projects or plans is limited. For example, the PRSPs, prepared before debt relief can be agreed under the Highly Indebted Poor Countries Initiative, require participatory exercises as inputs. Yet 39 organizations and regional networks in 15 African countries agreed at a meeting in Kampala, May 2001, that PRSPs "were simply window-dressing". The statement concluded that "the PRSP process is simply delivering repackaged structural adjustment programmes and is not delivering poverty-focused development plans and has failed to involve civil society and parliamentarians in economic policy discussions". The perceived lack of "scientificity" of the methods and their subjective nature, together with political economy considerations, undoubtedly contribute to this poor outcome.

A basic problem arises from heterogeneity in the community: in this case, the question is whose voices are being heard. Where there are conflicts within a community, the PPA has no agreed way of resolving them to arrive at a single community view. Moreover, certain groups are likely to be fearful of voicing opposition to powerful members of the community. It has been argued that PPA tends to condone and reinforce existing social relations (da Cunha and Junho Pena, 1997). Furthermore, some people are structurally excluded from "communities". For example, groups often identify others outside the group as being really poor. These outsiders generally consist of people who no longer have social relations with the rest of the community, typically the poorest who have fallen through the cracks of the reciprocity network (Howard and Millard, 1997, provide poignant examples). The method, by focusing on "the community", whether real or perceived, does not compensate for such exclusions. Furthermore, the intensive process involved in PPA often means that only small numbers are included, and these tend to be got together on an *ad hoc* basis and rarely constitute representative samples of the population.

There is a deeper problem about exclusive reliance on participatory methods, which goes back to Sen's criticisms of the utilitarian approach. People's own assessment of their own condition can overlook their objective condition, and can be biased as a result of limited information and social conditioning (i.e. these methods also suffer from "valuation neglect"). The generally public aspect of assessments may also make it difficult to get honest assessments, and could involve participants in some risk.

Some conclusions on PPA

The major advantage of this approach is that PPAs largely get away from externally imposed standards. They also provide a way of solving some of the problems encountered with the other methods. For example, they help to define an appropriate minimum basket of commodities for the monetary approach; a list of basic capabilities in the CA; and whether the concept of SE can be applied in a particular society and what its main elements might be.

There are two major differences from the other approaches. The main one is that the perspective is that of the poor, who, at least in theory, make the judgements which in other approaches are imposed from outside. The other is the small samples – even in scaled-up versions – relative to other methods. It is therefore difficult to carry out statistical significance tests on material gathered in this way. The method is complex and invariably contains multidimensional analysis. Like SE it includes processes, causes and outcomes of poverty, as perceived by the poor. The method is apparently cost-effective, but the community spends much more time on these exercises – estimated in one study at five times more than on a household survey (de Graft Agyarko, 1998) – which is not usually costed.

A comparative overview

Each of the approaches to poverty derives from a different perspective on what constitutes a good life and a just society. For operationalization, each requires methodological assumptions that are often not transparent. Because of the major differences in definition, who counts as poor is likely to differ according to the approach and the precise methods used by each approach. Moreover, the different approaches have different implications for policy, as considered below. Table 2.2 provides an overview of comparisons between the approaches on a number of the criteria discussed earlier.

Two important issues not yet discussed are data availability and policy implications. Currently for many countries data are available at regular intervals for the measurement of monetary poverty, from household consumer surveys and sometimes national income data. Moreover, the data are usually available on a continuum, so it is possible to vary the poverty line and measure the depth of poverty. In contrast, data for different types of capability poverty are often unavailable on a regular basis and rely on one-off surveys, with some capabilities not measured at all and others with deficient indicators. There are similar data deficiencies with respect to dimensions of SE. These deficiencies reflect prior preoccupation with monetary poverty, not any intrinsic property of the data. Participatory data are different in this respect. By their nature they require intensive dialogue with groups of the poor, and are difficult to organize nationally or at short intervals. However, a modified form of consultation can be carried out comprehensively and regularly, along with other surveys.

From a policy perspective, the approach adopted has important implications.
- The use of a monetary concept suggests that the solution is generation of money incomes. The development of capabilities might also be recommended, but only instrumentally as a means of increasing productivity and hence money incomes among the poor.
- The use of the CA in general suggests emphasis on a wider range of mechanisms – the social provision of goods, improved allocation of goods within the family and the more efficient use of goods to achieve health, nutrition and education, as well as money income as a means for promoting basic capabilities.
- Although basic capabilities have been interpreted in material terms in this chapter, potentially the approach can readily be extended to other spheres, such as political or cultural life, which is not the case with the monetary approach. Consequently, a much wider range of policies may emerge from the CA.
- Both monetary and capability approaches are fundamentally concerned with absolute poverty in most developing country contexts. Hence, one important policy response is to raise the level of the sea so that all boats may rise too ("Growth is good for the poor", according to Dollar

Table 2.2 A comparison of the four approaches to poverty

	Monetary poverty	Capability approach	Social exclusion	Participatory approach
Unit of analysis	Ideally the individual, *de facto* the household	The individual	Individuals or groups relative to others in their community/society	Groups and individuals within them
Required or minimum standard identified by	Reference to "external" information (defined outside the unit); central element food requirements	Reference to "lists" of dimensions normally assumed to be objectively definable	Reference to those prevailing in society and state obligations	Local people's own perceptions of well-being and ill-being
Sensitivity to social institutions	None, but assessments can be broken down by group	Emphasis on adequacy rather than sufficiency leaves space for (non-modelled) variations	Central element	Reflected in the way poor people analyse their own reality
Importance of processes	Not essential Increasing emphasis	Not clear	One of the main thrusts of the approach	Critical for achievement of satisfactory methods
Major weaknesses conceptually	Utility is not an adequate measure of well-being, and poverty is not an economic category	Elements of arbitrariness in choice of basic capabilities, problems of adding up	Broad framework, susceptible to many interpretations, difficult to compare across countries	Whose perceptions are being elicited, and how representative or consistent they are; how one deals with disagreements

Problems for cross-country comparisons	Comparability of surveys, of price indices, of drawing poverty lines	Fewer problems if basic capabilities are defined externally, but adding-up difficulties makes comparisons difficult with inconsistencies according to adding-up methodology	Lines of social exclusion essentially society-specific; also an adding-up problem	Cultural differences can make appropriate processes differ across societies, results may not be comparable
Data availability	Household surveys regularly conducted; omitted observations can be important. Use of national income data – but requires assumptions about distribution	Data less regularly collected, but could easily be improved	Currently have to rely on data collected for other purposes. If agreed on basic dimensions, data could be regularly collected	Generally only small purposive samples. Never available nationally; would be difficult to extend method for regular national data collection
Major weaknesses for measurement	Needs to be anchored to external elements. Arbitrary	Impossibility of set evaluation. How to deal with multidimensionality even if only of basic functionings	Problems with multidimensionality. Challenge of capturing process	How comparable? How representative?
Interpreted by policy-makers as requiring	Emphasis on economic growth and distribution of monetary income	Investments in extending basic capabilities/basic needs via monetary incomes and public services	Foster processes of inclusion, inclusion in markets and social process, with particular emphasis on formal labour market	Empowerment of the poor

and Kraay, 2001: 50). Distributional issues are present, but not at the forefront. In contrast, the relative element in poverty is at the forefront in the SE approach. Indeed, for this it is unlikely that growth alone can *ever* eliminate SE. Hence, redistributive polices and structural policies get priority.
- The monetary and capability approaches are essentially individualistic. Group features are consequently often ignored in policies, which tend to be focused on individual access to resources or transfers, and at best are regarded as instrumental. Yet in SE particularly, and also to a considerable extent in participatory approaches, the prime focus is on group characteristics. For SE, therefore, policies such as correcting racial discrimination or class barriers or citizenship restrictions are likely to play a central role in defining policy priorities.

Some empirical evidence on the approaches to poverty measurement

A critical issue for this comparison is whether the four approaches identify broadly the same people as poor, as if they do the theoretical differences may be unimportant in policy or targeting terms. Despite its theoretical deficiencies, monetary poverty could be used as a proxy for other types of poverty if essentially the same people are identified as poor under the different measures.

In any empirical comparison it first has to be decided how the particular approach is to be used, solving the difficult issues discussed above. In the comparisons adopted here the authors try to use commonly assumed solutions to these issues, since the aim is to explore differences that occur in practice when alternative methods are used.

For countries as a whole and for regions of the world, it appears that poverty rates differ significantly according to the approach adopted. Table 2.3 shows that country ranking differs in comparing capability poverty and both international and national monetary poverty lines. While at the country level different measures of deprivation are associated, and indeed one cannot reject the hypothesis that the different measures are not independent, what is striking is that low levels of poverty according to one measure are compatible with high levels of poverty according to another. This variability points to the potential lack of overlap in practice between different ways of measuring poverty, and calls for in-depth empirical assessment of the underlying causes of such differences. Such empirical tests can also show whether different measures capture different populations.

A study of India and Peru (Franco et al., 2002), drawing on both na-

Table 2.3 Monetary and capability poverty compared: Selected countries, percentage of population in poverty

	HPI[a] (HDR 2000)	Rank	International monetary poverty[b] 1983–2000	Rank	National poverty line 1978–2000	Rank
Costa Rica	4.0	1	12.6	4	22.0	5
Chile	4.1	2	<2.0	1	21.2	4
Mexico	9.4	3	15.9	6	10.1	2
Peru	12.8	4	15.5	5	49.0	9
Sri Lanka	17.6	5	6.6	3	25.0	7
China	14.9	6	18.8	7	4.6	1
Egypt	31.2	7	3.1	3	22.9	6
India	33.1	8	44.2	10	35.0	10
Morocco	35.8	9	<2.0	1	19.0	3
Zimbabwe	36.1	10	36.0	9	25.5	8
Uganda	40.8	11	NA	NA	55.0	11
Ethiopia	56.5	12	31.2	8	NA	NA

[a] Human poverty index (HPI) = geometric average of percentage of people not expected to live to 40 years; adult illiteracy rate; and average lack of access to safe water and sanitation.
[b] Monetary poverty = percentage of population living on less than $1 a day, valued at purchasing power parity.
NA = not available.
Source: UNDP (2002).

tional datasets and micro-surveys, found that significantly different people were identified as poor in the two countries according to whether the monetary, capability or participatory approach was adopted.

The national datasets showed that in India, using the national poverty line, monetary poverty, at 38 per cent, was below capability poverty: 52 per cent of adults were education poor (illiterate) and 26 per cent of children were education poor (not attending primary school); 70 per cent of children younger than 13 years old were undernourished, 44 per cent severely; but only 7 per cent of individuals between 7 and 59 suffered from chronic illness. In Peru, in contrast, monetary poverty at 54 per cent (again using a national poverty line) was greater than capability poverty: 20 per cent of adults and 7 per cent of children were education poor; 10 per cent of adults were health poor; and 29 per cent of the children below 5 years in age were undernourished.

The extent of the lack of overlap in individuals falling into monetary and capability poverty is shown in table 2.4. For example, in India 43 per cent of children and over half of adults who were capability poor using education or health as the indicator were not in monetary poverty; similarly, over half the nutrition-poor children were not in monetary pov-

Table 2.4 Lack of overlaps between monetary and CA poverty

Capability poverty measured as		Education		Nutrition/health	
		Children	Adults	Children	Adults
% of CA poor not in monetary poverty	India	43	60	53	63
	Peru	32	37	21	55
% of monetary poor not CA poor	India	65	38	53	91
	Peru	93	73	66	94

Source: Franco et al. (2002).

erty. In Peru around one-third of children and adults who were educationally capability poor were not monetary poor; while one-fifth of children and over half of adults who were capability poor (health/nutrition) were not monetary poor.

Are the large proportions of individuals who are monetary poor but not capability poor, or conversely, an artefact of the particular poverty lines selected? An investigation of the extent of capability poverty for different monetary deciles shows that altering the monetary poverty line would not greatly alter the results. For example, in India, although levels of education poverty were lower in higher deciles, 33 per cent of the richest tenth of the population (in terms of money incomes) were illiterate (compared with 64 per cent among the lowest decile). The proportion of health poor in the highest decile is quite similar to that in the lowest decile. Among those with incomes even as high as the seventh monetary decile more than 50 per cent are poor in either education or health. In Peru 12 per cent of the top decile are education poor among adults and 5 per cent among children – compared with 32 per cent in the lowest decile for adults and 9 per cent for children. The incidence of child undernutrition is 5 per cent for the top decile of money incomes compared with 9 per cent for the lowest decile. Hence changing the cut-off line for monetary poverty would not eliminate the weak overlaps with capability poverty in either country.

Micro-studies permitted a comparison of poverty magnitudes according to the capability and monetary approaches, and also using participatory methods. Again, big differences were apparent.

- In India, in the urban areas only around half of those ranked as "low well-being" by participatory methods were also monetarily poor. Even the highest monetary decile had 34 per cent of individuals ranked "low well-being". In Peru, in the rural areas, 48 per cent of the monetary non-poor were identified as poor according to the well-being ranking, while 39 per cent of the extremely poor by well-being ranking were

not monetary poor. In the urban areas, 49 per cent of the monetary non-poor were ranked as well-being poor while 44 per cent of those ranked as well-being poor were not monetary poor.
- In Peru, a lack of overlap also showed between self-perceptions of poverty and monetary poverty. In the rural area, 29 per cent of the self-declared poor were non-poor according to the monetary indicator, while of the monetary poor 42 per cent did not believe themselves to be poor. In the urban areas 40 per cent of the self-declared poor were not monetary poor, and 42 per cent of the monetary poor did not state that they were poor.

Both the Indian and Peruvian studies encountered problems in estimating SE. It had been intended that the participatory focus groups would define SE, and this definition would then be applied to the dataset. But none of the participatory activities generated a definition of SE – as none of the groups saw themselves as socially excluded. In India even those belonging to the lower castes, while aware of boundaries with upper castes, did not consider themselves to be socially excluded. The study thus did not generate a good definition of SE for these societies. In India, however, a rural group did suggest the concept of "social boycott" to describe (a very few) individuals who were no longer socially accepted by local people. The reasons for such a boycott were given as mixed marriage (across religions or castes) and suffering from leprosy.

Although the studies were unable to identify SE from participatory methods, the analysis of the incidence of different types of poverty pointed to certain groups as being particularly vulnerable to different types of poverty. In India these were people belonging to scheduled castes or tribes. For Peru, in rural areas they were the landless and those speaking local languages only, not Spanish; and in the urban areas those having only precarious (or no) employment.

The evidence from India and Peru thus points to significantly different populations being identified as poor according to the different approaches. The findings of substantially different distributions of people in monetary and capability poverty have been paralleled in research on Chile and Viet Nam (Ruggeri Laderchi, 1997; Baulch and Masset, 2003) and by earlier work in Peru using different indicators (Ruggeri Laderchi, 2001a). In Uganda participatory assessments of changes in poverty over time have differed from the monetary approach even over the direction of change (McGee, 2000). These large discrepancies in those defined as poor according to different methods mean that one cannot rely on a monetary indicator to identify those in other types of poverty, nor conversely. Consequently, theoretical differences between the various methods have serious practical implications for policy-making.

Conclusions

This review of the different approaches to the identification and measurement of poverty makes clear that there is no unique or "objective" way of defining and measuring poverty. There is a large element of "construction" involved in each of the poverty measures – by outsiders in the monetary, capability and SE approaches, and by a combination of outsiders and the people themselves in PPA. All definitions of poverty contain some arbitrary and subjective elements, often imposed by the outside observer. But this is of most concern with respect to conceptualization and measurement in the monetary approach, since this approach gives the (false) impression of being the most accurate and objective of the methods, while the judgements made in order to arrive at a measure of monetary poverty are generally not apparent. The limited empirical consistency of the monetary approach with the CA poses particular problems since it means that monetary poverty does not consistently point to failure to achieve certain material objectives, such as adequate nutrition. In contrast, capability poverty – albeit also subject to relatively arbitrary decisions – transparently means that people are unable to function in some ways that are universally accepted as important for human development. Capability poverty may not amount to everything we think we mean by poverty, but it definitely constitutes part of it, and the more one extends the basic capabilities included, the greater the range of deprivations covered. While participatory methods have a lot to offer when applied to poverty analysis, both in helping to make methodological decisions with respect to the other methods and in providing a valuable (but not exclusive) definition of poverty as perceived by the poor themselves, they should not be the exclusive approach as the perceptions of the poor (and even more the expression of these perceptions) can be conditioned by their circumstances.

A focus on measuring individual deprivation, whether it is monetary or capability, can neglect or even draw attention away from the fundamental causes of deprivation. In this respect the SE approach is particularly relevant. While the authors have found SE difficult to define in the developing country context, they believe the effort to do so is important because it points to processes of impoverishment, structural characteristics of societies responsible for deprivation and group issues that tend to be neglected in other approaches.

Conceptualization, definitions and measurement have important implications for targeting and policy. The considerable lack of overlaps between the different approaches means that targeting according to one type of poverty will involve serious targeting errors in relation to other types. Moreover, definitions also have implications for policy. While a monetary approach suggests a focus on increasing money incomes (by economic growth or redistribution), a capability approach tends to lead to more emphasis on the provision of public goods. SE draws attention to the need to break down exclusionary factors: for example by redistribution and anti-discrimination policies. Thus awareness of the conceptual apparatus underlying different practices, particularly in the case of the dominating paradigm of monetary poverty, is needed when adopting them. Furthermore, it suggests that identification and targeting of the poor with combined methods should be more widely adopted, reflecting the concerns for a broad characterization of poverty which currently form an important part of the development discourse.

Definitions do matter. Clearer and more transparent definitions of poverty are an essential prerequisite of any development policy that puts poverty reduction at its centre.

Acknowledgements

This is an edited version of an original paper, reprinted from *Oxford Development Studies* 31(3): 243–274, with the permission of the publisher, Taylor & Francis Ltd, www.tandf.co.uk/journals.

This chapter derives from research on "Alternative realities? An empirical investigation into alternative concepts of poverty" funded by the DFID. The authors have benefited greatly from comments and suggestions from the other members of the team, Barbara Harriss-White and Susana Franco. For more details on the approaches surveyed here see Ruggeri Laderchi (2000, 2001b) and Saith (2001a, 2001b). For an overview of the research see Franco et al. (2002). The authors would like to thank Abusaleh Shariff, Abhilasha Sharma and Rajesh Jaiswal of the NCAER in Delhi, the Academy of Science, Lucknow, Enrique Vásquezh, the Universidad del Pacífico, Instituto Cuanto, Araceli Roldan (CESA) and Francisco Díaz Canseco for help in the empirical work in India and Peru reported on in this chapter.

REFERENCES

Alkire, S. (2002) *Valuing Freedoms: Sen's Capability Approach and Poverty Reduction*, Oxford: Oxford University Press.

Anand, S., C. J. Harris and O. B. Linton (1993) "On the Concept of Ultrapoverty", Centre for Population and Development Studies, Working Paper No. 93.02, Harvard University, June.

Appasamy, P., S. Guhan and R. Hema (1996) *Social Exclusion from a Welfare Perspective*, Geneva: International Institute for Labour Studies.

Atkinson, A. B. (1989) *Poverty and Social Security*, London: Harvester Wheatsheaf.

─── (1998) "Social Exclusion, Poverty and Unemployment", in A. B. Atkinson and J. Hills, eds, *Exclusion, Employment and Opportunity*, CASE Paper 4, London: London School of Economics, Centre for Analysis of Social Exclusion.

Atkinson, A. B. and F. Bourguignon (1987) "Income Distribution and Differences in Needs", in G. Feiwel, ed., *Arrow and the Foundations of the Theory of Economic Policy*, London: Macmillan, pp. 350–370.

Baker, J. L. (1997) *Poverty Reduction and Human Development in the Caribbean: A Cross-country Study*, Washington, D.C.: World Bank.

Banks, J. and P. Johnson (1993) *Children and Household Living Standards*, London: Institute for Fiscal Studies.

Barry, B. (1998) *Social Exclusion, Social Isolation and the Distribution of Income*, CASE Paper 12, London: London School of Economics, Centre for Analysis of Social Exclusion.

Baulch, B. and E. Masset (2003) "Do Monetary and Non-monetary Indicators Tell the Same Story About Chronic Poverty? A Study of Vietnam in the 1990s", *World Development* 31: 441–453.

Booth, C. (1887) "The Inhabitants of Tower Hamlets (School Board Division), Their Condition and Occupations", *Journal of the Royal Statistical Society* 50: 326–340.

Booth, D., J. Holland, J. Hentschel, P. Lanjouw and A. Herbert (1998) *Participation and Combined Methods in African Poverty Assessments: Renewing the Agenda*, London: DFID Social Development Division Africa Division.

Bourguignon, F. and S. R. Chakravarty (2003) "The Measurement of Multidimensional Poverty", *Journal of Economic Inequality* 1(1): 25–49.

Burchardt, T., J. Le Grand and D. Piachaud (1999) "Social Exclusion in Britain 1991–1995", *Social Policy and Administration* 33: 227–244.

Cartaya, V., R. Magallanes and C. Dominiquez (1997) *Venezuela: Exclusion and Integration, A Synthesis in the Building?*, Geneva: International Institute for Labour Studies.

Chambers, R. (1994) "The Origins and Practice of PRA", *World Development* 22(7): 953–969.

─── (1997) *Whose Reality Counts? Putting the First Last*, London: Intermediate Technology Publications.

Clark, D. A. and M. Qizilbash (2002) "Core Poverty and Extreme Vulnerability in South Africa", paper presented to IARIW Conference, Djurhamn, Sweden, August, unpublished.

Clert, C. (1999) "Evaluating the Concept of Social Exclusion in Development Discourse", *European Journal of Development Research* 11: 166–199.

Cornwall, A. (2000) "Beneficiary, Consumer, Citizen Perspectives on Participation for Poverty Reduction", Institute of Development Studies, Sussex University.

da Cunha, P. V. and M. V. Junho Pena (1997) *The Limits and Merits of Participation*, Washington, D.C.: World Bank.

Dasgupta, P. (1993) *An Enquiry into Well-being and Destitution*, Oxford: Oxford University Press.
de Graft Agyarko, R. (1998) "Influencing Policy Through Poverty Assessments: Theoretical and Practical Overview of a Changing Process", PPA Topic Pack, Institute of Development Studies, Brighton.
Deaton, A. (1997). *The Analysis of Household Surveys: A Microeconometric Approach to Development Policy*, Washington, D.C.: Johns Hopkins University Press/World Bank.
Desai, M. (1995) "Poverty and Capability: Towards an Empirically Implementable Measure", in M. Desai, ed., *Poverty, Famine and Economic Development: The Selected Essays of Meghnad Desai*, Vol. II, Aldershot: Edward Elgar, pp. 185–204.
Dhatt, G. and M. Ravallion (1998) "Why Have Some Indian States Done Better Than Others at Reducing Rural Poverty?", *Economica* 65: 17–38.
Dollar, D. and A. Kraay (2001) "Growth is Good for the Poor", Policy Research Working Paper 2587, World Bank, Washington, D.C.
Doyal, L. and I. Gough (1991) *A Theory of Human Need*, London: Macmillan Education.
Drèze, J. and A. K. Sen (1995) *India: Economic Development and Social Opportunity*, New Delhi: Oxford University Press.
European Foundation (1995) *Public Welfare Services and Social Exclusion: The Development of Consumer Oriented Initiatives in the European Union*, Dublin: European Foundation.
Eurostat Taskforce (1998) *Recommendations on Social Exclusion and Poverty Statistics*, Luxembourg: Eurostat.
Foster, J., J. Greer and E. Thorbecke (1984) "A Class of Decomposable Poverty Measures", *Econometrica* 52: 761–766.
Franco, S., B. Harriss-White, C. Ruggeri Laderchi and F. Stewart (2002) "Alternative Realities? Different Concepts of Poverty, Their Empirical Consequences and Policy Implications", Queen Elizabeth House, Oxford, mimeo.
Grosh, M. E. and P. Glewwe (2000) *Designing Household Survey Questionnaires for Developing Countries: Lessons from 15 Years of the Living Standards Measurement Study*, Washington, D.C.: World Bank.
Howard, M. and A. V. Millard (1997) *Hunger and Shame: Poverty and Child Malnutrition on Mount Kilimanjaro*, London: Routledge.
Hulme, D. and A. Shepherd (2003) "Conceptualising Chronic Poverty", *World Development* 31: 403–423.
Lewis, G. W. and D. T. Ulph (1998) "Poverty, Inequality and Welfare", *Economic Journal* 98: 117–131.
Lipton, M. (1988) *The Poor and the Poorest. Some Interim Findings*, Washington, D.C.: World Bank.
Lipton, M. and M. Ravallion (1993) "Poverty and Policy", Policy Research Working Papers WPS 1130, World Bank, Washington, D.C.
McGee, R. (2000) "Analysis of Participatory Poverty Assessment (PPA) and Household Survey Findings on Poverty Trends in Uganda", unpublished mission report, 10–18 February.

Micklewright, J. (2002) *Social Exclusion and Children: A European View for US Debate*, Florence: UNICEF.
Morduch, J. (1995) "Income Smoothing and Consumption Smoothing", *Journal of Economic Perspectives* 9(3): 103–114.
Narayan-Parker, D. and R. Patel (2000) *Voices of the Poor: Can Anyone Hear Us?*, Oxford: Oxford University Press.
Nussbaum, M. (2000) *Women and Human Development: A Study in Human Capabilities*, Cambridge: Cambridge University Press.
Payne, P. R. (1993) "Undernutrition: Measurement and Implications", in S. Osman, ed., *Poverty, Undernutrition and Living Standards*, Oxford: Clarendon Press.
Qizilbash, M. (1998) *Poverty: Concept and Measurement*, Islamabad: Sustainable Development Policy Institute.
Ravallion, M. (1998) "Poverty Lines in Theory and Practice", LSMS Working Paper 133, World Bank, Washington, D.C.
―――― (2002) *How Not to Count the Poor. A Reply to Reddy and Pogge*, Washington, D.C.: World Bank.
Reddy, S. G. and T. W. Pogge (2002) *How Not to Count the Poor*, New York: Barnard College.
Rodgers, G., C. Gore and J. Figueiredo (1995) *Social Exclusion: Rhetoric, Reality, Responses*, Geneva: International Institute for Labour Studies.
Room, G. (1999) 'Social Exclusion, Solidarity and the Challenge of Globalisation', *International Journal of Social Welfare* 8: 66–74.
Rowntree, B. S. (1902) *Poverty. A Study of Town Life*, London: Macmillan.
Ruggeri Laderchi, C. (1997) "Poverty and its Many Dimensions: The Role of Income as an Indicator", *Oxford Development Studies* 25: 345–360.
―――― (2000) "The Monetary Approach to Poverty: A Survey of Concepts and Methods", Working Paper 58, Queen Elizabeth House, Oxford.
―――― (2001a) "Do Concepts of Poverty Matter? An Empirical Investigation of the Differences between a Capability and a Monetary Assessment of Poverty in Peru", unpublished PhD thesis, University of Oxford.
―――― (2001b) "Participatory Methods in the Analysis of Poverty: A Critical Review", Working Paper 62, Queen Elizabeth House, Oxford.
Saith, R. (2001a) "Capabilities: The Concept and its Operationalisation", Working Paper 66, Queen Elizabeth House, Oxford.
―――― (2001b) "Social Exclusion: The Concept and Application to Developing Countries", Working Paper 72, Queen Elizabeth House, Oxford.
Sen, A. K. (1976) "Poverty: An Ordinal Approach to Measurement", *Econometrica* 44: 219–231.
―――― (1985) *Commodities and Capabilities*, Amsterdam: North Holland.
―――― (1993) "Capability and Well-being", in M. C. Nussbaum and A. K. Sen, eds, *The Quality of Life*, Oxford: Clarendon Press, pp. 30–53.
――――, ed. (1997) *On Economic Inequality*, 2nd edn, Oxford: Clarendon Press.
―――― (1999) *Development as Freedom (DAF)*, Oxford: Oxford University Press.
Sen, A. K. and J. Foster (1997) "Inequality After a Quarter Century", in A. K. Sen, ed., *On Economic Inequality*, 2nd edn, Oxford: Clarendon Press.

Stewart, F. (1985) *Planning to Meet Basic Needs*, London: Macmillan.
——— (1995) "Basic Needs, Capabilities and Human Development", *Greek Economic Review* 17: 83–96.
Streeten, P. P., S. J. Burki, M. ul Haq, N. Hicks and F. Stewart (1981) *First Things First, Meeting Basic Human Needs in Developing Countries*, New York: Oxford University Press.
Sukhatme, P. V., ed. (1982) *Newer Concepts in Nutrition and Their Implications for Policy*, Pune: Maharashtra Association for the Cultivation of Science.
——— (1989) "Nutritional Adaptation and Variability", *European Journal of Clinical Nutrition* 43: 75–87.
Szekely, M., N. Lustig, J. A. Meijia and M. Cumpa (2000) *Do We Know How Much Poverty There Is?*, Washington, D.C.: IADB.
UNDP (1997) *Human Development Report 1997*, New York: Oxford University Press.
——— (2001) *Human Development Report 2001*, New York: Oxford University Press.
——— (2002) *Human Development Report 2002*, New York: Oxford University Press.
van Parijs, P., ed. (1992) *Arguing for Basic Income: Ethical Foundations for a Radical Reform*, London: Verso.

3
Economic well-being and non-economic well-being

Andrew Sumner

Introduction

Does "well-being" matter to economists? The answer is a resounding yes! Well-being has been of central interest: some have even placed it at the "heart" of development economics today, albeit labelled as "poverty reduction" (see, for example, Kanbur and Squire, 1999: 1). Such interest is not new, either. It drove not only the "founding fathers" of quantitative economics, such as Petty and Quesnay, but also the "pioneers" of political economy – Marx, Smith, Ricardo, Malthus and Mill (Anand and Sen, 2000: 2031). Furthermore, to this list we might also add the likes of Arthur Lewis and contemporary economists who have focused primarily on poverty and well-being, such as Paul Streeten, Amartya Sen, Martin Ravallion and Ravi Kanbur, to name but a few.

This chapter discusses the recent evolution of the debates on the meaning and measurement of well-being and poverty. It focuses on the post–Second World War era: that period of time when development economics emerged into a distinct subdiscipline as the "unfavoured child of two parental discourses" – mainstream economics and a general discourse on the human condition (Cameron, 2003: 2). The chapter is concerned with two questions over this period of time: first, how and why have the meaning and measurement of poverty and well-being evolved? And second, what are the comparative advantages (the relative efficiency in meeting objectives) of various indicators or groupings of indicators?

One thing is certain: the measurement and assessment of poverty and well-being have never been so high on the international agenda. The new results-based development discourse, exemplified in the UN Millennium Development Goals (MDGs) and the rewritten mission statements of the International Monetary Fund and the World Bank, coupled with the poverty reduction strategy papers (PRSPs) process and a mushrooming of new household surveys (the extension of the World Bank's demographic health and living standards measurement surveys and participatory poverty assessment, PPA) have all meant that the importance of assessing the well-being of the world's population has never been so high on the agenda.

This chapter considers what factors, policies and contexts have led well-being research. The defining characteristics of a poverty or well-being indicator are taken as a point of departure.

Characteristics of poverty and well-being indicators

What characteristics does a "good" poverty or well-being indicator exhibit? The UN's *Handbook on Social Indicators* (1989: 18) defines such indicators as accepted "standards" assessing "progress" through "measurement". This would seem non-contentious. Likewise, there is actually little disagreement on the characteristics of a "good" indicator. Most commonly noted are the following criteria: the measure should have an underlying conceptualization of well-being (we know human beings need food, for example), and be policy-relevant (i.e. meaningful to policy-makers), a direct and unambiguous measure of progress, specific to the phenomena, valid, reliable, consistent, measurable, user-friendly, not easily manipulated, cost-effective and up to date (DFID, 2002; United Nations, 1989; World Bank, 2002a, 2002b). Fine in theory, but what commonly used poverty indicators could jump through all these hoops?

It is worth taking a step backwards and reviewing the process that creates a poverty statistic. Indicators are the end product of a (lengthy) social process, which at every stage is shaped by the bias of agents involved. Errors are virtually certain to occur in both the sampling and non-sampling aspects of research. In the early stages bias appears in the choice of survey questions, and the interviewer may influence respondents' answers. There may be inaccurate reporting of consumption due to recall difficulties or concern over the use of the information. Underrepresenting of some groups in socio-economic surveys will happen because sample frames are often based on incomplete official records (such as national identity cards or electoral registers) that "hide" those without full "legal status", such as the homeless or slum dwellers. It is also likely that a disproportionate number of the "hidden" households will be poor and thus there will be a downward bias in the absolute number of the poor as calculated. Further, in the later stages, when the data are collated, processed and interpreted, bias and more errors are introduced in the stages of inputting and defining how the raw data fit the definition of a specific indicator. With this in mind, a list of salient questions for reflection when utilizing data might include the following. How are these social indicators created? Who collects them and for what purpose? How is the sample frame created? Who is omitted? What definitions are used? How are these indicators used? What are they used for?

Whilst these points are important, they are also somewhat academic when data availability is limited, and choice of indicators may simply be dictated by what is in existence.

The meaning and measurement of poverty and well-being

What are the most important characteristics of poverty and well-being and how are they best measured? Over the last 50 years the debate on this subject has moved from well-being as economically determined to broader conceptualizations of poverty, from considering the "means" of well-being to analysing the "ends", from identifying "needs" to identifying "rights", from no or few indicators to many and from (at best) an afterthought to a central focus of the development discourse. In each decade since the Second World War the dominant meaning and measurement of well-being have been shaped by the prevailing context and practice of development (see table 3.1).

In each decade the evolution of the meaning and measurement of poverty and well-being has also closely reflected the position of (development) economics within development studies and the tension between

Table 3.1 Evolution of the dominant meaning and measurement of well-being, 1950s–2000s

Period	Meaning of well-being	Measurement of well-being
1950s	Economic well-being	GDP growth
1960s	Economic well-being	GDP per capita growth
1970s	Basic needs	GDP per capita growth + basic goods
1980s	Economic well-being	GDP per capita but rise of non-monetary factors
1990s	Human development/capabilities	Human development and sustainability
2000s	Universal rights, livelihoods, freedom	MDGs and "new" areas: risk and empowerment

economic imperialism and multidisciplinarity. As development research has moved from being purely an economic pursuit to multidisciplinary approaches, so has well-being moved away from economic determinism to a multidimensional definition. However, tensions remain – why is it that economic measures of well-being are dominant in PRSPs despite the widespread acceptance of poverty as multidimensional?

In the 1950s economic growth dominated. Well-being was assumed to be improving if there was growth, because that growth would eventually reduce any poverty by a mechanistic trickle-down effect (Bourguignon, Da Silva and Stern, 2002). This was the era of "high development theory". At either end of the political spectrum, newly independent nations defined "development" as industrialization and catching up with the former colonial powers. It was this new independence and the search for "short-cuts" that created development economics as a distinct subdiscipline. Well-being was at this time, if measured at all, assessed by GDP growth.

However, in the 1960s well-being took on a greater importance. Economic emancipation was sought by many nationalist governments in the South, led by import substitution. "Development" itself was seen as raising standards of living for the local population. Social data gradually became available, but for many countries the indicator was still GDP, albeit per capita rather than just GDP growth. Only towards the end of the decade were there hints of the seismic shift at hand, beginning what was to become a Kuhnian shift in the conceptualization of poverty. The publication of Bauer's *Social Indicators* (1966) and a paper on "The Meaning of Development" by Dudley Seers in 1969 led the debate into *basic needs*. This shaped much of the 1970s, and discussions were led by scholars such as Nancy Baster (1979), Donald McGranahan (e.g. McGranahan, Pizarro and Richard, 1985), UNRISD (1970) and Paul Streeten (e.g. Hicks and Streeten, 1979; Streeten, 1984). Well-being was equated with the satisfaction of basic needs – physical necessities such as food, shelter and public goods, as well as the means to acquire these through employment. This broader definition became reflected in the availability of new data on health and education for many developing countries in the 1970s. The fact that statistics failed to show that the benefits of economic growth had trickled down created increased interest in this *basic needs approach*. Additionally, much research was led by the International Labour Organization (e.g. ILO, 1976, 1977). The culmination of all these efforts was the first composite measure of well-being – Morris's (1979) physical quality of life index (PQLI). For the first time there was a measure of well-being which took no account of income or economic well-being. The three components were life expectancy at birth, infant mortality and adult literacy.

In the early 1980s the publication of the Brandt Report (1980), Chambers's (1983) work on non-monetary poverty (in particular isolation and empowerment) and the coining of the phrase *well-being* and the 1980 *World Development Report* (*WDR*) appeared, in the first instance, to be shifting the debate further away from economic determinism. The *WDR* characterized well-being as beyond income and encapsulating nutrition, education and health (World Bank, 1980: 32). However, the debt crisis pushed non-economic concerns off the agenda and well-being was once again equated primarily to economic growth (Dagdeviren, Van der Hoeven and Weeks, 2001).

Despite this, towards the end of the decade there was a renewed interest in non-economic aspects of well-being, as the social impacts of adjustment programmes became more evident (see, for example, Cornia, Jolly and Stewart, 1987). What emerged was a synthesis of economic plus non-economic components of well-being. This was thanks to the highly influential work of Sen and Huq at the UNDP in establishing a new yearly report on well-being. The UNDP's *Human Development Report* (*HDR*) gave birth to the new concept of "human development" and a new set of composite indicators, led by the UNDP's human development index (HDI). The *HDR*s have since reoriented social development "from the periphery to the core" (Sagar and Najam, 1999: 743). In fact, by 2000 the *WDR* was quoting Sen on the first page of its opening chapter (World Bank, 2000: 15).

Sen (see in particular 1982, 1985, 1999) and the UNDP (1990–2005) have argued that well-being was not, as previously defined, based on "desire fulfilment" (utility or consumption measured by the proxy of income: GDP per capita) as this does not take account of the physical condition of the individual. Instead it was *the process of enlarging people's choices* (UNDP, 1990: 1). Sen (see also Nussbaum, 2000) provides an understanding of poverty as multidimensional. It is based on considering well-being as a set of freedoms that any particular individual values and his/her ability to attain them. Sen shifted the focus from *means* (such as having income to buy food) to *ends* (such as being well nourished). He noted there was a broad set of conditions (including being fed, healthy, clothed, educated) that together constitute well-being. According to Sen, individuals have a set of entitlements (command over commodities) which are created through a set of endowments (assets owned – physical and self) and exchange (trade and production by the individual). These entitlements are traded for a set of opportunities (capabilities) to achieve a set of functionings (outcomes of well-being). Thus "entitlements" can be transformed into "capabilities" which in turn can be transformed into "functionings". Poverty is "capability deprivation", and although Sen still refuses to endorse a list of capabilities, he did identify five "basic freedoms" – political/participative freedoms/civil rights; economic facilities; social opportunities; transparency guarantees; and protective security (Sen, 1999: 1, 18). The UNDP indices are, though, only a partial and somewhat uneven application of Sen's research on well-being.

It could be argued that the end of the Cold War and the decline of meta-narratives were instrumental in a new (post-modern) focus on the individual, the body, mortality and knowledge, a return to the fundamentals of well-being – people's bodies (Cameron, 2003: 32). What was certain was that the *HDR* and the HDI launch played a role in what was to become known as the decade in which social development would rise to prominence in academic and policy arenas. In the same year as the *HDR* launch, 1990, the World Bank also issued a new measure of (economic) well-being – the *dollar-a-day* poverty indicator. Throughout the decade there were numerous UN poverty conferences. Additionally, as the decade closed, as if to sum up, the 2000 *WDR* (World Bank, 2000) played a major role in solidifying the centrality of well-being in the discourse. Not only did the report accept a multifaceted model of well-being, it "promoted" well-being indicators to the early statistical tables and "relegated" economic indicators to later tables.

However, there was not complete consensus: the struggle between economic well-being and non-economic well-being continued, the debate over ranking various poverty dimensions continued (see a review in Hulme and McKay, 2005) and a further tension emerged – that between universal or "objective" measures of poverty and those measurements which sought to capture the "subjective" local experiences of well-being (for example, Narayan et al., 1999). The debate was simultaneously moving in opposite directions. The first direction was upwards towards universality. This was based on an international agreement in the UN MDGs and work on new *rights-based* approaches to development. The second was a move downwards towards locally based definitions of well-being. This was reflected in the increased prominence of both the *sustainable livelihoods approach* (SLA), a term first coined by Chambers and Conway (1991), and *participatory poverty assessments* (PPAs), a term claimed by the World Bank (1992). Originally the SLA did not include indicators, but measures have evolved since (see Norten et al., 2001 for greater detail).

In the former, development is the attainment of basic social, economic and political "human rights" as enshrined in the Universal Declaration of Human Rights and various internationally agreed treaties. This perspective is a shift from an adequate standard of living as a need (as in basic needs) to a right. The MDGs are then a universally agreed set of goals for 2015 that incorporate indicators for income poverty, education and gender equality in education, health and environmental poverty. At the same time, the meaning and measurement of well-being have evolved downwards to the local level. This can be observed in the predominance in much donor literature of micro-analysis, the SLA and the methodology of PPA. The SLA is an assessment of people's changing access to or ownership of the assets (known as the asset pentagon) of human capital, physical capital, social capital, financial capital and natural capital, and the impact of changes in these on livelihoods (see for more detail DFID, 2000).

PPAs have sought to elicit poor households' perspectives on well-being (albeit with the contradiction of having to use some definition of poverty to identify the poor sample beforehand). The largest study has been the Voices of the Poor (VOP), which included 60,000 people in 47 countries (Narayan et al., 1999). Much of the analysis was included in the *WDR 2000–2001* (World Bank, 2000). The VOP study concluded that the poor define poverty as multidimensional and beyond material well-being (although food security and employment were highlighted). In particular, two *new* psychological aspects of well-being were commonly highlighted: risk, vulnerability and chronic/transient poverty (see Hulme, Moore and Shepherd, 2001), and empowerment and participation. The first relates to economic well-being and the second to non-economic well-being.

However, the conversion of these new aspects into indicators is in its infancy (Alsop and Heinsohn, 2005: 5). Measures proposed include assessing risk, vulnerability and economic security through the variance of income (using household consumption surveys) and assets over time using the World Bank's demographic health surveys (see, for example, Pritchett, Surayadi and Sumarto, 2000). Indicators of empowerment and participation have been tentatively assessed by using qualitative and quantitative measures of inclusion in decision-making at various levels, access to information and the potential for civil society monitoring of development projects (see for more detail World Bank, 2000, 2002a, 2002b, 2003, 2005).

In sum, how and why have poverty and well-being indicators evolved? Over the last half-decade, if not longer, the meaning and measurement of well-being have shifted from purely economic metrics to include non-economic factors. It is worth noting at this stage that how poverty and well-being are measured is entirely dependent on the definition accepted. If poverty is defined as basic needs or material standard of living, then economic or money-metric measures might seem more appropriate (and growth the "solution"). However, if poverty is defined as capabilities or rights then non-economic or non-money-metric measures would seem more insightful (and public goods the "solution"). One implication of accepting a multifaceted definitions of well-being is that it is quite feasible for a person to be poor in one aspect but non-poor in another – i.e. the concept of "poor" is actually fragmented – thus having a very strong post-modern resonance regarding the loss of meaning in long-held concepts.

From the historical discussion, three clusters of well-being indicators can be identified and categorized: those that measure poverty as primarily economic well-being; those that measure poverty as primarily non-economic well-being; and those that measure poverty as composites. Each grouping is now discussed.

Economic well-being measures of well-being

Over the last 50 years, as noted above, economic or money-metric measures have struggled to remain central in the meaning of well-being. However, they have continued to dominate well-being in measurement. They define well-being as higher income or consumption per person and a raised material standard of living. Table 3.2 outlines the commonly used economic measures of well-being (as grouped by the author). A number are MDGs.

Nine commonly used well-being indicators can be identified and divided into three further subgroups: measures of income per capita, those utilizing an income poverty line and those assessing income inequality. The first includes GDP per capita, real wages per capita and the unemployment rate. Then there are three indicators based on an income poverty line (using the proxy of consumption) – the dollar-a-day mea-

Table 3.2 Most commonly used economic measures of well-being (grouped by author)

Indicators
Income per capita • GDP per capita • Real wages • Unemployment rate*
Income poverty lines • Percentage of the population living under a dollar-a-day per capita* • Percentage of the population living under the national poverty line (2,100 calories) • Percentage of the population vulnerable to poverty through variance of income or assets
Income inequality • Poverty gap and severity indices at a dollar-a-day per capita* • Expenditure of bottom quintile as percentage of total expenditure* • Gini coefficient

*Indicator is an MDG.

sure, the national poverty line (usually based on the cost of 2,100 calories per capita per day) and the relatively new measure of "vulnerability to income poverty" through variance of income or assets over a year. Finally, there are three inequality measures – the poverty gap and severity indices, the income share of the poorest quintile and the Gini coefficient.

The GDP per capita, the dollar-a-day poverty measure and national poverty lines are (although to a lesser extent than before) still the most commonly used poverty indicators (Booth and Lucas, 2002: 23; Kanbur and Squire, 1999: 4). Why is this, and what is the comparative advantage of measuring well-being in economic terms relative to non-economic terms? Economic measures of well-being are popular (with policy-makers in particular) because they are useful when quick, rough-and-ready, short-run, aggregate inferences are required to make an assessment. They are more responsive, changing much faster than non-economic social data (which suffer a time lag). They are likely to be more recent and readily available than non-economic measures and are also cheaper and less complex to collect than non-economic poverty data (World Bank, 2001a, 2001b).

It could be argued that the dominance of economic measures is additionally due to the preconception that economic measures are more precise and objective because they are amenable to quantification as they are tangible – consumption of a certain amount of rice in kilograms can be recorded (assuming there is no recall or respondent bias). In contrast, non-economic measures are somewhat less amenable to quantification and rely on more tenuous and subjective proxies – for example, equating being "educated" to the subjective concept of "literacy". It is perhaps assumed that what is more amenable to quantification is more objective (i.e. the same to all people). For example, 1 kilogram of rice or $1 a day is the same to everyone. But it could be argued that this is false, as the gain or loss of a dollar or a kilogram of rice has a different welfare impact on a poor/hungry person than on someone else better off/not hungry (Prennushi, Ferreira and Ravallion, 1998).

What is the comparative disadvantage of economic measures of well-being? There are several issues of contention. These are, first, omissions of non-market activity, of unrecorded informal sector work, of domestic housework or subsistence activity and environmental degradation and depletion. Second, they are static measures – only the vulnerability measures capture the dynamics of poverty, in that households may move in and out of poverty over the course of a year (see Kamanou and Murdoch, 2002).

Finally, the measures take only limited account of differential experiences (especially intra-household, as they are typically based on the household head). Only the inequality measures make any assessment of differential experiences. It could be added that inequality measures are open to question as the data tend to be based on the distribution of consumption expenditure rather than income itself, thus hiding savings of wealthier groups and underestimating inequality, whilst unemployment rates are also questionable where there is no social security system (i.e. people have to seek income somehow).

Given that income poverty lines – and in particular the dollar-a-day measure – dominate (as noted above), it is worthwhile giving some further consideration to them. There are several issues of contention on these measures alone: first, the lack of recent household survey data and second, the construction of the poverty line. The 2003 *HDR* (UNDP, 2003: 35) noted that there were 55 countries with no household survey since 1990 and 100 LDCs with no trend data (1990–2001). The World Bank takes the last available survey and extrapolates forward using GDP per capita, making the questionable assumption that income inequality is static (see discussion in Reddy and Pogge, 2002).

Second, poverty estimates based on a poverty line are highly sensitive to the construction of that line. The common observation of clustering of the poor around the poverty line means that reducing the value of calories or the monetary cost of a minimum consumption basket automatically reduces the number of people below the line. Although poverty lines typically have a starting point of 2,100 calories per capita per day, the pricing of items and basket weighting of component items can lead to widely differing poverty estimates from the same point of departure (for discussion see Ravallion, 1992, 1998).

Other problems include the purchasing power parity (PPP) conversion either understating (Reddy and Pogge, 2002) or overstating (Bhalla, 2003) poverty levels, depending on whether the poverty line is constructed on average consumption (as PPP conversion rates are) or consumption of the poor. Further issues include the lack of account of different costs of living within a country, problems with heterogeneous sizes and compositions of households, the comparability and consistency of national household surveys and different consumption patterns in different countries (Lipton and Ravallion, 1995).

The headcount ratios also lack information on the depth and severity of poverty and inequality among the poor; for example, two households may be defined as poor but one may be much further below the poverty line than the other. This led Foster, Greer and Thorbecke (1984) to calculate two further measures – the poverty severity index (the difference between the poverty line and the average income of the population under the poverty line) and the poverty gap (a combined measure of the incidence of poverty and the depth of poverty, calculated by multiplying the headcount and severity).

In sum, well-being measures based on economic well-being have had and continue to have enduring popularity despite debates over the meaning of poverty moving beyond purely economic measures.

Non-economic well-being measures of well-being

Non-economic or non-money-metric measures of well-being have increasingly dominated the discourse on the *meaning* of well-being. They define and measure well-being with some resonance to Sen's conceptualization of well-being. Table 3.3 lists the most commonly used measures in four subclusters (as grouped by the author). A number are MDGs. Under education the three indicators are enrolment rates, survival to final year/ completion of primary school and literacy rates (adult and youth). For health and nutrition the indicators are malnutrition rates/food or calorie consumption/the body mass index (weight in kilograms divided by height

Table 3.3 Most commonly used non-economic measures of well-being (grouped by author)

Indicators

Education
- Education enrolment rates*
- Survival to the final primary or secondary school grade/completion of primary or secondary school*
- Literacy rates*

Health and nutrition
- Malnutrition rates*/food or calorie consumption per capita/body mass index
- Mortality and morbidity rates*/life expectancy/not expected to survive to 40 years/infection rates*
- Health service usage – skilled personnel at birth*/contraceptive prevalence rate*/immunization rates*

Environment
- Access to "improved" water sources*
- Access to "adequate" sanitation*
- Household infrastructure – permanent material used for walls of home and electricity supply

Empowerment and participation (tentative)
- Participation in general and local election voting (decision-making at various levels)
- Extent of knowledge of local projects and district budgets (access to information)
- Number, size and revenue of active NGOs (potential for civil society monitoring)

*Indicator is an MDG.

in square metres), mortality and morbidity rates (including maternal, infant and under 5 years), life expectancy/not expected to survive to 40 years old and infection rates for various diseases (in particular HIV) and health service usage (skilled personnel at birth/contraceptive prevalence rate/immunization rates). Environmental indicators of well-being are made up of the living biosphere of households: infrastructure provided near or inside the household, such as access to "improved" water and "adequate" sanitation, as well as the infrastructure of the household itself – for example, permanent material used for the walls of living quarters, and electricity.

Also, there are empowerment and participation indicators. As noted previously, these are in their infancy (although the UNDP proposed a gender empowerment index – see below). For inclusion in decision-making, these could be measurement of participation in general and local elections through the percentage of the population who vote (and/or perhaps the number of political parties active in elections). Where surveys are possible, access to information could be assessed by the extent of people's knowledge of local projects and district budgets. The potential for civil society monitoring could be assessed by analysis of the number, size and revenue of active NGOs (for greater detail see World Bank, 2003, 2005).

What is the comparative advantage of measuring well-being in non-economic terms? Non-economic measures of well-being are more useful than economic measures when a medium- or longer-run assessment is required, because they address more directly the *ends* or outcomes of policy (being educated and healthy) rather than the inputs or *means* (greater income). Although they are slower and more expensive to collect (often requiring their own tailored surveys and/or combined methods) than economic data, they have the additional benefit of being amenable to disaggregation, making them instructive for assessing distributional impacts of policy changes (World Bank, 2001a, 2001b).

There are, in general, at least two significant limitations: the availability and quality of the data, and difficulties in precise measurement of the stated social phenomenon or capability. In terms of availability, there are a number of large gaps in non-economic social statistics. For example, the UNDP (2003: 35) noted that although only about 20 countries had no child malnutrition data, no net primary enrolment data and no "improved" water access data since 1990, trend data (two data points between 1990 and 2001) were not available for up to 100 countries depending on the indicator chosen.

Additionally, the quality of what is available is open to question because it fails even a basic test of consistency: the data on health presented in the *HDR* and *WDR* do not always tally. Loup and Naudet (2000: 11) cited a comparison of maternal mortality rates in the *HDR* and *WDR* in the mid-1990s. The *WDR* listed 56 countries with data and the *HDR* listed the same countries (minus one) and a further 48. Of the 55 listed in both, only a quarter were within a similar range (+/−50/100,000), about half were much higher in the *WDR* and a quarter were much lower. Booth and Lucas (2002: v) noted that a blind eye is being turned to poor data reliability in the PRSP process, especially when little else is available. As they also note, it is somewhat paradoxical that the poorest areas will probably have the least reliable data, because in these places the administrative support for surveying is weakest and least financially supported.

The second issue of contention is one of capturing precisely the nature of the well-being characteristic. For example, in terms of education, enrolment can be misleading as it does not necessarily mean daily attendance, quality teaching and resources or that "learning" is occurring. Also, enrolment may be over-reported through children repeating years or inaccurate records on the total number of children in age cohorts. Similarly, in terms of literacy, being "literate" is a relative concept – there is no defined cut-off point for "illiterate". Further, self-declared or household-head-declared literacy could also be misleading, as there may be a stigma in acknowledging illiteracy or literacy may be weak. Likewise, health, nutritional and environment measures are not without problems. For example, mortality data rely on accurate birth and death records that may not exist (and cause of death for maternal mortality rates), and individuals may be recorded as having access to water or sanitation even when the facilities are broken or the person is physically unable to reach them. There is also no internationally accepted definition of how far facilities need to be in order to be "accessible", and what is defined as "improved" or "safe" water or "adequate" sanitation differs between countries.

The new empowerment and participation indicators noted above are interesting extensions of measuring well-being, but also problematic to measure. They often require completely new and tailor-made surveys/PPAs to generate the statistics. Further, given the sensitive nature of power relations, the survey/PPA process may be more open to influence by local (or national) élites than other indicators.

In short, measures based on non-economic well-being are useful to assess well-being outcomes when longer-term trends or disaggregation are required. However, non-economic measures do suffer significant limitations. Given the flaws in both economic and non-economic well-being indicators, a pertinent question might be: do composite measures make up for deficiencies or exacerbate them?

Table 3.4 Commonly used composite indicators and their components

	Component indicators		
	Longevity	Knowledge	Decent standard of living
HDI	Life expectancy at birth	Adult literacy rate; combined enrolment rate	Adjusted income capita (US$ PPP)
GDI	Female and male life expectancy at birth	Female and male adult literacy rate; female and male combined enrolment ratio	Female and male earned income share
HPI	Percentage of people not expected to live to 40	Adult illiteracy rate	Percentage of the population without access to safe water; percentage of the population without access to health services; percentage of undernourished children under five

Source: UNDP (1990; 1995; 1997; 1998).

Composite measures of well-being

There are a number of composite measures of well-being. The best known are the WHO's quality of life (QOL) indicators and the UNDP's human development indices.

In line with the wider emergence of subjective and psychological poverty meanings, the WHO's QOL indicators consider six QOL domains: physical, psychological, independence, social relationships, environment and the spiritual. A survey instrument, known as QOL100, contains 100 questions covering the six domains and elicits the respondents' personal feelings on a scale of 1–5 relating to how they see their quality of life.

Finally, there are the well-known UNDP indices: the HDI, the gender-related development index (GDI) and the human poverty index (HPI). Table 3.4 outlines the components of each.

The HDI, GDI and HPI each take account of well-being related to longevity of life and health, knowledge and education and standard of living. There is also a gender empowerment measure (GEM). The GEM is a measure of gender equality in politics, business and wages. For greater detail on HDI methodology see UNDP (1990, 1998). For the GDI (and GEM) see UNDP (1995) and for the HPI see UNDP (1997).

What are the strengths and weaknesses of the WHO and UNDP composites? None of the measures actually tells us how many people are poor (Sen's aggregation problem) or who is poor (Sen's identification problem). The WHO QOL measures have strength in their deeper insights and depth of understanding of well-being, but they require the same survey in all countries in order to make comparisons.

There are a number of concerns relating to these UNDP measures: principally, the HDI and GDI show little more than income per capita (due to the heavy weighting of GDP per person in the indices) and the index components themselves correlate very closely. However, it is the faults in the component parts that more seriously undermine their validity – often data do not exist for a particular year, resulting in the nearest available year being used or estimated by UN country staff. For example, given the large gaps in recent health and education data, the 2002 HDI for many countries is made up of GDP per capita for 2002 but with education and health data from the mid-1980s (see UNDP, 2003: 35; for more detailed HDI critique see Desai, 1991; McGillivray, 1991; Srinivasan, 1994). In sum, composite measures cannot make up for the deficiencies in components. Although the WHO QOL provides deeper insights into the state of well-being, all composites lack an ability to pinpoint the poor and create a headcount figure. Finally, one might note that all the measures, to a varying degree, still include economic well-being. In the case of the HDI, some argue the indicator is little more than GDP per capita due to the weighting of this index.

Concluding discussion

What can be concluded from the above discussion? The evolution of the meaning and measurement of well-being has covered a vast amount of ground in 50 years. The area is very rich conceptually, but operationalization is lagging behind. Future directions could consolidate this conceptual work whilst waiting for the database to (hopefully) catch up.

In five decades the debate has shifted emphasis from meaning and measurement based purely on *means* (or economic welfare) to *ends* and broader definitions of well-being. When development was purely GDP growth, well-being was understandably economically determined. Now that development is beyond purely GDP growth, well-being has evolved in line with this.

What conundrums remain? First, despite the fact that measuring well-being has never been so popular, data availability (especially for key MDGs and particularly in sub-Saharan Africa) and quality remain a concern at least until present surveys yield new data. Even then, cross-temporal and cross-country consistency is problematic and existing statistics are questionable. Second, if it is now accepted that well-being is multidimensional, why do economic measures continue in prominence? It has been argued here that this question reflects ongoing discussions in development studies over economic imperialism versus multidisciplinarity, and the false dichotomy that "economics = quantitative = rigour = objective" whilst "non-economics = qualitative = non-rigorous = subjective" (see White, 2002). Arguably the resilience of economic measures is due to the (perhaps false) preconception that such indicators of well-being are more amenable to quantification (as they are more tangible) and objective (the same to all). In contrast, non-economic measures are somewhat less amenable to quantification and rely on more tenuous and subjective proxies to capture their characteristics – measuring "being educated" is an example of this.

So, how should one decide what indicator(s) to choose? Determining who is poor and how many poor people there are is critically dependent on the choice of indicator. It is certainly feasible, as the *HDR* continually shows, that a person may be poor in some facets and non-poor in others. Is there, then, a need for ranking importance (as PPAs have tried in an as yet non-generalizable way)? What are the comparative advantages (relative efficiency in meeting its objective) of various clusters of indicators? It could be argued "horses for courses" – that the choice of indicator should reflect its purpose. For example, economic measures are best when quick, rough-and-ready, short-run, aggregate inferences are required. In contrast, non-economic measures are better when medium- or longer-term trends on well-being and/or disaggregation are needed. The purpose of indicators as well as availability and the quality of what is available all need to play a role in choosing indicators. The alternative would be a *well-being profile* – a range of measures and/or a *hierarchy of indicators* where some indicators are judged to be more important than others. If well-being is multifaceted, it would seem appropriate that the selection of indicators should reflect this.

In their 1999 review of the evolution of thinking on poverty, Kanbur and Squire concluded by asking what Rowntree would have to say if he were alive today. They suggested he might be surprised, 100 years on, that income was still the main measurement for poverty, but would have probably agreed that health and education were important factors in well-being. What might some of the founding fathers of quantitative economics or classical political economy have to say if they were alive today?

All would probably have emphasized the essentialism of linking well-being to economic welfare, but Smith and Marx might have added that any overemphasis on this would be to deny the broader aspects of the human condition (Marx) and/or the corrupting influence on moral sentiments of overemphasis on the importance of money/income (Smith). One could speculate that Quesney, Ricardo and Malthus might take a closer interest in the importance of malnutrition given their shared interest in agricultural output, and Petty might well have focused on the provision of public goods such as health and education given his work on public finance and fiscal policy. However, it might be John Stuart Mill who would have the most to comment on the current well-being debates given his focus on the importance of economic, political and social freedoms. Certainly he can provide one of the most sobering thoughts (when taken to apply to the analysis of poverty) – "there are many truths of which the full meaning cannot be realized until personal experience has brought it home".

Acknowledgements

The author is grateful for the comments and suggestions of Chris Barrow, Eleanor Fisher, Gaim Kibreab, John Taylor, Jan Toporowski, Alan Thomas, Michael Tribe and participants at the World Institute for Development Economics Research (WIDER) Conference, "Inequality, Poverty and Human Well-being", held on 30–31 May 2003 in Helsinki, in particular Des Gasper, George Mavrotas and Mariano Rojas.

REFERENCES

Alsop, R. and N. Heinsohn (2005) "Measuring Empowerment in Practice: Structuring Analysis and Framing Indicators", Policy Research Working Paper No. 3510, World Bank, Washington, D.C.

Anand, S. and A. Sen (2000) "Human Development and Economic Sustainability", *World Development* 28(12): 2029–2049.

Baster, N. (1979) "Models and Indicators", in S. Cole and H. Lucas, eds, *Models, Planning and Basic Needs*, Oxford: Pergamon.

Bauer, R., ed. (1966) *Social Indicators*, Cambridge, Mass.: MIT Press.

Bhalla, S. (2003) *Imagine There's No Country: Poverty, Inequality, and Growth in the Era of Globalization*, Washington, D.C.: Institute for International Economics.

Booth, D. and H. Lucas (2002) "Good Practice in the Development of Poverty Reduction Strategy Papers Indicators and Monitoring Systems", Working Paper No. 172, Overseas Development Institute, London.

Bourguignon, F., L. Da Silva and N. Stern (2002) "Evaluating the Poverty Impact of Economic Policies: Some Analytical Challenges", World Bank, mimeo.

Brandt, W. (1980) *North-South: A Programme for Survival*, London: Pan Books.

Cameron, J. (2003) "Journeying in Development Economics: An Overview", paper presented at Fifty Years of Development Economics: Taking Stock of Controversies, London, 3 July, available at www.devstud.org.uk/studygroups/economics.htm.

Chambers, R. (1983) *Whose Reality Counts? Putting the First Last*, London: Longmans.

Chambers, R. and G. Conway (1991) "Sustainable Rural Livelihoods: Practical Concepts for the 21st Century", Discussion Paper 296, Institute for Development Studies, Brighton.

Cornia, G., R. Jolly and F. Stewart, eds (1987) *Adjustment with a Human Face*, New York: Oxford University Press.

Dagdeviren, H., R. Van der Hoeven and J. Weeks (2001) "Redistribution Matters: Growth for Poverty Reduction", Working Paper, International Labour Organization, Geneva.

Desai, M. (1991) "Human Development: Concepts and Measurement", *European Economic Journal* 35: 350–357.

DFID (2000) *Sustainable Livelihoods Guidance Sheets*, London: DFID.

—— (2002) *Statistics Matter: Eliminating World Poverty*, London: DFID.

Foster, J., J. Greer and E. Thorbecke (1984) "A Class of Decomposable Poverty Measures", *Econometrica* 52: 761–766.

Hicks, N. and P. Streeten (1979) "Indicators of Development: The Search for a Basic Needs Yardstick", *World Development* 7: 567–580.

Hulme, D. and A. McKay (2005) "Identifying and Understanding Chronic Poverty: Beyond Monetary Measures", paper presented at "The Future of Development Economics", 17–18 June, UNU-WIDER, Helsinki, unpublished.

Hulme, D., K. Moore and A. Shepherd (2001) "Chronic Poverty: Meanings and Analytical Frameworks", Working Paper 2, Chronic Poverty Research Centre, Manchester.

ILO (1976) *Employment, Growth and Basic Needs: A One-World Problem*, Geneva: ILO.

—— (1977). *Meeting Basic Needs: Strategies for Eradicating Mass Poverty and Unemployment*, Geneva: ILO.

Kamanou, G. and J. Murdoch (2002) "Measuring Vulnerability to Poverty", Discussion Paper 2002/58, UNU-WIDER, Helsinki.

Kanbur, R. and L. Squire (1999) "The Evolution of Thinking About Poverty: Exploring the Contradictions", Working Paper, Department of Economics, Cornell University, Ithaca, NY.

Lipton, M. and M. Ravallion (1995) "Poverty and Policy", in J. R. Behrman and T. N. Srinivasan, eds, *Handbook of Development Economics*, Vol. IIIB, Amsterdam: Elsevier.

Loup, J. and D. Naudet (2000) "The State of Human Development Data and Statistical Capacity Building in Developing Countries", Human Development Report Office Occasional Papers, UNDP, Geneva.

McGillivray, M. (1991) "The Human Development Index: Yet Another Redundant Composite Development Indicator?", *World Development* 19(10): 1461–1469.

McGranahan, D., E. Pizarro and C. Richard (1985) *Measurement and Analysis of*

Socio-economic Development: An Enquiry into International Indicators of Development and Quantitative Interrelations of Social and Economic Components of Development, Geneva: UNRISD.

Morris, D. (1979) *Measuring the Condition of the World's Poor: The Physical Quality of Life Index*, London: Cass.

Narayan, N., R. Patel, K. Schafft, A. Rademacher and S. Koch-Schulte (1999) *Can Anyone Hear Us? Voices from 47 Countries*, New York: Oxford University Press for the World Bank.

Norten, A., B. Bird, K. Brock, M. Kakande and C. Turk (2002) *A Rough Guide to Participatory Poverty Assessment: An Introduction to Theory and Practice*, London: DFID.

Nussbaum, M. (2000) *Women and Human Development: The Capabilities Approach*, Cambridge: Cambridge University Press.

Prennushi, G., F. Ferreira and M. Ravallion (1998) "Macroeconomic Crises and Poverty: Transmission Mechanisms and Policy Responses", Working Paper, World Bank, Washington, D.C.

Pritchett, L., S. Surayadi and S. Sumarto (2000) "Quantifying Vulnerability to Poverty: A Proposed Measure, With Application to Indonesia", Working Paper, Social Monitoring and Early Response Unit, Jakarta.

Ravallion, M. (1992) "Poverty Comparisons: A Guide to Concepts and Methods", Working Paper No. 88, World Bank, Washington, D.C.

——— (1998) "Poverty Lines in Theory and Practice", Working Paper No. 133, World Bank, Washington, D.C.

Reddy, S. and T. Pogge (2002) "How Not to Count the Poor", Working Paper, Department of Economics, Columbia University, New York.

Sagar, A. and A. Najam (1999) "Shaping Human Development: Which Way Next?", *Third World Quarterly* 20(4): 743–751.

Seers, D. (1969) "The Meaning of Development", *International Development Review* 11: 2–6.

Sen, A. (1982) *Choice, Welfare and Measurement*, Oxford: Basil Blackwell.

——— (1985) "Well-Being, Agency and Freedom: The Dewey Lectures", *Journal of Philosophy* 82(4): 169–221.

——— (1999) *Development as Freedom*, New York: Knopf.

Srinivasan, T. (1994) "Human Development: A New Paradigm or Reinvention of the Wheel?", *American Economic Review* 84: 238–243.

Streeten, P. (1984) "Basic Needs: Some Unsettled Questions", *World Development* 12(9): 973–980.

United Nations (1989) *Handbook on Social Indicators*, Geneva: United Nations.

UNDP (1990) *Human Development Report 1990*, New York: Oxford University Press.

——— (1995) *Human Development Report 1995*, New York: Oxford University Press.

——— (1997) *Human Development Report 1997*, New York: Oxford University Press.

——— (1998) *Human Development Report 1998*, New York: Oxford University Press.

—— (2003) *Human Development Report 2003*, New York: Oxford University Press.
UNRISD (1970) *Contents and Measurement of Socioeconomic Development*, Geneva: UNRISD.
White, H. (2002) "Combining Quantitative and Qualitative Approaches in Poverty Analysis", *World Development* 30(3): 511–522.
World Bank (1980) *World Development Report*, Washington, D.C.: World Bank.
—— (1990) *World Development Report*, Washington, D.C.: World Bank.
—— (1992) *Poverty Reduction Handbook*, Washington, D.C.: World Bank.
—— (2000) *World Development Report*, Washington, D.C.: World Bank.
—— (2001a) *Strengthening Statistical Systems for Poverty Reduction Strategies*, Washington, D.C.: World Bank.
—— (2001b) *Well-being Measurement and Analysis Technical Notes*, Washington, D.C.: World Bank.
—— (2002a) *Empowerment and Poverty Reduction: A Sourcebook*, Washington, D.C.: World Bank.
—— (2002b) *Poverty Reduction Strategy Papers Sourcebook*, Washington, D.C.: World Bank.
—— (2003) *Empowerment Sourcebook*, Washington, D.C.: World Bank.
—— (2005) *Measuring Empowerment*, Washington, D.C.: World Bank.

4
The four qualities of life: Ordering concepts and measures of the good life

Ruut Veenhoven

There are many words that are used to indicate how well we are doing. Some of these signify overall thriving; currently the terms *quality of life* and *well-being* are used for this purpose, and sometimes the word *health*. In the past the terms *happiness* and *welfare* were more commonly used. There are several problems with these terms.

One problem is that these terms do not have an unequivocal meaning. Sometimes they are used as an umbrella for all that is good, but on other occasions they denote specific merit. For instance, the term *well-being* is used to denote the quality of life as a whole and to evaluate life aspects such as dwelling conditions or employment chances. Likewise, the phrase *quality of life* refers in some contexts to the quality of society and in other instances to the happiness of its citizens. There is little consensus on the meaning of these words; the trend is rather to divergence. Over time, connotations tend to become more specific and manifold. Discursive communities tend to develop their own quality-of-life notions.

The second problem is in the connotation of inclusiveness. The use of the words as an umbrella term suggests that there is such a thing as *overall* quality of life and that specific merits can be meaningfully added in some wider worth; however, that holistic assumption is dubious. Philosophers have never agreed on one final definition of quality of life, and in the practice of empirical quality-of-life measurement we see comparisons of apples and pears.

The above problem of many meanings is partly caused by the suggestion of inclusiveness. One of the reasons why the meanings become more specific is that the rhetoric of encompassing crumbles when put into practice. The broad overall meaning appears typically unfeasible in measurement and decision-making. Hence connotations tend to become more specific and diverse. As a result, rhetorical denotation of the overall good requires new terms periodically. New expressions pop up, as opposed to narrower meanings. For instance, in the field of healthcare the term *quality of life* emerged to convey the idea that there is more than mere quantity of survival time. Likewise, the word *well-being* came into use in contrast to sheer economic *welfare*. Yet, in the long run, these new terms fall victim to their success. Once they are adopted as a goal for policy, analysts and trend-watchers start extracting palpable meanings and make the concepts ever more multidimensional.

Obviously, this communicative practice causes much confusion and impedes the development of knowledge in this field. In reaction there have been many proposals for standard definitions. Elsewhere the author has listed 15 definitions of happiness (Veenhoven, 1984: 16–17). More recently Noll (1999) listed many meanings of quality of life in nations.

Since we cannot really force the use of words, we can try to clarify their use better. We can elucidate the matter by distinguishing different meanings. An analytic tool for this purpose is proposed in this chapter. First, a fourfold classification of qualities of life is presented. By means of this taxonomy, common terms and distinctions are placed. The matrix is then used to chart substantive meanings in common measures of the good life. Finally the question is raised as to whether we can meaningfully speak about comprehensive quality of life.

Grouping qualities of life

A classic distinction is between *objective* and *subjective* quality of life. The first refers to the degree a life meets explicit standards of the good life as assessed by an impartial outsider – for instance, the result of a medical examination. The latter concerns self-appraisals based on implicit criteria; for example, someone's subjective feeling of health. These qualities do not necessarily correspond: someone may be in good health by the criteria of his doctor, but nevertheless feel bad. On the basis of this distinction, Zapf (1984: 25) has proposed a fourfold classification of welfare concepts. When conditions of life score well on objective measures and subjective appreciation of life is positive, he speaks of *well-being*; when both evaluations are negative, he speaks of *deprivation*. When objective quality is good but subjective appreciation is negative, the term *dissonance* is applied, and the combination of bad conditions and positive appreciation is labelled *adaptation*.

Though elegant, these distinctions have not proven particularly useful. The taxonomy does not explain much, mainly because the difference is more in observation than in substance. Objective health assessment aims at the same qualities as subjective appraisals, though by different means. Further, the labelling gives rise to misunderstanding. The word *objective* suggests indisputable truth, whereas the term *subjective* is easily interpreted as a matter of arbitrary taste. This suggestion is false: the fact that income can be measured objectively does not mean that its value is beyond question.

Chances and outcomes

A substantively more relevant distinction is between opportunities for a good life and the good life itself. This is the difference between potentiality and actuality, termed here as life chances and life results. Opportunities and outcomes are related, but are certainly not the same. Chances can fail to be realized, due to stupidity or bad luck. Conversely, people sometimes make much of their life in spite of poor opportunities.

This distinction is quite common in the field of public health research. Preconditions for good health, such as adequate nutrition and professional care, are seldom mixed up with health itself. Much research is aimed at assessing the relationships between these phenomena; for instance, by checking whether common nutritional advice really yields extra years lived in good health.

Yet in social policy discussions, means and ends are less well distinguished. For instance, in the Netherlands the term well-being is used for both social services, e.g. state pensions, and for the expected effects, satisfied citizens. This is not just sloppy thinking, it is also an expression of the ideology that there is quality to be found in the welfare society.

Outer and inner qualities

A second difference is between external and internal qualities. In the first case the quality is in the environment, in the latter it is in the individual. Lane (1994) made this distinction clear by emphasizing *quality of persons*. Likewise Musschenga (1994: 182) discerned *quality of conditions for living* from *the quality of being human*.

This distinction is also quite commonly made in public health. External pathogens are distinguished from inner afflictions, and researchers try to identify the mechanisms by which the former produce the latter and the conditions in which this is more and less likely. Yet again this basic insight is lacking in many social policy discussions. For instance, in the current discourse on city renewal, the phrase *quality of life* is used both for clean streets and feelings of being at home in the neighbourhood. All the

	Outer qualities	Inner qualities
Life chances	Liveability of environment	Life-ability of the person
Life results	Utility of life	Appreciation of life

Figure 4.1 Four qualities of life

research that found negligible relationships has not changed this use of words.

Four qualities of life

The combination of these two dichotomies yields a fourfold matrix (fig. 4.1). The distinction between chances and results is presented vertically, the difference between outer and inner qualities horizontally.

Two kinds of life chances

In the upper half of figure 4.1 we see two variants of potential quality of life, with the outer opportunities in one's environment and the inner capacities to exploit these. The environmental chances can be denoted by the term *liveability*, the personal capacities with the word *life-ability*. This difference is not new. In sociology the distinction between *social capital* and *psychological capital* is sometimes used in this context. In the psychology of stress the difference is labelled negatively in terms of *burden* and *bearing power*.

Liveability of the environment
The left top quadrant denotes the meaning of good living conditions. Often the terms *quality of life* and *well-being* are used in this particular meaning, especially in the writings of ecologists and sociologists. Economists sometimes use the term *welfare* for this meaning. Another term is *level of living*.

Liveability is a better word, because it refers explicitly to a characteristic of the environment and does not have the limited connotation of material conditions. One could also speak of the *habitability* of an environment, though that term is also used for the quality of housing in particular. Elsewhere the author has explored that concept of liveability in more detail (Veenhoven, 1996: 7–9).

Life-ability of the person
The right top quadrant denotes inner life chances: how well we are equipped to cope with the problems of life. This aspect of the good life is also known by different names. The words *quality of life* and *well-being*

are used to denote this specific meaning, especially by doctors and psychologists. There are more names, however. In biology the phenomenon is referred to as *adaptive potential*. On other occasions it is denoted by the medical term *health*, in the medium variant of the word, or by psychological terms such as *efficacy* or *potency*. Sen (1992) calls this quality-of-life variant *capability*. The present author prefers the simple term *life-ability*, which contrasts elegantly with "liveability".

Two kinds of life results

The lower half of the matrix is about the quality of life with respect to its outcomes. These outcomes can be judged by their value for one's environment and value for oneself. The external worth of a life is denoted by the term *utility of life*. The inner valuation of it is called *appreciation of life*. These matters are, of course, related. Knowing that one's life is useful will typically add to the appreciation of it. Yet not all useful lives are happy lives and not every good-for-nothing really cares. This difference has been elaborated in discussions on utilitaristic moral philosophy, which praises happiness as the highest good. Adversaries of that view hold that there is more worth to life than just pleasures and pains. Mill ([1863] 1990) summarized that position in his famous statement that he preferred an unhappy Socrates to a happy fool.

Utility of life

The left bottom quadrant represents the notion that a good life must be good for something more than itself. This presumes some higher values. There is no current generic for these external outcomes of life. Gerson (1976: 795) referred to these as transcendental conceptions of quality of life. Another appellation is *meaning of life*, which then denotes *true* significance instead of mere subjective sense of meaning. The author prefers the more simple *utility of life*, admitting that this label may also give rise to misunderstanding. Be aware that this external utility does not require inner awareness. A person's life may be useful from some viewpoint without them knowing.

Appreciation of life

Finally, the bottom right quadrant represents the inner outcomes of life; that is, the quality in the eye of the beholder. As we deal with conscious humans, this quality boils down to subjective appreciation of life. This is commonly referred to by terms such as *subjective well-being*, *life satisfaction* and *happiness* in a limited sense of the word. Life has more of this quality the more and the longer it is enjoyed. In fairy-tales this combination of intensity and duration is denoted with the phrase "they lived long and happily".

Ordering concepts of the good life

With the help of this matrix we can now place the various notions about the good life. This section starts with an overview of concepts that neatly fit the quality quadrants before confronting the matrix with some other classifications of qualities of life.

Meanings within quality quadrants

Most discussions of the good life deal with more specific values than the four qualities of life discerned here. Within each quadrant there is a myriad of submeanings, most of which are known under different names. It would need a voluminous book to record all the terms and meanings used in the literature. Some of the main variants are presented below.

Aspects of liveability

Liveability is an umbrella term for the various qualities of the environment which seem relevant for meeting human needs. In rhetoric use, the word refers mostly to specific kinds of qualities which typically root in some broader perception of the good society. The circumstantial qualities that are emphasized differ widely across contexts and disciplines.

Ecologists see liveability in the natural environment and describe it in terms of pollution, global warming and degradation of nature. Currently they associate liveability typically with *preservation*. City planners see liveability in the built environment and associate it with sewer systems, traffic jams and ghetto formation. Here the good life is seen as a fruit of human intervention.

In the sociological view, society is central. First, liveability is associated with the quality of society as a whole. Classic concepts of the *good society* stress material welfare and social equality, sometimes equating the concept more or less with the welfare state. Current notions emphasize close networks, strong norms and active voluntary associations. The reverse of that liveability concept is *social fragmentation*. Second, liveability is seen in one's position in society. For long the emphasis was on an *underclass*, but currently attention shifts to an *outer class*. The corresponding antonyms are deprivation and exclusion.

Kinds of life-ability

The most common depiction of this quality of life is the absence of functional defects. This is *health* in the limited sense, sometimes referred to as *negative health*. In this context, doctors focus on unimpaired functioning of the body while psychologists stress the absence of mental defects. In their language, quality of life and well-being are often synonymous with mental health. This use of words presupposes a "normal" level of functioning. Good quality of life is the body or mind working as designed. This is the common meaning used in curative care.

Next to absence of disease one can consider excellence of function. This is referred to as *positive health* and associated with energy and resilience. Psychological concepts of positive mental health involve also autonomy, reality control, creativity and inner synergy of traits and strivings. A new term in this context is *emotional intelligence*. Though originally meant for specific mental skills, this term has come to denote a broad range of mental capabilities. This broader definition is the favourite in the training professions.

A further step is to evaluate capability in a developmental perspective and include acquisition of new skills for living. This is commonly denoted by the term *self-actualization*; from this point of view a middle-aged man is not *well* if he behaves like an adolescent, even if he functions without problems at this level. This quality concept is also currently used in the training professions.

Lastly, the term *art of living* denotes special life-abilities; in most contexts this quality is distinguished from mental health and sometimes even attributed to slightly disturbed persons. Art of living is associated with refined tastes, an ability to enjoy life and an original style of life.

Criteria for utility of life

When evaluating the external effects of a life, one can consider its functionality for the environment. In this context, doctors stress how essential a patient's life is to his/her intimates. The life of a mother with young children is valued higher than the life of a woman of the same age without children. Likewise, indispensability at the workplace figures in medical quality-of-life notions.

At a higher level, quality of life is seen in contributions to society. Historians see quality as the addition an individual can make to human culture, and thus rate the lives of great inventors, for example, higher than those of anonymous peasants. Moralists see quality in the preservation of the moral order, and would deem the life of a saint to be better than that of a sinner.

In this vein the quality of a life is also linked to effects on the ecosystem. Ecologists see more quality in a life lived in a *sustainable* manner than in the life of a polluter. In a broader view, the utility of life can be seen in its consequences for long-term evolution. As an individual's life can have many environmental effects, the number of such utilities is almost infinite.

Apart from its functional utility, life is also judged on its moral or aesthetic value. Returning to Mill's statement that he preferred an unhappy

Socrates to a happy fool, Mill did not say this just because Socrates was a philosopher whose words have come down to us. It was also because he admired Socrates as an outstanding human being. Likewise, most of us would attribute more quality to the life of Florence Nightingale than to that of a drunk, even if it appeared that her good works had a negative result in the end. In classic moral philosophy this is called *virtuous living*, and is often presented as the essence of *true happiness*.

This concept of exemplary utility sometimes merges with notions of inner life-ability, in particular in the case of self-actualization. Self-development is deemed good, even if it might complicate life. In some philosophies of life, reaching a state of enlightenment is more important than departing from it.

This quality criterion is external; individuals need not be aware of their perfection or may actually despise it. It is an outsider who appraises the quality of the individual's life on the basis of an external criterion. In religious thinking such a judgement is made by God on the basis of eternal truth; in post-modern thought it is narrated by self-proclaimed experts on the basis of local conviction.

Clearly, the utility of life is not easy to grasp; the criteria and those who would judge are multifarious. Later we will see that this prohibits comprehensive measurement of this quality of life. This quadrant is typically the playground of philosophers.

Appreciation of life

Humans are capable of evaluating their life in different ways. As already noted, we have in common with all higher animals the ability to appraise our situation effectively. We feel good or bad about particular things and our mood level signals overall adaptation. As in animals these affective appraisals are automatic, but unlike other animals it is known that humans can reflect on that experience. We have an idea of how we have felt over the last year, while a cat does not. Humans can also judge life cognitively by comparing life as it is with notions of how it should be.

Most human evaluations are based on both sources of information: intuitive affective appraisal and cognitively guided evaluation. The mix depends mainly on the object. Tangible things such as our income are typically evaluated by comparison; intangible matters such as sexual attractiveness are evaluated by how it feels. This dual evaluation system probably makes the human experiential repertoire richer than that of our fellow creatures.

In evaluating our life, we typically summarize this rich experience in overall appraisals. For instance, we appreciate several domains of life. When asked how we feel about our work or marriage, we will mostly have an opinion. Likewise, most people form ideas about separate qualities of their life, for instance how challenging their life is and whether there is any meaning in it. Such judgements are made in different time perspectives, in the past, present and future. As the future is less palpable than the past and the present, hopes and fears depend more on affective inclination than on cognitive calculation.

Mostly such judgements are not very salient in our consciousness. Now and then they pop into mind spontaneously, and they can be recalled and refreshed when needed. Sometimes, however, life appraisals develop into pervasive mental syndromes such as depression or ennui.

Next to aspects of life, we also evaluate life as a whole. Jeremy Bentham ([1789] 2002) thought of this form of evaluation as a type of mental calculus, and currently most scholars in the field also see it as a cognitive operation. For instance, Andrews and Withey (1976) suggest that individuals compute a weighed average of earlier life-aspect evaluations, while Michalos's (1985) multiple discrepancy theory presumes comparisons of life as it is with various standards of how it should be. Many philosophers see it as an estimate of success in realizing one's life plan (e.g. Nordenfelt, 1989).

Yet there are good reasons to assume that overall life satisfaction is mostly inferred from affective experience (Veenhoven, 1997: 59–61). One reason is that life as a whole is not a suitable object for calculative evaluation. Life has many aspects, and there is usually not one clear-cut ideal model with which to compare. Another reason seems to be that affective signals tend to dominate: seemingly cognitive appraisals are often instigated by affective cues (Zajonc, 1980). This fits the theory that the affective system is the older in evolutionary terms, and that cognition works as an addition to that navigation system rather than a replacement.

This issue has important consequences for the significance of subjective appreciation of life as a criterion for quality of life. If appreciation is a matter of mere comparison with arbitrary standards, there is little of value in a positive evaluation; dissatisfaction is then an indication of high demands. If, however, happiness signals the degree to which innate needs are met, life satisfaction denotes how well we thrive.

Whatever the method of assessment, the fact that we are able to come to an overall evaluation of life is quite important. Later on we will see that this is the only basis for encompassing judgements of the quality of life.

Difference with other classifications of qualities of life

This is, of course, not the first attempt to chart concepts of the good life. A few examples will show how this matrix differs from other taxonomies.

Philosopher Dan Brock (1993: 268–275) also tried to grasp "the broad-

	Outer quality	Inner quality
Chances	Objective quality • Life meets normative ideals	
Results		Subjective quality • Life meets preferences • Life is enjoyed

Figure 4.2 Fit with Brock's classification

	Outer quality	Inner quality
Chances	Conditions for happiness • General happiness requisites • Idiosyncratic happiness requisites	
Results		Happiness

Figure 4.3 Fit with McCall's classification

est conception of ... what makes a life go best". He distinguishes three main concepts: the degree to which life fits current values and ideals; the degree to which life fits the individual's preferences; and the degree to which the individual enjoys life subjectively. He denotes the first concept as *objective* and the other two as *subjective*. Brock insists on the difference between satisfaction of preferences (contentment in the present author's terminology) and hedonic enjoyment (mood level).

These meanings are plotted in the matrix in figure 4.2. The difference is not so much in the appreciation quadrant, but in the other three. Brock's classification is less differentiated, and shovels all the objective meanings into one heap. As he is mainly concerned with healthcare, one can imagine that he leaves out societal liveability. Yet he does not distinguish either between *capability for life* and *utility of life*, though this distinction is quite relevant for medical decisions.

Sandoe (1999) proposes a similar classification which also separates realization of preferences and hedonic experience. The difference is that his *objective* qualities are limited to the development of potentials. He refers to that quality as *perfectionism*; the present author terms it *self-actualization*. In the matrix it is a part of the life-ability quadrant.

Storrs McCall (1975) also distinguishes two main concepts of quality of life (see fig. 4.3). Next to happiness itself, he emphasizes conditions for happiness. In his view life has quality if the necessary social conditions are available, even if an individual fails to exploit these chances or opts not to use them. Happiness is seen to result from need gratification, and hence the necessary conditions are linked to basic human needs. In this concept, human nature is the major yardstick, and not normative ideals. Consequently, the utility quadrant remains empty in this case. McCall does not distinguish between external and internal requisites, thus the two top quadrants are merged.

Ordering measures of the good life

The last decades have witnessed a surge in empirical research on the good life, in particular in the fields of social indicators research and medical quality-of-life assessment. This has produced a wealth of measures. Testbanks contain hundreds of them – see, for instance, Cummins (1993), Spilker (1996) and Veenhoven (2000a).

Most of these measures are multidimensional and are used to assess different qualities of life. Typically, the scores on the different qualities are presented separately in a "quality-of-life *profile*". Often they are also summed in a "quality-of-life *score*". Next, there are "unidimensional" measures which focus on one specific quality. Such single qualities are often measured by single questions; for instance, the condition of cancer patients is measured by simply asking them where they stand between the best and worst they have ever experienced (Bernheim and Buyse, 1983).

A lively discussion about the pros and cons of these measures is still going on. Psychometricians, who focus very much on factor loadings, reliability issues and inter-test correlations, dominate this discussion. There is less attention to matters of substance, so there is no clear answer to the question of what these measures actually measure. One of the reasons for this deficiency is a lack of a clear taxonomy of the qualities of life.

Now that we have a classification of meanings, we can give it another try. This section first outlines which of these qualities figure in measures that claim to cover the good of life inclusively, and then explores whether there are measures that fit one of the four qualities of life separately.

Meanings in comprehensive measures of quality of life

As there are so many measures of the good life, they cannot all be reviewed here: four examples must suffice to illustrate the approach. The examples are taken from different research fields: medical quality-of-life research, psychological well-being research, sociologically oriented research on welfare and socio-economic studies of national development.

	Outer quality	Inner quality
Life chances		• No limitations to work and social functioning • Not nervous • Energetic • General health good
Life results		• No pain • No bad feelings • Happy person

Figure 4.4 Meanings measured by Ware's SF-36 Health Survey

Example of a medical quality-of-life index

One of the most common measures in medical quality-of-life research is the SF-36 Health Survey (Ware, 1996). It is a questionnaire on the following topics:
- physical limitations in daily chores (10 items)
- physical limitations to work performance (4 items)
- bodily pain (2 items)
- perceived general health (6 items)
- vitality (4 items)
- physical and/or emotional limitations to social functioning (2 items)
- emotional limitations to work performance (3 items)
- self-characterizations as nervous (1 item)
- recent enjoyment of life (4 items).

Ratings on the first four topics are grouped in a "physical component subscore", ratings on the last four topics in a "mental component subscore". These components are added into a quality-of-life total score.

Most elements of this scale refer to performance potential and belong in the life-ability quadrant at the top right in figure 4.4. This will be no surprise, since the scale is aimed explicitly at health. Still, some of the items concern outcomes rather than potency, in particular the items on recent enjoyment of life (last on the list). Pain and bad feelings are typically the result of health defects. Happiness is clearly also an outcome. As a proper health measure the SF-36 does not involve outer qualities, so the left quadrants in figure 4.4 remain empty.

Several other medical measures of quality of life do involve items about environmental conditions that belong in the liveability quadrant. For instance, the Quality of Life Interview Schedule by Ouellette-Kuntz (1990) is about availability of services for handicapped persons. In this supply-centred measure of the good life, life is better the more services are offered and the more greedily they are used. Likewise, the quality-of-life index for cancer patients (Spitzer et al., 1981) lists support by family and friends as a quality criterion. Some medical indices also include outer effects that belong to the utility quadrant: typical items are continuation of work tasks and support provided to intimates and fellow patients.

Example of a psychological well-being scale

Cummins (1993) sees quality of life (QOL) as an aggregate of objective and subjective components. Each of these components is divided into the following seven domains:
- material well-being: measured by income, quality of house and possessions
- health: measured by number of disabilities and medical consumption
- productivity: measured by activities in work, education and leisure
- intimacy: contacts with close friends, availability of support
- safety: perceived safety of home, quality of sleep, worrying
- place in community: social activities, responsibilities, being asked for advice
- emotional well-being: opportunity to do/have things wanted, enjoyment of life.

Overall QOL is measured using a points system, objective QOL using simple scores amd subjective QOL using satisfaction with domains weighted by their perceived importance. Finally the scores on objective and subjective QOL are added.

The objective scores of this list represent typically life chances, though the safety items are subjective appraisals. This item is therefore placed between brackets in the matrix in figure 4.5. Most of the items concern

	Outer quality	Inner quality
Life chances	• Income, possessions • Social contacts • Social position (safety) • Opportunities	• Health • Productivity • Autonomy
Life results	• (Productivity) • (Social responsibility)	Satisfaction with • material life • social contacts • social position • safety • freedom

Figure 4.5 Meanings measured by Cummins's Comprehensive Quality of Life Scale

environmental chances and are placed in the liveability quadrant, top left. Two items concern inner capabilities and are placed in the life-ability quadrant, top right.

The subjective scores all refer to how the individual appreciates these aspects of life, and belong in the enjoyment quadrant on the bottom right. The Cummins scale has no items on overall satisfaction with life. The logic of his system produces the somewhat peculiar item "How satisfied are you with your own happiness?"

The bottom left quadrant remains empty in this interpretation; however, some of the life-chance items can also be seen as indicative of outer results. The measures of *place in community* imply not only better access to scarce resources, but can also denote contribution to society. Likewise, the productivity item may not only tap ability to work, but also the results of it. For this reason these items are placed in brackets in the meaning quadrant.

Example of a sociological measure of individual quality of life

One of the first attempts to chart quality of life in a general population was made in the Scandinavian Study of Comparative Welfare under the direction of Erik Allardt (1976). Welfare was measured using the criteria of income; housing; political support; social relations; irreplaceability; doing interesting things; health; education; and life satisfaction.

Allardt classified these indicators using his – now classic – distinction between *having*, *loving* and *being*. This labelling was appealing at that time, because it expressed the rising conviction that welfare is more than just material wealth, and because it fitted modish notions drawn from humanistic psychology. Though it is well known, the classification has not proven to be very useful.

These indicators can also be ordered in the fourfold matrix proposed here (see fig. 4.6). Most of the items belong in the top left quadrant

	Outer quality	Inner quality
Life chances	• Income (h) • Housing (h) • Political support (h) • Social relations (l)	• Health (h) • Education (h)
Life results	• Irreplaceable (b)	• Doing interesting things (b) • Life satisfaction (b)

Note: (h) = having, (l) = loving, (b) = being

Figure 4.6 Meanings measured by Allardt's "Dimensions of Welfare"

because they concern preconditions for a good life rather than good living as such, and because these chances are in the environment rather than in the individual. This is the case with income, housing, political support and social relations. Two further items also denote chances, but are internal capabilities: the health factor and level of education. These items are placed in the top right quadrant of personal life-ability. The item "irreplaceable" belongs in the utility bottom left quadrant: it denotes a value of a life to others. The last two items belong in the enjoyment bottom right quadrant. "Doing interesting things" denotes appreciation of an aspect of life, while life satisfaction concerns appreciation of life as a whole.

Example of a measure of quality in nations

Lastly comes illustration of measures used in cross-national comparisons of quality of life. The most commonly used indicator in this field is the human development index (HDI). This index was developed for the UNDP, which describes the progress in all countries of the world in its annual *Human Development Report* (UNDP, 1990). The HDI is the major yardstick used in these reports. The basic variant of this measure involves three items: public wealth, measured by buying power per head; education, as measured by literacy and schooling; and life expectancy at birth. Note that we deal now with scores drawn from national statistical aggregates instead of individual responses to questionnaires.

Later variants of the HDI involve further items: gender equality measured by the so-called "gender empowerment index", which involves male-female ratios in literacy, school enrolment and income, and poverty measured by prevalence of premature death, functional illiteracy and poverty.

In a theoretical account of this measure the UNDP claims to focus on how development enlarges people's choice, and thereby their chances for leading long, healthy and creative lives (UNDP, 1990: 9).

When placed in our fourfold matrix, this index can be seen to have three meanings (fig. 4.7). First, it is about living conditions, in the basic variant of material affluence in society, and in the variant of social equal-

	Outer quality	Inner quality
Life chances	• Material wealth • Gender equality • Income equality	• Education
Life results		• Life expectancy

Figure 4.7 Meanings measured by the UNDP's human development index

ity. These items belong in the top left quadrant. In the case of wealth it is acknowledged that this environmental merit is subject to diminishing utility; this, however, is not so with the equalities. Second, the HDI includes abilities. The education item belongs in the top right quadrant. Though a high level of education does not guarantee high mental health and pronounced ability in the art of living, it means that many citizens have at least basic knowledge.

Lastly, the item *life expectancy* is an outcome variable and belongs in the bottom right quadrant. The bottom left quadrant remains empty. The UNDP's measure of development does not involve specific notions about the meaning of life.

The HDI is the most concise measure of quality of life in nations. Extended variants in this family provide more illustration; for instance, Naroll's (1983: 73) "quality of life index" includes contributions to science by the country, which fits the utility quadrant. The index also includes suicide rates, which belong to the appreciation quadrant.

Measures for specific qualities of life

Next to these encompassing measures of quality of life, there are measures that denote specific qualities. These indicators can also be mapped on the matrix. Again, some illustrative examples will suffice.

Measures of liveability

Environmental life chances are measured in two ways: by the possibilities embodied in the environment as a whole, and by relative access to these opportunities. The former measures concern the liveability of societies, such as nations or cities. These indicators are typically used in developmental policy. The latter are about relative advantage or deprivation of persons in these contexts, and are rooted mostly in the politics of redistribution. These chance estimates are seldom combined.

Contents
Measures of liveability of society concern firstly nations; an illustrative example is Estes's (1984) "index of social progress". This measure involves aspects such as wealth of the nation, peace with neighbours, internal stability and democracy. The physical habitability of the land is also acknowledged. There are similar measures for quality of life in cities (e.g. Kunz and Siefer, 1995) and regions (e.g. Korczak, 1995). There are also liveability scores for more or less "total" institutions such as army bases, prisons, mental hospitals and geriatric residences.

Measures of relative deprivation focus on differences among citizens for such things as income, work and social contacts. Differences in command of these resources are typically interpreted as differential access to scarce resources (e.g. Townsend, 1979).

All these measures work with points systems and sum scores based on different criteria in some way. A part of the measures is based on objective assessments and is typically derived from social statistics. Others also include self-reports about living conditions and depend for this purpose on survey data.

Limitations
These inventories cannot really measure liveability comprehensively. First, the two kinds are seldom combined; second, both labour under serious limitations.

The first limitation is that the topics in these inventories do not exhaustively cover environmental conditions. The indices consist of some dozens of topics that are deemed relevant and happen to be measurable. The inventories obviously lack sections on conditions we do not know of as yet; note, for example, that the list of environmental pathogens is growing each year. Further, not all the conditions we are aware of are measurable. For instance, there are no measures for highly valued qualities like *social solidarity* and *cultural variety*.

Problem number two is the significance of topics that are included. Since there is no complete understanding of what we really need, we can only guess at the importance of a topic. Though it is evident that we need food and shelter, it is questionable whether we need holidays and a welfare state. The choice of topics to include in a liveability index is not based on evidence that we cannot thrive without something, but on the researcher's preconceptions of the good life. Elsewhere the author has proposed gauging the significance of liveability topics by their effects on health and happiness (Veenhoven, 1996). The case of the welfare state can be used to illustrate that point. Several liveability inventories include expenditures on social security, e.g. Naroll's (1983: 73) "quality of life index". Yet people appear not to thrive any better in nations with high social security expenditures than in comparable nations where state social security is modest (Veenhoven, 2000b). Freedom appears to add more to happiness, in particular economic freedom (Veenhoven, 2000c).

The third problem is the degree of opportunities required; how many should an environment provide to be liveable? With respect to food and temperature, we know fairly well what amounts we need minimally and what we can use maximally. Yet on matters of safety, schooling, freedom and wealth we know little about minimum and possible maximum needs. Lacking this knowledge, most indices assume that more is better.

Problem number four is that the significance of opportunities is not the same for everybody, but depends on capabilities. For instance, freedom in nations appears to add to happiness only when people are well educated (Veenhoven, 2000c). This means that topics should be given weights according to conditions. In practice that is hardly feasible.

Lastly there is the problem of aggregation. The aim is inclusion of all relevant opportunities, but the practice is a summing of a few topics. The assortment of topics differs considerably across inventories, and it is not clear whether one collection is better than another. In fact each ideology of the good life can compose its own liveability index.

Together this means that inclusive assessment of liveability is not feasible. The best we can do is to make promising condition profiles. Liveability sum scores make little sense.

Measures of life-ability

Capabilities for living are also measured in different ways. First there is a rich tradition of health measurement, which is rooted in the healing professions. Second there is a trade in skill measurement, which serves selection within education and at work. Third, capacities are also measured by performance at school and work.

Contents

Measures of health are, for the greater part, measures of negative health. There are various inventories of afflictions and functional limitations, several of which combine physical and mental impairments. Assessments are based on functional tests, expert ratings and self-reports. The above-mentioned SF-36 is an example of the latter kind of measure. In the self-report tradition, general health is also measured by single questions. For an overview of these health measures, see Spilker (1996). Next there are also some inventories for positive health, mainly self-report questionnaires in the tradition of personality assessment. Jahoda (1958) made the first selection of healthy traits; Verba (1988) reports a later attempt.

Measures of skilfulness concern mostly mental abilities, many of which are parts of so-called intelligence tests. Performance tests can be considered to be objective assessment. A new offspring of this tradition is testing for *emotional intelligence* (Mayer and Salovy, 1993), which is mostly a matter of subjective self-reporting. Next there are numerous tests for proficiency at work and in leisure, such as laying bricks or playing cards.

Lastly, many abilities manifest in real-life success. School success is measured in years of schooling and by the level of schooling achieved. People who do badly at school or receive no formal education in all probability lack several necessary abilities. In developing nations, literacy is a common topic. Life-ability is also inferred from apparent success at work and in love.

Limitations
As in the case of liveability, these measures do not provide a complete estimate of life-ability. Again the measures are seldom combined, and we meet the same fundamental limitations.

First, we cannot grasp all human capabilities; there are limitations to what we can conceive and what we can measure. Possibly the current measurement repertoire misses some essential talents, in particular aptitudes required for new challenges.

Second, we are again uncertain about the significance of topics in the inventories. Possibly some of the things we learn in school are irrelevant. Valued positive mental health traits may actually be detrimental for coping with the problems of life. Unlike the case of liveability, there is some significance testing in this field. Intelligence tests in particular are gauged by their predictive value for success at school and at work. Yet this validation criterion is not the most appropriate in this context, because success at school and work does not guarantee a happy life. Many of the other ability tests available lack any validation. Third, it is typically unclear how much of the ability is optimal; more is not always better. As there are limitations to skill acquisition, it is the right mix that counts. Fourth, the functionality of abilities is contingent to the situation and fit with other traits. For instance, assertiveness is more functional in an individualistic society than in a collectivist culture, and fits better with trait autonomy than with trait dependence. Lastly, we cannot adequately estimate general ability by adding up test scores. Though psychometrists dream about a general ability factor, this seems to be a statistical epiphenomenon rather than a reality.

Measures for utility of life
There are many criteria for evaluating the usefulness of a life, of which only a few can be quantified. When evaluating the utility of a person's life by the contribution that life makes to society, one aspect could be good citizenship. That quality can be measured by criteria such as law abidance and voluntary work. The author has not yet seen examples of such measures. When the utility of a life is measured by its effect on the environment, consumption is a relevant aspect. There are several measures of *green living*. It is less easy to quantify moral value. Though it is not difficult to see that some people's lives stand out, there are no tools to rate the common man.

On some criteria we have better information at the aggregate level. Wackernagel et al.'s (1999) measure of ecological footprint indicates the degree to which citizens in a country use irreplaceable resources. Patent counts per country give an idea of the contribution to human progress, and state participation in UN organizations could be seen as an equivalent of good citizenship.

Unlike the foregoing qualities of life, there have been no attempts to measure utility comprehensively. The obvious reason is that the criteria are too vague and varied. Utility is easier to conceive than measure.

Comprehensiveness is less of a problem when utility is measured subjectively. We can then assess the degree to which someone thinks of his/her life as useful. There are several questionnaires that measure subjective sense of meaning (for a review of some see Chamberlain and Zika, 1988). These questionnaires do not measure actual usefulness of life, but rather the person's satisfaction with his perception of the matter. Though these feelings may have some reality basis, the measures say more about the subjective appreciation of life; because the utility of one's life is so difficult to grasp, judgement is easily overshadowed by how much one likes or dislikes life.

Measures of appreciation of life

It is easier to measure the subjective appraisal of life. Since this is something people have in mind, we can simply ask them. Interrogation is mostly done by direct questioning via an interview or a written questionnaire. Since the focus is on *how much* the respondent enjoys life rather than *why*, the use of qualitative interview methods is limited in this field. Most assessments are self-reports in response to standard questions with fixed response options. As well as numerous single items, there are various questionnaires. Incidentally, subjective well-being is assessed by less obtrusive methods, such as analysis of diaries and projective tests.

Contents

Many of these measures concern specific appraisals, such as satisfaction with one's sex life or perceived meaning of life. As in the case of life chances, these aspects cannot be meaningfully added to a whole because, first, satisfactions cannot be assessed exhaustively and, second, satisfactions differ in significance. Yet humans are also capable of overall appraisals. As noted earlier, we can estimate how well we feel generally and report on that. So encompassive measurement is possible in this quality quadrant (fig. 4.8).

There are various ways to ask people how much they enjoy their life as a whole. One way is to ask them repeatedly how much they enjoy it right now, and to average the responses. This is called experience sampling. This method has many advantages, but is quite expensive. Another way is to ask respondents to estimate how well they feel generally or to strike the balance of their life. Almost all the questions ever used for this purpose are stored in the "Catalog of Happiness Measures", which is part of the author's "World Database of Happiness" (Veenhoven, 2000a).

Questions on enjoyment of life typically concern the current time. Most questions refer to happiness *these days* or *over the last year*. Obvi-

	Outer quality	Inner quality
Life chances	Quality of society • Liveability scores Position within society • Deprivation indices	• Impairment indices • Positive health inventories • Capability tests • Educational grade
Life results	?	• Satisfaction summations • Self-ratings of happiness • Happy life years

Figure 4.8 Inclusive measures for specific qualities of life

ously the good life requires more than this, hence happiness must also be assessed over longer periods. In several contexts we must know about happiness over a lifetime, or better, how long people live happily. Remember the above discussion of this criterion in the context of biology and system theory.

At the individual level it is mostly difficult to assess how long and happily people live, because we know only when they are dead; however, at the population level the average number of years lived happily can be estimated by combining average happiness with life expectancy. For details of this method, see Veenhoven (1996).

Limitations?

There are doubts about the value of these self-reports, in particular about interpretation of questions, honesty of answers and interpersonal comparability. Empirical studies, however, show reasonable validity and reliability; for details see Veenhoven (1996: 19–22, 1998) and Schyns (2003).

There are also qualms about comparability of average responses across cultures, and hence about the above-mentioned estimate of happy years of life. It is claimed that questions are differently understood and that response bias differs systematically in countries. These objections have also been checked empirically and appeared not to carry any weight. Many of these checks are reported in Veenhoven (1993).

In this case there is no problem of summation; the answer to the question about appreciation of life as a whole suffices.

Can quality of life be measured inclusively?

As noted in the introduction, terms like *quality of life* and *well-being* were circulated to denote *overall* worth of life. Hence the introduction of these terms was followed by attempts to measure the goodness of life comprehensively. The meanings addressed by these inventories was considered in the second section of this chapter. All assess overall quality of life by summing different merits, and in these summations the qualities discerned are merged. This adding of apples and pears yields a great variety of fruit salads, each with its special flavour and devotees. Unfortunately, this trade makes little sense.

Why cross-quadrant sum scores make no sense

First, three of the four separate qualities in the present scheme cannot be measured comprehensively. The author has argued that exhaustive assessment is not possible in the cases of liveability, life-ability and utility of life. Only happiness can be measured completely, because it is an overall judgement in itself. Where most of the components are incomplete, the sum cannot be complete either. Hence, sum scores are always selective, and therefore say more about *a* good life than about *the* good life.

Second, one cannot meaningfully add *chances* and *outcomes*. A happy and productive life is no better when lived in a perfect environment by a well-endowed person than when realized in difficult circumstances by someone handicapped.

Third, sum scores fail to appreciate the functional relationships between the qualities of life discerned. The value of environmental opportunities depends on personal capacities. An orchestra may be well equipped with violins, but if its members are horn players the musical performance will still be poor. Likewise, the worth of life-abilities depends on the environmental challenges for which they are needed. It is their fit that counts, rather than the mere amounts.

These contingencies are acknowledged in some concepts. For instance, Gerson (1976) defines quality of life as harmony of self-interest and *transcendent* utility. Yet this is easier said than measured. First, such harmony can hardly be quantified; for instance, the fit of individual and environmental potentialities cannot be observed as such, and at best we can infer fit from resulting enjoyment of life. Second, there is mostly not one best fit but several fitting configurations; for example, collectivist and individualistic arrangements can be equally harmonious but still represent quite different qualities.

The above problems could partly be met if one restricted oneself to the few conditions and capabilities for which the mutual fit can be estimated, for instance if we focus on sheer material subsistence. This is close to the basic needs approach, which is said to have formed the basis of the HDI (UNDP, 1990). Yet the HDI does not really solve the problem either.

Why there is most in happiness

When human capacities fit environmental demands, there is a good chance that human needs are gratified. Only bad luck or wilful deprivation can block that outcome. Gratification of basic needs will manifest in a stream of pleasant experiences. Biologically this is a signal that we are in the right pond. In human consciousness this manifests in good mood, and subsequently in satisfaction with life as a whole.

So, happiness is both a merit in itself and indicative of good life chances. Subjective happiness implies two things: first, the minimal conditions for humans thriving are apparently met and, second, the fit between opportunities and capacities must be sufficient. Hence happiness says more about the quality of life chances that the sum scores do.

This means that at least three of the four qualities of life can be meaningfully summarized by the degree and duration of happiness. This is how the good life is characterized in the closing sentence of many fairy-tales by stating that "they lived long and happily".

Why happiness is not all

The proposed fourfold matrix visualizes the main limitation of this view, ignoring the utility quadrant. As noted above, a life can be happy but not useful or useful but not happy. Though these qualities often go together, they do not necessarily do so.

Discussion

Use of this taxonomy

This exercise started with a discussion of the confusion surrounding words for *the good life*. As a remedy a fourfold matrix classification of the qualities of life was proposed. This taxonomy was used to clarify the substantive meanings denoted by current words and measures. This worked, though it was often not possible to place current notions in one particular quadrant. One can see this as a weakness (the scheme does not fit current concepts) or as a strength (it denotes new meanings).

Now there are more classifications of quality of life, which are also used to structure this complex field. The second section reviewed a few. Is this one any better? It would be too much to review all the alternative classifications. Let it suffice to note that the major distinctions in the field are between *objective* and *subjective* qualities and along disciplinary kinds, such as economic, social and psychological well-being. A great advantage of the proposed fourfold matrix is that it makes more sense theoretically. The distinction between *chances* and *results* positions the merits in a functional perspective; the distinction between *liveability* and *life-ability* brings the contingencies to mind. As such, this taxonomy helps us to see that overall quality of life cannot be seen as summed merits, but must rather be conceived as merit configurations.

Elusive utilities

In this taxonomy the utility quadrant is the most problematic. The criteria are quite diverse and elusive. One can see use in anything. Contrary to happiness there is no link with demands of human nature. The matter is in fact unmeasurable.

In an earlier paper on this subject the author therefore left the category out: this left a simpler three-step scheme of liveability, life-ability and life appreciation (Veenhoven, 2001). This is in line with the utilitarian idea that the ultimate value is in the greatest happiness of the greatest number. Bentham will nod in his glass case.

Though clear-cut, that three-step scheme misses an important class of qualities: the values that override sheer functionality and enjoyment. It is not possible to weave these meanings in as contributions to the happiness of other people, because many of them have no effect on happiness. The best we can do is acknowledge the existence of these many qualities, and mark the morass on our map. Without forewarning we get stuck in it over and over again.

Significance of happiness

The author concluded that the most comprehensive measure for quality of life is how long and happily a person lives. Though happiness was not proclaimed as the only quality criterion, it was presented as the best available summary indicator. Note that this is not a statement of belief, but a conclusion based on assumptions about the nature of happiness.

Subjective appreciation of life is not all, because happiness does not guarantee that other possible values are met. That latter position must be nuanced in two ways: both in favour and against. The favourable nuance is that happiness and utility do go together quite often. Both outcomes draw on the same opportunities. Useful living also requires tolerable environmental conditions and fair individual capabilities, in many cases similar to happiness. Further, objective utility is at least partly reflected in subjective awareness, and as such is part of the appraisal of life as a whole. In contrast, subjective enjoyment of life is not always appropriate in the given conditions. Though happiness works as a compass, it is not always an infallible tool for orientation: happiness sometimes results from cognitive distortion or chemical intoxication. Still, this is the exception rather than the rule, and in the long run dysfunctional happiness will destroy itself. So this problem applies more to short-term happiness than to happy life years.

Guide for research

The taxonomy does more than just map different qualities of life. It can also be used to help explore their interrelations. The first step is to distinguish qualities of life as different phenomena; the next steps will be to chart causal effects. As such the scheme suggests interesting research lines. One thing we can determine is those conditions for happiness that also promise desirable external effects. Since there are probably many ways to happiness, we can then select the most "useful" one.

Conclusion

One cannot meaningfully speak about *quality of life* at large. It makes more sense to distinguish four qualities: liveability of the environment, life-ability of the person, utility of life for the environment and appreciation of life by the person. These qualities cannot be added, hence sum scores make little sense. The best available summary indicator is how long and happily a person lives.

Acknowledgements

This is a shortened version of an article originally published in the *Journal of Happiness Studies* (2000), 1(1): 1–39, "The Four Qualities of Life: Ordering Concepts and Measures of the Good Life", by Ruut Veenhoven, © Kluwer Academic Publishers, and is included here with kind permission from Springer Science and Business Media.

REFERENCES

Allardt, E. (1976) "Dimensions of Welfare in a Comparative Scandinavian Study", *Acta Sociologica* 19: 227–239.
Andrews, F. and S. Withey (1976) *Social Indicators of Well-being: American Perceptions of Quality of Life*, New York: Plenum Press.
Bentham, J. (1789) "An Introduction into the Principles of Morals and Legislation", reprinted in John Bowring, ed. (2002) *The Works of Jeremy Bentham*, Chicago: University of Chicago Press.
Bernheim, J. L. and M. Buyse (1983) "The Anamnestic Comparative Self-

Assessment for Measuring Subjective Quality of Life for Cancer Patients", *Journal of Psychosocial Oncology* 1: 25-38.

Brock, D. W. (1993) *Life and Death: Philosophical Essays in Biomedical Ethics*, New York: Cambridge University Press.

Chamberlain, K. and S. Zika (1988) "Measuring Meaning in Life, Examination of Three Scales", *Journal of Personal and Individual Differences* 9: 589-596.

Cummins, R. A. (1993) *Comprehensive Quality of Life Scale for Adults. (ComQol-A4)*, 4th edn, Melbourne: Deakin University, School of Psychology.

Estes, R. (1984) *The Social Progress of Nations*, New York: Praeger.

Gerson, E. M. (1976) "On Quality of Life", *American Sociological Review* 41: 793-806.

Jahoda, M. (1958) *Current Concepts of Positive Mental Health*, New York: Basic Books.

Korczak, D., ed. (1995) *Lebensqualität Atlas*, Wiesbaden: Westdeutscher Verlag.

Kunz, M. and W. Siefer (1995) "Wo Sie am besten leben FOCUS", in D. Korczak, ed., *Lebensqualität Atlas*, Wiesbaden: Westdeutscher Verlag.

Lane, R. E. (1994) "Quality of Life and Quality of Persons. A New Role for Government?", *Political Theory* 22(2): 219-252.

Mayer, J. D. and P. Salovy (1993) "The Intelligence of Emotional Intelligence", *Intelligence* 17(4): 433-442.

McCall, S. (1975) "Quality of Life", *Social Indicators Research* 2: 229-249.

Michalos, A. (1985) "Multiple Discrepancy Theory (MDT)", *Social Indicators Research* 16: 347-413.

Mill, J. S. ([1863] 1990) *Utilitarianism*, 20th impression, Glasgow: Fontana Press.

Musschenga, A. W. (1994) "Quality of Life of Handicapped People", in L. Nordenfelt, ed., *Concepts and Measurement of Quality of Life in Health Care*, Dordrecht: Kluwer Academic, pp. 181-198.

Naroll, R. (1983) *The Moral Order. An Introduction to the Human Situation*, Beverley Hills: Sage.

Noll, H.-H. (1999) "Konzepte der Wohlfahrtsentwicklung: Lebensqualität und 'neue' Wohlfahrtskonzepte", Euro-reporting Paper No. 3, ZUMA, Mannheim.

Nordenfelt, L. (1989) "Quality of Life and Happiness", in S. Bjork and J. Vang, eds, *Assessing Quality of Life*, Health Service Studies No. 1, Stockholm: Samhall Klintland.

Ouellette-Kuntz, H. (1990) "A Pilot Study in the Use of the Quality of Life Interview Schedule", *Social Indicators Research* 23: 283-298.

Sandoe, P. (1999) "Quality of Life, Three Competing Views", *Ethical Theory and Moral Practice* 2(1): 11-23.

Schyns, P. (2003) *Income and Life Satisfaction. A Cross-National and Longitudinal Study*, Delft: Eburon.

Sen, A. (1992) "Capability and Well-Being", in A. Sen and M. Nussbaum, eds, *The Quality of Life*, Oxford: Clarendon Press, pp. 30-53.

Spilker, B., ed. (1996) *Quality of Life and Pharmaco-economics in Clinical Trials*, Philadelphia, Penns.: Leppincott-Raven Publishers.

Spitzer, W. O., A. J. Dobson, J. Hall, E. Chesterman, J. Levi and R. Shepherd (1981) "Measuring the Quality of Life of Cancer Patients", *Journal of Chronical Disease* 34(12): 585-597.

Townsend, P. (1979) *Poverty in the UK: A Survey of Household Resources and Standards of Living*, Harmondsworth: Penguin.
UNDP (1990) *Human Development Report 1990*, New York: Oxford University Press.
Veenhoven, R. (1984) *Conditions of Happiness*, Dordrecht: Kluwer.
—— (1993) *Happiness in Nations: Subjective Appreciation of Life in 56 Nations 1946–1992*, Rotterdam: RISBO.
—— (1996) "Happy Life-Expectancy", *Social Indicators Research* 39: 1–58.
—— (1997) "Progres dans la comprehension du bonheur", *Revue Quebecoise de Psychologie* 18(2): 29–74, available in English as "Advances in the Understanding of Happiness".
—— (1998) "Vergelijken van geluk in landen", *Sociale wetenschappen* 42: 58–84.
—— (2000a) "Catalog of Happiness Measures", World Database of Happiness, available at www1.eur.nl/fsw/happiness/index.html.
—— (2000b) "Well-being in the Welfare State: Level Not Higher, Distribution Not More Equitable", *Journal of Comparative Policy Analysis* 2: 91–125.
—— (2000c) "Happiness and Freedom", in E. Diener and E. Suh, eds, *Subjective Well-being across Cultures*, Boston, Mass.: MIT Press.
—— (2001) "Quality of Life and Happiness, Not Quite the Same", in G. DeGirolamo et al., eds, *Salute e qualità dell vida*, Turin: Centro Scientifico Editore, pp. 67–95.
Verba, S. K. (1988) "Measurement of Positive Mental Health, Some Theoretical and Practical Considerations", *International Journal of Clinical Psychology* 15: 6–11.
Wackernagel, M., L. Onislo, P. Bello, A. Linares, I. Fattan, J. Garcia, A. Guerrero and M. Guerrero (1999) "National Natural Capital Accounting with the Ecological Footprint Concept", *Ecological Economics* 29(3): 375–390.
Ware, J. E. Jr (1996) "The SF-36 Health Survey", in B. Spilker, ed., *Quality of Life and Pharmaco-economics in Clinical Trials*, Philadelphia, Penns.: Leppincott-Raven Publishers, pp. 337–345.
Zajonc, R. B. (1980) "Feeling and Thinking: Preference Needs No Inference", *American Psychologist* 35: 151–175.
Zapf, W. (1984) "Individuelle Wohlfahrt: Lebensbedingungen und wahrgenommene Lebensqualität", in W. Glatzer and W. Zapf, eds, *Lebensqualität in der Bundesrepublik. Objective Lebensbedingungen und subjectives*, Frankfurt am Main: Wohlbefinden, Campus Verlag, pp. 13–26.

5

Inequalities, agency and well-being: Conceptual linkages and measurement challenges in development

Douglas A. Hicks

Introduction: Inequalities and the capabilities approach

Inequality, agency and well-being are three fundamental interrelated concepts for understanding human and economic development. The capabilities approach, particularly the work of Amartya Sen, has helped to specify each of these complex terms. Although much of this chapter addresses conceptual issues, the central real-world problem that guides this analysis is the high level of inequality in many nations as well as inequality at the global level, the scale of which, in terms of income, is roughly that of the most unequal nations in the world (Milanovic, 2002; Hicks, 2000: 46–48). What is the impact of inequality on disadvantaged persons' well-being and agency?

Inequalities exist and can be analysed in various dimensions, including income, health, education and others. Scholars and policy-makers employ different metrics, such as money, primary goods or functionings, to frame and analyse such inequalities (Sen, 1992, 1997, 1999). Even within the capabilities approach, analysts and activists differ over which functionings and which inequalities to value (including how much to value them, and whether negatively or positively). Which inequalities matter economically, socially or morally – and why? Sen's own perspective intentionally leaves open the question of the naming and relative weighting of particular functionings. At the personal level he believes that individuals should have the freedom to determine what they themselves value, and at the society-wide level he holds that open, pluralistic debate should shape which basic functionings the collective should value (Sen, 1993, 1999). This chapter is not about which inequalities policy-makers or critics should address;[1] rather, it assumes that a few functionings – e.g. having basic income, being well educated, being in good health and being able to appear in public without shame – are normatively desirable.

Inequalities in these and other functionings can be analysed in multiple ways: through a comparison across individuals in a society (e.g. the Gini coefficient of income for individuals in Finland or some other country); as a differential-based comparison between social groupings, such as the difference between the average income of men and the average income of women in Finland; or as the comparison of inequality between such groups (such as comparing the degree of income inequality among men in Finland to the degree of income inequality among women in Finland). This chapter refers most frequently to the first two types: inequalities across all individuals in a society and differential-based inequality along gender-based lines.

The remaining sections of the chapter proceed as follows. The second section analyses the conceptual linkages between inequality and well-being. The third section offers a parallel analysis of inequality and agency. The fourth section considers ways in which the conceptual issues of attending to inequality and agency, alongside well-being, can be employed to expand development indicators. The final section presents conclusions and implications.

Inequality and well-being

Inequality, unlike absolute deprivation, is a relational phenomenon, concerning individuals across a distribution as a whole. In order to delineate how inequality – of income, for instance – affects an individual's well-being, that person's social or communal frame of reference must be named. It is possible, indeed likely, that a person's frame of reference entails more than one group: one's neighbourhood (as in observing one's next-door neighbour, famously depicted in James Duesenberry's ([1949] 1962) account of "keeping up with the Joneses"), one's village or city, one's nation and perhaps the "globalizing" world as a whole (see Hicks, 2001). If inequality is to be included in assessments of well-being, then relational, contextual factors must be taken into account. That is, an accurate understanding of personal well-being in the capabilities approach concerns not what one is able to achieve in some abstract location, but rather what a person can attain within his or her own social context(s).

The question of the relationship between inequality and well-being raises the fundamental issue of individual-level versus society-level well-being. It is important to note that a diverse set of indicators of development, including income per capita and the human development index (HDI), can each be calculated by the same general method for individuals or for societies.[2] Society-wide indicators offer a vision of the aggregate or "average" level of development for citizens of that society. While income figures focus on one sphere of development, the HDI expands the assessment to three spheres – basic income, education and health/longevity. Neither income per capita nor the HDI directly incorporates information about inequalities.[3] These measures do not include the distribution of income, health outcomes (affecting life expectancy figures) or school enrolments and literacy figures. Such distributional concerns can be incorporated in a variety of ways, but doing so requires adapting the standard approach.

A society-wide or an individual-based assessment of well-being can incorporate information about inequality in different ways. For example, a society-wide assessment, such as the *Human Development Reports'* determination of an HDI value for each nation, can include attention to inequality of one form or another as an indicator of its impact on the society as a whole. In most cases the incorporation of inequality into development measures has made a moral presumption that less inequality is preferable to more inequality.[4] As a prominent example, the *Human Development Report 1993* (UNDP, 1993) employed a country's Gini coefficient of income inequality to *discount* that country's average or aggregate income per capita figure within the HDI. In other words, for two countries with equal income per capita figures, the one with less income inequality is (relatively) rewarded *vis-à-vis* the other. The author's own work (Hicks, 1997) has incorporated inequalities in all three spheres of functioning in the HDI and demonstrated, employing data for 20 developing countries, how to calculate Gini coefficients for education and health/longevity. These inequality measures were employed, analogously to the income-based discounting of the income indicator in the *HDR 1993*, to discount the aggregate education and health/longevity components of the HDI. This method led to an inequality-adjusted human development index (IAHDI).

Using a differential-based method of attending to gender-based inequalities, the UNDP introduced, within the *Human Development Report 1995* (UNDP, 1995), the gender-related development index (GDI). The GDI is calculated by reducing a country's HDI figure according to the degree of gender-based inequalities in the three relevant spheres of well-being. This differential-based approach adapts the HDI to penalize countries with relatively high gender inequalities.[5]

In contrast to these society-level evaluations that attend to inequality, individual-based measures of well-being focus more directly upon the impact of inequality on a person's overall capability and specific freedoms and achievements. Individuals fall on a particular point of a society's distribution of any particular socio-economic good:[6] that is, a person is located at the 10th, 50th, 90th or some other percentile of an income distribution (or an educational attainment distribution, etc.). Analysts can ask whether and how an individual's location as a relatively poor, middle-class or wealthy person affects his or her well-being.

Critics of this approach could maintain that one's location in a socio-economic distribution does not directly affect one's well-being. Rather, in the objector's view, the relevant question is how much, in *absolute* terms, of a given good a person holds. Does the person have enough money, for instance, to meet his or her basic material needs? Whether a person falls at the 10th or the 50th percentile does not necessarily matter; it is important, instead, to know what the person is able to buy with his or her income because this is a crucial dimension of determining well-being. But purchasing power is contingent on a number of contextual factors. The critic is likely to concede that an adjustment for PPP is reasonable, since how many euros or dollars a person has is less important than what kind of housing and food the person is able to acquire with that money.

Beyond this type of contextual factor, however, what is required for adequate functioning in a given context is a matter of relational, indeed distributional, factors. For instance, it is necessary in the contemporary United States, as in many other countries, to have a telephone in order to experience adequate functioning in that social context. Indeed, it is by now arguably necessary to have internet access as well in order to be a full participant in many societies. Ready and regular access to both a telephone and the internet requires money-based expenditure. In general terms, as the average income of a society increases, the general social norms also change, requiring more financial expenditure, for instance, to purchase goods needed for any given level of functioning. The relationship between one's own holding of goods and the norms of the population is even more closely related when public goods are considered. In societies in which most people use public transportation, mass transport can be provided at some relatively low cost per passenger. As some or many people can afford and choose to use private transport (e.g. automobiles), the high fixed cost of mass transport is spread among fewer users, with the result that services are often cut or made more expensive for riders, who tend to be the relatively poor. If these assertions are correct, then as the average income of a society increases, persons whose income does not go up, other things being equal, see their well-being decrease.[7]

The functioning "having adequate income", in contrast to the simple good "income", can incorporate inequality directly. That is, the determination of precisely what income is adequate in any given context is influenced by the relational-relative factors noted above. Similarly, the functioning "being well educated" can also vary by social context. As with income, being located at some percentile of educational attainment is not in itself a direct indicator of whether a person is well educated in that society or not. But in general terms the duration and quality of education needed to attain any particular level of that functioning is affected by the mean and other characteristics of the distribution of years of education for a society.

One functioning that is often cited in the capabilities literature is what Sen, drawing upon Adam Smith, calls "being able to appear in public without shame" (Sen, 1983; see also Hicks, 2000: 192). Smith ([1776] 1976: 869–870) explains:

> By necessaries I understand not only the commodities which are indispensably necessary for the support of life, but what ever the custom of the country renders it indecent for creditable people, even of the lowest order, to be without. A linen shirt, for example, is, strictly speaking, not a necessary of life. The Greeks and Romans lived, I suppose, very comfortably though they had no linen. But in the present times, through the greater part of Europe, a creditable day-labourer would be ashamed to appear in public without a linen shirt, the want of which would be supposed to denote that disgraceful degree of poverty which, it is presumed, nobody can fall into without extreme bad conduct.

Smith's observation about the difference between eighteenth-century Europeans and more ancient peoples makes the point that this functioning varies by culture. In contemporary times the norms for appearing in public without shame clearly differ by culture and by level of affluence.

Consider a society with some degree of inequality of income, for instance, a level indicated by a Gini coefficient of approximately 0.30. Person L (Lazarus) is at the 10th percentile and person D (Dives) is at the 90th percentile of the income distribution. Under the current economic conditions, Lazarus is having a very difficult time making ends meet. He is barely able to afford the jacket that is customary in his society. Now consider that this society and economy change so that every person in the lower half of the distribution retains the same PPP-adjusted income but everyone in the upper half of the distribution doubles their PPP income.[8] The Gini coefficient and other indicators of inequality have thus increased dramatically. In this new situation, Lazarus can still afford what used to be the customary jacket. (Let us assume for this illustration that it is still possible to buy this jacket. If the market shifts in such a way that this older, simpler jacket is no longer produced, or produced only with a higher market cost, the situation is more grave for Lazarus.) Now Dives and his colleagues in the top half of society are wearing a new, sleeker jacket, one like the old one but with built-in connections and pouches for electronic devices, including cellphones, pagers, radios, etc. Lazarus cannot afford the new jacket, let alone the new electronic devices that everyone else seems to have. The new situation raises more than "merely" the question of Lazarus's feelings of social exclusion, significant as they may be. Indeed, the important role of social goods for achieving participation and social inclusion is a key point (Douglas and Isherwood, 1979). It also leads to difficulty in more tangible terms for Lazarus, for without the new jacket he appears dishevelled and inappropriately dressed when Dives interviews him for a job, and therefore is not offered a job. In broader terms, Lazarus finds it harder in this situation of increased inequality to participate in the life of his community.

As in this example, inequality often has a negative impact on the poorer person's well-being in direct and indirect ways. Some critics might object to assessing as part of well-being what could be considered "only" mental states like a person's sense of stake or participation in society. Or, even if it is agreed that these states are important, the critic could maintain that it is impossible to measure a person's sense of inclusion in any meaningful, empirically defensible way. In a similar vein, the functioning "being able to appear in public without shame" is generally seen to be difficult to assess, even by those who concede it is an important part of well-being. In these views, it is preferable to focus on more tangible (even material) outcomes of a person. The crucial point, in an inequality-incorporating perspective, is to acknowledge that relational-distributional factors do play a role in a person's well-being, whether subjectively or objectively measured. The practical evaluation of such factors is admittedly difficult, but to note this fact is different from stating that these factors are not worthy of attention. As possible measurements of well-being are considered below, this point will be revisited.

Inequality and agency

The question of what degree of participation a person perceives herself or himself to have – and actually has – is a matter not only of well-being but also of agency. Agency can be defined in this discussion as a person's capacity to achieve, within his or her social context, those things that he or she values. Agency (like well-being) can be analysed in terms of freedom to achieve and in terms of achievements. Agency freedom is "what the person is free to do and achieve in pursuit of whatever goals or values he or she regards as important" (Sen, 1985b: 203), and agency achievement is the actual attainment of those ends. One of the principal things that a person can (and should) value is his or her own well-being. But he or she can also value other things, including the well-being of family members, friends or even strangers, as well as aspects of life not necessarily directly connected to any specific person's well-being.[9]

Sen (1999: 19) contrasts the concept of the *agent* "as someone who acts and brings about change" with the *patient*, who is merely acted upon, albeit for that patient's own benefit. Throughout his corpus Sen emphasizes the value of agency, particularly for poor women and men, on intrinsic grounds as well as for its instrumental benefits for contributing to other vital functionings (Sen, 1990, 1999; see also Nussbaum, 2000). Indeed, along with the intrinsic value of agency, this literature has emphasized that women's increased agency contributes to increases in the well-being of others, especially their children (Sen, 1999; Buvinic, 1997).

Since agency has to do with the ability to bring about all of those things that a person values, and not only one's own well-being, the issue arises of how persons attribute relative value, or weight, to their various ends.[10] Much of the human development literature assumes that persons take their own well-being into account and give it some priority in their valuing of goals. But we must here consider the criticism that Sen, Elster and others aim at utilitarianism, namely that persons adjust their mental states and attitudes according to what is possible (Elster, 1983; Sen, 1999). Sen recognizes the problem of adjusting one's preferences to accept deprivation. He goes on to note the moral importance of creating social and economic conditions under which persons can make genuine determinations of value, free from oppressive conditions that constrain what they see as possible. This point suggests that along with considerations of persons' achievement of well-being, attention should also be paid to the social, cultural and economic factors that lead persons to give too little weight to their well-being in relation to other values they have. Thus, when speaking of agency goals in addition to well-being, it is important to try to distinguish those agency ends from ones that are imposed by oppressive social conditions.[11]

On this point of determining what agency is, Naila Kabeer (1999) rejects the view in which agency is readily equated to decision-making. It is not possible simply to count the number of decisions, for example, that women as housewives make within the household. It is, rather, a matter of how significant those decisions are and whether they merely perpetuate unjust social roles (see also Razavi, 1999). Kabeer cites an Egyptian study which found that men typically make the fundamental decision of whether or not the family will use contraception; if and when that decision is made in the affirmative, then (and only then) the woman typically has the power to choose the form of contraception (Kabeer, 1999: 447). She draws a distinction between *efficient agency* (making decisions within the given social constraints) and *transformatory agency* (making decisions that can change one's social or economic status) (Kabeer, 1999: 452). Only the latter form of agency, in her schema, can lead to poor women's empowerment.

Focusing on women's roles *vis-à-vis* men's roles in differing social contexts illuminates the impact of agency on inequality. It is now well established that increasing women's agency, including through education and entrance into the formal labour market, has a significant effect on women's well-being (Nussbaum, 2000; Sen, 1999). Sen argues that when women have the opportunity to enter the formal labour market, their agency tends to increase. This can be understood in terms of an increase in relative "negotiating power" *vis-à-vis* their husbands or others within the "cooperative conflicts" of the household (Sen, 1990; see also Hicks, 2002). In a related but broader understanding, access to educational institutions and the formal labour market expand one's understanding of, and ability to engage with, social contexts beyond the household.

A converse question concerns whether persons in situations of greater relative deprivation (e.g. in situations of more severe inequality) are more likely to adapt their attitudes and internalize unjust conditions rather than stand up for their own well-being. The literature on the role of women's relative empowerment or disempowerment supports an affirmative answer. One difficulty of measurement on this question is the fact that many potential indicators of lack of agency are also indicators of inequality – women's relatively low school enrolments or literacy, for instance. By the framework of cooperative conflict and negotiating power, women with the lowest relative status *vis-à-vis* their husbands (and *vis-à-vis* society as a whole) are in the worst position to effect change.

In making her distinction between effective agency and transformatory agency, Kabeer (1999) notes the finding that women's increased agency is seen to improve (i.e. reduce) excess female mortality *vis-à-vis* the boys' rate (while the boys' rate does not go up). This is a clear example of an increase of transformatory agency for females as a whole that leads to a reduction in gender-based inequalities. Indeed, the value of local women's cooperative and micro-lending initiatives – at least those that reshape structures – can be cast in broad terms of the effect that women's increased agency has on reducing gender-based disparities. Such programmes also have a direct effect on the well-being of many persons.

Incorporating agency and inequalities in development indicators: Challenges of measurement

If the previous sections are correct in asserting that both inequality in various forms and agency are important components of understanding development and are related in complex ways to well-being, the issue of how to attend to them empirically still remains. This section discusses the challenges confronted in designing development indicators that adequately take account of agency and inequality. The section focuses on poor persons, paying particular attention to poor *women* for two reasons. First, it is clear that many of the most prominent forms of discrimination in various societies are gender based. Second, this focus on one group of persons (i.e. females) *vis-à-vis* another group (i.e. males) is illustrative for other kinds of differential-based analysis as well.

One important effort to measure women's agency within discussions of development is the gender empowerment measure (GEM) introduced by the UNDP, along with the GDI, in 1995. The emphasis of the GEM is to evaluate the participation of women in economic and political life, particularly high-level decision-making (UNDP, 1995, 2002). But the kinds of participation measured are those that, in almost all cases, only élite women are able to attain: seats in parliament, positions as legislators, senior officials and managers. Variables for these forms of participation – high-level, formal leadership – make up two-thirds of the index. The additional component, counting as one-third of the index, is based upon the comparison of income shares for men and women; this is indeed an important variable that incorporates information about women *vis-à-vis* men across the socio-economic distribution (see UNDP, 2002: 257). But since it compares the mean estimated earned income for each gender, this indicator is not reflective in a specific way of the relative situation of *poor* women. The GEM's innovative focus on women's empowerment, then, sheds very little light on the agency of the most disadvantaged women.[12]

The challenge remains to focus on *poor* women's ability to have a positive impact on achieving what they value. As noted above, Kabeer (1999) demonstrates the problematic nature of the most relatively straightforward way of developing such an indicator, that of measuring the decision-making roles (e.g. through self-reporting surveys) that women hold. In order to reflect the ability of women to pursue what they would value if they did not unduly adapt to or accept social injustice, an indicator must not include those decisions that simply perpetuate a woman's position of relative deprivation.

The society-wide and individual-level distinction, noted above for discussions of inequality and well-being, is also relevant for agency. If the interest is to incorporate agency concerns into a society-level indicator, the question becomes: whose agency? Which persons (from the whole population or the population of all women) are included? The case of the GEM serves as an example of an agency-based indicator *not* particularly sensitive to persons with the least agency. What is needed, in contrast, is a measure most sensitive to the change in decision-making and voice-making power of persons who begin with little power in the first place.[13] In response to Kabeer's (1999) caution against including non-transformative decisions, it is necessary to make a choice about which decisions or actions reflect genuine voice and control over one's own life. This determination is likely to be highly context dependent, varying from one society to another (and perhaps even from village to village).

As a whole, such an exercise is necessarily and inescapably normative, both in the decisions and actions that are seen to be agential and in any weighting across a population to reflect greater sensitivity to the most disadvantaged. This is not especially controversial, for all discussions about which indicators to employ – even if one values only income per capita (a valuation that gives 100 per cent importance to income and 0 per cent direct importance to any other indicator of well-being) – are based on some assumption about what counts and what does not in social, economic or moral evaluation. Analysts of inequality have shown that the standard measures of inequality have normative assumptions built in (see Hicks, 2000: 247–251).

A further note about constructing an indicator of agency is in order. The previous section suggested that persons at the lower end of severely unequal socio-economic distributions are more likely than better-off persons in that distribution (or persons at the same place in a less severe distribution) to have adapted their attitudes to accept injustice, specifically to devalue their own well-being relative to concern for others. It would be a mistake, however, to imply that analysts should design an indicator that relates decreased concern for others as somehow desirable for well-being. In other words, the goal is not to decrease concern for others; it is to create social, economic and cultural conditions in which persons can properly attend to their own well-being and pursue other ends they value, including concern for others. Self-regarding and other-regarding behaviour need not be mutually exclusive, and analysts should not view the relationship as such in their modelling. At the same time, however, they should bear in mind that persons sometimes do make trade-offs between their own well-being and the well-being of others.

Alongside the consideration of agency, especially as it is affected by one's socio-economic position, development indicators can also attend directly to inequality. Should inequality itself be considered in development indicators – for example, either in the GDI (a female and male differential-based approach, as in UNDP, 1995) or in the IAHDI (based on Gini coefficients for the whole population, as in Hicks, 1997)? Or, alternatively, if analysts devise a more direct method to assess agency, especially that of disadvantaged persons, would this negate the need to incorporate inequality information in development measures? This chapter has suggested that inequality can have negative effects on both the well-being and the agency of persons at the lower end of socio-economic distributions. It may be possible to refine present indicators to assess more directly some of these well-being and agency effects. Although a precise account of inequality's myriad influences on a given society is context dependent and therefore beyond the scope of this chapter, severe disparity can have negative effects on social relations that in all likelihood cannot be completely captured in any other indicators. Importantly, rich and poor alike arguably experience the impact of severe inequalities on social solidarity.[14] Given the complexity of inequality's effects on social or communal life, data on inequalities of important social goods continue to provide important information for society-wide indicators of development.

In terms of individual (as opposed to society-wide) assessments of well-being or agency, the influences of inequality can be evaluated by more direct means. The decisions that persons make, and the ability to participate more generally in society, can be determined in terms of functionings. More simply stated, for a given person in a specific social context, the response to the question "Is she well educated?" will take into account the relational information, along with other information, about that person. The determination of more complex functionings, such as being able to appear in public without shame, also considers contextual factors.

It is easier to assess degree of functioning at the individual level than at the society-wide level because for individuals these functioning determinations can "build in" relevant relational information. It is conceptually possible, at the society-wide level as well, to aggregate individual information in such a way as to focus on functionings and not goods. But in practice, given the limitations on data availability as well as the importance placed on easy cross-national comparisons, the human development approaches continue to focus on goods – such as basic income or years of education – as proxies of functioning.[15] Inequality-based information about the distribution of income, schooling or years of life within a population can help improve the estimation of actual functioning and capability for society-wide determinations of agency and well-being. This same kind of information is needed for individual-level assessments of development, but it may be incorporated into the functionings themselves.

Conclusions and implications

This chapter has sought to delineate the complex interrelationships of inequality, agency and well-being, especially as they pertain to the efforts by policy-makers and activists to understand and evaluate development. One way to harness effective efforts against absolute and relative deprivation is located in the positively reinforcing circle between reducing inequality and improving agency. In Sen's language, the best hope for improving human well-being of the most disadvantaged persons in our societies and globalizing world is not for leaders and development experts to rescue patients; rather, development efforts should equip persons to be agents of their own improvement.

The language of agency, empowerment and even participation is currently not as precise as it could be in the development literature (see Cleaver, 1999). Agency is more fundamental than simple decision-making; it is about the ability to make those decisions and to exercise one's voice in ways that can help persons and groups remove disadvantage. While there is good reason to value increasing agency in terms of (élite) women's participation in high-ranking leadership positions, such as in the GEM measure of the UNDP, attention must also focus on the less obvious shifts in the lives of persons with little or no voice as they incrementally develop their ability to participate in the life of their society.

The analysis of this chapter helps to show that the capabilities approach, although it is based upon what *individuals* can and do achieve (see Gore, 1997; Craig, 2003), certainly can incorporate focus upon social structures. Indeed, to examine Sen's and Nussbaum's respective writings on gender-based discrimination is to see that the capabilities approach concentrates on questioning (and transforming) social structures of injustice that keep individuals and groups from attaining agency and well-being (Hicks, 2003). This chapter builds upon the capabilities approach to clarify ways in which persons' concern for others, within structures of injustice, sometimes negatively impacts on their own well-being. The emphasis on the positive relationship between the agency of women and the well-being of their children (see Sen, 1999: 195–198) must remain where Sen and Nussbaum intend it – within a framework that acknowledges the *intrinsic* importance of women's well-being and agency. This framework requires critical reflection on discrimination and social justice.

This chapter has not specified particular indicators of agency that can be used, either at the society-wide or individual levels. More work – theoretical and empirical – is needed to find specific indicators of agency. Which decisions and actions reflect genuine voice and influence? More important than any list of agency indicators is the social reflection about what conditions must be necessary for agency to exist. Indeed, the very creation of public discussion in local contexts about what agency, participation and empowerment look like is a way to increase the agency of those who take part in it.

Finally, alongside attention to agency, the chapter calls for an expanded use of inequality indicators within measures of development. At the society-wide level, inequality indicators can be integrated (in different ways) with indicators of aggregate achievement. At the individual level, distributional information – specifically, information that accounts for one's location at a point in the distribution – can be incorporated into the determination of particular functionings. Viewed together, inequality and agency expand our understanding of development. The admittedly complex task of modelling development in ways that account for these concepts will yield more precise perspectives on who benefits, and in what ways, from the processes of development.

Acknowledgements

This was an invited paper delivered at the Inequality, Poverty and Human Well-Being conference, sponsored by the World Institute for Development Economics Research (WIDER) of the United Nations University, in Helsinki, 30 May 2003. The author would like to thank conference attendees and Jonathan B. Wight, Terry L. Price, G. Scott Davis and Rebecca Todd Peters for helpful comments on this chapter.

Notes

1. The author has elsewhere argued for the moral significance of the negative effects that severe inequalities of certain functionings have on persons at the lower end of those distributions (Hicks, 2000, 2001; Hicks and Price, 1999).
2. For the HDI, the component index for education, when calculated for a sole individual, would take on either a 0 or 1 value: "1" if the child is enrolled in school or if the adult is literate, and "0" otherwise. PPP-adjusted income could be discounted (for values above gross world product per capita) in the same way it is for the national figure. Life expectancy at birth might require employment of society-wide medical figures (and thus it would be a relational exercise in a limited sense), but the individual's particular features (e.g. gender, health at birth) could be incorporated into this determination. The calculation of the HDI is explained in UNDP, 2002 (Technical Note 1: 253).
3. For a fuller discussion of the HDI and distributional concerns see Hicks (1997).
4. Often, however, the moral or social reasons to support the claim that less inequality is preferable to more inequality are not fully presented. The author has offered a normative account for constraining inequality in Hicks (2000).
5. For a fuller discussion of the calculation of the GDI see Anand and Sen (1995). For discussions of the GDI's shortcomings see Bardhan and Klasen (1999) and Saith and Harriss-White (1999: 485–488).
6. Of course, a society's own figure – whether aggregate (e.g. GDP/capita) or distributional (e.g. Gini coefficient for income) – can be compared internationally. For instance, Finland's GDP/capita can be placed on a distribution of income per capita (with each

country's figure being weighted either equally or according to population), or its Gini coefficient for income can be ranked with that of other nations.
7. It may well be the case that less relevant than one's location at a percentile is some other measure of disparity – for instance, one's standard deviation distance from the mean. This technical question is worthy of further work, but it does not affect the general point about relative position and well-being.
8. In nominal terms, the incomes of persons in the lower half may well have increased in order to maintain their purchasing power.
9. Sen (1985a) lists "commitment", such as to moral ideals or a religious community, as an influence that can lead persons to pursue activities that are not beneficial to their own well-being. He contrasts commitment with sympathy, by which one's concern for other persons is also (positively) related to one's own well-being. Importantly, Sen's use of the word "commitment" and its contrast with "sympathy" should not be taken to mean that religious or moral commitments in the more common use of the term cannot also positively influence one's own well-being. Actual commitments (in contrast to Sen's usage) can certainly entail the sense of sympathy that Sen (following Adam Smith) invokes.
10. Sen (1999: 19) acknowledges that one's agency might not be judged exclusively in terms of what that person values. He notes that one's agency-based "achievements can be judged in terms of her own values and objectives, whether or not we assess them in terms of some external criteria as well".
11. This task, by definition, requires an external means of valuation that reflects a set of normative assumptions about what is to be valued. This external means does not need to be a universal or even fully objective one; it might be based, for example, upon the statements and convictions of local persons whom other local persons consider to be wise. These issues strike at the heart of the standard economic assumption that each individual person is the best judge of his or her own well-being, but this rethinking is necessary in order for these social influences upon agency to be taken into account.
12. See Bardhan and Klasen (1999) for a related criticism of the GEM.
13. If scholars studied the women in the bottom 20 per cent (or 40 per cent or 50 per cent) of a distribution – thus focusing on those experiencing the most disadvantage – they would find it difficult to monitor the women's progress over time, because persons who acquire agency tend to move out of the bottom portion of the population. For this reason it is preferable to choose indicators that attend to all women (or the population as a whole), but with weighting that gives preferential attention to persons closer to the bottom of a distribution.
14. As one possible example, wealthy persons in a society of vast inequality may experience a lack of agency in terms of their ability to help reduce poverty. Public discourse in the United States about global and domestic poverty often includes reference to the belief that even if persons had the conviction to help the poor, their own efforts would be nearly futile. It would be valuable for scholars to undertake further study on the effects on agency of rich and poor alike of increasing (or decreasing) inequalities.
15. Life expectancy is admittedly a closer reflection of (projected) functioning than income figures are an indicator of having basic access to goods and services.

REFERENCES

Anand, S. and A. Sen (1995) "Gender Inequality in Human Development: Theories and Measurement", Occasional Paper No. 19, UNDP Human Development Report Office, New York.

Bardhan, K. and S. Klasen (1999) "UNDP's Gender-Related Indices: A Critical Review", *World Development* 27(6): 985–1010.

Buvinic, M. (1997) "Women in Poverty: A New Global Underclass", *Foreign Policy* (Fall): 38–53.

Cleaver, F. (1999) "Paradoxes of Participation: Questioning Participatory Approaches to Development", *Journal of International Development* 11: 597–612.

Craig, D. (2003) "Comment [on Hicks (2002) and Beckley]", *Journal of Religious Ethics* 31(1): 153–158.

Douglas, M. and B. Isherwood (1979) *The World of Goods: Towards an Anthropology of Consumption*, New York: Basic Books.

Duesenberry, J. ([1949] 1962) *Income, Saving, and the Theory of Consumer Behavior*, Cambridge, Mass.: Harvard University Press.

Elster, J. (1983) *Sour Grapes: Studies in the Subversion of Rationality*, Cambridge: Cambridge University Press.

Gore, C. (1997) "Irreducibly Social Goods and the Informational Basis of Amartya Sen's Capability Approach", *Journal of International Development* 9(2): 235–250.

Hicks, D. A. (1997) "The Inequality-Adjusted Human Development Index: A Constructive Proposal", *World Development* 25(8): 1283–1298.

—— (2000) *Inequality and Christian Ethics*, Cambridge: Cambridge University Press.

—— (2001) "Inequality, Globalization, and Leadership: 'Keeping Up with the Joneses' across National Boundaries", *Annual of the Society of Christian Ethics* 21: 63–80.

—— (2002) "Gender, Discrimination, and Capability: Insights from Amartya Sen", *Journal of Religious Ethics* 30(1): 137–154.

—— (2003) "The Author Replies [to David Craig (2003)]", *Journal of Religious Ethics* 31(1): 163–165.

Hicks, D. A. and T. L. Price (1999) "An Ethical Challenge for Leaders and Scholars: What Do People Really Need?", in *Selected Proceedings of the Leaders/Scholars Association*, University of Maryland, College Park: James MacGregor Burns Academy of Leadership.

Kabeer, N. (1999) "Resources, Agency, Achievements: Reflections on the Measurement of Women's Empowerment", *Development and Change* 30: 435–464.

Milanovic, B. (2002) "True World Income Distribution, 1988 and 1993: First Calculations Based on Household Surveys Alone", *Economic Journal* 112(1): 51–92.

Nussbaum, M. C. (2000) *Women and Human Development: The Capabilities Approach*, Cambridge: Cambridge University Press.

Razavi, S. (1999) "Gendered Poverty and Well-being: Introduction", *Development and Change* 30: 409–433.

Saith, R. and B. Harriss-White (1999) "The Gender Sensitivity of Well-being Indicators", *Development and Change* 30: 465–497.

Sen, A. (1983) "Poor, Relatively Speaking", *Oxford Economic Papers* 35: 153–169.

—— (1985a) "Goals, Commitment and Identity", *Journal of Law, Economics, and Organization* 1(2): 341–355.

—— (1985b) "Well-Being, Agency and Freedom: The Dewey Lectures 1984", *Journal of Philosophy* 82(4): 169–221.
—— (1990) "Gender and Cooperative Conflict", in I. Tinker, ed., *Persistent Inequalities*, New York: Oxford University Press, pp. 123–149.
—— (1992) *Inequality Reexamined*, Cambridge, Mass.: Harvard University Press and Russell Sage.
—— (1993) "Capability and Well-Being", in M. Nussbaum and A. Sen, eds, *The Quality of Life*, Oxford: Clarendon Press, pp. 30–53.
—— (1997) *On Economic Inequality*, expanded edition with a substantial annexe by J. E. Foster and A. Sen, Oxford: Clarendon Press.
—— (1999) *Development as Freedom*, New York: Alfred A. Knopf.
Smith, A. ([1776] 1976) "An Inquiry into the Nature and Causes of the Wealth of Nations", in R. H. Campbell, A. S. Skinner and W. B. Todd, eds, *Glasgow Edition of the Works and Correspondence of Adam Smith*, New York: Oxford University Press.
UNDP (1993) *Human Development Report 1993*, New York: Oxford University Press.
—— (1995) *Human Development Report 1995*, New York: Oxford University Press.
—— (2002) *Human Development Report 2002*, New York: Oxford University Press.

Part II
Well-being measures and applications

6

On the measurement of human well-being: Fuzzy-set theory and Sen's capability approach

Mina Baliamoune-Lutz

Human development is the end – economic growth the means. (UNDP, 1996)

Introduction

The UNDP's view that human development constitutes an end while economic growth is the means may seem to be in line with Amartya Sen's capability approach (CA). However, Sen's view of capabilities encompasses a much greater scope than the one covered by the mainstream view of human development. The CA underlines the importance of focusing on the advancement of humanity.

Amartya Sen's influential work on the role of functionings and capabilities in defining human well-being emphasizes freedom: freedom of doing and freedom of being. This is a clear "upgrade" of the way we view human development, but the measurement of capabilities is complex. The first difficulty arises from the multiplicity of components included in well-being and the potential double (multiple) counting that may result. Second, we must take into account the fact that there are non-uniform weights given by different societies (and different individuals within the same society) to different components of well-being. Third, the weights given to different levels of achievements in the overall achievement and in different components should not necessarily be the same. Fourth, and perhaps more importantly, in deciding what dimensions to involve in the computation of a well-being index, we are making assumptions about preferences and relating outcomes to preferences which are, in essence, vague. For example, if we consider freedom, and given country-specific preferences, would a society that has an index of 1 (on a scale of 1 to 10, with 1 being the worst) be much worse off or equally worse off as a society that has a score of, say, 4? Should a society that has achieved a score of 6 up from 1 get more or the same credit as one that improved its score from 5 to 6? Does it make sense to have a *linear* scoring method, such as the one employed in the computation of the UNDP's human development index (HDI)?[1] Conventional measures of treatment of achievements (or scores for those achievements) imply accounting even for irrelevant variation. For example, variation in education levels among the richest countries is quite irrelevant, and the same statement applies to variation in life expectancy. Similarly, variation in freedom indicators and democracy among the clearly democratic countries has little or no usefulness for the analysis of well-being.[2]

The main purpose of this chapter is to review Sen's CA and the UNDP's human development indices, and propose a measurement framework that would reconcile these approaches and the fuzziness of the preferences and outcomes that are inherently imbedded in what constitutes human well-being.

The chapter proceeds as follows. In the next section Sen's CA and the UNDP's HDI are discussed. The third section develops a framework based on fuzzy-set theory and outlines how certain indices can be derived. In the fourth section, using this framework, a well-being index for a group of countries is constructed and the resulting indices are discussed. The last section contains concluding remarks.

Human well-being, human development and Sen's capability approach

Human well-being is not exclusively the realm of economists. While economic well-being is an important part of human well-being, several other dimensions are equally (if not more) crucial. These dimensions have traditionally been researched in the fields of philosophy, psychology, sociology, religion and political science. These disciplines are, in general, critical of the way the concept of well-being has been treated in mainstream economics.[3]

In the early economic literature well-being was equated with welfarism and focused on the concept of "utility", derived from consumption and based on (assumed) preferences. In this theory, human beings were viewed as self-interested. Welfarism does not allow for some crucial dimensions to be included and does not consider changes in preferences, thus it was strongly criticized in many disciplines. Hausman and McPherson (1996: 73) point out that "there are such obvious objections to a preference satisfaction view of well-being that one wonders how economists could possibly endorse it".

In view of the strong criticism addressed to welfarism, another theory of well-being developed; the so-called basic needs approach (see the important body of research of Mahbub Ul Haq, Paul Streeten and Frances Stewart). This approach focuses on whether countries are achieving satisfactory levels of "meeting" specific basic needs. The major criticism to this line of thought lies in the fact that it is not clear how many needs should be included.

Amartya Sen's theory, which was intended to replace welfarism as a theory of well-being, is normative and centres on capabilities and functionings or states of being (see, for example, Sen, 1977, 1979, 1982, 1985). The idea of capabilities and functionings is quite old and can be traced back to Aristotle. Major aspects of the Aristotelian view are examined in the work of Martha Nussbaum on capability. In modern economics, capabilities and functionings were first formalized and operationalized by Amartya Sen in his well-known "capability approach".[4]

Sen's influential work on human development has led economists to explore new areas that have become increasingly important for well-being. Sen stresses the "capabilities" and "functionings" that an individual achieves. On the subject of capability, Sen (1990: 114) writes:

[I]ndividual claims are to be assessed not by the resources or primary goods the persons respectively hold, but the freedoms they actually enjoy to choose between different ways of living that they can have reason to value. It is this actual freedom that is represented by the person's "capability" to achieve various alternative combinations of functionings, or doings and beings.[5]

Sen's CA has become equivalent to a well-being theory and has been praised by many scholars (see, for example, Crocker, 1992; Nelson, 1996; Anderson, 1999; Atkinson, 1999; Pressman and Summerfield, 2000). Other scholars, on the other hand, have criticized the approach on the grounds that it fails to account for many crucial dimensions. Gasper (2002: 436) contends that "viewed from outside economics, the [capability approach] seems primitive in some ways, insufficient as a theory of well-being, and hardly a theory of the human development". Moreover, Sen's approach does not outline some important aspects of the practicability of the capability view. In particular, as explained by Sen himself, issues related to the assessment of capability and the applicability of this approach need to be seriously addressed (Sen, 1993).

In 1990 the UNDP introduced the HDI, primarily as a response to the criticism that GDP is not an adequate measure of human development. The HDI is an index that combines a measure of income with measures of longevity and education/literacy (a proxy for knowledge). All three dimensions have equal weight. Since the early 1990s several aspects of the HDI have been criticized by numerous scholars (Desai, 1991; McGillivray, 1991; Dasgupta and Weale, 1992). In general the criticism focused on the composition of the index, the statistical construction and data quality. Ogwang (1994: 2013) finds that life expectancy is "the variable which best represents the three human deprivation variables". Yet Anand and Sen (2000: 102) maintain that income "plays a part that the other two components of HDI cannot serve". On the other hand, Hopkins (1991) views literacy as the weakest indicator since "it is impossible to have the same standards for abilities to read and write given language differences". According to Sen's theory of "capability and functionings", literacy (education) is also in the set of capability, so it is very important to be able to undertake an appropriate measurement of this dimension and also to have the ability to make meaningful comparisons. However, as pointed out by Hopkins (1991), that is not possible. In many societies the written language (the language one learns in school) is very different from the spoken language or dialect.

Several researchers have proposed adjustments and the UNDP, indeed, made some changes. For example, the *Human Development Report 1994* (*HDR*) introduced a change in the threshold income level to underscore the fact that the poverty level of industrialized countries is "not an appropriate income target for developing countries" (UNDP, 1994: 91). In 1995 the HDI was adjusted in order to incorporate improvements in the computation method. More recently the UNDP has added other indices, such as the human poverty index (HPI), a gender empowerment measure (GEM) and a gender-related development index (GDI).[6] These indices reflect the extent of inequality in distribution, gender inequality and female participation in politics and policy-making. Thus it may appear that the notion of a set of indicators covering basic needs as well as social justice is imbedded in these measures. However, nothing has been done to address properly the vagueness of the variables included in the computation of the index.

A fuzzy-set-based approach for HDI computation

A "social indicator" is not very useful because it helps in categorizing the achievements or the state of well-being of countries into high, medium and low. Its true usefulness stems from the fact that such an indicator could provide relevant information for policy-making. If the indicator fails to do so, it becomes useless. Furthermore, a measurement technique is only useful in so far as it allows a better understanding and analysis of well-being. As stated in the previous section, Sen stresses the importance of the "freedom to choose". Freedom, however, is not always a crisp outcome, and membership in the freedom space can take place gradually. Sen himself agrees that "well-being and inequality are broad and partly opaque concepts" (Sen, 1992: 48). Fuzzy sets allow for gradual transition from one state to another while also allowing one to incorporate rules and goals, and hence are more suitable for modelling preferences and outcomes that are ambiguous. For example, fuzzy-set theory is particularly appropriate for measuring vulnerability to poverty and famine.

The application of fuzzy sets to economic issues is relatively new. Moreover, in the area of well-being the applications are rather limited in number and are exclusively focused on micro-level data and predominantly on poverty measurement. For example, Qizilbash (2002) uses fuzzy logic to construct poverty measures in order to explore vulnerability to poverty in South Africa. Other studies that used fuzzy-set theory to measure poverty include Cheli and Lemmi (1995), Cheli (1995) and Chiappero (1996, 2000). To this author's best knowledge, there has never been an application of fuzzy-set theory to assess well-being using macro-level data.

The use of household surveys and other micro-level data is useful and does have the potential to yield important insight into disparities among groups, but tends to be of little value when trying to compare across countries. Furthermore, it may not allow one to assess how the country as a whole is improving (or not improving) over time, since the focus is on "parts" that may evolve in different directions.

This is not the first attempt to apply fuzzy-set theory to macroeconomic data. Von Furstenberg and Daniels (1991) and Baliamoune (2000) use this theory to assess the degree of country compliance with the G7 economic summit commitments. The main contribution of the present chapter lies in the fact that this is the first time an application of fuzzy-set theory to macroeconomic and social indicators of well-being is undertaken. In addition, the only other study that has applied fuzzy logic in conjunction with Sen's CA is Lelli (2001). Using data from a representative sample of Belgian individuals, Lelli applied fuzzy sets and factor analysis to well-being measurement and found that the "fuzzy aggregates" were insensitive to the choice of the form of the membership function. However, the author does recommend that one explore with other membership functions. More importantly, Lelli (2001: 25) finds both methods (factor analysis and fuzzy sets) show that "income accounts only for a very limited part of the story and this should definitely be seen as a reason to follow multidimensional approaches like Sen's one".

The notion of fuzzy sets was conceptualized by Lotfi Zadeh. The publication of Zadeh's seminal paper ("Fuzzy Sets") in 1965 marked a milestone in the modern research on uncertainty and ambiguity. In his paper, Zadeh defined fuzzy sets as "a class of objects with a continuum of grades of membership". While the early applications of fuzzy logic were in science and engineering, such as biology and artificial intelligence, fuzzy-set theory has more recently been increasingly applied to many issues in various social science and business fields.

Degrees of membership or compliance with goals are commonly expressed by numbers belonging to the interval [0, 1]. Fuzzy sets allow one to model gradual transition from membership to non-membership and vice versa. It is a concept that permits a meaningful representation of ambiguous and vague objects or outcomes. Fuzzy sets are appropriate when, for example, we examine literacy or education in a country. What is the degree of membership of individuals with primary education or some secondary education in the fuzzy set of "educated"? It cannot be zero because the person has some education, but we cannot say the individual is educated because that would imply treating a college graduate the same way we treat a high school drop-out.

The present chapter uses a fairly common fuzzy membership function, which is expressed as follows:[7]

$$\mu(x) = \frac{1}{1 + e^{-a(x-b)}} \qquad (1)$$

The parameters a and b can be derived as follows. Let μ_h be the membership degree of the highest achievement (x_h) of the goal. Similarly, let μ_l be the membership degree of the lowest achievement (x_l) of the goal. From equation (1), and given μ_h and μ_l, we can solve a and b.

It turns out that[8]

$$a = \frac{\ln\left(\frac{\mu_h}{1-\mu_h}\right) - \ln\left(\frac{\mu_l}{1-\mu_l}\right)}{x_h - x_l} \qquad (2)$$

and

$$b = \frac{x_l \ln\left(\frac{\mu_h}{1-\mu_h}\right) - x_h \ln\left(\frac{\mu_l}{1-\mu_l}\right)}{\ln\left(\frac{\mu_h}{1-\mu_h}\right) - \ln\left(\frac{\mu_l}{1-\mu_l}\right)} \qquad (3)$$

It is worth noting that the parameters a and b serve to *operationalize* certain concepts associated with the fuzzy membership function. The slope a represents the extent of vagueness and b may be viewed as the identification threshold. The parameter b "represents the point at which the tendency of the subject's attitude changes from rather positive into rather negative" (Zimmermann, 1987: 205).

In the present context, taking for example education, b would represent the threshold at which a country changes from rather negative (dismal) to a rather positive (there is hope) achievement, say an index greater than 0.5. In the case of GDP per capita, the threshold may represent the poverty line or any other level deemed appropriate to serve as a dividing line between poor and adequate or satisfactory performance. One useful aspect of having such a parameter is the ability it gives the policy-maker or researcher to conduct sensitivity analysis when the threshold changes. The membership degrees μ_h and μ_l, as well as the parameters a and b used to compute the three dimensions of HDI, are reported in table 6.1.

Once we obtain values for a and b, we can compute the degree of membership (adherence) for each country. First, fuzzy-set theory is applied to three components of the HDI. Second, other dimensions are included to examine a more encompassing concept of well-being (see the next section).

Table 6.2 reports degrees of membership for a large group of countries. There is no rationale to selecting this group of countries except that they represent different levels of economic development, institutional structure and/or geographical areas and cultures. The data used to compute the indices are from UNDP (2002).

The results reported in tables 6.2 and 6.3 show that the ranking of some countries based on fuzzy membership is different from that associated with the HDI. It is important to stress that fuzzy-set scores convey information that does not readily transpire from the HDI. The membership degrees (scores) underline the extent of deprivation and the "lagging behind". For example, the UNDP measures indicate that the GDP index for Sierra Leone (the poorest country in the group) is 0.265 while that of Norway is 0.952. This implies that Sierra Leone's GDP index is 27 per cent of that in Norway, which may lead to a misleading interpretation (in the sense that one may consider 27 per cent of the index of income in Norway as still not a very bad outcome!). On the other hand, the fuzzy-set computation indicates that Sierra Leone's GDP index is 0.34 per cent of Norway's. This clearly conveys the idea that there is absolute deprivation in this area in Sierra Leone.

Another feature worth highlighting is that the fuzzy-set approach em-

Table 6.1 Parameters for computing degrees of membership*

		μ_h	μ_l	a	b
Life expectancy					
	(1)	0.99	0.294	7.8609	0.4054
	(2)	0.95	0.46	6.3363	0.4853
Education					
	(1)	0.9999	0.0001	18.4242	0.5000
	(2)	0.9999	0.16	12.9402	0.2881
GDP					
	(1)	0.99	0.0025	10.7181	0.5613
	(2)	0.85	0.01	7.5354	0.6198

*Computation of the HDI based on fuzzy membership.
Notes
Life expectancy
a) The numbers in row (1) are derived as follows. Based on the UNDP's assumption of 85 years as the goal (maximum), we use 0.99 (age that is 99 per cent of 85 years) as the highest possible achievement μ_h. The UNDP's assumption of 25 years as the worst (minimum) achievement is used to generate μ_l equal to 0.294 (age that is 25 as a percentage of the maximum age 85).
b) The numbers in row (2) are derived as follows. The highest life expectancy in the world is 81 (Japan). That number, as a percentage of 85 (the UNDP's goal) yields μ_h equal to 0.95. The lowest life expectancy is 38.9 (Sierra Leone), which represents 46 per cent of the goal (85 years). Thus, μ_l is equal to 0.46.
c) In order to get consistent measurement units, the actual achievement X is computed as a percentage of the goal (85 years).
Education
a) The numbers in row (1) are derived as follows. Based on the UNDP's assumption of the "100 per cent education rate" as the goal and zero as the worst achievement, we use 0.9999 (for computation feasibility) as μ_h and 0.0001 as μ_l.
b) The numbers in row (2) are derived using μ_h equal to 0.9999 and μ_l equal to 0.16 which is the lowest achievement (Niger).
c) Consistent with the UNDP, a weight of two-thirds is placed on adult literacy and a weight of one-third is placed on primary, secondary and tertiary gross enrolment.
GDP
a) The numbers in row (1) are derived as follows. The highest achievement is assigned μ_h equal to 0.9999, and the lowest achievement is assigned μ_l equal to 0.0025 (100/40,000), since the UNDP uses a maximum of US$40,000 and a minimum of US$100.
b) The numbers in row (2) are derived as follows. The highest GDP achieved is US$34,142 (PPP), which represents 85 per cent of the maximum (US$40,000) that the UNDP uses to derive the HDI. Thus μ_h equals 0.85. Similarly, the lowest GDP per capita (Sierra Leone) as a percentage of 40,000 is used as value for μ_l.
c) In order to get consistent measurement units, the actual achievement X is computed as a percentage of the goal (US$40,000).

phasizes relevant variation and downgrades (or even ignores) irrelevant variation. For the reasons explained earlier (see the introduction), this is an improvement over other widely used computation methods. For example, while the HDI shows different scores (indices) for education in the group with high HDI, the fuzzy-set approach yields indices that are the same (1.00) for countries included in this group. As we move to low HDI countries, membership degrees (indices) drop dramatically.

It is worth noting that the extreme cases (very high and very low levels) are not, in general, affected but the middle ones (because of the fuzziness) are affected, as some countries which are borderline on development either fall to a lower level (for example, Argentina, Slovakia, Poland, Morocco) or move to a higher rank (for example, Zambia).[9] This is, however, expected given the construction of the fuzzy membership function, which is context-specific.

Computation of fuzzy-set-based human well-being subindices: A simple illustration

The model developed in the previous section can be used to derive an index of well-being that is consistent with Sen's CA. However, two major questions arise. First, do we need an indicator (similar to the HDI) that measures well-being and summarizes the result in one *composite* index or a set of indicators (indices) that could be more useful in understanding well-being in different countries and could be used to do some sort of country ranking? Second, what are the major non-income components of well-being?

While the UNDP's HDI is a useful indicator for researchers concerned with how countries fare in relative income (mainly), literacy and life expectancy, it is by no means a good indicator for well-being. There is a large body of debate regarding what we should include in well-being. Perhaps the most encompassing measure is the genuine progress index (GPI) which covers dimensions traditionally ignored in the computation of GDP and the HDI. These components take into account negative outcomes usually associated with higher GDP (and more common in some wealthy nations), such as crime, natural disasters, divorce rates, reduction in leisure time and pollution.

An important goal of this chapter is to illustrate how fuzzy sets can be used to compute a well-being index. It is not claimed that such an index is inclusive. Rather, it is hoped that the proposed methodology will serve as a framework that can be expanded to include policy goals, identification thresholds and other dimensions deemed useful for assessing well-being. Table 6.4 reports the degrees of membership for several well-being com-

Table 6.2 UNDP and fuzzy-set-based indices

	UNDP			Fuzzy membership					
	Life expectancy index	Education index	GDP index	Life expectancy index		Education index		GDP index	
				(1)	(2)	(1)	(2)	(1)	(2)
High HDI									
Norway	0.892	0.983	0.952	0.983	0.941	1.000	1.000	0.881	0.724
Sweden	0.912	0.993	0.917	0.985	0.946	1.000	1.000	0.620	0.476
Canada	0.897	0.983	0.940	0.984	0.943	1.000	1.000	0.809	0.640
Australia	0.898	0.993	0.926	0.984	0.943	1.000	1.000	0.704	0.542
US	0.867	0.977	0.974	0.981	0.981	1.000	1.000	0.958	0.853
Japan	0.933	0.933	0.933	0.987	0.951	1.000	1.000	0.760	0.591
Finland	0.877	0.993	0.921	0.982	0.938	1.000	1.000	0.662	0.508
France	0.893	0.973	0.916	0.983	0.942	1.000	1.000	0.617	0.473
UK	0.878	0.993	0.911	0.982	0.938	1.000	1.000	0.570	0.440
Austria	0.885	0.960	0.933	0.983	0.940	1.000	1.000	0.761	0.592
Germany	0.878	0.973	0.922	0.982	0.938	1.000	1.000	0.671	0.515
Singapore	0.877	0.968	0.910	0.982	0.938	1.000	1.000	0.560	0.433
Korea	0.832	0.986	0.861	0.977	0.925	1.000	1.000	0.204	0.198
Argentina	0.807	0.922	0.804	0.973	0.917	1.000	1.000	0.063	0.088
Slovakia	0.805	0.920	0.788	0.973	0.916	1.000	1.000	0.047	0.072
Poland	0.805	0.945	0.752	0.973	0.916	1.000	1.000	0.027	0.049
Costa Rica	0.857	0.861	0.744	0.980	0.932	0.999	0.999	0.024	0.046
Kuwait	0.853	0.743	0.845	0.979	0.931	0.989	0.997	0.144	0.155
Qatar	0.743	0.791	0.874	0.963	0.892	0.995	0.999	0.273	0.244
Medium HDI									
Mexico	0.793	0.846	0.751	0.971	0.912	0.998	0.999	0.027	0.049
Malaysia	0.792	0.803	0.752	0.971	0.911	0.996	0.999	0.027	0.049
Saudi Arabia	0.777	0.712	0.790	0.969	0.906	0.980	0.996	0.049	0.074

Brazil	0.712	0.835	0.723	0.956	0.878	0.998	0.999	0.018	0.038
Turkey	0.747	0.774	0.708	0.963	0.894	0.994	0.998	0.016	0.034
China	0.758	0.804	0.615	0.966	0.898	0.996	0.999	0.007	0.019
Tunisia	0.753	0.720	0.693	0.965	0.896	0.983	0.996	0.013	0.030
Algeria	0.743	0.685	0.663	0.963	0.892	0.968	0.994	0.010	0.025
South Africa	0.452	0.879	0.758	0.836	0.692	0.999	1.000	0.029	0.052
Egypt	0.705	0.622	0.600	0.954	0.875	0.904	0.987	0.006	0.018
Gabon	0.462	0.760	0.690	0.855	0.701	0.992	0.998	0.013	0.029
Morocco	0.710	0.499	0.596	0.955	0.877	0.497	0.939	0.006	0.018
India	0.638	0.565	0.527	0.935	0.838	0.767	0.973	0.005	0.014
Botswana	0.255	0.748	0.713	0.632	0.482	0.990	0.997	0.016	0.035
Zimbabwe	0.298	0.808	0.546	0.686	0.531	0.997	0.999	0.005	0.015
Ghana	0.530	0.617	0.497	0.888	0.761	0.896	0.986	0.004	0.013
Cameroon	0.417	0.649	0.473	0.808	0.658	0.939	0.991	0.004	0.013
Low HDI									
Pakistan	0.583	0.421	0.494	0.914	0.802	0.190	0.849	0.004	0.013
Sudan	0.517	0.499	0.482	0.880	0.750	0.494	0.938	0.004	0.013
Yemen	0.593	0.479	0.365	0.918	0.809	0.403	0.922	0.003	0.011
Bangladesh	0.573	0.399	0.463	0.909	0.795	0.134	0.807	0.004	0.013
Nigeria	0.445	0.576	0.366	0.831	0.685	0.802	0.976	0.003	0.011
Uganda	0.317	0.597	0.416	0.707	0.551	0.857	0.982	0.003	0.012
Zambia	0.273	0.684	0.343	0.655	0.503	0.967	0.994	0.003	0.011
Angola	0.337	0.357	0.515	0.730	0.573	0.067	0.708	0.004	0.014
Chad	0.345	0.387	0.361	0.739	0.582	0.111	0.783	0.003	0.011
Burundi	0.260	0.380	0.297	0.638	0.488	0.099	0.766	0.003	0.010
Niger	0.337	0.159	0.335	0.730	0.573	0.002	0.159	0.003	0.011
Sierra Leone	0.232	0.330	0.265	0.601	0.456	0.042	0.632	0.003	0.010

Table 6.3 HDI: Composite index and country ranking

	(1)		(2)
High human development			
US	0.98	US	0.93
Norway	0.95	Norway	0.89
Canada	0.93	Canada	0.86
Japan	0.92	Japan	0.85
Austria	0.91	Austria	0.84
Australia	0.90	Australia	0.83
Germany	0.88	Germany	0.82
Finland	0.88	Finland	0.82
Sweden	0.87	Sweden	0.81
France	0.87	France	0.80
UK	0.85	UK	0.79
Singapore	0.85	Singapore	0.79
Qatar	0.74	Qatar	0.71
Korea	0.73	Korea	0.71
Kuwait	0.70	Kuwait	0.69
Medium and low human development			
Argentina	0.68	Argentina	0.67
Slovakia	0.67	Slovakia	0.66
Costa Rica	0.67	Costa Rica	0.66
Poland	0.67	Saudi Arabia	0.66
Saudi Arabia	0.67	Poland	0.65
Mexico	0.67	Mexico	0.65
Malaysia	0.66	Malaysia	0.65
Brazil	0.66	Turkey	0.64
Turkey	0.66	Tunisia	0.64
China	0.66	China	0.64
Tunisia	0.65	Brazil	0.64
Algeria	0.65	Algeria	0.64
South Africa	0.63	Egypt	0.63
Egypt	0.62	Morocco	0.61
Gabon	0.62	India	0.61
Ghana	0.60	Ghana	0.59
Cameroon	0.58	South Africa	0.58
India	0.57	Yemen	0.58
Zimbabwe	0.56	Gabon	0.58
Botswana	0.55	Sudan	0.57
Zambia	0.54	Nigeria	0.56
Nigeria	0.55	Pakistan	0.55
Uganda	0.52	Cameroon	0.55
Morocco	0.49	Bangladesh	0.54
Sudan	0.46	Uganda	0.51
Yemen	0.44	Zimbabwe	0.51
Pakistan	0.37	Botswana	0.50
Bangladesh	0.35	Zambia	0.50
Chad	0.28	Chad	0.46
Angola	0.27	Angola	0.43
Burundi	0.25	Burundi	0.42
Niger	0.24	Sierra Leone	0.37
Sierra Leone	0.22	Niger	0.25

ponents (data used in the computation of these indices are for the year 2000).

The first three components displayed in table 6.4 are the ones derived earlier and reported in table 6.2, columns labelled (1). These components are consistent with the dimensions included in the HDI. Perhaps it is useful to provide a brief review of the rationale for their inclusion.

Income represents an important aspect of command over resources and is a type of functioning. It also serves as a means to achieve a capability that would help to make functionings happen (for example, a life without hunger or disease). Health and knowledge (or education) are examples of capabilities to achieve functionings.

However, there are diminishing returns to income, so that returns (impact) may become nil at moderate to high levels of income. Anand and Sen (2000: 86) argue that "The income level enjoyed, especially close to poverty lines, can be very crucial information on the causal antecedents of basic human capabilities." The use of the logarithm transformation (as in the HDI) of the purchasing power parity (PPP) value of GDP per capita is meant to reflect diminishing returns as income rises.

The information and communication technology (ICT) index measures both functionings and capability (knowledge and freedom to communicate). This index may also be used as an indicator of the extent of social exclusion. The ICT index is constructed using four components (data are from ITU, 2002): cellphones per 100 inhabitants, internet hosts per 10,000 people, internet users per 10,000 people and personal computers per 100 inhabitants.

The dimension labelled "other" is constructed based on four components: infant mortality rates, under-five mortality rates, percentage of population with access to urban sanitation and percentage of population with access to an improved water source. Data are from the World Bank (2002).

The last two components represent freedom dimensions. They include political liberties and civil rights (Freedom House, 2001). The relationship between freedom and income (GDP) or other socio-economic indicators is not always clear. For example, Dasgupta and Weale (1992) construct a measure of well-being that includes political and civil liberties and find that per capita income and life expectancy are positively correlated with improvements in political and civil liberty, while infant mortality and – oddly – improvements in literacy show a negative correlation with political and civil liberties. Similarly, some researchers have shown that, as income reaches high levels, so do some factors that have a negative impact on well-being. Many wealthy societies have higher suicide rates, divorce rates, pollution and crime rates compared to poorer societies. For example, Jungeilges and Kirchgässner (2002) examined the

Table 6.4 Degrees of membership for selected human well-being components

Rank	Life expectancy index		Education index		GDP index		ICT index		Other		Political rights		Civil rights	
1	Japan	0.987	Sweden	1.000	US	0.958	Norway	0.998	Sweden	0.981	Norway	1.00	Norway	1.000
2	Sweden	0.985	Australia	1.000	Norway	0.881	Finland	0.991	Singapore	0.981	Sweden	1.00	Sweden	1.000
3	Australia	0.984	Finland	1.000	Canada	0.809	Sweden	0.991	Norway	0.981	Canada	1.00	Canada	1.000
4	Canada	0.984	UK	1.000	Austria	0.761	Australia	0.976	Japan	0.980	Australia	1.00	Australia	1.000
5	France	0.983	Korea	1.000	Japan	0.760	US	0.967	Finland	0.980	US	1.00	US	1.000
6	Norway	0.983	Norway	1.000	Australia	0.704	Singapore	0.919	France	0.980	Japan	1.00	Finland	1.000
7	Austria	0.983	Canada	1.000	Germany	0.671	Canada	0.903	Germany	0.979	Finland	1.00	Austria	1.000
8	UK	0.982	US	1.000	Finland	0.662	Japan	0.861	Austria	0.979	France	1.00	Japan	0.950
9	Germany	0.982	France	1.000	Sweden	0.620	Austria	0.830	Australia	0.979	UK	1.00	France	0.951
10	Finland	0.982	Germany	1.000	France	0.617	UK	0.811	Canada	0.979	Austria	1.00	UK	0.951
11	Singapore	0.982	Singapore	1.000	UK	0.570	Germany	0.790	UK	0.979	Germany	1.00	Germany	0.951
12	US	0.981	Austria	1.000	Singapore	0.560	Korea	0.688	US	0.977	Argentina	1.00	Korea	0.951
13	Costa Rica	0.980	Poland	1.000	Qatar	0.273	France	0.609	Slovakia	0.976	Slovakia	1.00	Argentina	0.951
14	Kuwait	0.979	Japan	1.000	Korea	0.204	Malaysia	0.265	Korea	0.972	Poland	1.00	Slovakia	0.951
15	Korea	0.977	Argentina	1.000	Kuwait	0.144	Slovakia	0.242	Costa Rica	0.972	Costa Rica	1.00	Poland	0.951
16	Argentina	0.973	Slovakia	1.000	Argentina	0.063	Kuwait	0.231	Malaysia	0.967	South Africa	1.00	Costa Rica	0.951
17	Slovakia	0.973	South Africa	0.999	Saudi Arabia	0.049	Qatar	0.194	Poland	0.967	Korea	0.951	South Africa	0.951
18	Poland	0.973	Costa Rica	0.999	Slovakia	0.047	Turkey	0.158	Kuwait	0.965	Mexico	0.951	Botswana	0.951
19	Mexico	0.971	Mexico	0.998	South Africa	0.029	Poland	0.139	Saudi Arabia	0.957	India	0.951	Mexico	0.729
20	Malaysia	0.971	Brazil	0.998	Malaysia	0.027	South Africa	0.132	Argentina	0.957	Botswana	0.951	Brazil	0.729
21	Saudi Arabia	0.969	Zimbabwe	0.997	Poland	0.027	Costa Rica	0.127	Mexico	0.924	Ghana	0.951	India	0.729
22	China	0.966	China	0.996	Mexico	0.027	Argentina	0.121	Tunisia	0.918	Brazil	0.721	Ghana	0.729
23	Tunisia	0.965	Malaysia	0.996	Costa Rica	0.024	Mexico	0.091	Brazil	0.913	Bangladesh	0.721	Gabon	0.271
24	Turkey	0.963	Qatar	0.995	Brazil	0.018	Brazil	0.086	Algeria	0.910	Kuwait	0.271	Morocco	0.271
25	Qatar	0.963	Turkey	0.994	Botswana	0.016	Botswana	0.069	China	0.904	Turkey	0.271	Bangladesh	0.271
26	Algeria	0.963	Gabon	0.992	Turkey	0.016	Saudi	0.056	Turkey	0.902	Nigeria	0.271	Nigeria	0.271

27	Brazil	0.956	Botswana	0.990	Tunisia	0.013	Gabon	0.053	Egypt	0.864	Niger	0.271	Zambia	0.271
28	Morocco	0.955	Kuwait	0.989	Gabon	0.013	Morocco	0.048	Morocco	0.831	Sierra Leone	0.271	Niger	0.271
29	Egypt	0.954	Tunisia	0.983	Algeria	0.010	China	0.047	Bangladesh	0.727	Singapore	0.049	Singapore	0.049
30	India	0.935	Saudi Arabia	0.980	China	0.007	Egypt	0.038	South Africa	0.725	Malaysia	0.049	Kuwait	0.049
31	Yemen	0.918	Algeria	0.968	Egypt	0.006	Tunisia	0.037	Qatar	0.716	Gabon	0.049	Malaysia	0.049
32	Pakistan	0.914	Zambia	0.967	Morocco	0.006	Zimbabwe	0.036	Sudan	0.699	Morocco	0.049	Turkey	0.049
33	Bangladesh	0.909	Cameroon	0.939	Zimbabwe	0.005	Zambia	0.033	India	0.679	Yemen	0.049	Tunisia	0.049
34	Ghana	0.888	Egypt	0.904	Cameroon	0.005	Cameroon	0.032	Ghana	0.645	Zambia	0.049	Algeria	0.049
35	Sudan	0.880	Ghana	0.896	India	0.004	India	0.032	Yemen	0.643	Qatar	0.007	Egypt	0.007
36	Gabon	0.855	Uganda	0.857	Angola	0.004	Uganda	0.032	Zimbabwe	0.621	Tunisia	0.007	Zimbabwe	0.007
37	South Africa	0.836	Nigeria	0.802	Ghana	0.004	Algeria	0.032	Pakistan	0.600	Algeria	0.007	Pakistan	0.007
38	Nigeria	0.831	India	0.767	Pakistan	0.004	Ghana	0.032	Cameroon	0.545	Egypt	0.007	Uganda	0.007
39	Cameroon	0.808	Morocco	0.497	Sudan	0.004	Nigeria	0.032	Gabon	0.532	Zimbabwe	0.007	Chad	0.007
40	Chad	0.739	Sudan	0.494	Cameroon	0.004	Pakistan	0.031	Nigeria	0.522	Pakistan	0.007	Sierra Leone	0.007
41	Angola	0.730	Yemen	0.403	Bangladesh	0.004	Angola	0.031	Uganda	0.502	Uganda	0.007	Qatar	0.007
42	Niger	0.730	Pakistan	0.190	Uganda	0.003	Sudan	0.031	Zambia	0.499	Angola	0.007	China	0.007
43	Uganda	0.707	Bangladesh	0.134	Nigeria	0.003	Yemen	0.031	Niger	0.485	Chad	0.007	Cameroon	0.007
44	Zimbabwe	0.686	Chad	0.111	Yemen	0.003	Bangladesh	0.031	Angola	0.403	Burundi	0.007	Yemen	0.007
45	Zambia	0.655	Burundi	0.099	Chad	0.003	Sierra Leone	0.031	Botswana	0.393	Saudi Arabia	0.001	Angola	0.001
46	Burundi	0.638	Angola	0.042	Zambia	0.003	Burundi	0.031	Burundi	0.351	China	0.001	Burundi	0.007
47	Botswana	0.632	Sierra Leone	0.042	Niger	0.003	Chad	0.031	Chad	0.347	Cameroon	0.001	Saudi Arabia	0.001
48	Sierra Leone	0.601	Niger	0.002	Sierra Leone	0.003	Niger	0.031	Sierra Leone	0.149	Chad	0.001	Sudan	0.001

link between suicide rates and economic welfare (economic growth and per capita income) and civil liberties. They found a positive relationship between suicide rates and economic welfare, and a negative relationship between suicide rates and civil liberty. Thus, freedom dimensions are very important for well-being. Indeed, the foreword to the *HDR* (UNDP, 2002: v) states:

> This *Human Development Report* is first and foremost about the idea that politics is as important to successful development as economics. Sustained poverty reduction requires equitable growth – but it also requires that poor people have political power.

It is clear that the inclusion of other components of well-being yields useful insight in this area. For example, based on the HDI, Costa Rica, Kuwait and Qatar were ranked 17, 18 and 19 respectively and were included in the high development group (UNDP ranking). According to the measure of well-being employed here (table 6.4), Costa Rica will still be included in this group, based on an average rank or Borda ranking. On the other hand, Qatar and Kuwait will drop to the next group since their membership degrees in most dimensions of well-being are relatively low. One observes similar outcomes in the case of other countries with low membership degrees in the component "freedom".

The fuzzy-set membership approach handles both saturation levels (diminishing, or even no, returns) and minimum requirements (threshold levels). For example, we observe that membership degrees for countries with low income drop abruptly. If one consider ICT indicators as a type of functioning that helps to achieve a specific capability, namely knowledge and freedom to communicate, one can see that 35 out of 48 countries are far below what would be a satisfactory achievement. Concerning freedom indicators, at least half the countries in the group have below satisfactory levels.

In addition, the fuzzy-set methodology indicates that the inter-country ranking is different from the HDI ranking. A more significant point, however, is the fact that several countries that had been labelled as "high or medium development" countries (UNDP, 2002) seem to fit more in the "low human well-being" subgroup (for example, Qatar, Kuwait, Cameroon and Morocco).

The membership approach used in this chapter allows comparison over time in order to see if a country has reached a "critical" level with regard to a well-being component. For example, an acceptable membership degree in the space "freedom" requires moving from a score of 0.271 to one of 0.729, implying a *non-transformed* freedom index equal to 3 (or less) which, according to Freedom House (2001), is interpreted as "partly free".

Concluding remarks

This chapter has developed a framework that uses fuzzy-set theory to measure human well-being in consistency with Sen's CA. Fuzzy sets allow for gradual transition from one state to another while also allowing one to incorporate rules and goals, and hence are more appropriate for modelling preferences and outcomes that are ambiguous. The fuzzy-set-based indices suggest that several countries that had been included in the high (or medium) human development group in various *HDR*s seem to score much lower on the *human well-being* front. Application of the model to data from a large group of developing and developed countries indicates that the UNDP's HDI and well-being as measured using fuzzy-set theory yield different country rankings. This raises significant questions regarding the potential policy implications of empirical results obtained from different measurement methodologies. In particular, it is important to bear in mind that preferences and choices underlying both objective and subjective indicators of well-being are, in essence, broad and vague; and that such vagueness can have major implications for the outcome of social and economic policies. Thus the present findings have clear policy implications for governments and international agencies.

The chapter has derived several well-being indices and has deliberately left the question of how to compute a composite well-being index (and whether a composite index can be useful) open. The underlying rationale is that individual indicators (indices) may be able to convey more relevant information about the state and components of a country's human well-being. Separate indicators could be more useful than one composite index if the aggregation procedure is based on shaky grounds. Using individual indicators one could produce an overall country ranking, for example using Borda ranking or another method that is deemed appropriate given the context of the analysis.

Finally, it is worth pointing out that human well-being is sometimes interpreted as human happiness. In economics – as well as in other behavioural and social sciences – there are some interesting debates regarding happiness, economic performance and well-being (see, for example, Oswald, 1997). Perhaps the question of whether wealth (income) ensures happiness has been best addressed by the French philosopher Jean-Jacques Rousseau ([1782] 1953) when he confessed:

It was only in my happiest days that I travelled on foot, and ever with the most unbounded satisfaction; afterwards, occupied with business and encumbered with baggage, I was forced to act the gentleman and employ a carriage, where care, embarrassment, and restraint, were sure to be my companions, and instead of being delighted with the journey, I only wished to arrive at the place of destination.

Notes

1. In setting a dimension index equal to (value of actual − minimum value)/(maximum value − minimum value), as in the HDI computations, it is assumed that the vulnerability (non-vulnerability) to underachievement (or deprivation) varies linearly between the upper and lower bounds.
2. Ragin (2000: 161) provides an interesting discussion of the issue of relevant versus irrelevant variation.
3. Tomer (2002) provides an insightful overview of how different dimensions of human well-being are examined in other fields.
4. It is worth noting that some elements of the CA had been spelled out in the works of Adam Smith and Karl Marx.
5. Sen was greatly influenced by John Rawls's theory of justice and its implication on individual freedom.
6. UNDP's (2002) *HDR* actually discusses a wide range of other issues or indicators, but the emphasis changes from year to year.
7. One is trying to determine the degree of achievement, given a certain (defined) standard or goal. Thus the distance between the achievement and the goal becomes an indicator of the extent of the success in meeting the target (achievement or underachievement). If $d(x) = 0$, there is full membership ($\mu(x) = 1$). If $d(x) > 0$, then $\mu(x) < 1$. So we can write μ as:

$$\mu(x) = \frac{1}{1 + d(x)}$$

Noting that, in general, the relationship between physical objects and perceptions takes an exponential form (see Zimmermann, 1987), $d(x)$ can be expressed as:

$$d(x) = e^{-a(x-b)}, \quad \text{so that} \quad \mu(x) = \frac{1}{1 + e^{-a(x-b)}}$$

8. From equation (1) it follows that $\ln(\mu/(1-\mu)) = a(x-b)$.
9. In fact, had the cut-off point been 0.800 (as in the *HDR*'s ranking method) Korea, Kuwait and Qatar would have dropped to the next level of human development (table 6.3, column 1).

REFERENCES

Anand, S. and A. Sen (2000) "The Income Component of the Human Development Index", *Journal of Human Development* 1(1): 83–106.

Anderson, E. (1999) "What is the Point of Equality?", *Ethics* 109: 287–337.

Atkinson, A. B. (1999) "The Contributions of Amartya Sen to Welfare Economics", *Scandinavian Journal of Economics* 101: 173–190.

Baliamoune, M. N. (2000) "Economics of Summitry: An Empirical Assessment of the Economic Effects of Summits", *Empirica* 27: 295–314.

Cheli, B. (1995) "Totally Fuzzy and Relative Measures of Poverty in Dynamic Context", *Metron* 53(3/4): 183–205.

Cheli, B. and A. Lemmi (1995) "A 'Totally' Fuzzy and Relative Approach to the Multidimensional Analysis of Poverty", *Economic Notes* 24(1): 115–134.

Chiappero, M. E. (1996) "Standard of Living Evaluation Based on Sen's Approach: Some Methodological Suggestions", *Notizie di Politeia* 12: 37–53.

—— (2000) "A Multidimensional Assessment of Well-Being Based on Sen's Functioning Approach", *Rivista Internazionale di Scienze Sociali* 2: 207–239.

Crocker, D. A. (1992) "Functioning and Capability: The Foundation of Sen's and Nussbaum's Development Ethics", *Political Theory* 20: 584–612.

Dasgupta, P. and M. Weale (1992) "On Measuring the Quality of Life", *World Development* 20: 19–131.

Desai, M. (1991) "Human Development, Concepts and Measurement", *European Economic Review* 35: 350–357.

Gasper, D. (2002) "Is Sen's Capability Approach an Adequate Basis for Considering Human Development?", *Review of Political Economy* 14(4): 435–461.

Freedom House (2001) *Freedom in the World*, available at www.freedomhouse.org/ratings/index.htm.

Hopkins, M. (1991) "Human Development Revisited: A New UNDP Report", *World Development* 19(10): 1469–1473.

Hausman, D. M. and M. S. McPherson (1996) *Economic Analysis and Moral Philosophy*, Cambridge: Cambridge University Press.

ITU (International Telecommunication Union) (2002) *International Telecommunication Indicators*, available at www.itu.int/ITU-D/ict/statistics.

Jungeilges, J. and G. Kirchgässner (2002) "Economic Welfare, Civil Liberty, and Suicide: An Empirical Investigation", *Journal of Socio-Economics* 31: 215–231.

Lelli, S. (2001) "Factor Analysis vs. Fuzzy Set Theory: Assessing the Influence of Different Techniques on Sen's Functioning Approach", available at www.econ.kuleuven.ac.be/ew/academic/econover/Papers/DPS0121.pdf.

McGillivray, M. (1991) "The Human Development Index: Yet Another Redundant Composite Development Indicator?", *World Development* 19(10): 1461–1468.

Nelson, J. A. (1996) *Feminism, Objectivity and Economics*, London: Routledge.

Ogwang, T. (1994) "The Choice of Principal Variables for Computing the Human Development Index", *World Development* 22(12): 2011–2014.

Oswald, A. J. (1997) "Happiness and Economic Performance", *Economic Journal* 107: 1815–1831.

Pressman, S. and G. Summerfield (2000) "The Economic Contributions of Amartya Sen", *Review of Political Economy* 12: 89–113.

Qizilbash, M. (2002) "A Note on the Measurement of Poverty and Vulnerability in the South African Context", *Journal of International Development* 14: 757–772.

Ragin, C. C. (2000) *Fuzzy-Set Social Science*, Chicago: University of Chicago Press.

Rousseau, J.-J. ([1782] 1953) *The Confessions of Jean-Jacques Rousseau*, trans. J. Cohen, London: Penguin.

Sen, A. (1977) "Social Choice Theory: A Re-examination", *Econometrica* 45(1): 53–89.

―――― (1979) "Personal Utilities and Public Judgements: Or What's Wrong with Welfare Economics?", *Economic Journal* 89(355): 537–558.

―――― (1982) *Choice, Welfare and Measurement*, Oxford: Basil Blackwell.

―――― (1985) "Well-Being, Agency and Freedom: The Dewey Lectures 1984", *Journal of Philosophy* 82(4): 169–203.

―――― (1990) "Justice: Means versus Freedoms", *Philosophy and Public Affairs* 19: 111–121.

―――― (1992) *Inequality Reexamined*, Cambridge, Mass.: Harvard University Press.

―――― (1993) "Capability and Well-Being", in M. Nussbaum and A. Sen, eds, *The Quality of Life*, Oxford: Clarendon Press.

Tomer, J. F. (2002) "Human Well-being: A New Approach Based on Overall and Ordinary Functionings", *Review of Social Economy* LX: 23–45.

UNDP (1994) *Human Development Report 1994*, Oxford: Oxford University Press.

―――― (1996) *Human Development Report 1996*, Oxford: Oxford University Press.

―――― (2002) *Human Development Report 2002*, Oxford: Oxford University Press.

Von Furstenberg, G. M. and J. P. Daniels (1991) "Policy Undertakings by the Seven Summit Countries: Ascertaining the Degree of Compliance", *Carnegie-Rochester Conference Series on Public Policy* 35: 267–308.

World Bank (2002) *World Bank Indicators*, CD, Washington, D.C.: World Bank.

Zadeh, L. A. (1965) "Fuzzy Sets", *Information and Control* 8: 338–343.

Zimmermann, H. J. (1987) *Fuzzy Sets, Decision Making, and Expert Systems*, Boston, Mass.: Kluwer Academic Publishers.

7
Benchmarking sustainable development: A synthetic meta-index approach

Laurens Cherchye and Timo Kuosmanen

Introduction

Benchmarking is a well-established tool for measuring the performance of business and public sector organizations (see e.g. Cox and Thompson, 1998; Auluck, 2002 for discussion). The benchmarking practice typically starts with the identification of peers (e.g. competing firms in the same sector, firms in other industries or other comparable organizational units) which exemplify the best practice in some activity, function or process. These best-practice peers represent reference points against which actual performance is evaluated. Reference points are often selected from external comparison partners; external benchmarking usually works effectively in drawing attention to areas of underperformance that may be ignored in internal audits.

Benchmarking is now widely applied in various types of *sustainable development* (SD) projects, mainly in the field of public administration and at the level of local communities. The benchmarking practice is typically based on *performance indices*, which aggregate various performance dimensions into a single numerical figure. Consequently, a whole literature has emerged on the construction of an operational *index of sustainable development* (ISD) which should be easy to understand and use in the context of political decision-making.[1] In this respect, major research efforts are currently targeted at developing ISDs at the local, national and international levels; e.g. the International Institute for Sustainable Development lists more than 200 voluntarily submitted ISD initiatives (see www.iisd.ca). At the global scale, well-known ISD initiatives include Prescott-Allen's (2001) well-being index, the ecological footprint of Wackernagel et al. (2002), the environmental sustainability index of the World Economic Forum (WEF, 2002) and the human development index (HDI) of the UNDP (2001), among many others.

Despite the generally recognized importance of a well-defined ISD for effective policy-making and the considerable research effort devoted to the construction of an *ideal* ISD, we are still far from reaching consensus on the standard indicators and benchmarking methodologies. One immediate explanation for the observed heterogeneity of ISDs proposed in the literature pertains to the vague definition of the SD concept (see e.g. Lélé, 1991 for a critical discussion of various interpretations). For example, the most frequently cited definition, which comes from the Brundlandt Commission Report (BCR) (World Commission on Environment and Development, 1987: 54), describes SD as "development that meets the needs of the present without compromising the ability of future generations to meet their own needs". This definition most clearly illustrates the diverse, multidimensional character of SD.

A second problem concerning the practical construction of an encompassing ISD relates to the choice of operational indicators associated with the selected SD dimensions. These indicators generally provide imperfect proxies for what we would really like to measure. We inevitably have to trade off alternative "proxy indicators" in terms of multiple criteria such as reliability, relevance, validity, cost and coverage of data. This means that currently there exist numerous ISDs which differ according to the selection of SD dimensions and/or the indicators to represent those dimensions. Consequently, the results reported in the aforementioned studies are all but unisonous.

Despite these difficulties, the benchmarking approach offers new possibilities for promoting sustainable policies and practices at the international and national levels. Even though many important aspects related to the "organizational learning" side of benchmarking do not directly apply in the international context, explicit international benchmarks could provide some – necessary? – political pressure for governments to pay more attention to SD. Perhaps most importantly, benchmarking could promote SD through facilitating diffusion of experiences and expertise from the leading countries in SD to the less developed and under-performing countries.

This chapter proposes a *meta-index* of sustainable development (MISD) which combines existing knowledge into a single synthesizing index of SD. All existing ISD efforts provide useful information about at least some SD aspects, in terms of the dimensions/indicators that are selected. On the other hand, each ISD can be criticized in that it only partially captures overall SD, as the number of dimensions/indicators that are included is necessarily limited. Hence the basic motivation of the MISD is to combine and structure the information captured in the existing ISDs, rather than add yet another index to already quite a long list. In line with the principles of benchmarking, this index is a comparative index: we cannot infer whether any particular country is genuinely on the SD path or not; we can solely identify the best performance in *relative* terms.

The main challenge in constructing the MISD pertains to the aggregation of the constituent ISDs. Clearly, the aggregation method has a decisive impact on the index values, and hence it should be based on explicitly stated, scientifically sound premises. This chapter proposes a so-called "benefit-of-the-doubt" weighting method as a potentially useful aggregation method. More specifically, in the absence of an a priori weighting scheme, it *endogenously* selects those weights that yield the highest MISD value for each country under investigation. Putting it differently, as it is a priori not clear which ISD is the most appropriate to evaluate SD, for each country higher weights are attached to those ISDs for which the country under evaluation performs relatively well. This weighting method, which is inspired by the data envelopment analysis (DEA) technique for productivity and efficiency analysis (Charnes, Cooper and Rhodes, 1978), has been successfully applied for similar aggregation problems in the context of macro-level policy performance assessment. For example, Melyn and Moesen (1991) used it for constructing synthetic indicators that merge performance indicators for heterogeneous economic dimensions like GDP growth, inflation, unemployment and balance of payment surplus/deficit (see e.g. Cherchye, 2001 for a general discussion). It is argued that the multidimensional nature of the method easily allows extension to the more complex setting of SD.

The next section presents the methodology for constructing the MISD. To describe the data sources, the third section reviews existing ISDs, with special attention to the selection of SD dimensions that underlie each proposal. In addition it presents a classification of existing ISDs, based on Munasinghe's (1993) triangle. The fourth section presents and discusses the empirical MISD values. The fifth section compares the MISD results to those of more standard approaches, and analyses the impact of the different ISD components on the meta-index values. The final section summarizes the main conclusions and sets out a number of avenues for further research.

Meta-index of sustainable development

Consider the general case of a cross-section of m ISDs for n countries, and let y_{ij} be the value of ISD i in country j. One assumes all ISDs satisfy the following two properties (possibly after some appropriate normalization): $y_{ij} \in [0, 1]$ $\forall i, j$; and $y_{ij} > y_{ik} \Rightarrow$ country j performs better than country k for ISD i.

We want to merge these individual ISDs into a single-valued MISD, defined as the weighted average of the m ISDs. Given that each ISD has been developed by a team of experts, it is reasonable to assert that one cannot rate any ISD to be superior to the other ISDs by any objective grounds. This means that we are generally unable to specify a priori any generally acceptable weights to be accorded to each ISD. (The chapter will return to the lack of agreement among experts on the issue of SD priorities below.)

Benefit-of-the-doubt weighting

The benefit-of-the-doubt weighting method resolves this weighting problem by selecting those weights that maximize the index value for each country, subject to the constraint that no other country yields an index value greater than 1 when applying those same weights. Formally, the general MISD for country j is defined as the weighted average:

$$\mu_j \equiv \sum_{i=1}^{m} y_{ij} \cdot w_{ij}^*$$

where the weights $w_{ij}^* = \arg\max_{w_{ij}} M$ are obtained from the optimal solution to the linear programming problem

(objective: *weighted ISD sum*) $M = \max\limits_{w_{ij}} \sum_{j=1}^{n} \left(\sum_{i=1}^{m} y_{ij} w_{ij} \right) v_j$

s.t.

(*scaling constraint*) $\sum_{i=1}^{m} y_{ij} w_{ik} \leq 1$ $\forall j, k = 1, \ldots, n$

(*non-negativity constraint*) $w_{ij} \geq 0$ $\forall i = 1, \ldots, m; j = 1, \ldots, n$

In this problem, the objective function reveals that the (endogenously selected) ISD weights maximize the weighted sum of country-specific MISD values. As in the classic index theory, each country j ($j = 1, \ldots, n$) is weighted by the a priori specified weight v_j for that country. The interpretation of the weight v_j is analogous to that of expenditure share or volume-based weights in the construction of price indices.[2] Most importantly, each w_{ij} ($i = 1, \ldots, m; j = 1, \ldots, n$) represents the weight accorded to ISD i for computing the MISD value of country j. Unlike the v_j, the w_{ij} are not fixed a priori, but are endogenously selected in a way that maximizes the index value of the country. To guarantee an index with an intuitive degree of interpretation, one imposes that no country in the sample can achieve an SD index value greater than 1 under these weights; see the *scaling constraint*. Finally, the individual ISD weights cannot be negative, and hence the MISD is a non-decreasing function of the ISDs; see the *non-negativity constraint*. All this implies that $0 \leq \mu_j(\cdot) \leq 1$ for each country j, where higher values can be interpreted as better overall SD performance.

The interpretation of the benefit-of-the-doubt weighting (or the selection of *most favourable* weights for each country) is immediate: highest relative weights will be accorded to those ISDs for which the country j performs best (in relative terms) when compared to other countries in the sample. This prevents policy-makers from claiming that an unfair weighting scheme is employed for evaluating their country; any other weight profile can only worsen the position of the country *vis-à-vis* the other countries in the sample. In a way the proposed methodology allows the policy-makers of each country to define "their own weights"; the method reveals the optimal priority orderings for each evaluated country.[3] The result $\mu_j(\cdot) = 1$ means that there exists at least one weighting scheme under which country j yields the highest attainable MISD value over all countries in the sample. Alternatively, $\mu_j(\cdot) < 1$ gives the proportion of the actual MISD value (under optimal weights) over the highest attainable value in the sample of countries under investigation.

Of course, a possible criticism of this benefit-of-the-doubt approach is that it makes SD performance "look better" than it really is, since the selected weights can deviate from the "true" (but unknown) priorities. Still, given the complexity of biological and physical systems that underlie objective priorities in terms of SD, it is very unlikely that experts will ever agree on appropriate weights/priority orderings (compare with Ludwig, Hilborn and Waters, 1993). Therefore, this chapter opts for a second-best route, letting the data "speak for themselves" and determining the weights endogenously rather than resorting to specific a priori weights for each ISD.

Finally, while the use of specific a priori *values* for the ISD weights is problematic, it may well be that there is consensus on "generally acceptable" a priori *restrictions* regarding the acceptable domain of ISD weight values, which are stronger than the mere non-negativity restriction in the above model. Interestingly, the proposed methodology naturally allows for imposing such "general" weight bounds. This issue is next discussed in greater detail, proposing some new approaches for setting upper and lower bounds for the weight domain.

Methodological extensions

In the basic MISD model the only restriction on the ISD weights is that they should be non-negative. Somewhat inconveniently, this does not exclude extreme scenarios. For example, all the relative weight can be assigned to a single ISD, which would then completely determine the overall SD performance value; the other ISDs would "not matter" as their relative weight equals zero. Of course, such extreme weighting schemes can hardly be regarded as realistic or relevant. There is hence a need for further restricting the endogenously selected ISD weights.

This issue of imposing additional a priori weight bounds has attracted considerable attention in the closely related DEA literature; see e.g. Pedraja-Chaparro, Salinas-Jimenez and Smith (1997) for a review. The conventional approach in that literature is to set bounds on the variability of the weights at the level of individual performance indicators (*in casu* the ISDs). In this analysis, bounds are also imposed at the levels of countries and ISD categories (introduced below). Suppose for the moment that ISDs can be classified in p mutually exclusive categories $S_1, \ldots, S_p$; each category represents a certain orientation or focus (such as economic development, social/political equity or environmental sustainability). Imposing weight bounds on these categories involves a relatively straightforward extension of the more standard ISD weight bounds, but is particularly interesting in this specific context, as explained below. To the best of the authors' knowledge, the type of country weight bounds constitutes a new innovation.

Formally, one can distinguish three types of supplementary weight bounds:

(weight bound: ISDs) $\quad \dfrac{1}{\alpha} \leq \dfrac{w_{hj}}{w_{ij}} \leq \alpha \quad \forall h, i = 1, \ldots, m; \ j = 1, \ldots, n$

(weight bound: categories) $\quad \dfrac{1}{\beta} \leq \dfrac{\sum_{i \in S_k} w_{ij}}{\sum_{i \in S_l} w_{ij}} \leq \beta \quad \forall k, l = 1, \ldots, p; \ i = 1, \ldots, m; \ j = 1, \ldots, n$

(weight bound: countries) $\quad \dfrac{1}{\gamma} \leq \dfrac{w_{ij}}{w_{ik}} \leq \gamma \quad \forall i = 1, \ldots, m; \ j, k = 1, \ldots, n$

These bounds are incorporated in the original model by simply adding the corresponding constraints to the programming problem. To enhance intuition, the weight restrictions are written here in the ratio form. The appendix shows how these constraints are normalized to preserve the linear structure of the optimization problem. For simplicity the lower bound is written here as the reciprocal of the upper bound; in the general case, the upper and the lower bounds may be set independently.

In the above restrictions the parameters $\alpha, \beta, \gamma \geq 1$ define upper and lower weight bounds at respectively the ISD level (see *weight bound: ISDs*), the category level (see *weight bound: categories*) and the country level (see *weight bound: countries*). These weight bounds are motivated as follows.

- Weight bounds for *ISDs* limit the variability of ISD weights by means of the parameter α, and directly exclude "unrealistic" cases where extremely high relative weights are accorded to only one ISD (or a very limited number of ISDs); lower values of α imply more stringent weight bounds.
- Weight bounds for *categories* of ISDs guarantee that different aspects of SD (e.g. economic, environmental and social-political) are adequately represented in the index; again, lower values of β imply more stringent weight bounds.
- Weight bounds for *countries* determine the extent to which the ISD weights can vary over countries; as before, lower γ levels imply more stringent weight bounds.

The idea of incorporating category and country bounds originates from the observation that it is often difficult to define weight bounds on the level of individual ISDs (i.e. weight bounds of the standard type) a priori. It seems a much simpler task to put intuitive limits on the weight variability at the level of ISD categories or countries. Indeed, categorical weights directly reflect the importance of the key components of SD in the eventual MISD value. On the other hand, country weight bounds simply reflect the extent to which categorical and country-specific weight values can differ from the mean weight levels in the sample.

Existing ISDs: A selective survey

As discussed in the introduction, numerous ISDs have been presented, and it is practically impossible to provide an exhaustive survey of all these proposals. Attention will be restricted to a selection of ISDs, following three criteria induced by the specific scope of this study (i.e. providing a SD-based cross-country comparison that synthesizes existing ISD results). (Still, it is worth stressing at this point that the methodology is, of course, easily applied to alternative ISDs, if this seems recommendable from the specific orientation of the study.) An evident first criterion is availability of calculated values. The second criterion is that the ISD should have large country coverage. Finally, to ensure meaningful and fair comparisons across countries, one requires that the data underlying the selected ISDs are obtained by using a uniform methodology across countries, and are thus preferably based on objectively measured quantitative statistics. Table 7.1 lists the ISD initiatives that meet these three conditions.

For the sake of brevity the chapter refrains from a detailed discussion of each ISD. It primarily focuses on the SD dimensions that are covered, which are instrumental for the further discussion. In this respect, Munasinghe's (1993) triangle is used as a framework for classifying the presented ISDs. Munasinghe classifies sustainability issues into three categories: economic issues (efficiency, growth and stability), social-political issues (poverty, consultation/empowerment, culture/heritage) and environmental issues (biodiversity/resilience, natural resources, pollution); thus each ISD is labelled as "social-political", "environmental" or "economic" (see also table 7.1).

Human Development Report (2001)

The first five indices considered were adopted from the UNDP's (2001) *Human Development Report*.
- The HDI is a summary measure of human development. It measures the average achievement of a country in three basic dimensions: a long and healthy life, knowledge and standard of living;
- While the HDI measures average achievement, the human poverty index for developing countries (HPI-1) and the human poverty index for selected OECD countries (HPI-2) measure deprivation in terms of human development, respectively, for developing countries and for a set of selected OECD countries. More specifically, the HPI-1 captures vulnerability to death at a relatively early age, exclusion from the world of reading and communications and lack of access to overall economic provisioning. The HPI-2 measures deprivation in the same way as the HPI-1, somewhat differently defined, and includes an additional dimension of social exclusion.
- Next, the gender-related development index (GDI) adjusts the HDI to reflect the inequalities between men and women in the dimensions captured by the HDI.
- Finally, in contrast to the GDI, the gender empowerment measure (GEM) focuses on women's opportunities, rather than capabilities, in

Table 7.1 Summary of selected ISDs

Index	Source	Year (publication/reference)	Country coverage	Primary focus
Human development index (HDI)	UNDP	2001/1999	162	Economic
Human poverty index-1 (HPI-1)	UNDP	2001/1999	162	Economic
Human poverty index-2 (HPI-2)	UNDP	2001/1999	162	Economic
Gender-related development index (GDI)	UNDP	2001/1999	162	Social-political
Gender empowerment measure (GEM)	UNDP	2001/1999	162	Social-political
Human well-being index (HWI)	Prescott-Allen	2001/n.a	180	Economic
Ecosystem well-being index (EWI)	Prescott-Allen	2001/n.a	180	Environmental
Environmental sustainability index-1 (ESI-1)	WEF	2002/+−2000	142	Environmental
Environmental sustainability index-2 (ESI-2)	WEF	2002/+−2000	142	Environmental
Environmental sustainability index-3 (ESI-3)	WEF	2002/+−2000	142	Social-political
Environmental sustainability index-4 (ESI-4)	WEF	2002/+−2000	142	Social-political
Environmental sustainability index-5 (ESI-5)	WEF	2002/+−2000	142	Social-political
Health-adjusted life expectancy (HALE)	WHO	2001/2000	191	Social-political
Ecological footprint (EF)	Redefining Progress	2000/1996, 1998	142	Environmental

three dimensions: political participation and decision-making power, economic participation and decision-making and power over economic resources.

Index values have been calculated for 162 countries. The HDI, GDI and GEM are constructed in such a way that higher values indicate better performance. The opposite interpretation holds for the HPI-1 and HPI-2 values. In the discussion below, 1 minus the original values is used to convert these "bads" into "goods"; the HPI-1 and HPI-2 are percentage indices, so this conversion procedure preserves the informational contents of the original indices. The HDI mainly captures economic aspects of SD; to some extent it could be argued that it also (indirectly) includes social-political SD aspects. A similar interpretation holds for HPI-1 and HPI-2. Finally, the GDI and GEM have almost exclusively a social-political orientation.

The well-being of nations (2001)

Two further ISDs proposed by Prescott-Allen (2001) have been selected.[4]
- The human well-being index (HWI) gives an overall measure of socio-economic conditions; its interpretation is similar to that of the HDI index presented above.
- The ecosystem well-being index (EWI) is a broad measure of the state of the environment.

These indices are computed for 180 countries. Again, higher values always indicate better performance. Like the HDI, the HWI can be considered as a measure for economic SD performance. Obviously the EWI can be regarded as a measure for the environmental aspects of SD.

Environmental sustainability index (2002)

Next one can look at the indices suggested by the WEF (2002); this institution proposes an overall environmental sustainability index (ESI), which is intended "to measure overall progress towards environmental sustainability". The following discussion considers the five core components of the ESI, which pertain to different aspects of environmental sustainability.
- The state of the environmental systems (ESI-1), which captures air quality, water quantity, water quality, biodiversity and land.
- The stresses on those systems (ESI-2), measured in terms of air pollution, water stress, ecosystem stresses, waste and consumption pressures and population growth.

- Human vulnerability to environmental change (ESI-3), in the form of basic human sustenance and environmental health.
- Social and institutional capacity to cope with environmental challenges (ESI-4), pertaining to science and technology, the capacity for debate, environmental government and eco-efficiency.
- Global stewardship (ESI-5), as reflected in participation in international collaborative efforts, greenhouse gas emissions and reducing transboundary environmental pressures.

The associated index values are available for 142 countries. The five indices are constructed so that higher values reflect better performance. While the first two ESI components are almost exclusively concerned with environmental aspects, the last three components have a more social-political orientation.

World Health Report *(2001)*

The WHO (2001) provides an index for the health-adjusted life expectancy (HALE) which was reported for 191 countries in the year 2000. This HALE indicator combines losses from premature death (defined as the difference between the actual age of death and life expectancy at that age in a low-mortality population) and loss of healthy life resulting from disability. Clearly this index primarily captures social-political aspects of SD, while it also indirectly reflects the economic and environmental aspects. Higher values can be interpreted as better SD performance.

Ecological footprint (1996–1998)

National estimates of the ecological footprint (EF) per capita, proposed and discussed by Wackernagel et al. (2002), are calculated by the public policy organization Redefining Progress and are reported in the WWF (2000) *Living Planet Report* for 142 countries in 1996; Redefining Progress provides updated figures for a subsample of 48 countries (www.rprogress.org).[5] This footprint statistic measures the land and water area that are needed to support a defined human population and material standard indefinitely, using prevailing technology. Clearly, this ISD can also be interpreted as measuring "the burden of human lifestyle to the ecology, i.e. the area of 'average quality' land needed to support one human being by the ecological services he needs". Hence, lower EF values indicate better environmental SD performance. For convenience, a transformation of the original data will be employed in the discussion below so that better performance is associated with higher values. Specifically, $1 - f/\max(f)$ is used, where f denotes the original EF index.

Empirical results

Model specification

The original MISD model described in the second section allows for full weight flexibility. In principle, it is even possible that only a single ISD is weighted in the eventual index value, which makes the overall SD performance dependent on that ISD. Such extreme weight scenarios seem all the more problematic in view of the relatively large number of performance dimensions in the present study; see the 14 ISDs reviewed in the previous section. Indeed, it seems hardly reasonable to evaluate SD in terms of only a single ISD if one selects not less than 14 ISDs in total. For these reasons, some additional weight bounds are imposed in this MISD application, which reflect an a priori judgement about the relative importance of different ISDs and ISD categories and put normative limits on the variation of weights across countries.

As for the ISD categories, it is widely held that all three dimensions of sustainability (social-political, economic and environmental) should be equally represented in the index. This would suggest the parameter value $\beta = 1$ in the weight bound of the ISD categories. However, in view of the numerous shortcomings in the international data from which the ISDs are calculated, some flexibility is allowed in the group weighting and the bound parameter is set at $\beta = 1.2$.

Next, it is reasonable to impose that, for any ISD, the weight of one country should not depart too much from that of another country. Indeed, while the operational conditions and the policy preferences of countries can differ considerably, the authors think it recommendable from a normative point of view that countries should conform to the most rudimentary ideals and values of SD. Clearly, the trade-off between conformity to universal weighting and freedom for country-specific deviations is not easy to resolve. This study thus opts for a so-called "conservative" bound and puts $\gamma = 3$, implying that the maximum weight (over countries) in any particular ISD can only be three times higher than the minimum weight.

Finally, it is most difficult to set acceptable bounds for the relative ISD weights that are selected for each country. The authors believe all ISDs should get a positive weight in the index, but also want to let the data speak for themselves, i.e. to exploit fully the attractive benefit-of-the-doubt interpretation that underlies this MISD model. Adopting again a conservative perspective, the bound parameter is specified as $\alpha = 10$. This means that, for each country, the maximum weight of an ISD is at most 10 times greater than the minimum ISD weight.

In sum, one ends up with the following bound specifications:

- $\alpha = 10$, i.e., $0.1 \leq w_{hj}/w_{ij} \leq 10$ for all ISDs h, i and countries j
- $\beta = 1.2$, i.e., $0.833 \leq \sum_{i \in S_k} w_{ij} / \sum_{i \in S_l} w_{ij} \leq 1.2$ for all ISD categories S_k, S_l
- $\gamma = 3$, i.e., $0.333 \leq w_{ij}/w_{ik} \leq 3$ for all countries j, k and all ISDs i.

Next the MISD values for a sample of 154 countries were calculated. All countries for which at least 6 out of 14 ISDs are reported were included in the sample. The large amount of missing data, especially for developing countries, causes some difficulties for this analysis. Of course, one could limit attention to those countries for which the complete data are available, but this would yield a sample consisting of only 15 countries. Given that the methodology (which – to recap – directly builds on the observed data) generally requires a large sample, there is no option other than to proceed with the unbalanced data. The missing entries are then simply discarded from the analysis by inserting the value of zero in the data matrix. Clearly this creates a possible positive bias in the results, since data unavailability may signal problems in that particular area. Still, the minimum number of six ISDs, all of which contain valuable information, should suffice to provide a reasonably balanced overall SD picture.

From the technical perspective, the standard DEA weighting model will automatically match the missing entries with a weight of zero, i.e. the missing ISDs for a given country are *ipso facto* excluded from the analysis of that particular country. However, one also needs to account for the missing data when defining the weight bounds, to avoid zero entries arbitrarily influencing the results. Interestingly, one can circumvent the problem of missing/zero entries in the data matrix by means of a simple modification of the weight bounds: one multiplies the inequality constraints by the product of the corresponding ISDs, which is a constant (see Kuosmanen, 2002 for a more detailed discussion). For example, the resulting weight bound for ISDs reads:

$$\frac{1}{\alpha} \cdot y_{hj} \cdot y_{ij} \leq \frac{w_{hj}}{w_{ij}} \cdot y_{hj} \cdot y_{ij} \leq \alpha \cdot y_{hj} \cdot y_{ij}$$

Clearly, if either one of the data entries equals zero the inequalities become redundant, and hence the missing entries cannot flaw the relative weights. On the other hand, if both ISD values are strictly positive then this simple modification has no impact whatsoever on the original inequalities.

Country rankings

Although all countries were treated equally in the pooled sample, it is most illustrative to view the results from the perspective of the proper

Table 7.2 MISD rankings, high-income countries

Rank	Country	MISD	Rank	Country	MISD
1	Norway	1.000	15	Slovenia	0.944
2	Sweden	1.000	16	Greece	0.939
3	Austria	1.000	17	Australia	0.922
4	Switzerland	0.991	18	Belgium	0.918
5	Finland	0.983	19	Israel	0.914
6	Netherlands	0.983	20	United Kingdom	0.909
7	Iceland	0.976	21	Denmark	0.907
8	Spain	0.964	22	Ireland	0.900
9	France	0.960	23	New Zealand	0.897
10	Portugal	0.959	24	United States	0.804
11	Canada	0.957	25	Luxembourg	0.748
12	Japan	0.953	26	Singapore	0.699
13	Germany	0.948	27	Kuwait	0.692
14	Italy	0.948	28	United Arab Emirates	0.605

peer groups. The countries were therefore classified in different groups (high income – gross national income per capita greater than US$9,266 in 2000; upper-middle income – GNI per capita between US$2,996 and US$9,266; lower-middle income – GNI per capita between US$755 and US$2,996; and low income – GNI per capita less than US$755) according to the World Bank classification (www.worldbank.org/data/databytopic/class.htm). This classification makes the comparison and ranking of countries more meaningful and allows one to identify more appropriate benchmarks for each country (although it should be stressed that the MISD scores are, in principle, also comparable across the income groups).

Table 7.2 lists the MISD rankings of the 28 high-income countries in the sample. Norway, Sweden and Austria show up, for example, as the leading countries on the way towards more sustainable development.[6] Overall, the country rankings do not offer any major surprises. Northern and Western European countries strongly dominate the index. The oil-producing countries (i.e. Kuwait and the United Arab Emirates) distinguish as a low-performing subgroup among the richest countries. Finally, the relatively low score of the United States, which may be somewhat surprising at first, is solely due to the weak performance in terms of the environmental dimensions. A somewhat similar qualification applies for Luxembourg, although missing data may also partly explain the low rank of that country.

It is firmly stressed that these country-specific results should be interpreted with sufficient caution. For example, one cannot directly conclude from these results that the top-ranked countries are on the SD path. Indeed, the MISD is by construction a comparative index which assesses

Table 7.3 MISD rankings, upper-middle-income countries

Rank	Country	MISD	Rank	Country	MISD
1	Costa Rica	1.000	14	Trinidad & Tobago	0.888
2	Uruguay	1.000	15	Lebanon	0.887
3	Panama	1.000	16	Poland	0.886
4	Croatia	0.984	17	South Korea	0.886
5	Chile	0.977	18	Botswana	0.854
6	Hungary	0.971	19	South Africa	0.852
7	Slovakia	0.966	20	Libya	0.847
8	Brazil	0.963	21	Oman	0.839
9	Venezuela	0.962	22	Gabon	0.825
10	Mexico	0.960	23	Saudi Arabia	0.785
11	Turkey	0.930	24	Argentina	0.725
12	Estonia	0.920	25	Mauritius	0.662
13	Czech Republic	0.892			

SD performance of any country relative to that of other countries in the sample. It does not directly account for the burden of technological and economic processes to the world's ecosystem. Still, the authors strongly believe that this comparative approach – when correctly interpreted – has its own merits. Probably most importantly in that respect, the MISD evaluates SD performance in terms of what is actually achieved (by the countries in the sample), which indeed seems an attractive second-best route in the absence of full information about the true physical, technological and economic possibilities.

Table 7.3 presents the results and rankings of the upper-middle-income group. In this group the index also identifies three leading nations: Costa Rica, Uruguay and Panama. More generally, the Central and South American nations perform especially well. The good performance of the EU candidates – Croatia, Hungary and Slovakia – is equally encouraging. In certain areas of SD the top-ranked countries of this group can act as benchmarks for the countries in the middle-income group. However, also in this case one cannot directly infer from the comparative indices that these countries are on a truly sustainable path; for example, non-governmental organizations have expressed concern about the violence against women in all three benchmark countries of this group (see e.g. UN Economic and Social Council, 1999a) and it is well known that pesticides are intensively used in Costa Rican banana plantations (see e.g. UN Economic and Social Council 1999b).

The MISD rankings of the lower middle-income countries are reported in table 7.4. Apparently, none of the countries in this group can be distinguished as a global benchmark. Still, Colombia, Peru and Latvia do come very close to the top-ranked richer nations. Further, and in line with the

Table 7.4 MISD rankings, lower-middle-income countries

Rank	Country	MISD	Rank	Country	MISD
1	Colombia	0.991	24	El Salvador	0.911
2	Peru	0.976	25	Romania	0.911
3	Latvia	0.974	26	Lithuania	0.907
4	Cuba	0.973	27	Moldova	0.907
5	Armenia	0.970	28	Jamaica	0.906
6	Dominican Republic	0.969	29	China	0.904
			30	Morocco	0.900
7	Sri Lanka	0.963	31	FYR Macedonia	0.892
8	Bolivia	0.961	32	Guatemala	0.885
9	Thailand	0.955	33	Syria	0.879
10	Paraguay	0.954	34	Egypt	0.874
11	Philippines	0.949	35	Namibia	0.871
12	Ecuador	0.946	36	Papua New Guinea	0.859
13	Albania	0.938	37	Kazakhstan	0.853
14	Jordan	0.932	38	Russia	0.848
15	Algeria	0.924	39	Turkmenistan	0.800
16	Belarus	0.922	40	Iraq	0.774
17	Bulgaria	0.922	41	Bosnia & Herzegovina	0.712
18	Iran	0.920	42	Belize	0.690
19	Indonesia	0.914	43	Fiji	0.671
20	Honduras	0.912	44	Guyana	0.654
21	Viet Nam	0.912	45	Cape Verde	0.633
22	Malaysia	0.911	46	Maldives	0.604
23	Tunisia	0.911			

results in table 7.3, the Latin American countries perform relatively well. More generally, one observes that the overall distribution of the MISD values in this group is fairly well comparable to that of the upper-middle-income group. The good overall performance of the countries in the middle-income group as a whole becomes especially apparent by comparing these countries to those of the high-income group: as many as 19 middle-income countries perform better than Japan, and no less than 60 countries (including Russia) outperform the United States.

The results in table 7.5, which pertain to the 55 countries of the low-income group, are more disappointing. Eritrea, Lesotho and Yemen are distinguished as the least developed countries in the entire sample. Still, despite the obvious economic and social problems, a number of countries of this group (e.g. Myanmar) perform relatively well in terms of environmental indicators that capture emissions and material flows. In fact, these findings rather make one doubt whether the original ISD indicators, which are essentially constructed from the perspective of the high-income economies, are well adapted to give a reasonably balanced picture of the SD performance of low-income nations. It seems that some countries

Table 7.5 MISD rankings, low-income countries

Rank	Country	MISD	Rank	Country	MISD
1	Myanmar	0.900	29	Mozambique	0.815
2	Nicaragua	0.898	30	Congo, Dem. Rep. (Zaire)	0.813
3	Kyrgyzstan	0.887			
4	Ghana	0.885	31	Gambia	0.801
5	Bhutan	0.882	32	Zambia	0.801
6	Congo, Rep.	0.881	33	Senegal	0.800
7	Cameroon	0.869	34	Ukraine	0.798
8	Azerbaijan	0.865	35	Chad	0.793
9	Zimbabwe	0.859	36	Côte d'Ivoire	0.792
10	Bangladesh	0.858	37	Mali	0.786
11	Laos	0.857	38	Guinea	0.773
12	Kenya	0.856	39	Angola	0.769
13	Cambodia	0.855	40	Guinea-Bissau	0.767
14	Tanzania	0.848	41	Ethiopia	0.765
15	Tajikistan	0.848	42	Burkina Faso	0.760
16	Uzbekistan	0.844	43	Rwanda	0.760
17	Benin	0.844	44	Nigeria	0.751
18	India	0.841	45	Burundi	0.734
19	Sudan	0.840	46	Mauritania	0.732
20	Central African Republic	0.837	47	Niger	0.729
			48	Sierra Leone	0.703
21	Nepal	0.832	49	Somalia	0.622
22	Madagascar	0.829	50	North Korea	0.619
23	Mongolia	0.822	51	Liberia	0.615
24	Togo	0.822	52	Comoros	0.510
25	Uganda	0.822	53	Yemen	0.483
26	Haiti	0.817	54	Lesotho	0.477
27	Malawi	0.816	55	Eritrea	0.458
28	Pakistan	0.815			

rank relatively high only because of economic collapse, which reflects positively in the environmental indicators. In this regard, it should be borne in mind that the results this method (or any method for that matter) can produce are only as good as the data one puts in the model. Some of the index values and relative rankings cast a serious doubt on the reliability of the underlying ISDs.

Notwithstanding some strange results for some individual countries, the overall picture conforms reasonably well with prior expectations. The group of leading countries appears among the top in almost all individual ISDs, but a large number of countries come very close to the best performers. Indeed, one of the striking features of this index is that the differences between the highly developed countries and the developing countries do not seem as insurmountable as one might expect.

Table 7.6 Summary statistics of MISD values, four income classes

	High	Upper middle	Lower middle	Low
GNI per capita (US$)	>9,266	2,996–9,266	755–2,995	<755
Number	28	25	46	55
Minimum	0.605	0.662	0.604	0.458
Maximum	1.000	1.000	0.991	0.900
Average	0.908	0.898	0.881	0.783
Standard deviation	0.103	0.087	0.098	0.106
Skewness	−1.731	−1.027	−1.579	−1.779

As a note of caution, one should keep in mind that the rankings of individual countries can be highly biased due to data errors in the underlying ISDs. Rather than comment on every single country ranked in the tables, it is more fruitful to compare the performance at the level of groups or clusters of countries sharing similar characteristics.

Cluster-level analysis

From the previous rankings it is difficult to distinguish any obvious groups of especially well or poorly performing countries without reference to secondary criteria such as the income level or the geographic location. Therefore the chapter next takes a closer look at a number of summary statistics at the level of country clusters, which are defined on the basis of these two criteria.

Table 7.6 summarizes the results at the level of income groups. The shapes of the MISD distributions appear rather similar in all four income groups; the most interesting differences concern the position of the distributions. Not surprisingly, the average MISD values tend to be higher for higher-income groups. As noted above, however, the two middle-income classes do not fall very far apart from the high-income group; the average MISD score of the lower-middle-income group is only 0.027 points below that of the high-income group. The difference is much more pronounced for the low-income countries. Overall, one can conclude that, abstracting from the poorest countries, high GDP is not a prerequisite for SD.

Next one can compare the differences between the developed and the developing countries, classifying the developing countries according to their geographical location (following the World Bank classification). The group of developed countries is the same as the high-income group above (these countries are not included in the geographic classification of the World Bank). Table 7.7 reports the summary statistics for each group of countries.

Table 7.7 Developed versus developing countries, by region

	Developed countries	Developing countries					
		Europe and Central Asia	Latin America and Caribbean	East Asia and Pacific	Middle East and North Africa	South Asia	Sub-Saharan Africa
Number	28	25	24	14	13	7	43
Minimum	0.605	0.712	0.654	0.619	0.483	0.604	0.458
Maximum	1.000	0.984	1.000	0.955	0.932	0.963	0.885
Average	0.908	0.894	0.913	0.858	0.843	0.828	0.768
Standard deviation	0.103	0.064	0.098	0.098	0.119	0.110	0.104
Skewness	−1.731	−0.938	−1.650	−1.716	−2.604	−1.502	−1.598

Comparing the average MISD values, there are no great differences between the developing countries of Europe, Asia and the Pacific. Interestingly, the Latin American and Caribbean countries seem to outperform the European and Central Asian countries; in fact, the former group of countries does even slightly better than the group of high-income developed countries. Finally, the sub-Saharan African countries stand out as a group with a significantly lower average MISD value than the other country groups. Indeed, the development problems of this region are well known, but appropriate solutions remain undiscovered.

Next, turning to the other summary statistics in table 7.7, one observes that the Middle East and North Africa group has the highest standard deviation and the lowest skewness in the MISD distribution. This is entirely due to the weak performance of Yemen; the other countries of this group have a profile that is very similar to that of the neighbouring group of Europe and Central Asia.

In fact, the group of developed, high-income countries proves to be the most diverse in terms of the associated performance values. Not only does this group include the benchmark countries of Norway, Sweden and Austria, it also includes the low-ranked Arab nations of Kuwait and the United Arab Emirates. Apart from Yemen, Kuwait and the United Arab Emirates fall behind all other countries in the Middle East and North Africa region in the MISD index.

Weights

Besides the index values, the optimal solution of the MISD problem also provides valuable information about the implicit policy weights w. In this respect, recall that the benefit-of-the-doubt weighting scheme uses weights that maximize the relative index value for each country.

Let us first consider the classification of ISDs in terms of economic, social-political and environmental indices. The restriction was imposed that the sum of weights in each category should not exceed the sum of weights in any other category by more than 20 per cent. This constraint proved to be binding in the optimal solution. Surprisingly, however, the countries in the sample would actually have been accorded a higher weight in the environmental category than in the economic or the social-political oriented ISDs had one not imposed this additional weight bound: the environmental indicators were assigned the maximum weight (37.5 per cent of the total sum of weights), while the minimum weight (31.2 per cent) was given to both the economic indicators and the social-political indicators.

The most plausible explanation for this result lies in the relative nature of the MISD. It appears that the inequalities are more pressing in the economic and social dimensions than in the environmental indicators. In general, the leading high-income countries have made considerable investments in cleaner technologies, which show up as good performance in "emissions per capita" types of indicators. On the other hand, many of the middle- and low-income nations do well in terms of the "lifestyle" indicators because of their low consumption of resources. Admittedly, great differences in the environmental performance of nations remain. Still, the good or the bad environment is more evenly distributed than economic wealth, thus the majority of countries benefit if the environmental SD dimensions are emphasized in the assessment. Still, the environment is not the only aspect of SD; the category weight restrictions guarantee that the economic and social-political SD dimensions are also important in the calculated index values.

To give an idea about the general importance of each ISD in the MISD, table 7.8 reports the average weight of each ISD, together with the associated standard deviation. The standard deviations reveal substantial country-specific variations within the specified bounds. Still, the average weights provide at least a rough impression of the overall impact of each ISD. In that respect, the EF and the HDI turn out to be rather influential for the calculated MISD values, while the ESI-4 and the GEM have a more moderate impact; the latter only attracts about 10–15 per cent of the weights accorded to the former. It is important to interpret these results correctly: the fact that one ISD gets a higher average weight than another does not necessarily mean that is more reliable or important for overall SD, but rather that it is generally advantageous for countries to attach a higher weight to the first ISD in the index.

Table 7.8 Summary statistics of the weights

ISD	Mean	Std dev.	Orientation
EF	0.227	0.065	Environmental
HDI	0.206	0.082	Economic
ESI-2	0.153	0.062	Environmental
HALE	0.152	0.064	Social-political
ESI-5	0.127	0.064	Social-political
HPI-1 (developing countries)	0.114	0.093	Economic
GDI	0.044	0.025	Social-political
ESI-1	0.041	0.045	Environmental
HWI	0.039	0.020	Economic
EWI	0.036	0.018	Environmental
HPI-2 (developed countries)	0.033	0.058	Economic
ESI-3	0.032	0.015	Social-political
GEM	0.029	0.010	Social-political
ESI-4	0.027	0.006	Social-political

Discriminatory power and correlation analysis

This section assesses the performance of the proposed MISD by comparing it to the results of the two more standard alternatives: the equally weighted average of the ISDs, and the index resulting from basic benefit-of-the-doubt weighting without additional weight bounds. The first method is frequently used in context of the sustainability indices; see e.g. the UNDP's development indices or Prescott-Allen's (2001) well-being index. The latter method, widely known as data envelopment analysis (DEA), is often applied in similar weighting problems in decision sciences; from the methodological perspective, the DEA analysis can be viewed as an intermediate step towards the MISD proposal. In the following exposition the SD index obtained as the arithmetic average of the ISDs is labelled the "average" index; the index obtained from benefit-of-the-doubt weighting without additional weight restrictions is labelled the DEA index; and the weight-restricted index advocated in the current chapter is again labelled MISD.

This empirical assessment first considers the discriminatory power of the empirical criteria. Subsequently it will consider the correlation between the alternative overall SD indices (average, DEA and MISD) and the correlation between these indices and the constituent ISDs.

Discriminatory power

Obviously, a well-defined MISD should have sufficient discriminatory power. The performance of the MISD is compared to the two standard

Table 7.9 Summary statistics: Average, DEA and MISD

	Average	DEA	MISD
Minimum	0.474	0.701	0.458
Maximum	0.901	1.000	1.000
Average	0.657	0.978	0.854
Standard deviation	0.102	0.0489	0.113
% efficiency	0.00	83.00	6.00

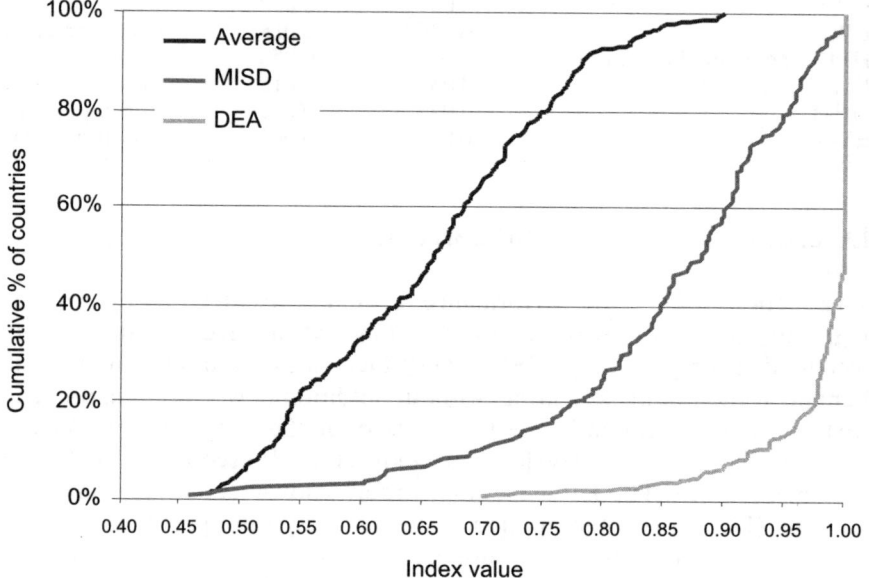

Figure 7.1 Cumulative distribution functions: Average, DEA and MISD

alternatives by looking at the descriptive statistics associated with each variant (average, standard deviation, minimum and maximum) and the percentage of "efficient" countries (i.e. countries with a relative performance score of 100 per cent); also, one can consider the distribution histogram associated with each index.

A first step is to compare the average results with the DEA results. The associated descriptive statistics are given in table 7.9; figure 7.1 highlights the corresponding distribution histograms. From these results one learns that the DEA model has very low discriminatory power; e.g. figure 7.1 shows that almost all countries are efficient or almost efficient. As compared to the average index, the average performance value rises from 62 per cent to almost 98 per cent. In addition, standard deviation is only 5 per cent and the minimum performance value is 70 per cent. These somewhat disappointing results for the DEA model suggest imposing additional weight bounds as a promising avenue.

This is indeed confirmed by the results, which clearly illustrate the intermediate nature of the MISD. By imposing intuitive, widely acceptable normative weight bounds (on the ISD level, the ISD category level and the country level), this measure excludes cases where the performance score is fully determined by a single ISD value only, which entails considerably higher discriminatory power than the DEA index. Also, it does not resort to the overly restrictive weighting scheme where each ISD gets the same weight, which is reflected in the fact that the MISD values are generally higher than the average values.

Overall, the discriminatory power of the MISD is satisfactory. Only 6 of the 154 countries in the sample are declared as (relatively) efficient, as opposed to as many as 83 countries for the unrestricted DEA index. In addition, while average efficiency naturally increases as compared to the average index (from 66 per cent to 85 per cent), standard deviation of the MISD remains somewhat above that of the average index (from 10 per cent to 11 per cent), and higher standard deviation can be interpreted as evidence of more discriminatory power. Finally, the minimal efficiency value is even slightly below that of the average index (and, even more, is below 50 per cent), which indicates that overall poor performance (i.e. in terms of the economic, environmental and social-political ISDs) remains severely penalized. These features are also graphically illustrated in figure 7.1.

Correlation analysis

It can be argued that a well-defined MISD should adequately reflect the information captured by each of its ISD components. We therefore look next at the correlation between the three overall SD indices (average, DEA and MISD) and the corresponding values of the constituent ISDs, reported in table 7.3. Note that this also "penalizes" MISDs whose values are based on a single ISD for which the evaluated country performs relatively well while performing generally poorly for the other ISDs. Of course, this criterion also demands that a well-defined MISD should give a "balanced" indication of the "aggregate" performance in the three dimensions of SD performance (social-political, economic and environmental).

Ideally, an MISD should correlate at least moderately with all or at least a majority of the underlying ISDs. Still, high correlation is not desirable *per se*: typically a high correlation with a few ISDs would cause a low or negative correlation with other ISDs, implying a disproportionate

Table 7.10 MISD-ISD (Spearman rank) correlation matrix (%)

	Average	DEA	MISD
Average	100.00		
DEA	41.47	100.00	
MISD	71.80	49.82	100.00
Economic			
HDI	84.91	34.26	61.36
HPI-1	74.94	53.57	56.60
HPI-2	76.78	(n.c.)	52.73
HWI	87.56	36.76	62.22
Environmental			
EWI	1.82	−5.77	−10.01
EF	−72.83	−20.60	−51.16
ESI-1	29.99	17.08	23.48
ESI-2	0.50	13.79	18.67
Social-political			
GDI	86.03	36.69	59.40
GEM	70.15	54.39	35.57
HALE	82.11	30.93	62.40
ESI-3	84.85	33.16	67.13
ESI-4	70.95	45.35	56.66
ESI-5	−12.21	13.18	−0.23

representation of ISDs in the overall index; generally, there is a trade-off between the degree of correlation with one ISD and the degree of correlation with another ISD when the two ISDs are negatively interrelated. A well-balanced MISD would require that the correlation coefficients across ISDs should converge to some common level.

As a preliminary step one first looks the correlation between the average index, the DEA index and the MISD, reported in table 7.10. The results clearly illustrate the intermediate position of the MISD; it correlates more strongly than the DEA index with the average index and more strongly than the average index with the DEA index. Further, the MISD correlates more strongly with the average index than with the DEA index. At least this suggests that imposing some restrictions on the endogenously determined ISD weights implies a ranking that is considerably different from that obtained from the extreme model that uses no weight bounds at all; the corresponding correlation coefficient amounts to merely 50 per cent. Still, the obtained ranking also differs quite substantially from that resulting from the other extreme model where fixed (equal) weights are used to value each ISD in the index; the corresponding correlation coefficient is no more than 72 per cent.

Let us then have a closer look at the correlations between the presented overall SD indices and the underlying ISDs, also reported in table

7.10. The average model systematically correlates relatively strongly with the economic and social-political ISDs (the only exception is ESI-5). The intuition of the result lies in the fact that economic indicators and social-political indicators are strongly positively interrelated, while there appears to be some trade-off between economic and social-political performance on the one hand and environmental performance on the other (see the third section). This means that the average index, which gives an equal weight to each indicator, will tend in the direction of these predominant economic and social-political indicators.

High correlation with environmental and social-political indicators makes this index correlate rather poorly with environmental indicators. This poor correlation is most pronounced in the EF indicator; the associated correlation coefficient is −73 per cent, which is the worst correlation in the table. This falls in line with the earlier point that high correlation with constituent ISDs should not be desirable *per se*, because it necessarily implies poor correlation with other ISDs.

There are more moderate correlation patterns for the DEA index and the MISD index. When comparing these two "more balanced" measures, the correlation coefficient associated with the MISD is above that corresponding to the DEA index in 9 out of the 14 cases; the difference is even quite pronounced in many cases.

In the authors' opinion, these results give an argument in favour of the MISD as a "well-balanced" measure of overall SD when compared to the extreme average and DEA indices. This argument is further strengthened by identifying, for each ISD, the overall SD measure with the lowest correlation: this is the MISD only in the case of the EWI and the GEM, while it is the average index in three cases (footprint, ESI-2 and ESI-5) and the DEA index in the remaining nine cases (HDI, HPI-1, HWI, ESI-1, GDI, HALE, ESI-3 and ESI-4).

The general conclusion of this empirical assessment is favourable for the MISD: it has satisfactory discriminatory power, and a relatively well-balanced pattern of correlation with the constituent ISDs. These findings are all the more attractive in view of the intuitively appealing methodological starting points that underlie the MISD, i.e. benefit-of-the-doubt weighting (by letting the data speak for themselves) complemented by generally acceptable weight restrictions.

Concluding discussion

Sustainable development is a complex, multidimensional concept. The need for quantifying SD is widely accepted, but the vague definition of SD leaves room for different interpretations and hence for different SD indices. This chapter approached the quantification problem from the perspective of comparative evaluation and benchmarking. It proposed to synthesize the information of various existing indices of SD and its subcomponents in a *meta*-index, which is constructed as an unequally weighted average of the underlying ISDs. The methodology builds on an intuitive benefit-of-the-doubt weighting principle which allows countries to accord a higher weight to those SD dimensions in which they perform relatively well.

The main focus of the current study is methodological. The proposed methodology was applied to a sample of 154 countries, which demonstrates the practical usefulness of the approach. It is worth stressing at this point that this application mainly serves illustrative purposes and the results are best regarded as a "rough screening" of the country sample under study. Indeed, some of the results obtained may seem debatable to some. At least this shows the necessity of confronting "measurement" with "opinion" (and vice versa). Of course, such surprising results may also reflect poor data quality (which is an important concern for countries like Sierra Leone, Liberia or Turkmenistan); this in turn may suggest conducting the SD comparison exercise for different subsamples of countries (e.g. grouped by data quality). Further, counterintuitive country results may indicate the need for a different selection of underlying ISDs (that are merged in the MISD). For example, one may want to add simple economic indicators such as GDP per capita growth; guaranteeing a minimum weight for growth prevents countries in a state of collapse (e.g. Myanmar, Cuba and Armenia) from being identified as sustainable. Or one may include a measure based on the subjective policy evaluation by the population (such as the net migration rate). Sustainability requires that a large share of the population is not trying to escape. Next, one may construct an MISD directly from the single indicators that constitute the aggregated ISDs underlying the current proposal; this applies the benefit-of-the-doubt weighting already at the level of the very basic ingredients of the MISD. To keep the discussion focused (and avoid a highly normative discussion), the authors have deliberately refrained from such practical fine-tuning of the empirical analysis. Attention was limited to the already published ISDs with large country coverage. But it should be clear that such extensions are readily carried out by using the presented methodology.

A further note concerns the exact interpretation of the reported MISD values. It is firmly stressed that the proposed MISD is essentially *comparative* in its nature. In particular, one cannot directly infer whether a particular country is on the SD path or not; one can only assess overall SD in comparison to other countries. Hence, the comparative indices alone are clearly insufficient for thorough SD monitoring. Still, the authors strongly believe that they can be particularly useful for identifying and promoting sustainable policies and practices.

In particular, the MISD can be employed for *benchmarking* purposes. For example, by taking a highly aggregate perspective, the application identifies a handful of countries exemplifying the best practices and policies towards SD in not just one but many (if not all) aspects of SD. In this respect the MISD rankings can stimulate governments and policy-makers in both the top- and the low-ranked countries to engage into active dialogue in order to share knowledge and experiences, and so speed up the diffusion of sustainable policies and practices from the leading countries of SD towards the less developed nations. It is not claimed that all countries should mimic and replicate *every* policy, for instance, of Sweden or Norway (i.e. two benchmark countries), especially since we have limited insight into the driving factors behind the MISD results. Still, given the large coverage of existing SD indices, the authors are confident that the current policy practice in Sweden and Norway can provide useful inspiration for identifying sustainable (economic, social-political or environmental) policies which could be applied in other countries as well. Essentially, the authors plead for country-level implementation of the benchmarking approach, which has already become an influential business paradigm and has also seen extensive application in the public sphere in local-level administration. This evidently constitutes a worthwhile topic for follow-up research.

Appendix

The programming problem presented in the second section is non-linear. In order to turn it into a more standard linear programming problem, one needs to adjust the different weight bounds, which are originally expressed in ratio form. A linear programming version of the optimization problem is the following:

$$\max_{w_{ij}} \sum_{j=1}^{n} \left(\sum_{i=1}^{m} y_{ij} w_{ij} \right)$$

s.t.

$$1 - \sum_{i=1}^{m} y_{ij} w_{ik} \geq 0 \qquad \forall j, k = 1, \ldots, n$$

$$(\alpha w_{ij} - w_{hj}) \cdot y_{ij} \cdot y_{hj} \geq 0 \qquad \forall h, i = 1, \ldots, m; \; j = 1, \ldots, n$$

$$\gamma \sum_{i \in S_l} w_{ij} - \sum_{i \in S_k} w_{ij} \geq 0 \quad \forall k, l = 1, 2, 3; \ i = 1, \ldots, m; \ j = 1, \ldots, n$$

$$(\beta w_{ik} - w_{ij}) \cdot y_{ij} \cdot y_{ik} \geq 0 \quad \forall i = 1, \ldots, m; \ j, k = 1, \ldots, n$$

This formulation also incorporates the proposed technical solution for dealing with zero data entries in the weight restrictions (see the fourth section).

Acknowledgements

This study forms a part of the NOMEPRE research programme. The financial support for this programme from the Emil Aaltonen Foundation, Finland, is gratefully acknowledged.

Laurens Cherchye thanks the Fund for Scientific Research, Flanders (Belgium) (FWO-Vlaanderen) for his post-doctoral fellowship.

The authors thank the participants of the WIDER conference on Inequality, Poverty and Human Well-Being (Helsinki, 30–31 May 2003) for helpful discussions. In addition, the authors owe special thanks to Rob Dellink, Marcus Stronzik and Frank Vöhringer for constructive comments. The usual disclaimer applies.

Notes

1. An alternative approach for measuring sustainable development tries to *correct* national accounts (and their main aggregates like the GDP and GNI) for the cost of depleting environmental and natural resources (which is ignored in the standard national accounting system), following the classical work of Nordhaus and Tobin (1972). See e.g. Gerlagh et al. (2002) for a detailed discussion and references.
2. In the present context, equality of nations supports assigning equal weights v_j for each country. Alternatively, proportioning weights to the population could better reflect equality of human beings, while weighting by the GDP shares would reflect the economic power.
3. In a way, this weighting method reflects the assumption that good performance in a particular policy dimension (relative to the selected sample of countries) is an indicator of a high policy priority accorded to that dimension. This idea of the "benefit-of-the-doubt" weights comes very close in spirit to the "natural" weighting idea formulated by Hardin (1968: 1244). In fact, the authors believe the proposed procedure of implicit weighting suggests an attractive and easily implemented approach for addressing the problem put forward by Hardin: "It is when the hidden decisions are made explicit that the arguments begin. The problem for the years ahead is to work out an acceptable theory of weighting."
4. Prescott-Allen (2001) also proposes an overall "well-being index" (WI) which is obtained as an equally weighted average of the HWI and EWI. As the MISD similarly com-

bines the HWI and EWI (using an unequal weighting procedure), this WI will not be directly considered in the following discussion.
5. To strike a balance between the problem of missing data and the intention of using the most recent data, the arithmetic average of the 1996 and 1998 figures was used in all computations.
6. In case of ties, countries were ranked using the arithmetic average of ISDs as a secondary criterion. For Norway and Sweden the arithmetic averages were equal.

REFERENCES

Auluck, R. (2002) "Benchmarking: A Tool for Facilitating Organizational Learning?", *Public Administration and Development* 22(2): 109–122.
Charnes, A., W. Cooper and E. Rhodes (1978) "Measuring the Efficiency of Decision Making Units", *European Journal of Operational Research* 2: 429–444.
Cherchye, L. (2001) "Using Data Envelopment Analysis to Assess Macroeconomic Policy Performance", *Applied Economics* 33: 407–416.
Cox, A. and I. Thompson (1998) "On the Appropriateness of Benchmarking", *Journal of General Management* 23(4): 1–20.
Gerlagh, R., R. Dellink, M. Hofkes and H. Verbruggen (2002) "A Measure of Sustainable National Income for the Netherlands", *Ecological Economics* 41: 157–174.
Hardin, G. (1968) "The Tragedy of the Commons", *Science* 162: 1243–1248.
Kuosmanen, T. (2002) "Modeling Blank Entries in Data Envelopment Analysis", EconWPA working paper, available at http://econwpa.wustl.edu:8089/eps/em/papers/0210/0210001.pdf.
Lélé, S. M. (1991) "Sustainable Development: A Critical Review", *World Development* 19: 607–621.
Ludwig, D., R. Hilborn and C. Waters (1993) "Uncertainty, Resource Exploitation, and Conservation: Lessons from History", *Science* 260: 36.
Melyn, W. and W. Moesen (1991) "Towards a Synthetic Indicator of Macroeconomic Performance: Unequal Weighting When Limited Information Is Available", Public Economics Research Paper 17, Center for Economic Studies, Leuven.
Munasinghe, M. (1993) "Environmental Economics and Sustainable Development", Environment Paper 3, World Bank, Washington, D.C.
Nordhaus, W. D. and J. Tobin (1972) *Economic Growth: Is Growth Obsolete?*, New York: Columbia University Press.
Pedraja-Chaparro, F., J. Salinas-Jimenez and P. Smith (1997) "On the Role of Weight Restrictions in Data Envelopment Analysis", *Journal of Productivity Analysis* 8: 215–230.
Prescott-Allen, R. (2001) *The Wellbeing of Nations: A Country-by-Country Index of Quality of Life and the Environment*, Washington, D.C.: Island Press.
UNDP (2001) *Human Development Report 2001: Making New Technologies Work for Human Development*, Oxford and New York: Oxford University Press.
UN Economic and Social Council (1999a) "Integration of the Human Rights of Women and the Gender Perspective: Violence against Women, Report

of the Special Rapporteur", E/CN.4/1999/68, available at www.hri.ca/fortherecord1999/documentation/commission/e-cn4-1999-68.htm.

——— (1999b) "Adverse Effects of the Illicit Movement and Dumping of Toxic and Dangerous Products and Wastes on the Enjoyment of Human Rights, Report of the Special Rapporteur", E/CN.4/1999/46/Add.1, available at www.hri.ca/fortherecord1999/documentation/commission/e-cn4-1999-46-add1.htm.

Wackernagel, M., N. Schultz, D. Deumling, A. Linares, V. Kapos, C. Montfredo, J. Loh, N. Myers, R. Norgaard and J. Rardis (2002) "Tracking the Ecological Overshoot of the Human Economy", *Proceedings of the National Academy of Science* 99(14): 9266–9271.

WEF (2002) *2002 Environmental Sustainability Index; Main Report*, Global Leaders of Tomorrow Environmental Task Force, World Economic Forum, available at www.ciesin.columbia.edu/indicators/ESI.

WHO (2001) *World Health Report: Mental Health: New Understanding, New Hope*, Geneva: WHO.

World Commission on Environment and Development (1987) *Our Common Future*, Oxford: Oxford University Press.

WWF (2000) *Living Planet Report 2000*, Gland: WWF.

8
Adjusting human well-being indices for gender disparity: Insightful empirically?

Mark McGillivray and J. Ram Pillarisetti

Introduction

There has been considerable progress in recent years concerning the range and inter-country coverage of development indicators. This is particularly so with what can be loosely described as social indicators. No longer are we confined to such indicators as life expectancy, literacy and mortality. Data on such indicators as the share of earned income by gender, parliamentary representation and access to health services are now available for reasonably large numbers of countries, both developing and developed. The UNDP has played a major role in reporting and publicizing these data in its *Human Development Reports* (*HDR*s, UNDP, 1990–2004). In particular, the UNDP has been a leader in combining a number of these indicators to form new composite indicators of development. Its human development index (HDI) is well known, originally appearing in the *HDR 1990*. Since 1995 it has reported values of composites for the gender-related development index (GDI) and the gender empowerment measure (GEM). The UNDP has been especially keen to promote the GDI and the GEM, and made gender aspects of development the main focus of its *HDR 1995*.

Development clearly fails (or cannot be said to have occurred) if its fruits are not equitably distributed between females and males. The GDI and GEM are thus important contributions by emphasizing gender issues in development. Yet at a purely empirical level there is reason to question the insightfulness of these new indices. Research conducted by Hicks and Streeten (1979), Larson and Wilford (1979), McGillivray (1991), McGillivray and White (1993), Srinivasan (1994) and Cahill (2005) has shown that social and composite indicators of development tend to be very highly correlated with income per capita. On the basis of this outcome it has often been concluded that these indicators, at best, offer limited additional empirical insights into inter-country development levels or, at worst, are empirically redundant. This finding is especially pointed in the case of composite indicators, as they have often been devised to move attention away from income per capita by revealing insights that they cannot.[1] Should we draw similar conclusions for the GDI and GEM? That is, do they provide insights into inter-country development levels that pre-existing indicators cannot?[2]

This is the issue to which the current chapter turns. Specifically, it looks at the extent to which the GEM and GDI provide information that non-gender-specific indicators cannot provide. It is especially interested in whether these indicators tell us more than the HDI can alone tell us. It should be stressed that the chapter does not question the ideological basis of the GDI and GEM, nor their roles in bringing attention to gender issues or in mobilizing effort to reduce gender imbalances. The non-gender-specific indicators under consideration are income per capita (measured using PPP GDP) and the HDI. A range of simple yet insightful and powerful parametric and non-parametric statistical tests are employed. Unlike most other studies the chapter also considers explicitly the statistical basis on which an indicator is deemed non-insightful or redundant.

The GDI and GEM

It is helpful from the outset to describe the composition and design of the HDI, GDI and GEM as this is an issue returned to later in this chapter.[3] The HDI is defined as follows:

$$HDI_i = \frac{1}{k}\sum_{j=1}^{k} I_{j,i} \qquad (1)$$

where $I_{j,i}$ is the jth index of a specific dimension of human development in country i, and $i = 1, \ldots, n$. There are three dimensions and hence component indices: longevity $(I_{1,i})$, educational attainment $(I_{2,i})$ and income or (material) standard of living $(I_{3,i})$. Each of the variables comprising these indices is scaled within the range of zero to one using the equation:

$$X_{j,i} = \frac{x_{j,k,i} - x_{j,k}^{\min}}{x_{j,k}^{\max} - x_{j,k}^{\min}} \qquad (2)$$

where $X_{j,k,i}$ is the kth component of $I_{j,i}$ for country i, $x_{j,k,i}$ is the value of that component prior to scaling, $x_{j,k}^{\max}$ is a so-called "maximum" value of $x_{j,i}$ and $x_{j,k}^{\min}$ is a so-called "minimum" value, although these values are fixed by the UNDP (UNDP, 1997).

The longevity index $(I_{1,i})$ is a linear function of one variable only: the number of years a newborn infant would be expected to live based on current mortality patterns. The minimum and maximum values used to scale this variable are 25 and 85 years, respectively. The educational attainment index $(I_{2,i})$ is defined as follows:

$$I_{2,i} = \alpha_1 X_{2,1,i} + \alpha_2 X_{2,2,i} \qquad (3)$$

where α_1 and α_2 are weights set at two-thirds and one-third respectively, $X_{2,1,i}$ is country i's adult literacy rate and $X_{2,2,i}$ is that country's combined primary, secondary and tertiary enrolment ratio. The maximum and minimum values used to transform $x_{2,1,i}$ into $X_{2,1,i}$ and $x_{2,2,i}$ into $X_{2,2,i}$ are 0 and 100 per cent for each, respectively. Note, however, a number of countries record values of $x_{2,1,i}$ and $x_{2,2,i}$ that exceed 100 per cent: the UNDP caps these values at unity. The material standard of living index $(I_{2,i})$ is also based on a single variable $(x_{3,1,i})$ obtained by adjusting purchasing power parity (PPP) GDP per capita (y_i). In the 1995–1998 HDRs the adjustment is as follows:

$$\begin{aligned} x_{3,1,i} &= y_i & &\text{for } 0 < y_i \leq y^*, \\ &= y^* + 2[(y_i - y^*)^{1/2}] & &\text{for } y^* \leq y_i \leq 2y^* \text{ and} \\ &= y^* + 2[(y_i - y^*)^{1/2}] + 3[(y_i - 2y^*)^{1/3}] & &\text{for } 2y^* \leq y_i \leq 3y^* \end{aligned} \qquad (4)$$

and so on, where y^* is the average PPP per capita world income of PPP\$5,711. The minimum and maximum values of $x_{3,1}$ used to obtain $X_{3,1,i}$ are PPP\$100 and PPP\$6,400, respectively (UNDP, 1997). In the 1999–2001 HDRs $x_{3,1,i}$ is obtained by taking the logarithm of y_i and the minimum and maximum values used in scaling at the logarithms of PPP\$100 and PPP\$40,000, respectively. Luxembourg's actual PPP GDP per capita exceeds the latter value. Thus in calculating the HDI it is capped at PPP\$40,000 (UNDP, 2001).[4]

The GDI is defined as follows:

$$GDI_i = \frac{1}{k}\sum_{j=1}^{k} I^g_{j,i} \qquad (5)$$

where $I^g_{j,i}$ is the jth gender-disparity-adjusted indicator of human development in country I, $i = 1, \ldots, p$. These indicators are adjusted indices of longevity $(I^g_{1,i})$, educational attainment $(I^g_{2,i})$ and income $(I^g_{3,i})$. The adjusted longevity and educational attainment indices are defined as:

$$I^g_{j,i} = [p^f_i(I^f_{j,i})^{1-\varepsilon} + p^m_i(I^f_{j,i})^{1-\varepsilon}]^{1/(1-\varepsilon)} \quad j = 1, 2 \qquad (6)$$

where p^f_i is the share of females in the total population of i, p^m_i is the male share of population in i, $I^f_{1,i}$ is the female value of the particular index of human development in i, $I^m_{1,i}$ is the male value of that index in i and ε is an inequality aversion parameter set at two. $I^f_{1,i}$ and $I^m_{1,i}$ are obtained in the same manner as their aggregate counterparts in the HDI. That is, the longevity index is based solely on life expectancy, educational attainment is defined on the basis of literacy and combined school enrolment rates and each of these variables is scaled with the range of zero and one. In the case of life expectancy, for women the maximum value is 87.5 years and the minimum is 27.5 years; for men the corresponding values are 82.5 and 22.5 years. In the case of school enrolment ratios the maximum and minimum values are 100 and 0 per cent, respectively, in all instances (UNDP, 1997).

The gender-disparity-adjusted income index is defined as follows:

$$I^g_{3,i} = \frac{x^g_{3,1,i} y_i - x^{\min}_{3,1}}{x^{\max}_{3,1} - x^{\min}_{3,1}} \qquad (7)$$

where $x^g_{3,1,i}$ is an equally distributed equivalent income index, y_i is unadjusted PPP GDP per capita and $x^{\max}_{3,1}$ and $x^{\min}_{3,1}$ are "maximum" and "minimum" values of PPP GDP per capita, respectively, the corresponding values being those used to obtain the HDI's $X_{3,1,i}$. In the HDRs for 1995–1998 PPP GDP per capita was adjusted according to equation (4), while in the 1999–2001 HDRs the logarithm of this value is used instead. $x^g_{3,1,i}$ is defined as follows:

$$x^g_{3,1,i} = \left(p^f_i \left[\frac{w^f_i}{w_i} a^f_i \frac{1}{p^f_i} \right]^{1-\varepsilon} + p^m_i \left[\frac{w^m_i}{w_i} a^m_i \frac{1}{p^m_i} \right]^{1-\varepsilon} \right)^{1-\varepsilon} \qquad (8)$$

where w^f_i and w^m_i denote average female and male wages, respectively, in i, w_i is the average wage in i and a^f_i and a^m_i denote the ratios of economically active females and males, respectively, to the economically active total population in i (UNDP, 1997, 2001).

The GEM is defined as:

$$GEM_i = \frac{1}{k}\sum_{j=1}^{k} G_{j,i} \qquad (9)$$

where $G_{j,i}$ is the jth index of gender empowerment in country i and $i = 1,\ldots,q$. Empowerment is defined in terms of indices of economic participation and decision-making power $(G_{1,i})$, political decision-making power $(G_{2,i})$ and power over economic resources $(G_{3,i})$. The first of these indices is defined as follows:

$$G_{1,i} = \beta_1 g_{1,1,i} + \beta_2 g_{1,2,i} \qquad (10)$$

where β_1 and β_2 are weights each set at 0.5 and

$$g_{1,1,i} = \frac{1}{50}[p_i^f(am_i^f)^{1-\varepsilon} + p_i^m(am_i^m)^{1-\varepsilon}]^{1-\varepsilon} \quad \text{and} \qquad (11)$$

$$g_{1,2,i} = \frac{1}{50}[p_i^f(pt_i^f)^{1-\varepsilon} + p_i^m(pt_i^m)^{1-\varepsilon}]^{1-\varepsilon} \qquad (12)$$

where am_i^f and am_i^m are the shares of administrative and managerial positions held by females and males, respectively, and pt_i^f and pt_i^m are the shares of professional and technical positions held by females and males, respectively. α has the same interpretation as in the GDI and is again set to two. As the maximum values of $g_{1,1,i}$ and $g_{1,2,i}$ (and $G_{1,i}$) are 50, which implies perfect equality between men and women, each is multiplied by 1/50 to show the degree of inequality in empowerment (UNDP, 1997).

The political decision-making power index $(G_{2,i})$ is defined as:

$$G_{2,i} = \frac{1}{50}[p_i^f(pr_i^f)^{1-\varepsilon} + p_i^m(pr_i^m)^{1-\varepsilon}]^{1-\varepsilon} \qquad (13)$$

where pr_i^f and pr_i^m are the shares of total parliamentary seats held by women and men, respectively, in country i. The power over economic resources index $(G_{3,i})$ is defined as:

$$G_{3,i} = \frac{x_{3,1,i}^g y_i - y^{\min}}{y^{\max} - y^{\min}} \qquad (14)$$

where y^{min} and y^{max} are the minimum and maximum values of actual PPP GDP per capita, respectively. The corresponding values used by the UNDP are PPP$100 and PPP$40,000 respectively (UNDP, 1997).

Data and statistical methods

Data are taken from the *HDR 2001* (UNDP, 2001). Three samples are employed, each determined by data availability: a sample of 174 countries for which data on the HDI and income per capita are available; a sample of 148 countries for which data on income per capita and the HDI and GDI are available; and a sample of 102 countries for which data on each of income per capita and the HDI, GDI and GEM are available. Each of these samples is divided into subsamples defined according to whether a country is classified as high human development, medium human development, low human development, high income, medium income or low income. Country classifications are available in UNDP (2001). Most of the data used to calculate index values relate to 1999 (UNDP, 2001).

Three test statistics were utilized: the Pearson zero-order correlation coefficient; the Spearman rank-order correlation coefficient; and the Kendall tau-beta coefficient. The use and interpretation of these coefficients require elaboration. Of issue here is the level of these coefficients which deems the new indicator sufficiently insightful for it not to be redundant. Srinivasan (1994) reminds us that there are two extremes in assessing whether an indicator provides additional statistical information as compared to others. An indicator will provide no more information than another if they are perfectly correlated with each other. In this case the new indicator is perfectly redundant with respect to the other. At the other extreme, the new insights are at a maximum if the two indicators are mutually orthogonal. It follows that one can test for the perfect redundancy of an indicator by evaluating the null hypothesis that the particular coefficient's value is one. Failure to reject is evidence of perfect redundancy. In practice, however, this test will almost always be passed.

A more appropriate question is whether the extent of redundancy justifies the effort involved in calculating and reporting the new indicator. This involves a threshold to differentiate between redundancy and non-redundancy. McGillivray and White (1993) provide two thresholds – 0.90 and 0.70 – and hence evaluate the nulls that the particular coefficient equates to these values, which are termed as type I and type II redundancy respectively. These thresholds are of course arbitrary, but would appear to be reasonable. The current chapter therefore evaluates the following hypotheses:

- $H_0^{\text{I}}: \rho \geq 0.90$
- $H_1^{\text{I}}: \rho < 0.90$

and

- $H_0^{\text{II}}: \rho \geq 0.70$
- $H_1^{\text{II}}: \rho < 0.70$

where ρ is the chosen coefficient of statistical association. The null hypothesis, in each case, is of redundancy, either types I or II. The chapter also evaluates the null of perfect redundancy, that the coefficient is equal to one.

Results

All results are reported in tables 8.1–8.4. Table 8.1 provides results obtained using the first of the above-mentioned samples and gives information on the HDI and income per capita only. From table 8.1 we observe that the HDI is redundant with respect to PPP GDP per capita at either levels I or II for all samples, based on the Pearson and Spearman coefficients, with the exception of the high-income country group. Based on the Spearman coefficient, it is redundant at level I in the full country sample. Very similar correlation coefficients are reported by McGillivray (1991), McGillivray and White (1992) and Cahill (2005).

Striking results are reported in tables 8.2–8.4. The GDI is practically indistinguishable empirically from the HDI for the full country samples, reported in tables 8.2 and 8.4, of 143 and 95 countries respectively. The Pearson coefficient between the HDI and GDI for both samples is 0.999, indicating redundancy at level I (and II, therefore). The Spearman and Kendall coefficients for the 143-country sample are 0.997 and 0.973

Table 8.1 Coefficients of statistical association between PPP GDP per capita and the HDI

	Pearson (zero order)	Spearman (rank order)	Kendall tau-beta
All countries ($n = 174$)	0.76*	0.93**	0.78*
High human development ($n = 45$)	0.70*	0.68*	0.53*
Medium human development ($n = 94$)	0.59*	0.69*	0.52*
Low human development ($n = 35$)	0.51*	0.49*	0.32
High income ($n = 32$)	0.32	0.35	0.25
Medium income ($n = 82$)	0.64*	0.70*	0.54
Low income ($n = 60$)	0.76*	0.77*	0.58*

Notes
*denotes redundancy at level II.
**denotes redundancy at levels I and II.

Table 8.2 Coefficients of statistical association between PPP GDP per capita, the HDI and GDI

Country sample		PPP GDP per capita			HDI		
		Pearson (zero order)	Spearman (rank order)	Kendall tau-beta	Pearson (zero order)	Spearman (rank order)	Kendall tau-beta
All countries ($n = 143$)	HDI ($n = 143$)	0.778*	0.939**	0.789*	–	–	–
	GDI	0.774*	0.931**	0.776*	0.999**	0.997**	0.973**
High human development	HDI ($n = 43$)	0.691*	0.660*	0.502	–	–	–
	GDI ($n = 43$)	0.658*	0.623*	0.463	0.994**	0.990**	0.942**
Medium human development	HDI ($n = 72$)	0.635*	0.708*	0.530*	–	–	–
	GDI ($n = 72$)	0.594*	0.667*	0.495*	0.993**	0.983**	0.929**
Low human development	HDI ($n = 28$)	0.491*	0.477*	0.322	–	–	–
	GDI ($n = 28$)	0.488*	0.463*	0.316	0.990**	0.979**	0.912**
High income ($n = 31$)	HDI ($n = 31$)	0.296	0.303	0.222	–	–	–
		0.267	0.250	0.182	0.993**	0.997**	0.931**
Medium income GDI ($n = 62$)	HDI ($n = 62$)	0.695*	0.692*	0.525*	–	–	–
		0.646*	0.658*	0.496*	0.990**	0.979**	0.926**
Low income GDI ($n = 50$)	HDI ($n = 50$)	0.735*	0.722*	0.550*	–	–	–
		0.728*	0.712*	0.537*	0.998**	0.995**	0.959**

Notes
* denotes redundancy at level II.
** denotes redundancy at levels I and II.

respectively. For the 102-country sample the corresponding coefficients are 0.999 and 0.983 respectively. Each of these coefficients indicates level I redundancy. Slightly lower coefficients between the HDI and GDI for the subsamples were obtained, but all indicate level I redundancy. Adjusting the HDI for gender disparity based on these statistics is not an empirically insightful exercise. Correlation coefficients between PPP GDP per capita and the GDI were usually of a level indicating type II redundancy (see tables 8.2 and 8.4). The main exceptions to this are the coefficients obtained from the high-income country samples, which do not indicate redundancy at either level I or II. In general the GDI is redundant, usually at level II, with respect to both GDP per capita and the HDI for most samples under consideration.

The GEM is the most insightful indicator *vis-à-vis* GDP per capita (see table 8.3). While often redundant at level II for the larger samples, it is not redundant in this sense at any level for the subsamples under consideration. Indeed, it is negatively correlated with GDP per capita for the low human development country group (see tables 8.3 and 8.4), based on values of the Pearson, Spearman and Kendall coefficients. The Spearman rank correlation coefficients are the lowest, and are actually statistically significant (that is, they are significantly different from zero). Rather than being redundant for the low human development country, the GEM would appear to provide some strikingly new insights compared to what income per capita reveals. The GEM is often reasonably highly correlated with the HDI, although not to the extent that the GDI is. These correlations deem the GEM redundant, at level II, with the HDI in most subsamples. From table 8.3 the subsamples in which it is not redundant are the low human development, middle-income and low-income country samples. From table 8.4 it is not redundant for the low human development and middle-income country samples. The GEM and the HDI are negatively correlated in table 8.4's middle-income country sample, although the coefficients are not significantly different from zero.

Conclusion

The central question considered in this chapter was whether the GDI and the GEM provide insights into ordinal and cardinal country well-being achievement which differ greatly from non-gender-adjusted indicators. The non-gender-adjusted indicators under specific consideration were PPP GDP per capita and the HDI. Based on simple measures of statistical association (Spearman, Pearson and Kendall coefficients), the answer to these question is rather mixed. In general, the GDI does not add many empirical insights *vis-à-vis* income per capita and the HDI. The GDI is

Table 8.3 Coefficients of statistical association between PPP GDP per capita, the HDI and GEM

Country sample		PPP GDP per capita			HDI		
		Pearson (zero order)	Spearman (rank order)	Kendall tau-beta	Pearson (zero order)	Spearman (rank order)	Kendall tau-beta
All countries	HDI ($n = 102$)	0.783*	0.942**	0.806*	–	–	–
	GEM ($n = 102$)	0.701*	0.712*	0.522	0.723*	0.768*	0.586*
High human development	HDI ($n = 37$)	0.753*	0.707*	0.562*	–	–	–
	GEM ($n = 37$)	0.408	0.442	0.294	0.675*	0.691*	0.511*
Medium human development	HDI ($n = 52$)	0.634*	0.700*	0.540*	–	–	–
	GEM ($n = 52$)	0.422	0.424	0.294	0.560*	0.548*	0.401
Low human development	HDI ($n = 13$)	0.625*	0.626*	0.452*	–	–	–
	GEM ($n = 13$)	−0.550	−0.621	−0.477	0.301	0.412	−0.308
High income	HDI ($n = 29$)	0.428	0.486*	0.356	–	–	–
	GEM ($n = 29$)	0.217	0.227	0.167	0.717*	0.642*	0.495*
Medium income	HDI ($n = 48$)	0.693*	0.710*	0.544*	–	–	–
	GEM ($n = 48$)	0.192	0.254	0.162	0.406	0.413	0.294
Low income	HDI ($n = 25$)	0.873*	0.911**	0.740*	–	–	–
	GEM ($n = 25$)	0.319	0.281	0.187	0.365	0.326	0.224

Notes
* denotes redundancy at level II.
** denotes redundancy at levels I and II.

Table 8.4 Coefficients of statistical association between PPP GDP per capita, the HDI, GDI and GEM

Country sample		PPP GDP per capita			HDI			GDI		
		Pearson (zero order)	Spearman (rank order)	Kendall tau-beta	Pearson (zero order)	Spearman (rank order)	Kendall tau-beta	Pearson (zero order)	Spearman (rank order)	Kendall tau-beta
All countries	HDI (n = 95)	0.790*	0.943**	0.804*	–	–	–	–	–	–
	GDI (n = 95)	0.789*	0.939**	0.799*	0.999**	0.999**	0.983**	–	–	–
	GEM (n = 95)	0.707*	0.727*	0.534	0.757*	0.794*	0.607*	0.766*	0.803*	0.617*
High human development	HDI (n = 36)	0.753*	0.691*	0.550*	–	–	–	–	–	–
	GDI (n = 36)	0.725*	0.655*	0.516*	0.995**	0.985**	0.938**	–	–	–
	GEM (n = 36)	0.393	0.422	0.286	0.683*	0.695*	0.515*	0.725*	0.743*	0.564*
Medium human development	HDI (n = 47)	0.653*	0.704*	0.540*	–	–	–	–	–	–
	GDI (n = 47)	0.650*	0.702*	0.544*	0.997**	0.907**	0.971**	–	–	–
	GEM (n = 47)	0.392	0.387	0.264	0.570*	0.552*	0.392	0.595*	0.565*	0.401
Low human development	HDI (n = 12)	0.602*	0.650*	0.473*	–	–	–	–	–	–
	GDI (n = 12)	0.586*	0.615*	0.443*	0.997**	0.993**	0.970**	–	–	–
	GEM (n = 12)	−0.512	−0.587	−0.473	−0.213	−0.364	−0.273	0.204	0.322	0.242
High income	HDI (n = 28)	0.400	0.442	0.330	–	–	–	–	–	–
	GDI (n = 28)	0.366	0.375	0.282	0.991**	0.969**	0.914**	–	–	–
	GEM (n = 28)	0.135	0.159	0.122	0.709*	0.623*	0.473*	0.760*	0.688*	0.537*
Medium income	HDI (n = 45)	0.697*	0.715*	0.543*	–	–	–	–	–	–
	GDI (n = 45)	0.689*	0.711*	0.548*	0.997**	0.997**	0.975**	–	–	–
	GEM (n = 45)	0.167	0.227	0.138	0.416	0.408	0.283	0.441	0.411	0.286
Low income	HDI (n = 22)	0.903**	0.915**	0.758*	–	–	–	–	–	–
	GDI (n = 22)	0.906**	0.911**	0.752*	0.999**	0.997**	0.980**	–	–	–
	GEM (n = 22)	0.418*	0.343	0.196	0.478*	0.401*	0.269	0.500*	0.420*	0.290

Notes
* denotes redundancy at level II.
** denotes redundancy at levels I and II.

practically indistinguishable empirically from the HDI for larger samples of countries. Adjusting the HDI for gender disparity adds little empirically, it seems. The GEM offers more original insights than the GDI, especially for country subsamples, in which is can be negatively correlated with both income per capita and the HDI. Evidence is thus mixed on whether adjusting well-being indicators for gender disparity matters empirically – in some instances it does and in others it does not. This does not, however, diminish the conceptual and ideological case for such adjustments. From a practitioner or policy-maker perspective, it follows that if they want to use a national-level gender-adjusted development indicator that provides different information to the HDI, the GEM is preferable to the GDI.

Notes

1. Note that this finding has not stopped the UNDP and others from making claims to the contrary. Typically these claims are based on comparing extreme cases where a country's rank based on one indicator differs radically from that generated by another, rather than on large samples of countries.
2. Saith and Harriss-White (1999) also ask this question, based on the findings of McGillivray (1991) and McGillivray and White (1992), but do not pursue it empirically.
3. While the aim of this chapter is not to critique the UNDP's indicators, it is not blind to the various limitations identified in the literature. Relevant studies include Dasgupta (1990), McGillivray (1991), McGillivray and White (1992), Ogwang (1994), Gormely (1995), Streeten (1995), Hicks (1997), Ivanova, Arcelus and Srinivasan (1998), Sagar and Najam (1998), Noorbakhsh (1998a, 1998b), Pillarisetti and McGillivray (1998), Bardhan and Klasen (1999), Saith and Harriss-White (1999), Neumayer (2001) and Morse (2003). One should not forget these limitations, and the various caveats emerging from them, in interpreting the results reported here.
4. See Anand and Sen (2000) for an excellent discussion of income in the HDI.

REFERENCES

Anand, S. and A. Sen (2000) "The Income Component of the Human Development Index", *Journal of Human Development* 1: 83–106.

Bardhan, K. and S. Klasen (1999) "UNDP's Gender-related Indices: A Critical Review", *World Development* 27: 985–1010.

Cahill, M. (2005) "Is the Human Development Index Redundant?", *Eastern Economic Journal* 31: 1–5.

Dasgupta, P. (1990) "Well-being in Poor Countries", *Economic and Political Weekly*, 4 August: 1713–1720.

Gormely, P. J. (1995) "The Human Development Index in 1994: Impact of Income on Country Rank", *Journal of Economic and Social Measurement* 21: 253–267.

Hicks, D. A. (1997) "The Inequality Adjusted Human Development Index: A Constructive Proposal", *World Development* 25: 1283–1298.

Hicks, N. and P. Streeten (1979) "Indicators of Development: The Search for a Basic Needs Yardstick", *World Development* 7: 567–580.

Ivanova, I., F. J. Arcelus and G. Srinivasan (1998) "An Assessment of the Measurement Properties of the Human Development Index", *Social Indicators Research* 46: 157–179.

Larson, D. A. and W. T. Wilford (1979) "The Physical Quality of Life Index: A Useful Social Indicator?", *World Development* 7: 581–584.

McGillivray, M. (1991) "The Human Development Index: Yet Another Redundant Composite Development Indicator?", *World Development* 19: 1451–1460.

McGillivray, M. and H. White (1992) "Measuring Development? A Statistical Critique of the Human Development Index", Working Paper 135, Institute of Social Studies, The Hague.

────── (1993) "Measuring Development? The UNDP's Human Development Index", *Journal of International Development* 5: 183–192.

Morse, S. (2003) "For Better or For Worse, Till the Human Development Index Do Us Part?", *Ecological Economics* 45: 281–296.

Neumayer, E. (2001) "The Human Development Index and Sustainability – A Constructive Proposal", *Ecological Economics* 39: 101–114.

Noorbakhsh, F. (1998a) "A Modified Human Development Index", *World Development* 26: 517–528.

────── (1998b) "A Human Development Index: Some Technical Issues and Alternative Indices", *Journal of International Development* 10: 589–605.

Ogwang, T. (1994) "The Choice of Principal Variables for Computing the Human Development Index", *World Development* 22: 2011–2114.

Pillarisetti, J. R. and M. McGillivray (1998) "Human Development and Gender Empowerment", *Development Policy Review* 16: 197–203.

Sagar, A. and A. Najam (1998) "The Human Development Index: A Critical Review", *Ecological Economics* 25: 249–264.

Saith, R. and B. Harriss-White (1999) "The Gender Sensitivity of Well-being Indicators", *Development and Change* 30: 465–498.

Srinivasan, T. N. (1994) "Human Development: A New Paradigm or Reinvention of the Wheel?", *American Economic Review Papers and Proceedings* 84: 238–243.

Streeten, P. (1995) "Human Development: The Debate about the Index", *International Social Science Journal* 47: 25–37.

UNDP (1990–2004) *Human Development Report*, New York: Oxford University Press.

9
Well-being and the complexity of poverty: A subjective well-being approach

Mariano Rojas

Introduction

The lessening of poverty is a central concern. Many resources are allocated to the study of poverty and the design of abatement policies. The definition of poverty is critical in this concern. It is reasonable to accept that a poor person is one whose well-being is low; thus poverty depends on the specific concept of human well-being. It is therefore imperative to study human well-being before measuring poverty and designing policies towards its abatement.

This chapter borrows from the literature on subjective well-being to expand and enrich the concept of poverty. Subjective well-being refers to well-being as declared by a person. It is understood and measured from a subjective well-being/happiness approach, which is common in the relevant literature.

The investigation shows that the relationship between subjective well-being and the traditional indicators of well-being (income, consumption, socio-economic situation and access to public services) is weak. Thus subjective well-being has additional information, not contemplated in the traditional indicators, which is useful for studying human well-being and, in consequence, poverty.

The investigation goes on to explore some possible reasons for the existence of a weak relationship between subjective well-being and some socio-economic indicators. Three topics are studied. First, the fact that a person is much more than a consumer is studied through the domains-of-life literature; second, the role of human perceptions is examined; and third, the existence of heterogeneity in the purpose of life is studied through the *conceptual referent theory of happiness*.

The domains-of-life literature allows for the introduction of a multidimensional approach to human well-being and, in consequence, to poverty. The recognition that human beings are much more than economic agents leads to the study of life satisfaction in domains different from the economic one. It is shown that human well-being comes from a person's condition in all domains of life, while traditional indicators of poverty are related only to satisfaction in the consumption domain. Thus poverty, as a situation lacking in well-being, is better understood as a multidimensional phenomenon.

There are also important differences across persons in the perception of objectively identical circumstances. Perceptions play an important role in subjective well-being, so the common practice of associating traditional poverty indicators to the lack of human well-being is questionable on the basis of heterogeneity of perceptions across people.

In addition, people do have different life purposes, and a person's evaluation of his/her well-being is contingent on his/her life purposes. Thus, when evaluating their well-being, people tend to focus on different considerations. The conceptual referent theory of happiness studies the conceptual referent which is behind a person's subjective well-being. It states that people have different conceptual referents in the subjective evaluation of their well-being. This heterogeneity in the well-being conceptual referent across persons implies that socio-economic indicators, which are commonly used as proxies of well-being, are not equally pertinent for everybody.

An empirical investigation is done in Mexico. A large survey was applied in five states of south-central Mexico and in the Federal District. The empirical findings suggest that improvement in human well-being would be better served by a well-being concept which is based on the wholeness and complexity of human beings. The investigation suggests that subjective well-being indicators can enrich the understanding of the concept of poverty, at least if it is meant to reflect a situation lacking in well-being.

The literature on subjective well-being

On the approach

Human well-being is measured from a subjective well-being (SWB) approach. SWB refers to well-being as declared by a person. It is based on a person's answer to either a single question or a group of questions about their well-being. It is a self-reported measure of well-being.

SWB has been extensively studied in disciplines such as psychology (Kahneman, Diener and Schwarz, 1999; Argyle, 2002) and sociology (Veenhoven, 1988, 1993, 1997; Veenhoven, DenBuitelaar and de Heer, 1995). It is a relatively new area of study in economics (Easterlin, 1974, 1995, 2001; Clark and Oswald, 1994; Di Tella, MacCulloch and Oswald, 2001; Frey and Stutzer, 2000; McBride, 2001; Oswald, 1997; Pradhan and Ravallion, 2000; van Praag and Frijters, 1997). It has some noteworthy advantages over alternative well-being measures and concepts.

The well-being of a person

SWB is well-being as declared by a person; hence it is a measure of a person's well-being that incorporates all life events, aspirations, achievements, failures, emotions and relations of human beings, as well as their neighbouring cultural and moral environment. Hence SWB differs substantially from alternative well-being concepts that are inspired by academic discipline approaches. The academic discipline concepts, such as economic well-being, psychological well-being, political well-being and so on, are inherently incomplete because they are based on an analytical theory of knowledge. Thus they cannot entirely capture the well-being of a human being.[1] SWB constitutes an enhancement in the understanding of human well-being because it provides a direct measure of the well-being of a person.

Inferential approach

The SWB literature is based on an inferential rather than a doctrinal approach. Because SWB refers to well-being as declared by a person, it is neither the researcher nor the philosopher who assesses a person's well-being, but the person himself.[2] In other words, SWB implies a bottom-up rather than a top-down approach. Thus SWB differs substantially from other approaches that put forward sophisticated arguments to justify an assessment of a person's well-being on the basis of an external set of criteria. Doctrinal approaches, rather than inferential ones, have dominated the history of well-being studies. These approaches have had little interest in testing empirical validation, rather they assume both the specific concept of human well-being and its explanatory factors.

SWB approaches just require a person to be able to assess his/her life satisfaction or happiness level; the rest of the analysis – for example, the importance of some presumed well-being explanatory factors – is based on inferential techniques.[3]

Inherently subjective

A person's well-being necessarily implies a subjective appraisal, because it is based on a person's assessment of his/her life. Academic disciplines such as economics have always stressed the use of objective measures of well-being for the sake of objectivity itself. However, from an SWB point of view, objective indicators of well-being can be deceiving, because well-being is inherently subjective. Besides, objective indicators, being chosen by researchers and public officers, are based on subjective, arbitrary and somewhat paternalistic criteria. In addition, objective indicators do tend to impose the same standards on everybody, while SWB does not face this problem, allowing for heterogeneity across persons in this respect.

Transdisciplinary approach

Academic disciplines focus on partial aspects of a person's life, since they do not really use the human being as their unit of study. SWB measures a person's well-being and not the well-being of an academically constructed agent. Thus it is difficult to seize the complexity of SWB measures from any single discipline, and a transdisciplinary, or at least an interdisciplinary, approach is preferred.

On the measurement of SWB

SWB is associated with the concept of *life satisfaction* or *happiness in life* (Ferrer-i-Carbonell, 2002; Cummins, 1997, 1999; Veenhoven, 1988).[4] Veenhoven (1984) states that subjective well-being can be measured only on the basis of a person's answer to a direct question about his/her well-being; there is no room for speculation based on a person's possessions, facial expressions or other extrinsic behaviour.[5]

This investigation uses the happiness approach to measure a person's well-being.[6] The following direct question was applied: "Taking everything in your life into consideration, how happy are you?" A Likert ordinal scale with seven options, from very unhappy to extremely happy, was used to capture people's answers.[7]

On the main findings in the literature and their explanations

Since the pioneering study of Easterlin (1974) several investigations have studied the topic of subjective well-being or happiness and its relationship to economic variables, including Mullis, 1992; Veenhoven, 1988, 1993, 1997; Heady, 1991; Douthitt, MacDonald and Mullis, 1992; Diener et al., 1993; Diener, 2002; Diener and Oishi, 2000; Diener and Suh, 1997;

Frey and Stutzer, 2000; Fuentes and Rojas, 2001; Rojas, Fuentes and Oplotnik, 2001; Oswald, 1997; van Praag, Frijters and Ferrer-i-Carbonell, 2000, 2002; Argyle, 1999, 2002.

A weak relationship between income and happiness is a common finding in the literature.[8] Thus traditional objective indicators of well-being, such as income, do not seem to pass an external validation as good proxies of well-being on the basis of the SWB approach.[9] In consequence, a low income level is not necessarily associated with a lack of human well-being, nor do high income levels necessarily imply high well-being levels. As a result, traditional measures of poverty, which are based on a person's income or purchasing power, would not necessarily imply lack of well-being according to an SWB approach. Different theories have been advanced to explain the existence of a weak relationship between SWB and income.

The *relative theory* states that the impact of income on a person's subjective well-being depends on changing standards based on his/her expectations and social comparisons (Meadow et al., 1992; Diener and Diener, 1996; Parducci, 1968, 1995; Easterlin, 1974, 1995; Diener et al., 1993; Hagerty, 1999).

The *absolute theory* assumes that basic needs satisfaction is related to subjective well-being; it suggests the existence of a threshold beyond which the impact of income on subjective well-being is not important.

The *adaptation theory* focuses on the ability of persons to adapt to positive and negative events; thus persons with higher adaptation capabilities tend to be happier, even in situations where income is low (Brickman, Coates and Janoff-Bulman, 1978).

The *aspiration theory* states that the degree of satisfaction/dissatisfaction experienced by a person is related to the ratio of his/her satisfied total desires. Persons who believe that their desires are fully satisfied tend to be happier than persons who have unsatisfied desires, regardless of their income levels (Michalos, 1985).

The *conceptual referent theory* stresses the importance of heterogeneity in the SWB conceptual referent; because of this, the relevance of some explanatory factors of happiness differs across persons. Thus while for some people income would be a relevant proxy for well-being, for others it would be completely irrelevant (Rojas, 2005, 2006a).

The database

A survey was conducted in five states of central and south Mexico[10] as well as in the Federal District (Mexico City) during October and November 2001. A stratified random survey was designed to collect information from a sample of persons. The survey was controlled by household income, gender and urban-rural areas. The sample size is acceptable for inference in central Mexico; 1,540 questionnaires were properly completed.

The survey gathered information regarding the following quantitative and qualitative variables.

- Demographic and social variables: education, age, gender, civil status, religion, family composition, health condition, occupation and working situation.
- Economic variables: current household income,[11] consumption expenditure, access to public services, size of house and possession of durable commodities.
- Subjective well-being: a seven-option happiness-with-life scale is used. The scale's answering options are extremely happy, very happy, happy, somewhat happy, neither happy nor unhappy, unhappy and very unhappy. Happiness was handled as an ordinal variable, with values between one and seven, where one was assigned to the lowest level of happiness and seven to the highest.[12]
- Life domains: a large set of questions was used to enquire about satisfaction in life domains. Six life domains were constructed on the basis of principal component techniques: health satisfaction, material/consumption satisfaction, job satisfaction, family satisfaction, interpersonal/friendship relations and personal satisfaction.
- Perception variables: the survey inquired on perceptions about poverty, social class, capacity of income to satisfy material needs and economic well-being.
- Conceptual referent for happiness: the survey also asked about the conceptual referent to the happiness question. This variable is explained further later in this chapter.

Poverty and sample inference

National deciles for household income distribution were constructed on the basis of the 2001 National Income and Expenditure Survey. Table 9.1 shows the sample distribution along the national deciles. It is observed that the sample distribution follows closely the Mexican income distribution, and it is thus a representative sample.

Approximately 55 per cent of the persons in the sample could be considered as poor according to the traditional measures of poverty used by the Mexican Social Development Secretariat. Do these persons declare low levels of well-being? Are they poor from an SWB approach? In addition, do persons considered as non-poor declare high levels of well-being?

Table 9.1 Sample distribution across national deciles of income

National decile	Sample %	Cumulative %
1	9.0	9.0
2	11.5	20.5
3	9.5	30.0
4	11.8	41.8
5	11.8	53.6
6	9.5	63.1
7	4.7	67.8
8	13.2	81.0
9	12.7	93.7
10	6.3	100.0
Total	100.0	

Table 9.2 Subjective well-being distribution

Simplified four-categories scale	Original seven-options scale	%
	Very unhappy	0.2
Not happy	Unhappy	1.1
	Neither happy nor unhappy	3.6
Somewhat happy	Somewhat happy	6.0
Happy	Happy	37.4
Very happy	Very happy	46.3
	Extremely happy	5.5
Total		100.0

Subjective well-being in the survey

The distribution of happiness in the survey is not very different from most findings in the literature (Argyle, 1999, 2002; Veenhoven, 1993; Diener and Diener, 1996). Most of the people are either happy or very happy. Table 9.2 shows the happiness distribution in the survey according to the original seven-options scale. A four-categories scale is constructed for simplification in the presentation of the information.

Less than 5 per cent of the persons in the sample declared having a not-happy life. Almost 90 per cent of the persons in the survey declared that their life is either happy or very happy. This finding, together with the fact that more than 50 per cent of the people in the survey could be considered as poor according to their household income, suggests that the relationship between income (a conventional indicator of poverty) and subjective well-being (an indicator of human well-being) is not strong. The following section explores this relationship further.

Table 9.3 Subjective well-being and household income in percentages, simplified SWB scale

Quintile of income	Not happy	Somewhat happy	Happy	Very happy	Total
1	1.3	18.2	42.6	37.9	100
2	2.0	8.5	44.6	44.9	100
3	1.6	8.0	38.8	51.6	100
4	0.7	7.4	33.7	58.2	100
5	0.7	5.4	23.6	70.4	100

Subjective well-being and socio-economic indicators

Socio-economic indicators such as income, possession of durable goods and access to public services have commonly been used as proxies of well-being. The previous section hints that the relationship between these indicators and subjective well-being is not strong. This section, using different objective indicators, studies the relationship further.

Subjective well-being and income

Table 9.3 shows the subjective well-being situation for every income quintile. This table enables a comparison of well-being to be made across different income groups. A strong relationship between income and subjective well-being should imply that most happy and very happy people are in the higher quintiles, and most not-happy and somewhat happy people are in the lower quintiles.

As can be seen in table 9.3, a relationship between income and subjective well-being exists. Higher income quintiles have more people located in the happy and very happy categories. For example, 80 per cent of the people in the lower quintile declare themselves to be happy or very happy, while in the higher quintile the figure rises to 94 per cent. Thus income does seem to have a positive influence on subjective well-being. However, the influence is not a determinant, as is shown by the fact that even in the lower quintile (where, according to conventional measures of poverty, all people are poor), 80 per cent of the people express high SWB levels.

In consequence, income does have an influence on SWB, but income by itself is not a good proxy of SWB. There are persons who are happy with their lives at all income levels, and an increase in income does not ensure greater happiness. Therefore income is not a good proxy of well-being; it is just a means for well-being, and as such its effectiveness in

Table 9.4 Subjective well-being and socio-economic position* in percentages

Quintile	Not happy	Somewhat happy	Happy	Very happy	Total
1	3.3	16.0	45.4	35.3	100
2	1.3	8.9	44.4	45.4	100
3	0.3	9.0	36.9	53.8	100
4	0.7	5.9	31.9	61.5	100
5	0.8	7.2	26.4	65.6	100

*Socio-economic position measured with variable Soc_1, which is related to the ownership of traditional electronic commodities such as a radio, TV and refrigerator.

increasing well-being should not be presumed but should be empirically validated.

Subjective well-being and other socio-economic indicators

Socio-economic indicators are also used as proxies of well-being. This investigation constructs three indicators of a person's socio-economic position on the basis of a large group of questions about quality of housing, ownership of durable goods and so on. Principal component techniques were used to obtain the three socio-economic indicators. Soc_1 is associated with the ownership of traditional electronic commodities such as a radio, TV and refrigerator. Soc_2 is related to the ownership of commodities such as computers, microwave ovens and cable/satellite TV, as well as size of house (measured by number of bedrooms and number of lights). Soc_3 relates to access to services such as potable water and electricity.

Table 9.4 shows the subjective well-being situation for every socio-economic position as measured by variable Soc_1.[13] The observations are divided in quintiles according to the person's socio-economic position, with quintile 1 for the worst situation and quintile 5 for the best situation. Results are quite similar as in the case of income. Socio-economic position does have an influence on SWB; it is not, however, a determinant influence. Moving towards higher socio-economic quintiles implies a rise in the percentage of people who are happy and very happy with their lives. However, even in the lower quintiles a very large percentage of people declare themselves to have happy or very happy lives.

Subjective well-being and access to public services

The provision of more and better public services is considered to be a fundamental social task. Access to these services is presumed to be highly

Table 9.5 Subjective well-being and access to public services in percentages

Quintile	Not happy	Somewhat happy	Happy	Very happy	Total
1	2.6	15.5	36.8	45.1	100
2	1.6	8.5	40.0	49.8	100
3	1.6	9.8	38.7	49.8	100
4	0.0	5.7	37.0	57.2	100
5	0.0	9.1	30.0	60.9	100

Table 9.6 Correlation matrix – Socio-economic indicators and SWB

	SWB	Income	Soc_1	Soc_2	Soc_3	Serv
SWB	1					
Income	0.1257	1				
Soc_1	0.1509	0.5635	1			
Soc_2	0.1847	0.2468	0.4509	1		
Soc_3	0.2202	0.1964	0.3392	0.5222	1	
Serv	0.1341	0.0805	0.0995	0.1400	0.2210	1

correlated to well-being. To study this issue, a variable that captures access to public services and their perceived quality was constructed. The public services considered are trash collection, public transport, potable water, public lights, drainage, neighbourhood safety and road conditions. Principal component techniques were used to create a single variable of access to public services (*Serv*). This variable ranks people from those in the worst situation to those in the most favourable.

Table 9.5 shows the SWB distribution for every access-to-public-services quintile. The first quintile includes the 20 per cent of population in the worst situation and the fifth quintile refers to the 20 per cent in the most favourable situation. Results do not differ substantially from previous ones. Access to more and better public services tends to increase SWB, but it does not have a strong impact.

Subjective well-being and socio-economic indicators: Correlation analysis

Table 9.6 shows the correlation matrix between the socio-economic indicators and the SWB indicator. All correlations are positive, indicating a direct relationship between each socio-economic indicator and SWB.[14] Thus it seems that SWB tends to increase with a rise in the socio-economic position. However, all correlations are relatively low; in the case of income and SWB the correlation is 0.12.

Table 9.7 Regression analysis – Socio-economic indicators and SWB

Parameter	Variable	Coefficient	Probability > t
α_0	Intercept	1.617	0.000
α_1	Income	0.004	0.074
α_2	Soc_1	0.004	0.377
α_3	Soc_2	0.037	0.030
α_4	Soc_3	0.263	0.000
α_5	Serv	0.051	0.002
R^2	0.0676		

Subjective well-being and socio-economic indicators: Regression analysis

The following regression was estimated to explore further the relationship between socio-economic indicators and SWB:

$$H = \alpha_0 + \alpha_1 Y + \alpha_2 Soc_1 + \alpha_3 Soc_2 + \alpha_4 Soc_3 + \alpha_5 Serv + \mu$$

where H stands for the happiness level, Y for household income, Soc_1, Soc_2 and Soc_3 for the principal components constructed socio-economic variables and $Serv$ for the principal components constructed access-to-public-services variable.

Table 9.7 presents the results from the linear regression analysis.[15] It is noteworthy that R^2 is 0.067. In other words, the group of socio-economic variables, commonly used as proxies of well-being, explains less than 7 per cent of the variability in SWB. Thus it is clear that SWB and the socio-economic position are not only different concepts, but they are not strongly correlated. In consequence, SWB indicators can make an important contribution to the study of well-being and poverty beyond that which the traditional socio-economic indicators provide.

The following sections study three factors that partially explain the nature of subjective well-being and its weak relationship to socio-economic indicators.

Subjective well-being and heterogeneity in perceptions

Perceptions play an important role in SWB. As stated by Lin (1940: 9), "What matters is everyone's point of view."

A person's SWB is closely related to his/her own perception of life's conditions. The relationship between socio-economic indicators and SWB is mediated by a person's perception of his/her socio-economic

Table 9.8 Personal expenditure and poverty perception in percentages

Quintile of personal expenditure	Poor	Not poor	Total
1 (lower)	47.4	52.6	100
2	27.7	72.3	100
3	27.8	72.2	100
4	27.7	72.3	100
5 (higher)	16.2	83.8	100

situation. If a person's perception of this socio-economic situation follows the objective conditions closely, a strong relationship between socio-economic indicators and SWB would be expected. However, two persons can perceive differently certain objectively identical socio-economic situations, while some socio-economic situations that are objectively different can be perceived as identical (Parducci, 1984).

To study the existence of heterogeneity in perceptions, people were asked in the survey about the following perceptions: poverty perception (do you consider yourself to be a poor person?); economic well-being perception (how is your economic well-being?); and perception of material needs satisfaction (what is the capacity of your income to satisfy your material needs?).

Personal expenditure is used as a socio-economic indicator,[16] and quintiles are constructed to study the role of a person's socio-economic position. The first quintile includes the 20 per cent of people with the lowest personal expenditure, while the fifth quintile includes those with the largest personal expenditure.

Personal expenditure and poverty perception

Table 9.8 shows the relationship between personal expenditure and poverty perception. It is remarkable that most people, even in the lower quintiles of personal expenditure, do not consider themselves as poor. For example, 72 per cent of those in the second quintile do not consider themselves poor even though, according to conventional measures, they would be considered poor. It is also surprising that 16 per cent of those in the fifth quintile (those with higher expenditures) do consider themselves poor. It suggests that the concept of poverty used by people is not similar to the concept used by economists. There may be many reasons for this. People, for example, may evaluate their situation on the basis of their relative rather than absolute position, or they may take into account other aspects of life that are not considered in the traditional definition of poverty or may even assess their situation on the basis of different life purposes.

Table 9.9 Personal expenditure and perception of economic well-being in percentages

Quintile of personal expenditure	Very bad	Bad	Good	Very good	Total
1 (lower)	2.2	25.8	64.7	7.3	100
2	1.8	12.5	77.1	8.6	100
3	1.5	17.5	71.5	9.5	100
4	0.9	15.6	75.5	8.1	100
5 (higher)	0.4	4.9	72.4	22.4	100

Table 9.10 Personal expenditure and perception of degree of satisfaction of material needs in percentages

Quintile of personal expenditure	Very insufficient	Insufficient	Some needs	Most needs	All needs	Total
1 (lower)	30.4	49.2	4.2	10.7	5.5	100
2	20.5	44.3	9.2	16.5	9.5	100
3	19.3	37.4	10.7	23.0	9.6	100
4	18.7	39.9	13.4	19.3	8.7	100
5 (higher)	12.6	26.6	15.5	28.1	17.3	100

Personal expenditure and perception of economic well-being

Similar results show up in a question about economic well-being perceptions. Table 9.9 indicates that the perception of having a good or very good economic situation tends to increase with personal expenditure. However, what is really noteworthy is that 70 per cent of the people in the first quintile of personal expenditure perceive their economic well-being to be good or very good. The figure goes up to about 85 per cent for people in the second quintile. Hence there is no strong correlation between the economic situation of a person and his/her own perception of that situation.

Personal expenditure and perception of material needs' satisfaction

Fuentes and Rojas (2001) find that the perception of unsatisfied material needs is an important explanatory variable for SWB. They also note that as a person's income increases, his/her own perception of satisfied needs does not rise significantly.

Results from table 9.10 corroborate these findings. There are persons in the lower quintiles of expenditure who state that most or all their needs are being satisfied, while almost 40 per cent of the persons in the higher quintile say that their income is insufficient or very insufficient to satisfy all their material needs. Consequently, it seems that the fact that a person has high expenditure levels is not enough to ensure a perception of satisfying all material needs.

On perceptions, subjective well-being and socio-economic indicators

SWB is influenced by a person's perception of his/her own socio-economic position and satisfaction of material needs.[17] Nonetheless, perceptions are not strongly related to the objective socio-economic indicators which are commonly used as indicators of well-being.

There are disparities between the information provided by objective socio-economic indicators and a person's perception of their socio-economic condition. For example, a number of people who, according to conventional indicators, are considered poor do not consider themselves as such. If the understanding of human well-being is a main objective, it is necessary to go beyond the apparent neutrality of objective indicators to recognize and study the large heterogeneity that exists in human perception.

Domains of life and subjective well-being

The fact that there is more to life than the standard of living is captured by the concept of subjective well-being and not by socio-economic indicators. A person is much more than an economic agent, and the construct of *domains of life* constitutes an attempt to study the complexity of a person's being.[18] A person's well-being is related to his/her own situation in all domains of life, and this relationship is neither a linear nor a single-equation one (Rojas, 2006b).

A taxonomy of domains of life

The classification of a person's activities, feelings and thoughts into a set of domains of life is inherently arbitrary. Some authors argue in favour of having just a few categories, while others prefer to extend the number of categories (Cummins, 1999). Nevertheless, independently of the demarcation used, recognition of the multidimensionality in human lives allows for a better understanding of human well-being.

On the basis of a large set of questions about life satisfaction in many areas, and using factor analysis and principal component techniques,[19] this investigation constructs six domains of life which are measured on a 1–7 scale (from *very unsatisfied* to *very satisfied*).

Table 9.11 Satisfaction in the domains of life average and standard deviation on a 1–7 scale

Domain of life	Average	Standard deviation
Health	5.07	1.02
Consumption	4.45	1.21
Job	4.65	2.23
Family		
Partner	5.14	2.44
Children	5.53	2.80
Rest of family	5.24	1.12
Friendship	4.69	1.18
Personal	4.43	1.33
Subjective well-being	5.40	0.95

- Health, associated with a person's perceived health and access to medical services.
- Consumption, associated with the capacity for purchasing goods and services, financial situation and house ownership.
- Job, associated with a person's relationship with his/her boss and colleagues, job responsibilities and job environment.
- Family, which is divided into three areas: relationship with partner, relationship with own children and relationship with rest of the family.
- Friendship, associated with the existence of interpersonal relations and access to a social network.
- Personal, associated with the possibility of pursuing one's own goals and having time for personal interests.

Satisfaction in the domains of life

Table 9.11 shows the average satisfaction in each domain of life. It is in the *family* domains where people in the survey claim, on average, to be more satisfied. People are less satisfied in the consumption, personal and job domains. These results provide a hint about the sources of SWB; it seems that well-being comes from having not only a high standard of living but also from good interpersonal relations, which could be more important than income in the generation of well-being.[20]

Life domains and subjective well-being

Are all domains of life equally important for well-being? Table 9.12 presents the correlation coefficients for SWB and satisfaction in the domains of life. All correlations are positive, which indicates that greater

Table 9.12 Subjective well-being and domain satisfaction correlation coefficients

Domain of life	Correlation coefficient
Health	0.30
Consumption	0.30
Job	0.21
Family	
Partner	0.35
Children	0.31
Rest of family	0.24
Friendship	0.18
Personal	0.25

Table 9.13 Socio-economic indicators and domain satisfaction regression coefficient: R^2

Domain of life	R^2
Health	0.047
Consumption	0.147
Job	0.070
Family	
Partner	0.016
Children	0.022
Rest of family	0.021
Friendship	0.034
Personal	0.038

satisfaction in any domain is associated with greater SWB. However, correlation coefficients are relatively low; thus, even though all domains are important, none of them in itself is an important determinant of SWB. It seems that family satisfaction, at least with respect to satisfaction with partner and children, is important, followed by health and consumption.

Socio-economic indicators and satisfaction in the domains of life

A regression analysis was used to study the impact of a person's socio-economic position in each domain-of-life satisfaction. Eight regressions were estimated using the following specification:

$$D_i = \alpha_0 + \alpha_1 Y + \alpha_2 Soc_1 + \alpha_3 Soc_2 + \alpha_4 Soc_3 + \alpha_5 Serv$$

where D_i stands for satisfaction in domain of life i.

Table 9.13 shows the R^2 obtained from the regression analysis. It is noted that the socio-economic indicators have a mutual explanatory power only in the *consumption* domain of life; their impact in the other domains is negligible. These results suggest another explanation for the weak relationship between socio-economic indicators and well-being as declared by a person. While SWB depends on the situation in all domains of life, a person's socio-economic position has an impact in only one domain of life: *consumption*. Besides, *consumption* is not a central domain in explaining SWB (Rojas, 2006b). Consequently, it is possible to state that there is more in life than the standard of living.

Heterogeneity in the purpose of life: Conceptual referent theory

SWB refers to the degree to which a person appraises the overall quality of his/her life favourably (Veenhoven, 1984). A subjective judgement or evaluation of life as a whole is involved in this appraisal. The conceptual referent theory studies what is appraised when a person makes a judgement about his/her happiness. The conceptual referent theory also stresses the importance of heterogeneity; that is, the conceptual referent may vary considerably across persons.[21] This heterogeneity in the conceptual referent extends to the explanatory structure of SWB. Rojas (2006a) finds that the relationship between socio-economic variables and SWB is contingent on a person's conceptual referent. Thus income and other socio-economic variables are significant explanatory variables of SWB for only some people, while for others they are completely irrelevant.

A conceptual referent theory study

Rojas (2005, 2006a) studies the conceptual referent for happiness. What do people have in mind when they appraise their life as a whole in order to answer a typical subjective well-being question? Does everybody have the same conceptual referent?

A typology of conceptual referents was created on the basis of an extended survey of philosophical essays on happiness.[22] The typology defines eight conceptual referents for happiness. Each conceptual referent is associated with a group of philosophical schools of though.[23] Simple phrases associated with each conceptual referent were used in the survey to enquire about what people have in mind when appraising their lives and expressing an SWB level.[24] Once a person answered the happiness-level question, he/she was presented with eight phrases and asked to identify the phrase he/she relates to happiness in life.

Table 9.14 presents the distribution of the conceptual referent for hap-

Table 9.14 Conceptual referent for happiness sample distribution across referents

Conceptual referent	Associated phrase	%
Stoicism	Happiness is accepting things as they are	14.6
Virtue	Happiness is a sense of acting properly in our relations with others and with ourselves	8.2
Enjoyment	Happiness is to enjoy what I have got in life	14.0
Carpe diem	Happiness is to enjoy every moment in life; seize the day	11.6
Satisfaction	Happiness is being satisfied with what I have and what I am	24.2
Utopian	Happiness is an unreachable ideal we can only try to approach	7.7
Tranquillity	Happiness is in living a tranquil life, not looking beyond what is attainable	8.1
Fulfilment	Happiness is in fully developing our abilities.	11.7
Total		100.0

piness across the sample. It is noted that not everybody has the same referent when they respond to the happiness question. In the Mexican case, approximately one-quarter of the people in the survey related happiness to the concept of satisfaction ("happiness is being satisfied with what I have and what I am"). Following in importance are referents related to stoicism ("happiness is accepting things as they are") and enjoyment ("happiness is to enjoy what I have in life"). However, what really matters is not which referents are selected most often, but that there exists a large dispersion across persons in the conceptual referent for happiness. This finding proves the hypothesis of heterogeneity in the conceptual referent.

The existence of heterogeneity in the conceptual referent for happiness partially explains the weak relationship between socio-economic indicators and SWB. Rojas (2006a) studies this relationship, showing that the explanatory power of socio-economic indicators is contingent on a person's conceptual referent for happiness. In other words, for some people income and other socio-economic variables are significant explanatory variables and hence good proxies for SWB. However, for other persons these socio-economic variables are irrelevant in explaining SWB and are therefore not good proxies of SWB.

A common implicit assumption in most of the well-being literature is that everybody has the same conceptual referent for a happy life and there is universality in the explanatory factors of well-being. The conceptual referent theory of happiness stresses the idea of heterogeneity and

Table 9.15 Subjective well-being by conceptual referent for happiness: Average and standard deviation on a 1–7 scale

Conceptual referent	Average	Standard deviation
Stoicism	5.32	1.03
Virtue	5.41	0.89
Enjoyment	5.47	0.83
Carpe diem	5.25	0.92
Satisfaction	5.54	0.92
Utopian	5.19	0.96
Tranquillity	5.45	0.86
Fulfilment	5.35	1.09
Total	5.40	0.95

rejects the universality assumption; it states that the understanding of human well-being and its causes is better served if heterogeneity is recognized.

SWB by conceptual referent

The following question emerges once heterogeneity in the conceptual referent for happiness is recognized: "Is there a dominant conceptual referent?" A conceptual referent is said to be dominant if it is associated to greater SWB levels. Table 9.15 shows the average SWB (on a 1–7 scale) for people embracing every conceptual referent. It is clear that there is not a definite dominant conceptual referent. Conceptual referents such as *satisfaction, enjoyment, tranquillity* and *virtue* show slightly greater SWB averages; while referents such as *carpe diem* and *utopian* are a little bit lower. Thus, it can be stated that the nature of heterogeneity is horizontal rather than vertical; in other words, it is incorrect to argue in favour of a particular conceptual referent on the basis of the pursuit of greater happiness. Hence recognition, tolerance and even encouragement of heterogeneity in the conceptual referent for happiness seem to be an appropriate attitude.

Conceptual referent heterogeneity, SWB and socio-economic indicators

Rojas (2006a) shows that socio-economic variables are strongly related to SWB for those persons with conceptual referents such as *satisfaction* and *carpe diem*. However, the socio-economic variables are completely irrelevant for persons with conceptual referents such as *tranquillity* and *virtue*. Thus, it is not proper to use the same well-being proxies for everybody.

Conclusions

This investigation uses the SWB approach, well-being as it is described by the person herself, to measure the well-being of persons. The investigation finds out that SWB and socio-economic position are not only different concepts, but they are also not strongly correlated. In consequence, SWB indicators can make an important contribution to the study of well-being and poverty because they can provide new information beyond what traditional socio-economic indicators provide.

It is not correct to assess a person's well-being only on the basis of income and other socio-economic indicators. It is clear that human well-being depends on many factors beyond the ordinary standard-of-living indicators, such as income, consumption, wealth, socio-economic position and access to some public services. Thus income (and its rate of growth over time) must be considered as one of the many alternatives available for increasing well-being, and its capacity to generate well-being is a matter of empirical corroboration rather than of presumption. The effectiveness of income to generate well-being, in comparison to other alternative means, must also be empirically studied.

This investigation studied three potential explanations for the existence of a not-so-strong relationship between well-being and the socio-economic indicators which are traditionally used as its proxies: the perceptions that people have about their objective socio-economic conditions; the role of heterogeneity in life purposes, which heterogeneity extends to the sources of well-being; and the fact that well-being depends on satisfaction in many domains of life, not just on the consumption domain.

There are discrepancies between the information provided by objective socio-economic indicators and a person's perception of his/her socio-economic condition. For example, many people who are considered poor according to conventional indicators do not consider themselves as such. If the understanding of human well-being is a main objective, then it is necessary to go beyond the apparent neutrality of objective indicators to recognize and study the large heterogeneity that exists in human perception. It seems that people employ a different concept of poverty than economists. There may be many reasons for this. For example, a person may evaluate his/her situation on the basis of a relative rather than absolute position; one may also consider other aspects of life that are not considered in the traditional definition of poverty; and it is possible that not everyone evaluates their own situation on the basis of the same life purpose.

A person is much more than an economic agent. The construct of *domains of life* constitutes an attempt to study the complexity of a person's life. SWB is related to a person's situation in all the domains of life. Independent of the demarcation used, the recognition of multidimensionality in human domains of life allows for a better understanding of human well-being. Thus another explanation for the weak relationship between socio-economic indicators and the personal declaration of well-being is that while SWB depends on the situation in all domains of life, a person's socio-economic position is related to just a few domains. In consequence, it can be stated that there is more in life than the standard of living.

It is common in the literature to assume that everybody has the same life purpose. However, the conceptual referent theory of happiness stresses the idea of heterogeneity and rejects the universality assumption. This heterogeneity extends to the explanatory factors of SWB. The importance of a person's socio-economic position in his/her well-being is contingent on his/her conceptual referent. Income and other socio-economic variables could be significant explanatory variables, and good proxies, of well-being for some people, but not for everybody. For other people these socio-economic variables are irrelevant in explaining SWB and thus are not good proxies of well-being.

The empirical findings from this investigation suggest that the understanding and abatement of poverty would be better served by a concept of well-being which is based on the wholeness and complexity of human beings, and that SWB indicators do provide useful information in this respect.

Notes

1. These well-being concepts are based on an analytical theory of knowledge, which compartmentalizes the way of understanding human beings and generates partial and incomplete knowledge about their well-being (see Capra, 1983).
2. Thus SWB avoids the subjectivity, the arbitrariness and the paternalistic approach of the so-called objective indicators of well-being.
3. Fuentes and Rojas (2001) find that people may underestimate or overestimate the impact that different factors have in their SWB. Loewenstein and Schkade (1999) also argue that people have difficulties in estimating the well-being impact of some actions. Thus it is not convenient to ask people to assess which factors contribute the most to their well-being and what changes they would benefit from the most. If a person takes decisions on the basis of his/her (wrongly) estimated well-being impact, then it is incorrect to use a person's behaviour to reach well-being conclusions. Therefore, the revealed preference theory has limitations as an inferential tool to assess human well-being.
4. In the psychological literature the SWB concept is also associated with a person's psychological health.
5. It is common within economics to reject the direct question approach on the basis of the revealed preference theory, which states that well-being can be studied from a person's actions. For a critique on the former and a justification for the latter see van Praag and

Frijters (1997). Kahneman, Diener and Schwarz (1999: x) state that "questions can be raised about the accuracy of people's predictions of their future pleasures and pains, and about their intuitive understanding of the rules of hedonic psychology ... The evidence available suggests that people may not have the ability to predict their future tastes and hedonic experiences with the accuracy that the economic model requires."

6. The research project also has information on the life satisfaction approach; however, it is not used in this chapter.
7. For a discussion of SWB measures see Cummins (1999).
8. A logarithmic specification has a better goodness of fit and increases the significance of income with respect to a linear specification.
9. There are no previous studies going beyond income to include other socio-economic indicators such as possession of durable goods, access to public services and so on.
10. The states considered are Oaxaca, Veracruz, Puebla, Tlaxcala and the state of Mexico. The survey was applied in both rural and urban areas.
11. Household income is used as a proxy of income. Other proxies such as personal income and per capita household income were also calculated and used, with relatively similar conclusions.
12. The survey also enquired about happiness using a 1–10 scale. Results using the 1–10 scale do not differ substantially from the results from the 1–7 scale, which are shown in this chapter.
13. Similar results are obtained when using other proxies of socio-economic position such as Soc_2 and Soc_3.
14. Some authors have expressed doubts on the issue of causality. Is it because a better socio-economic position leads to an increase in SWB, or is it because people with greater SWB tend to achieve better socio-economic positions? See Argyle (2002) and Diener and Oishi (2000).
15. A logarithm specification has better goodness of fit. See Fuentes and Rojas (2001) and Rojas (2006b) on the issue of specification.
16. Results do not differ substantially when using household income or socio-economic position.
17. Regression analysis shows that there is a stronger relationship between SWB and perception variables of socio-economic position than between SWB and socio-economic variables. Hence a person's perception of his/her own socio-economic position, rather than the socio-economic position itself, has a much greater capacity to explain SWB.
18. For an explanation of the domains of life and their relationship to happiness see van Praag, Frijters and Ferrer-i-Carbonell (2000, 2002).
19. A variable replacement technique was used in this case. See Hair et al. (1999).
20. Rojas (2006b) studies the impact of each domain of life on SWB.
21. The reasons for heterogeneity in the conceptual referent for happiness need further examination. Why do very similar people have different conceptual referents? Is there a role played by socio-demographic and economic variables? Is it a matter of culture or family background? Nevertheless, the existence of heterogeneity in human values, ideas and conceptual referents should not be a surprise to any human being. Rojas (2005) studies the relationship between the conceptual referent of happiness and socio-demographic and economic variables.
22. The author is grateful to Lourdes Rodríguez for his work in the construction of the philosophical survey (2001). Being a topic so widely discussed, this survey cannot claim to be exhaustive.
23. One of the main advantages in the study of happiness is that it is a common word in many cultures. People easily understand the word; common wisdom talks about what happiness is, about true and deceiving happiness and about how to be happy. The sub-

ject is central in both romantic and tragic songs; it is also common in movies and soap operas, as well as in poetry, literature, plays and even in fairy-tales. Being such an important aim, it attracts a lot of human attention and has also attracted philosophers everywhere and at every time. Thousands of pages have been written by philosophers about what happiness is and the proper way to pursue it. Being a main topic of reflection and debate for almost 3,000 years, it is no surprise that philosophers do not agree on what happiness is and how to achieve it.

24. It was a difficult task to translate the intricate philosophical arguments into simple phrases people can understand and relate to. A focus-group approach was used to design simple phrases that were easily understood by common people while keeping an essence of the philosophical school of thought.

REFERENCES

Argyle, M. (1999) "Causes and Correlates of Happiness", in D. Kahneman, E. Diener and N. Schwarz, eds, *Well-being: The Foundations of Hedonic Psychology*, New York: Russell Sage Foundation Publications.

────── (2002) *The Psychology of Happiness*, London and New York: Routledge.

Brickman, P., D. Coates and R. Janoff-Bulman (1978) "Lottery Winners and Accident Victims: Is Happiness Relative?", *Journal of Personality and Social Psychology* 36(8): 917–927.

Capra, F. (1983) *The Turning Point: Science, Society and the Rising Culture*, New York: Bantam Books.

Clark, A. E. and A. J. Oswald (1994) "Subjective Well-being and Unemployment", *Economic Journal* 104: 648–659.

Cummins, R. (1997) "Comprehensive Quality of Life Scale", in *Adult Manual*, 5th edn, Melbourne: Deakin University.

────── (1999) *Directory of Instruments to Measure Quality of Life and Cognate Areas*, Melbourne: School of Psychology, Deakin University.

Di Tella, R., R. J. MacCulloch and A. J. Oswald (2001) "Preferences Over Inflation and Unemployment: Evidence from Surveys of Subjective Well-being", *American Economic Review* 91: 335–341.

Diener, E. (2002) "Will Money Increase Subjective Well-being?", *Social Indicators Research* 57: 119–169.

Diener, E. and C. Diener (1996) "Most People are Happy", *Journal of Psychological Science* 7: 181–185.

Diener, E. and S. Oishi (2000) "Money and Happiness: Income and Subjective Well-being Across Nations", in E. Diener and E. Suh, eds, *Subjective Wellbeing Across Cultures*, Cambridge, Mass.: MIT Press, pp. 185–218.

Diener, E. and E. Suh (1997) "Measuring Quality of Life: Economic, Social and Subjective Indicators", *Social Indicators Research* 40: 189–216.

Diener, E., E. Sandvik, L. Seidlitz and M. Diener (1993) "The Relationship between Income and Subjective Well-being: Relative or Absolute?", *Social Indicators Research* 28: 195–223.

Douthitt, R. A., M. MacDonald and R. Mullis (1992) "The Relationship between

Measures of Subjective and Economic Well-being: A New Look", *Social Indicators Research* 26: 407–422.

Easterlin, R. A. (1974) "Does Economic Growth Improve the Human Lot? Some Empirical Evidence", in P. A. David and M. W. Reder, eds, *Nations and Households in Economic Growth*, New York: Academic Press.

——— (1995) "Will Raising the Incomes of All Increase the Happiness of All?", *Journal of Economic Behavior and Organization* 27(1): 35–47.

——— (2001) "Subjective Well-being and Economic Analysis: A Brief Introduction", *Journal of Economic Behavior and Organization* 45(3): 225–226.

Ferrer-i-Carbonell, A. (2002) "Subjective Questions to Measure Welfare and Well-being: A Survey", Discussion Paper TI2002-020/3, Tinbergen Institute, Amsterdam.

Frey, B. and A. Stutzer (2000) "Subjective Well-being, Economy and Institutions", *Economic Journal* 110: 918–938.

Fuentes, N. and M. Rojas (2001) "Economic Theory and Subjective Well-being: Mexico", *Social Indicators Research* 53: 289–314.

Hagerty, M. (1999) "Unifying Livability and Comparison Theory: Cross-national Time-series Analysis of Life Satisfaction", *Social Indicators Research* 47(3): 343–356.

Hair, J., R. Anderson, R. Tatham and W. Black (1999) *Análisis Multivariante*, Englewood Cliffs, N.J.: Prentice Hall.

Heady, B. (1991) "An Economic Model of Subjective Well-being: Integrating Economic and Psychological Theories", *Social Indicators Research* 28: 97–116.

Kahneman, D., E. Diener and N. Schwarz, eds (1999) *Well-being: The Foundations of Hedonic Psychology*, New York: Russell Sage Foundation Publications.

Lin, Yutang (1940) *La Importancia de Vivir*, Buenos Aires: Editorial Sudamericana.

Loewenstein, G. and D. Schkade (1999) "Wouldn't It Be Nice? Predicting Future Feelings", in D. Kahneman, E. Diener and N. Schwarz, eds, *Well-being: The Foundations of Hedonic Psychology*, New York: Russell Sage Foundation Publications.

McBride, M. (2001) "Relative-income Effects on Subjective Well-being in the Cross Section", *Journal of Economic Behavior and Organization* 45: 251–278.

Meadow, H. L., J. Metzer, D. R. Rahtz and J. Sirgy (1992) "A Life Satisfaction Measure Based on Judgement Theory", *Social Indicators Research* 26: 23–59.

Michalos, A. (1985) "Multiple Discrepancy Theory", *Social Indicators Research* 16: 347–413.

Mullis, R. (1992) "Measures of Economic Well-being as Predictors of Psychological Well-being", *Social Indicators Research* 26: 119–135.

Oswald, A. J. (1997) "Subjective Well-being and Economic Performance", *Economic Journal* 197: 1815–1831.

Parducci, A. (1968) "The Relativism of Absolute Judgments", *Scientific American* 219: 84–90.

——— (1984) "Perceptual and Judgmental Relativity", in V. Sarris and A. Parducci, eds, *Perspectives in Psychological Experimentation: Toward the Year 2000*, Mahwah, N.J.: Lawrence Erlbaum Associates.

────── (1995) *Happiness, Pleasure, and Judgment: The Contextual Theory and Its Applications*, Mahwah, N.J.: Lawrence Erlbaum Associates.

Pradhan, M. and M. Ravallion (2000) "Measuring Poverty Using Qualitative Perceptions of Consumption Adequacy", *Review of Economics and Statistics* 82(3): 462–471.

Rodríguez, L. (2001) "Bienestar e Ingreso: Un Estudio sobre el Concepto de Felicidad", unpublished licentiate thesis, Universidad de las Américas, Puebla.

Rojas, M. (2005) "A Conceptual-referent Theory of Happiness: Heterogeneity and its Consequences", *Social Indicators Research* 74(2): 261–294.

────── (2006a) "Income and Happiness: A Conceptual-referent-theory Explanation", *Journal of Economic Psychology*, forthcoming.

────── (2006b) "The Complexity of Well-being: A Life-satisfaction Conception and a Domains-of-life Approach", in I. Gough and A. McGregor, eds, *Researching Well-being in Developing Countries*, Cambridge: Cambridge University Press.

Rojas, M., N. Fuentes and Z. Oplotnik (2001) "Economic Growth and Prosperity", *Our Economy* 47(1/2): 29–43.

van Praag, B. M. and P. Frijters (1997) "Choice Behaviour and Verbal Behaviour: A Critical Assessment of their Relevance for Practical Policy", Discussion Paper TI1997-119/1, Tinbergen Institute, Amsterdam.

van Praag, B. M., P. Frijters and A. Ferrer-i-Carbonell (2000) "A Structural Model of Well-being", Discussion Paper TI2000-053/3, Tinbergen Institute, Amsterdam.

────── (2002) "The Anatomy of Subjective Well-being", Discussion Paper TI2002-022/3, Tinbergen Institute, Amsterdam.

Veenhoven, R. (1984) *Conditions of Happiness*, Boston, Mass.: Kluwer Academic.

────── (1988) "The Utility of Happiness", *Social Indicators Research* 20: 333–354.

────── (1993) "Happiness in Nations: Subjective Appreciation of Life in 56 Nations, 1946–1992", RISBO Studies in Social and Cultural Transformation, Erasmus University, Rotterdam.

────── (1997) "Quality-of-life in Individualistic Society: A Comparison of 43 Nations in the Early 1990s", *Social Indicators Research* 48(2): 91–125.

Veenhoven, R., C. DenBuitelaar and H. de Heer (1995) *World Database of Happiness. Correlates of Happiness*, Rotterdam: Department of Social Sciences, Erasmus University.

10
International inequality in human development dimensions

Mark McGillivray

Introduction

The human development index (HDI) is without doubt the best known and most widely reported multidimensional national well-being measure. Combining life expectancy, adult literacy, the gross combined school enrolment ratio and the logarithm of PPP GDP per capita, the HDI first appeared in the *Human Development Report 1990* (UNDP, 1990). HDI data have subsequently been published annually, with index values now being available for more than 170 countries, and the index has generated a vast literature. Researchers and policy-makers alike have made extensive use of the index, despite its well-documented shortcomings. Most attention has been given to various aspects of national well-being achievement at single points in time, through the examination of HDI values or rankings. Inter-temporal comparisons in HDI values have also been made. A relatively small subset of the first group of studies has looked at inter-country HDI inequality (Ram, 1992; Pillarisetti, 1997; McGillivray and Pillarisetti, 2004).

The preceding studies provide estimates of HDI inequality for various years using a number of inequality measures. While this information is important and policy-relevant, it needs to be remembered that this index is a statistical construct providing summary information on well-being. Interventions designed to reduce HDI inequality among countries must focus on its component variables. Yet inter-country inequalities in these components have received little or no attention in the literature on multidimensional well-being. Looking at inequalities in these variables also side-steps some of the criticisms of the HDI, in particular the weighting and scaling of each variable.

This chapter seeks to address the above-mentioned omission in the literature on multidimensional well-being. It reports estimates of the inequality of the HDI's four component variables for more than 170 countries during the period 1997–2001. The estimates are obtained using six inequality indices, including the Gini coefficient, the squared coefficient of variation and two Theil measures. Each measure is population weighted. By reporting inequality in this variable and the HDI as a whole, the chapter updates the work of McGillivray and Pillarisetti (2004), who report inequality estimates for the period 1992–1998.

This chapter consists of a further three sections. The second section outlines the inequality concept under consideration and the inequality measures employed. The third section outlines the data used and provides estimates of the inequality of these variables, together with that of the HDI and PPP GDP per capita. The fourth section concludes, highlighting the policy relevance of the results.

Inequality concept and measures

Milanovic (2002) distinguishes between three types of global income inequality: inequality between countries in terms of GDP per capita; inequality between countries in terms of GDP per capita weighted by population size; and inequality among world citizens, irrespective of the country in which they live. These concepts can also be applied to well-being indicators other than GDP per capita. Type III is ruled out for this chapter given that the HDI is not applied at the level of individuals. Type II inequality is preferred, given that country-level HDI data are used. As Firebaugh (1999) and others have argued, a nation's contribution to world inequality should be relative to its population size. Large countries like China and India should have a greater impact on an inequality measure than smaller ones like Luxembourg or the Solomon Islands. Thus all measures outlined below are weighted by country population size.

It has become commonplace in studies of inequality to report results from the application of a range of inequality indices. These indices have different properties and can yield different insights. This chapter follows that approach, using a number of inequality measures. The following measures are used: Theil-Bourguignon measure (TB), Theil Entropy measure (L), the Wolfson exponential measure (W), the Gini coefficient (G), the squared coefficient of variation (CV) and the variance of logarithms measure (VL). These measures may be written as follows, for the rth well-being measure.

$$TB_r = \sum_{i=1}^{n} p_i \left(\frac{p_i}{H_{r,i}}\right),$$

$$L_r = \sum_{i=1}^{n} H_{r,i} \ln\left(\frac{H_{r,i}}{p_{r,i}}\right),$$

$$W_r = \sum_{i=1}^{n} p_i e^{-h_{r,i}/\mu_{h,r}},$$

$$G_r = \sum_{i=1}^{n} p_i \left(\frac{h_{r,i}}{\mu_{h,r}}\right)(q_{r,i} - Q_{r,i}),$$

$$CV_r = \sum_{i=1}^{n} p_i \left(\frac{h_{r,i}}{\mu_{h,r}} - 1\right)^2 \quad \text{and}$$

$$VL_r = \sum_{i=1}^{n} p_i \left(\ln\frac{h_{r,i}}{\mu_{h,r}} - E\left[\ln\frac{h_{r,i}}{\mu_{h,r}}\right]\right)^2.$$

where p_i is the ratio of the population of country i to total population among n countries, $H_{r,i}$ is country i's share of the world value of the rth human development indicator, $h_{r,i}$ is the rth human development indicator for country i, $\mu_{h,r}$ is the mean value of indicator r among n countries, $q_{r,i}$ is the proportion of population among n countries that has lower human development achievement in indicator r than country i and $Q_{r,i}$ is the proportion of population among n countries that has higher human development achievement in indicator r than country i. The formulae for the above measures are taken from Ram (1992), Wolfson (1994), Pillarisetti (1997), Firebaugh (1999) and Lambert (2001).

A brief comment on the ordering principle, in this case $h_{r,i}$, is warranted. In previous studies of HDI inequality (Ram, 1992; Pillarisetti, 1997; McGillivray and Pillarisetti, 2004) the ordering principle is not $h_{r,i}$ but $h_{r,i}$ multiplied by i's population size. These studies have in essence followed the approach typically used in studies of the distribution of incomes by household within countries, which uses total family income rather than average family income. This approach would appear to be questionable in the context of inter-country human development or well-being comparisons.

Data and results

The main variables under consideration, as mentioned, are the four components of the HDI. Life expectancy is intended as a measure of the health dimension to well-being. Adult literacy and the school enrolment ratio are intended to capture the knowledge dimension, while the logarithm of PPP GDP per capita is intended to capture material standards of living not captured by the other dimensions (UNDP, 2004). Also considered is inequality in the HDI and in (non-logarithmic values of) PPP GDP per capita.

All data were taken from the *HDR*s for the years 1999 to 2003 (UNDP, 1999–2003). There is usually a two-year lag between the year of publication and the year to which the data relate. The data relate, therefore, to the years 1997 to 2001.[1] Data from earlier periods are not used as the HDI from 1999 is not compatible with those for earlier periods owing to changes in the index's design. The sample for each year consists of 174 countries ($n = 174$, therefore). This sample comprises all countries for which data are available. It is tempting to refer to this as world inequality, though emphasizing that this is a rather loose usage of the term "world" as it does not take into account inequality within nations, only between them (Ram, 1992).

A further comment is required prior to turning to the results. While the aim of this chapter is not to critique the HDI and its components, one should not be blind to the various limitations identified in the literature. Relevant studies include McGillivray (1991), McGillivray and White (1993), Streeten (1995), Hicks (1997), Ivanova, Arcelus and Srinivasan (1998), Noorbakhsh (1998a, 1998b) and Morse (2003). Some of these limitations, and the various caveats emerging from them, should not be forgotten when interpreting the results reported below. Among the various criticisms are the weighting of components, high correlations among components, the scaling of components, the dominance of the income components, the treatment of income and the choice and interpretation of components.

The results are reported in tables 10.1 and 10.2. Table 10.1 shows inequalities in what might be described as the raw HDI component variables. As described elsewhere (see chap. 8, this volume), the HDI variables are capped and scaled prior to being weighted and summed to form the index. The raw component variables are neither capped nor

Table 10.1 International inequality in human development dimensions

	Life expectancy						Adult literacy						School enrolment					
	TB_r	T_r	W_r	G_r	CV_r	VL_r	TB_r	T_r	W_r	G_r	CV_r	VL_r	TB_r	T_r	W_r	G_r	CV_r	VL_r
1997	1.639	1.729	0.364	0.065	0.015	0.018	1.719	1.764	0.392	0.138	0.064	0.093	1.664	1.647	0.372	0.142	0.066	0.087
1998	1.638	1.725	0.369	0.065	0.015	0.018	1.712	1.753	0.395	0.133	0.059	0.083	1.667	1.742	0.379	0.149	0.072	0.092
1999	1.635	1.733	0.363	0.068	0.016	0.019	1.711	1.770	0.389	0.130	0.056	0.080	1.664	1.748	0.374	0.148	0.071	0.093
2000	1.631	1.733	0.363	0.068	0.017	0.019	1.713	1.778	0.391	0.128	0.055	0.078	1.666	1.743	0.374	0.149	0.072	0.094
2001	1.631	1.735	0.363	0.072	0.019	0.024	1.711	1.776	0.391	0.126	0.054	0.078	1.701	1.752	0.387	0.140	0.065	0.079
1997–2001	1.634	1.727	0.364	0.067	0.016	0.020	1.713	1.764	0.391	0.131	0.057	0.085	1.672	1.741	0.376	0.144	0.067	0.089

	PPP GDP per capita (log)						HDI						PPP GDP per capita					
	TB_r	T_r	W_r	G_r	CV_r	VL_r	TB_r	T_r	W_r	G_r	CV_r	VI_r	TB_r	T_r	W_r	G_r	CV_r	VL_r
1997	1.671	1.721	0.376	0.065	0.014	0.014	1.683	1.763	0.380	0.122	0.048	0.057	2.337	2.243	0.573	0.482	1.172	1.003
1998	1.666	1.717	0.380	0.064	0.014	0.014	1.677	1.759	0.383	0.121	0.047	0.056	2.310	2.227	0.575	0.477	1.155	0.963
1999	1.666	1.733	0.375	0.064	0.014	0.014	1.675	1.772	0.377	0.122	0.047	0.056	2.303	2.240	0.564	0.480	1.151	0.982
2000	1.663	1.737	0.374	0.064	0.014	0.014	1.673	1.774	0.377	0.120	0.047	0.055	2.310	2.275	0.566	0.477	1.140	0.987
2001	1.663	1.731	0.375	0.062	0.013	0.013	1.676	1.776	0.379	0.119	0.045	0.054	2.301	2.289	0.565	0.458	1.078	0.931
1997–2001	1.665	1.724	0.375	0.064	0.014	0.014	1.676	1.764	0.378	0.121	0.047	0.058	2.306	2.246	0.566	0.474	1.135	0.996

scaled. Also shown in table 10.1 are inequalities in the HDI and (non-logarithmic) values of PPP GDP per capita. The most striking result is the similarity in the inequalities revealed by the HDI and each of its component variables. Consider the results based on variable averages for the five years under consideration. Based on the Wolfson (1994) indices, for example, the HDI yields an inequality index value of 0.378. Those yielded by its raw components vary from 0.364 to 0.391 in the respective cases of life expectancy and adult literacy. Similarly, the Gini coefficient for the five-year averages of the raw components varies from 0.064 to 0.144 for the logarithm of GDP per capita and school enrolment, respectively. The Gini coefficient for the average values of the HDI is 0.121. PPP GDP per capita (non-logarithmic) yields substantially higher inequality index values. The Gini coefficient, for example, for 1997–2001 average GDP per capita values is 0.474. That the HDI exhibits quite low inequality, and various measures of income per capita much higher inequality, has been also been reported in previous studies (Ram, 1992; Pillarisetti, 1997; McGillivray and Pillarisetti, 2004).

The results for per capita GDP are especially interesting. Most previous research has generally tended to compare inequalities in non-transformed values of this variable with various indicators, including the HDI, and has reported much higher inequalities in the former compared with all variables in the latter group. It is totally obvious that taking the log of a variable will result in it exhibiting lower inequality. It is also reasonably obvious that income per capita prior to a logarithmic transformation will display higher inequality than life expectancy, adult literacy and school enrolment. It is an upwardly continuous variable in the sense that it has no statistical upper limit. This is not the case with most other development indicators. Life expectancy has an upper biological limit, and adult literacy and school enrolment are expressed as percentages and as such have an upper theoretical limit of 100. Many countries are as close to reaching these limits as one could reasonably expect. But it is not obvious that the log of PPP GDP per capita will exhibit strikingly similar levels of inequality as a number of non-economic (or income-based) components, as reported in table 10.1. Moreover, if the results of table 10.1 are any indication, it might be concluded that using any one of a number of non-economic measures of well-being, or summary measures containing economic and non-economic variables, would produce largely the same picture regarding inter-country inequalities.

Results for the transformed components, as they appear in the HDI, are shown in table 10.2. The interest here is whether the same sorts of results, as reported in table 10.1, hold after these transformations, and therefore whether the transformations (capping and scaling) alter inequality levels. The answer to the first of these questions is "yes", as ba-

Table 10.2 International inequality in transformed human development dimensions

	Life expectancy						Adult literacy					
	TB_r	T_r	W_r	G_r	CV_r	VL_r	TB_r	T_r	W_r	G_r	CV_r	VL_r
1997	1.644	1.771	0.365	0.105	0.039	0.056	1.719	1.764	0.392	0.138	0.064	0.093
1998	1.643	1.767	0.370	0.104	0.039	0.056	1.712	1.753	0.395	0.133	0.059	0.083
1999	1.646	1.749	0.366	0.108	0.041	0.058	1.717	1.791	0.391	0.129	0.056	0.080
2000	1.634	1.774	0.363	0.110	0.043	0.061	1.713	1.778	0.391	0.127	0.055	0.078
2001	1.638	1.788	0.364	0.116	0.050	0.081	1.711	1.776	0.391	0.125	0.054	0.078
1997–2001	1.640	1.775	0.365	0.108	0.042	0.062	1.714	1.768	0.391	0.130	0.057	0.085

	Gross school enrolment						PPP GDP per capita (log)					
	TB_r	T_r	W_r	G_r	CV_r	VL_r	TB_r	T_r	W_r	G_r	CV_r	VL_r
1997	1.664	1.747	0.372	0.142	0.066	0.087	1.722	1.785	0.394	0.146	0.072	0.076
1998	1.665	1.743	0.378	0.148	0.071	0.091	1.711	1.784	0.396	0.143	0.069	0.073
1999	1.675	1.778	0.376	0.145	0.068	0.092	1.719	1.837	0.393	0.024	0.066	0.074
2000	1.664	1.745	0.373	0.011	0.070	0.093	1.705	1.808	0.389	0.024	0.066	0.071
2001	1.702	1.765	0.388	0.137	0.062	0.078	1.703	1.803	0.389	0.134	0.062	0.067
1997–2001	1.672	1.751	0.376	0.143	0.065	0.087	1.711	1.799	0.391	0.140	0.066	0.074

Table 10.3 Correlations between the HDI and its component variables

	Life expectancy	Adult literacy	Gross enrolment	PPP GDP per capita (log)
1997	0.934	0.882	0.882	0.915
1998	0.935	0.887	0.887	0.930
1999	0.932	0.883	0.883	0.926
2000	0.925	0.872	0.881	0.923
2001	0.922	0.857	0.861	0.912
1997–2001	0.933	0.881	0.888	0.926

sically the same general picture emerges. This is notwithstanding mixed answers to the second question. The transformations to the raw HDI components largely leave inequality levels unchanged in the case of adult literacy and gross school enrolment, although very slight declines in inequality in the former can be observed. Slight increases in inequality in life expectancy and the logarithm of PPP GDP per capita resulting from the transformations can be observed. It must, however, be emphasized that in most cases the transformations only result in slight changes in observed inequalities, hence the answer to the first of the above-mentioned questions.

Ram (1992) and Pillarisetti (1997) observe that one would expect similar levels of inequality between the HDI and other variables if they are highly correlated. While noting that a high simple correlation coefficient between two variables is a necessary but not sufficient condition for them having similar inequalities (it is necessary and sufficient if accompanied by a slope coefficient between the variables of close to 1.0), a comment in passing on the statistical association between the HDI and its components would appear warranted. Simple correlation coefficients between the HDI and each of its raw component variables are shown in table 10.3. All coefficients are rather high, typically either just above or just below 0.90.

Conclusion

This chapter has examined inter-country inequality in the HDI and each of its four component variables. A range of inequality indices was used for this purpose. Data for more than 170 countries for the period 1997–2001 reveal strikingly similar inequalities in the HDI and its four components, consistent with the quite high correlations between these variables. Just as any one of these variables paints a similar picture about inter-country well-being levels, so too do they about inter-country inequalities in well-being. Indeed, they tell virtually the same story about inequalities, so much so that researchers are justified in looking at either the index as a whole or any one of its components. From the perspective of policy interventions, it follows that there is no obvious signal as to which component should be targeted if overall HDI inequality reductions are the objective. The contribution of each component to inequality in the HDI will be a function of that component's inequality and its mean value. Each has rather similar means given their transformations. Some other criteria or criterion should therefore be used in determining which variable to target. If we treat each as equally worthy, in terms of the human development dimension they represent, then a possible criterion should be the relative extent to which they can be influenced by policy interventions.

Note

1. Both the 2001 and 2002 *HDR*s provide 1999 gross school enrolment data only, but for different sample sizes. As a consequence, in tables 10.1 and 10.2 the statistics reported for this variable for 2000 actually relate to 1999.

REFERENCES

Firebaugh, G. (1999) "Empirics of World Income Inequality", *American Journal of Sociology* 104: 1597–1630.

Hicks, D. A. (1997) "The Inequality Adjusted Human Development Index: A Constructive Proposal", *World Development* 25: 1283–1298.

Ivanova, I., F. J. Arcelus and G. Srinivasan (1998) "An Assessment of the Measurement Properties of the Human Development Index", *Social Indicators Research* 46: 157–179.

Lambert, P. (2001) *The Distribution and Redistribution of Income*, Manchester: Manchester University Press.

McGillivray, M. (1991) "The Human Development Index: Yet Another Redundant Composite Development Indicator?", *World Development* 19: 1451–1460.

McGillivray, M. and H. White (1993) "Measuring Development? The UNDP's Human Development Index", *Journal of International Development* 5: 183–192.

McGillivray, M. and J. R. Pillarisetti (2004) "International Inequality in Human Well-being", *Journal of International Development* 16: 563–574.

Milanovic, B. (2002) *Worlds Apart: Inter-national and World Inequality 1950–2000*, Washington, D.C.: World Bank.

Morse, S. (2003) "For Better or for Worse, Till the Human Development Index Do Us Part?", *Ecological Economics* 45: 281–296.

Noorbakhsh, F. (1998a) "A Modified Human Development Index", *World Development* 26: 517–528.

―― (1998b) "A Human Development Index: Some Technical Issues and Alternative Indices", *Journal of International Development* 10: 589–605.

Pillarisetti, J. R. (1997) "An Empirical Note on Inequality in the World Development Indicators", *Applied Economics Letters* 4: 145–147.

Ram, R. (1992) "International Inequalities in Human Development and Real Income", *Economics Letters* 38: 351–354.

Streeten, P. (1995) "Human Development: The Debate about the Index", *International Social Science Journal* 47: 25–37.

UNDP (1990–2004) *Human Development Report*, New York: Oxford University Press.

Wolfson, M. C. (1994) "When Inequalities Diverge", *American Economic Review, Papers and Proceedings* 84: 353–358.

11
Assessing well-being using hierarchical needs

Matthew Clarke

Introduction

Determining whether well-being in developing countries has improved is an important multidisciplinary task. Numerical measures of well-being are becoming increasingly common and numerous methods of measurement now exist. This chapter provides a systematic empirical study of well-being in South-East Asia.

Common measures of well-being include single representative indicators such as GDP per capita, life expectancy or literacy rates, or composite indicators using various combinations of these, such as the human development index (HDI) (UNDP, 2003) or the physical quality of life index (PQLI) (Morris, 1979). This chapter argues that widely accepted measures of well-being, both representative (that is, GDP per capita) and composite (that is, the HDI) fail to capture fully actual movements of well-being within nations across time. The weaknesses of both are well known within the literature (see for example McGillivray, 1991; Clarke and Islam, 2004). Therefore it is important that well-being measures reflect a wide spectrum of human needs. One way to represent this multidimensionality is to consider hierarchical human needs. Whilst some relative reporting in terms of well-being in the form of hierarchical needs has been undertaken (Daly, 1996), the empirical implication of this approach to determine and measure well-being in terms of hierarchical needs is limited.

Improving well-being within this approach requires progressive satisfaction of hierarchical needs. This hierarchical approach is underpinned by a rigorous psychological theory of human motivation (Maslow, 1970), where hierarchical human needs are classified into various categories, including basic, safety, belonging and self-esteem needs. The highest level of need is self-actualization. Becoming self-actualized is predicated on the attainment or fulfilment of the lower-level needs, thus the concept of self-actualization can be considered analogous with Sen's concept of capabilities (Sen, 1985, 1987a, 1987b) and Doyal and Gough's (1991) concept of social and critical participation. Within this chapter therefore, well-being is defined as a function of the extent to which society facilitates the attainment or fulfilment of the ultimate hierarchical need: self-actualization.

It is possible to operationalize this approach by identifying outcomes and indicators that represent or correspond to the four lower levels of needs upon which the achievement of self-actualization is predicated. Eight indicators have been chosen to reflect these four hierarchical categories. A composite indicator of these eight indicators will be calculated using an approach similar to that of the HDI. Weights will also be assigned to the different levels within this hierarchy to reflect the shift from minimally adequate standards to higher levels of well-being within nations. This chapter empirically applies this new measure of well-being to eight South-East Asian countries for the period 1985–2000. The countries surveyed are Cambodia, Indonesia, Lao PDR, Malaysia, the Philippines, Singapore, Thailand and Viet Nam. In addition, results for Australia are provided as a comparative benchmark.

The results of this new approach show a general increase of well-being based on the attainment of hierarchical needs recorded across the region over the past 16 years. This chapter concludes that policy-makers must consider multidimensional human needs and motivation when seeking to improve well-being through economic and social development activities.

The chapter is divided into six sections. The second section introduces Maslow's framework of hierarchy of needs before the third section discusses how this approach could be utilized to measure well-being. The fourth section discusses how this new approach is operationalized. The findings of this new approach to well-being measurement based on the fulfilment of hierarchical needs are reviewed in the fifth section, and the final section summarizes the chapter.

Maslow's hierarchical framework

A universally accepted definition of well-being does not exist. However, it is possible to list various components that must be considered when developing a measure of well-being. For example, Nussbaum (2000) identified emotions, bodily integrity and health, social basis of self-respect, freedom from discrimination and control over environment, and Doyal and Gough (1991) identified physical security, economic security, opportunities to participate and cognitive and emotional capacity.

Maslow's (1970) hierarchy of human needs and motivation theory was initially proposed to explain human motivation. It was a psychological theory focusing on workplace behaviour rather than a theory of well-being. Within the *hierarchy of human needs*, human well-being is bounded by the fulfilment of a given set of ascending needs that can be divided into five categories (from lowest to highest): basic, safety, belonging, self-esteem and self-actualization (Maslow, 1970). Human effort is exerted to achieve each level. The primary needs that must be fulfilled are those basic needs such as food, shelter and water. Until these needs are fulfilled, higher needs are not considered. However, once these needs are achieved, consideration moves to the next tier of needs. The ultimate need to which humans aspire is self-actualization. All behaviour is therefore motivated by the desire to fulfil one's own potential.

Maslow's theory of human need and motivation is suited to underpin a measure of well-being, as it provides an explanation of what is required to improve life outcomes. This hypothesis argues that the fundamental or ultimate needs of all human beings do not differ nearly as much as do their conscious everyday desires. A measure of well-being that focuses on these fundamental needs can be applied across societies and time as fundamental needs are universal, whereas daily desires differ both intertemporally and interspatially. This approach is not dissimilar to that presented in Doyal and Gough (1991) and Nussbaum (1992, 1993, 2000). Whilst local cultures may determine specific roads to achieve these ends, these ends themselves can be considered universal (Maslow, 1970). Thus needs are achieved through what Max-Neef (1991) coins "satisfiers" (see Kamenetsky, 1981 for a similar approach). Satisfiers change according to each culture and even differ within each culture, but the underlying needs remain constant.

The first set of hierarchical needs identified by Maslow is *basic needs*. Basic (or physiological) needs include air, water, food, sleep and sex. Unsatisfied basic needs cause feelings of pain, illness and discomfort. Until these needs are satisfied, attention to higher needs is not possible. The attainment of basic needs occurs at a low level of income. Their satisfaction is an absolute outcome and not dependent on increasing income (also see Hirsch, 1995 for a description of the "paradox of affluence" where higher income and consumption do not increase well-being). The second group is *safety needs*. These needs are psychological rather than physiological, and take the form of home and family. Within the approach used in this chapter, the attainment of safety needs is not specifically dependent on income. Indeed, other than basic needs, income levels are specifically not important in increasing well-being within this hierarchical needs-fulfilment approach. The third level of need is *belonging needs*: human desire to belong to groups such as clubs, work groups, families or gangs. This level of needs incorporates the need to feel (non-sexual) love and acceptance by others. Closely related to this is the fourth level, *self-esteem needs*. Once people belong to groups, they seek to be admired by those around them. Self-esteem can be brought about through the mastery of skills or attention and recognition from others. Finally, once these four levels of needs have been satisfied, a person can become self-actualized. *Self-actualization* is an ongoing process. It is the need to be what one was born to be. It is self-fulfilment of one's own potential. Self-actualization can be considered analogous to capability (Sen, 1985, 1987a, 1987b; Nussbaum, 1988) and social and critical participation (Doyal and Gough, 1991).

The concept of hierarchy can be criticized, however. Whilst Doyal and Gough (1991) utilize a hierarchical concept in their theory of human needs, they do so only in a methodological sense. They argue that health and autonomy are fundamental universal needs in a thin, Kantian sense. Then, using codified knowledge, it is possible to identify universal satisfier characteristics that everywhere contribute to these. But all are simultaneously necessary even for low levels of functioning. Similarly, Max-Neef (1991) argues that a range of human needs (subsistence, protection, affection, understanding, participation, idleness, creation, identity and freedom) exist, but they do so simultaneously and are therefore non-hierarchical.

This divergence between hierarchical and non-hierarchical can be bridged, though. Maslow (1970) notes that the dominant need is always shifting, so that a self-actualized person does become hungry and tired and this basic need becomes the priority. The implication of this shifting dominant need or non-hierarchy of needs is that policies aimed at maximizing well-being must be more sophisticated to consider explicitly the various forms of needs and their relative significance in achieving optimal well-being. Developing a social welfare function on Maslow's approach to hierarchical need fulfilment encourages this outcome.

Fulfilment of hierarchical needs and well-being

This approach does not seek to use the Maslow approach to predict patterns of economic development; rather, it draws on Maslow's (1970) description of needs to measure well-being. Rather than predicting paths of development, this chapter is interested in measuring well-being in a manner which until now has not been undertaken. Maslow did not intend his theory of needs to be used outside of management psychology, but recent studies (Sirgy, 1986; Hagerty, 1999) have widened its use to consider development and well-being issues.

Hindrances constructed by society can prevent people reaching the highest level of self-actualization. That is why hierarchical needs fulfilment can be applied to well-being measures. This approach can demonstrate whether a society is assisting or hindering its citizens from becoming self-actualized. Societies that enable their members to achieve each level of this hierarchy will have higher levels of well-being.

As this approach to well-being is underpinned by a theory of hierarchical needs, appropriate weights are given to the different levels of needs. In this approach, therefore, needs at the higher level of the hierarchy are given more weight than those at the lower end of the hierarchy. The use of weights in this fashion demonstrates that the hierarchical structure of needs has been explicitly considered in the conceptualization and measurement of well-being, since different hierarchical structures of needs provide different types and levels of well-being.

Table 11.1 summarizes the well-being outcomes associated with each level of need.

It is possible to operationalize this approach by identifying outcomes and indicators that represent or correspond to the four lower levels of needs upon which the achievement of self-actualization is predicated. Eight indicators have been chosen to reflect these four hierarchical categories.

Table 11.1 Selected well-being outcomes and indicators that correspond to Maslow's categories of needs

Maslow's categories of needs	Some well-being outcomes that correspond with this need
Basic (physiological)	– Healthy
	– Vitality
Safety	– Safe
	– Settled
	– Secure
Belonging	– Included
	– Loved
	– Participating
Self-esteem	– Empowered
	– Confident
	– Convivial
Self-actualization	– Actively seeking knowledge
	– Inspired to reach potential

- Basic: daily calories available per person; access to safe water.
- Safety: infant mortality; life expectancy.
- Belonging: telephone mainlines; fertility rates.
- Self-esteem: adult illiteracy; unemployment.

Significant literature exists regarding the identification of basic needs (see Streeten, 1995, for a summary of the issues surrounding this area). Two measures have been chosen as indicators for this first level of need: calories per person and access to safe water. Without sufficient food or sufficient water quality, long-term survival is not possible. Having attained the lowest level of needs required, attention would focus on achieving a feeling of safety. Two indicators of safety have been chosen to measure this: infant mortality and life expectancy. Infant mortality reflects the safety of society's most vulnerable members (unborn and new-born babies), and life expectancy is a reasonable measure of how safe one's life is across society. The relationship one has with one's own family is often rated highly as a factor of self-reported happiness. In this sense fertility rates represent belonging to a family. Belonging to the wider society is represented by telephone mainline connections. Adult illiteracy rates and unemployment rates have been selected to represent the concept of self-esteem.

Whilst Hagerty (1999) proposed the indicators that form the basis for this new measure, the ultimate choice of indicators must based on society's preferences and value judgements. To this end, Doyal and Gough (1991: 141) adopt a dual strategy of social policy formation in which decisions are made using "both the codified knowledge of experts and the experimental knowledge of those whose basic needs and daily life world are under consideration". This approach bears a strong resemblance to normative social choice theory (Clarke and Islam, 2004). Normative social choice theory is concerned with how the preferences, value judgements and choices of society can be identified and measured. Traditionally, voting systems were the primary focus within this theory. However, it is possible to extend the theory to measure well-being. Normative social choice theory should be applied to well-being measures as it highlights social preferences and value judgements. It is concerned with economic and non-economic activities that are important in determining well-being levels, quality and composition. The theory can highlight changes within society and how these changes impact on well-being. Applying normative social choice theory to measuring well-being is dependent upon four operations determining whose well-being is being measured; whether the well-being of the group is different or equal to the sum of well-being of the group's individual members; how distribution of the individual well-being affects the group's well-being; and how to aggregate individual well-being to determine the level of group well-being (Bonner, 1986).

It is acknowledged that all indicators have limitations. However, it is argued that the selected indicators are robust enough to provide a solid basis for this application and subsequent analysis. Each indicator has been selected to represent the various concepts encapsulated in each level of need. The choice of indicators representing or corresponding to the four hierarchical levels of need is constrained by availability both across countries and within countries but across time. The choice of indicators fulfils the criteria of reliability, availability, reliance and timeliness (Baster, 1972), but also draws heavily on Hagerty (1999), who first conceptualized the use of Maslow's (1970) hierarchy of needs as a measure of development. As noted, it is acknowledged that no indicator is perfect and strong arguments for alternative choices could be made. However, utilizing normative social choice theory allows society's preferences and value judgements to be utilized when selecting representative indicators based on expert or analyst opinion (Clarke and Islam, 2004). It is therefore argued that the indicators selected reasonably represent the four levels of hierarchical needs.

Operationalizing the fulfilment of hierarchical needs index

Having determined the indicators representing each set of hierarchical needs leading to well-being or self-actualization, it is necessary to construct a social welfare function to operationalize the fulfilment of hierarchical needs index (FHNI).

The social welfare function is:

$$WB = SA(\alpha_1 BN, \alpha_2 SN, \alpha_3 BlN, \alpha_4 SEN)$$

where WB = well-being, SA = self-actualization, BN = basic needs, SN = safety needs, BlN = belonging needs, SEN = self-esteem needs and $\alpha_1, \ldots, \alpha_5$ are the weights assigned to each set of needs.

Weights

If well-being (or self-actualization) is achieved through the attainment of various hierarchical components, a decision must be made as to the importance of the different components with respect to their impact on well-being. This means deciding the relative importance between the hierarchical components within that functional relationship.

As an aggregation of different components or as a function of separate forms, weighting is an important issue when measuring different levels of well-being.

The determination of weights is dependent on various value judgements made explicit within the social welfare function, and is based on normative social choice theory (Clarke and Islam, 2004). Even when explicit weights are not defined, a value judgement has been made in that all components are equally weighted. This decision is just as much a value judgement as setting separate weights for each component.

No agreement exists as to how these weights should be determined. A number of methods have been suggested. First, the decision-maker unilaterally sets the weights according to his/her own value judgements on equity (Dasgupta and Pearce, 1972). Equity may refer to income levels only, or be considered greater than just income and incorporate issues such as access to social services, ascetic environments or satisfactory mental health. Second, the weights may be set to reflect society's preferences on equity reflected in such policy instruments as marginal taxation rates. The justification for this approach is that society, represented through successive governments, has determined that through progressive tax rates the benefits of those on higher incomes should be weighted less than the benefits of those on lower incomes. As such, the calculation of well-being should be biased in favour of those on lower incomes rather than those on higher incomes as this is society's preference (Dasgupta and Pearce, 1972). Third, a similar approach, first suggested by Foster (1966), has that the aggregation of well-being based on individual well-being weighted by the ratio of the average national income to the individual's income. Fourth, rather than use the ratio of national average income to individual income, the shape and elasticity of the marginal utility of income could determine the weights. The major difficulty of this approach, however, rests in the assumption that such a calculation of utility can be determined. Whilst some estimates have been made (see Theil and Brooks, 1970, for an example of an early attempt), "most economists remain unshaken in their belief in the impossibility of measuring differences in the marginal utility of income across individuals" (Pearce and Nash, 1981: 27).

Clearly, then, weights can take any reasonable form, being only dependent on the value judgements upon which they are based.

Within this chapter, the weights are based on a value judgement that the appropriate weights should reflect a hierarchical and linear progression. As the fulfilment of these needs is hierarchical, greater weight is given to the higher needs. As a simple linear progression is used, basic needs are weighted least ($\times 1$), safety needs are weighted as twice as important ($\times 2$), belonging needs three times as important ($\times 3$) and self-esteem needs four times as important ($\times 4$). This decision is consistent with normative social choice theory in which society's preferences and value judgements are interpreted by the analyst (Bonner, 1986).

Aggregation

The estimation of this measure of well-being relies on aggregating changes in illiteracy rates, calorie intake, access to water, fertility and so on. Such an aggregation requires finding a common denominator. A *normalized* index for each component can be calculated in order to find this common denominator. A normalized index is calculated by dividing each year's figure by the highest figure occurring throughout the time series. Such an index therefore compares movements within a span of numbers rather than the numbers themselves. By using this approach, different indicators can be compared (and aggregated).

This approach is similar to that used in calculating the HDI (UNDP, 2003), with one significant difference. Within the HDI the normalized number is calculated by comparing one country's performance against the performance of all other countries for that year. Thus countries are ranked against one another. In the approach taken in this chapter, a country is compared against itself over the period being reviewed (1985–2000). Thus comparisons between countries are actually comparisons of how countries have improved (or worsened) relative to their own standards. Therefore, whilst the indicators across all levels of needs may be substantially higher in "rich" developed countries, the measurement of well-being will not necessarily be higher in these countries than in countries with lower indicators. This is because well-being is based on movements within these indicators, not on their absolute numbers. Thus a country with a poor record of infant mortality (of, say, 100 in every 1,000) will improve in terms of well-being if infant mortality is reduced over the specified time period compared to a country with a low level of infant mortality (of, say, 10 in every 1,000) that remains static.

This outcome could be considered a significant flaw in the calculation of the index of well-being based on the fulfilment of hierarchical needs. It appears to reward countries with low starting points and penalize countries that are already developed. However, this outcome can also be seen as a major advantage. Human beings are adaptive by nature. Small mercies can be found in the most miserable of circumstances and tedium found in lavish surrounds (Sen, 1990; Hirsch, 1995). If an increase in wealth leads to happiness it is only a temporary situation; a disequilibrium of sorts. "Happiness is not the results of being rich, but a temporary consequence of having recently become richer" (Inglehart, 1990, cited in Myers, 1999: 3; also see Travers and Richardson, 1993; Brekke, 1997; Pusey, 1998. Ng 2001 provides an extensive review of this literature). Equilibrium will soon return and people's levels of satisfaction will subsequently fall. Thus increasing well-being is partly dependent upon regular improvements in satiating various hierarchical needs. It therefore may be that well-being within developed nations does plateau at a certain point when all hierarchical needs have been reached. It is not difficult to accept that there maybe a cap on levels of human happiness or well-being (Cummins et al., 2001).

Analysis

As this new measure of well-being is based on fulfilling hierarchical needs within society, it is able to provide useful insights into the structure of society in terms of those needs. It provides information on which needs are being successfully attained and which are failing to be met. Alternative measures of well-being do not adequately provide such information (Islam and Clarke, 2000, 2001).

As discussed in the previous section, the components of the FHNI have been weighted in a linear manner so that the highest need (self-esteem) is four times as important as the lowest need (basic) and so forth. The results (fig. 11.1) show that the well-being of all countries discussed, as defined by the FHNI, has risen over the period 1985–2000.

Interestingly, though, this general increase occurs for most countries in a series of rises and falls. Thailand recorded the most striking falls between 1989–1991 and 1997–1998, the latter being linked to the Asian financial crisis.

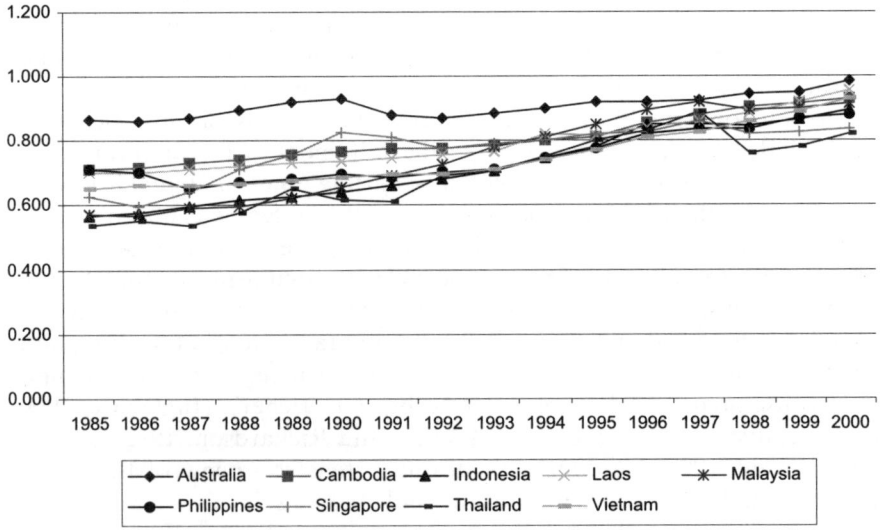

Figure 11.1 Comparison of FHNI, 1985–2000

FHNI and GDP per capita

Well-being is often measured by a single, representative indicator – GDP per capita (see for example Gylfason, 1999; World Bank, 2001). The increase in GDP per capita (constant in 1995 US$) normalized in the same manner for this period can be seen in figure 11.2. The increase in constant GDP per capita is greater than that experienced in the FHNI. Following the Asian financial crisis, the rate of growth within these countries shrank, and was actually negative in a number of countries.

Compared to the large increases in well-being as measured by constant GDP per capita, the rise in well-being as measured by the fulfilment of hierarchical needs is quite modest. The average increase in FHNI between 1985 and 2000 was 39 per cent, compared to an average increase in GDP of 70 per cent. The smallest increase in the FHNI was 14 per cent (Australia) compared to 18 per cent for GDP constant per capita (Philippines), but the gap between the maximum increases ranges from 61 per cent for the FHNI (Malaysia) to 117 per cent for constant GDP per capita (Singapore).

It may be argued that economic growth therefore has a limited impact on well-being, or at the very least the relationship between economic growth and well-being is overstated. For all countries, the FHNI actually rose and fell independently of the accelerated growth in GDP per capita

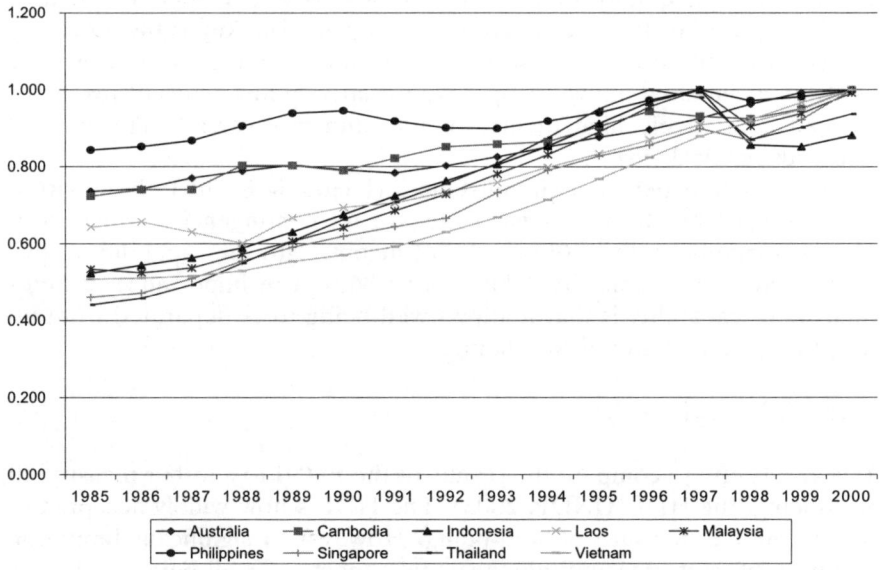

Figure 11.2 Comparison of GDP per capita (1995 US$), 1985–2000

recorded during this period. If well-being is able to fall or remain unchanged during periods of strong economic growth, such growth has an arguably limited impact on well-being.

Comparing well-being (measured by the FHNI) and economic growth (measured by constant GDP per capita) may provide some new insights into the efficiency of converting income (Y) into well-being:

$$WB = Y\alpha$$

where α is the efficiency rate of converting income into well-being.

Ruskin, writing in the mid-nineteenth century, defined well-being not simply as the measurement of economic possessions but the capability of utilizing them in an appropriate manner (Smith, 1993). Cochrane and Shaw Bell's (1956: 95) definition of well-being is based on a similar approach: "The consuming unit buys food, clothing, shelter, and recreation and transforms them into satisfaction, or utility." Sen (1985, 1987a, 1987b) takes this approach further and argues that well-being is not measured by the possession of a commodity, nor the utility of the commodity, but rather by what the person actually does with the commodity. Sen terms this the "functioning" of a commodity. Increasing attempts have been made to operationalize Sen's functioning and capability concept (see Comin, 2001; Martinetti, 2001). Lovell et al. (1993) found that resources are not related strongly to capabilities and therefore the attainment of a high quality of life (capabilities) is not dependent on high levels of material standard of living (resources). The key is the efficiency by which people use their resources (Denison, 1971). Thus efficiency or skills or social habit allow "people with relatively low levels of resources to lead a relatively high quality of life, and vice-versa" (Travers and Richardson, 1993: 48).

Issues such as personal circumstances (including health), the environment, social climate and social state are all contingencies which "can lead to variation in the 'conversion' of income into the capability to live a minimally acceptable life" (Sen, 1999: 360). The importance of Sen's analysis of capability is that it allows well-being to be separated from income levels and material well-being.

The FHNI and the HDI

It is also useful to compare the results of the FHNI to another measure of well-being: the HDI (UNDP, 2003). The HDI is now widely accepted as an alternative measure of well-being. However, a significant limitation in terms of capturing multidimensional aspects of well-being is that its three component indicators (life expectancy, literacy and income) are

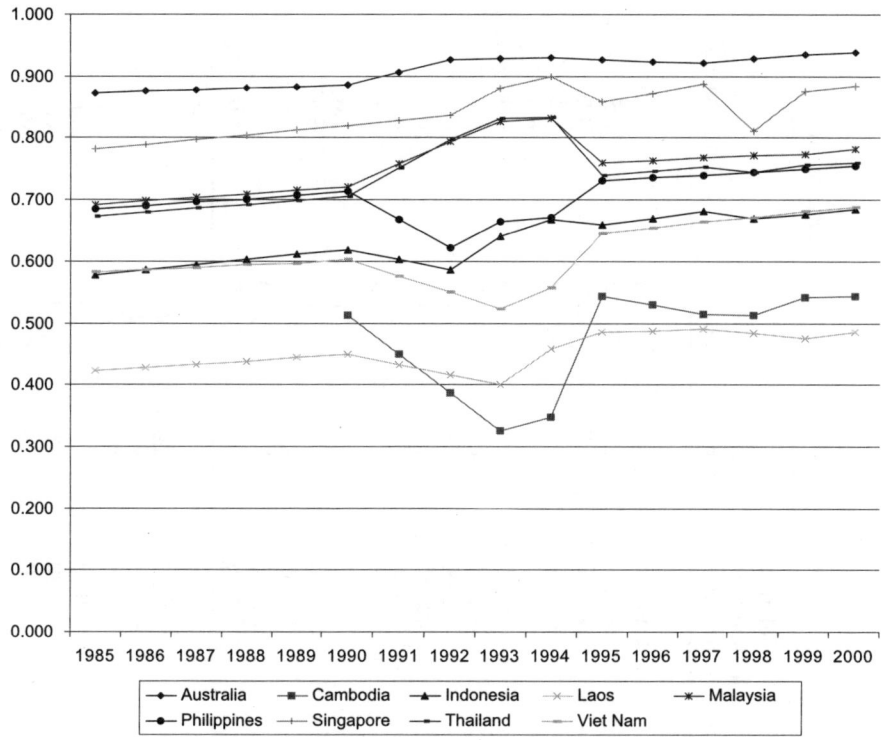

Figure 11.3 Comparison of HDI, 1985–2000

closely correlated to one another and give rise to claims of redundancy (McGillivray, 1991).

The general movement in well-being, as measured by the HDI, is a slight increase over the time period (with the notable fall of Cambodia in the early 1990s: see fig. 11.3 and table 11.2). The greatest increase in the HDI was 18 per cent, achieved by Viet Nam and Indonesia. The smallest increase was 6 per cent (Cambodia) and the average increase across all nine countries was only 13 per cent (compared to 39 per cent for the FHNI and 70 per cent for GDP per capita). It is important to note, though, that movement of the HDI represents inter-country comparisons across the three component indicators. This differs significantly from how the FHNI has been developed, in which movements are reflections of intra-country movements across eight indicators. This may account for the larger general shift in the FHNI compared to the HDI.

This focus on intra-country comparisons should be considered a strength of the FHNI, as the relevancy of the well-being indicators rests upon their authority in representing shifts in well-being actually experi-

Table 11.2 Data

	Basic needs		Safety		Belonging		Self-esteem	
	Daily calorie intake	Access to safe water	Infant mortality	Life expectancy	Telephone mainlines per '000	Fertility rate	Illiteracy rate	Unemployment
Australia								
1985	3,091	99.9	9.9	75.7	391.80	1.9	1.0	8.0
1986	3,160	99.9	9.9	75.9	405.80	1.9	1.0	8.5
1987	3,178	99.9	9.8	76.1	419.10	1.9	1.0	8.1
1988	3,196	99.9	9.2	76.4	429.30	1.8	1.0	7.2
1989	3,216	99.9	7.7	76.7	441.50	1.8	1.0	6.9
1990	3,385	99.9	8.0	77.0	456.30	1.9	1.0	6.9
1991	3,305	99.9	7.1	77.2	465.50	1.9	1.0	9.6
1992	3,316	99.9	7.0	77.5	472.00	1.9	1.0	10.8
1993	3,338	99.9	6.1	77.6	483.50	1.9	1.0	10.9
1994	3,288	99.9	5.9	77.7	495.60	1.9	1.0	9.7
1995	3,200	99.9	5.7	77.9	492.40	1.8	1.0	8.5
1996	3,231	99.9	5.8	78.0	500.70	1.8	1.0	8.6
1997	3,224	99.9	5.3	78.1	512.70	1.8	1.0	8.6
1998	3,220	99.9	5.0	78.6	509.30	1.8	1.0	8.0
1999	3,210	99.9	5.6	78.7	515.30	1.8	1.0	7.2
2000	3,298	99.9	4.9	78.9	524.60	1.8	1.0	6.6
Cambodia								
1985	1,784	19	95.0	47.1	0.25	6.0	41.6	n/a
1986	1,804	19	92.0	47.8	0.25	5.9	40.9	n/a
1987	1,893	19	89.0	48.5	0.30	5.8	40.1	n/a
1988	2,002	20	86.0	49.1	0.30	5.7	39.3	n/a
1989	2,166	20	83.0	49.7	0.30	5.6	38.6	n/a
1990	2,114	22	80.0	50.3	0.30	5.6	38.0	n/a

1991	2,089	25	81.6	50.9	0.40	5.5	37.5	n/a
1992	2,021	25	83.2	51.5	0.40	5.4	37.0	n/a
1993	2,030	36	84.8	52.0	0.40	5.2	36.6	n/a
1994	2,197	36	86.4	52.5	0.60	5.0	36.1	n/a
1995	2,011	36	88.0	52.9	0.80	4.7	35.5	n/a
1996	2,045	36	89.4	53.4	1.50	4.5	34.9	n/a
1997	2,048	36	90.8	53.9	1.90	4.3	34.2	n/a
1998	2,078	38	92.2	53.8	2.10	4.2	33.5	n/a
1999	2,103	37	93.6	53.7	2.20	4.1	32.7	n/a
2000	2,119	37	95.0	53.8	2.36	4.0	32.0	n/a
Indonesia								
1985	2,398	19	69.5	58.6	3.60	3.6	25.4	n/a
1986	2,412	22	67.6	59.4	4.00	3.5	24.4	n/a
1987	2,572	35	65.7	60.2	4.40	3.3	23.4	n/a
1988	2,598	46	63.8	60.7	4.80	3.2	22.4	n/a
1989	2,750	46	61.9	61.2	4.90	3.1	21.5	n/a
1990	2,631	47	60.0	61.7	5.90	3.0	20.5	n/a
1991	2,763	47	57.2	62.2	7.10	3.0	19.7	n/a
1992	2,755	48	54.4	62.7	8.90	2.9	18.9	n/a
1993	2,790	51	51.6	63.1	9.90	2.8	18.0	n/a
1994	2,812	62	48.8	63.6	12.90	2.8	17.2	n/a
1995	2,896	62	46.0	64.1	16.80	2.8	16.5	n/a
1996	2,900	63	43.8	64.6	21.10	2.8	15.8	4.0
1997	2,886	61	41.6	65.1	24.70	2.8	15.2	4.7
1998	2,873	60	39.4	65.4	27.00	2.7	14.5	5.5
1999	2,909	64	37.2	65.7	29.00	2.6	13.9	5.5
2000	2,893	69	35.0	66.0	32.30	2.5	13.2	5.5
Laos								
1985	2,205	22	127.5	47.2	1.60	6.5	47.6	n/a
1986	2,088	22	126.0	47.7	1.60	6.4	46.7	n/a
1987	2,256	22	124.5	48.2	1.60	6.3	45.9	n/a

Table 11.2 (cont.)

	Basic needs		Safety		Belonging			Self-esteem	
	Daily calorie intake	Access to safe water	Infant mortality	Life expectancy	Telephone mainlines per '000	Fertility rate	Illiteracy rate	Unemployment	
1988	2,398	25	123.0	48.7	1.60	6.2	45.1	n/a
1989	2,630	27	121.5	49.2	1.50	6.1	44.3	n/a
1990	2,475	29	120.0	49.7	1.60	6.0	43.5	n/a
1991	2,378	32	117.0	50.2	1.60	5.9	42.7	n/a
1992	2,259	34	114.0	50.7	1.90	5.8	41.9	n/a
1993	2,233	36	111.0	51.0	1.90	5.7	41.0	n/a
1994	2,198	45	108.0	51.4	3.90	5.6	40.2	n/a
1995	2,175	39	105.0	51.8	3.50	5.5	39.4	n/a
1996	2,056	44	102.0	52.1	4.10	5.4	38.6	n/a
1997	2,108	44	99.0	52.5	4.80	5.3	37.7	n/a
1998	2,100	45	96.0	52.9	5.50	5.2	36.9	n/a
1999	2,099	49	93.0	53.3	6.60	5.1	36.1	n/a
2000	2,106	48	90.0	53.7	7.78	5.0	35.2	n/a
Malaysia								
1985	2,684	44	23.5	68.8	61.40	4.1	23.7	6.9
1986	2,617	48	22.0	69.1	65.20	4.1	22.8	8.3
1987	2,698	59	20.5	69.5	68.40	4.0	22.0	7.3
1988	2,701	51	19.0	69.8	73.60	3.9	21.1	7.2
1989	2,774	51	17.5	70.1	80.00	3.9	20.2	6.3
1990	2,697	58	16.0	70.5	89.20	3.8	19.3	5.1
1991	2,765	65	15.5	70.8	99.10	3.7	18.6	4.3
1992	2,884	71	15.0	71.2	111.40	3.6	17.9	3.7
1993	2,876	78	13.7	71.3	125.40	3.6	17.2	3.0
1994	2,893	78	12.3	71.6	145.60	3.5	16.4	2.9

Year								
1995	2,873	88	11.0	71.7	165.70	3.4	15.7	2.8
1996	2,938	90	10.3	71.8	178.10	3.3	15.1	2.5
1997	2,977	93	9.5	71.8	194.80	3.3	14.5	2.5
1998	2,970	93	8.3	72.0	201.50	3.2	13.8	3.2
1999	2,986	92	7.9	72.3	202.90	3.1	13.2	3.4
2000	2,964	92	7.9	72.5	199.16	3.0	12.6	3.1
Philippines								
1985	2,309	68	55.0	63.4	9.30	4.5	10.0	6.1
1986	2,204	68	53.0	63.8	9.50	4.4	9.7	6.4
1987	2,284	67	51.0	64.2	9.50	4.3	9.3	9.1
1988	2,340	70	49.0	64.7	9.70	4.2	9.0	8.3
1989	2,375	71	47.0	65.1	9.90	4.2	8.7	8.4
1990	2,452	75	45.0	65.6	10.00	4.1	8.3	8.1
1991	2,386	75	43.2	66.0	10.40	4.1	7.9	9.0
1992	2,258	79	41.4	66.5	10.30	4.0	7.6	8.6
1993	2,205	82	39.6	66.9	12.10	3.9	7.2	8.9
1994	2,309	83	37.8	67.3	16.50	3.9	6.9	8.4
1995	2,373	85	36.0	67.7	20.50	3.8	6.5	8.4
1996	2,363	83	34.8	68.1	25.50	3.7	6.2	7.4
1997	2,425	85	33.6	68.5	28.60	3.6	5.9	7.9
1998	2,469	85	32.4	68.7	34.10	3.6	5.6	9.6
1999	2,860	85	31.2	69.0	38.80	3.5	5.4	9.6
2000	2,801	87	30.0	69.2	40.02	3.4	5.1	10.1
Singapore								
1985	3,098	99.9	9.4	72.8	294.20	1.6	14.4	4.1
1986	3,080	99.9	7.4	73.2	307.80	1.4	13.8	6.5
1987	3,087	99.9	7.4	73.5	319.30	1.6	13.1	4.7
1988	3,105	99.9	7.0	73.8	329.80	2.0	12.5	3.3
1989	3,198	99.9	7.5	74.0	340.50	1.8	11.8	2.2
1990	3,114	99.9	6.7	74.3	349.40	1.9	11.2	1.7
1991	3,167	99.9	5.5	74.5	356.30	1.8	10.9	1.9

Table 11.2 (cont.)

	Basic needs		Safety		Belonging		Self-esteem	
	Daily calorie intake	Access to safe water	Infant mortality	Life expectancy	Telephone mainlines per '000	Fertility rate	Illiteracy rate	Unemployment
1992	3,186	99.9	5.0	74.8	367.80	1.8	10.5	2.7
1993	3,204	99.9	4.7	75.5	382.10	1.8	10.1	2.7
1994	3,195	99.9	4.7	76.3	395.90	1.8	9.7	2.6
1995	3,220	99.9	4.0	76.4	411.90	1.7	9.3	2.7
1996	3,244	99.9	3.6	76.7	432.60	1.7	9.0	3.0
1997	3,282	99.9	3.6	77.0	450.90	1.6	8.8	2.4
1998	3,299	99.9	4.1	77.4	459.90	1.5	8.4	3.1
1999	3,266	99.9	3.2	77.5	481.90	1.5	8.1	4.1
2000	3,244	99.9	2.9	77.9	484.48	1.5	7.7	4.4
Thailand								
1985	2,178	38	39.5	65.8	12.60	2.8	9.8	3.7
1986	2,116	47	38.4	66.0	15.80	2.7	9.3	3.5
1987	2,284	55	37.3	66.2	17.50	2.6	8.9	5.9
1988	2,209	66	36.2	67.0	19.10	2.5	8.5	3.1
1989	2,316	59	35.1	67.7	21.60	2.4	8.1	1.4
1990	2,271	63	34.0	68.5	24.20	2.3	7.6	2.2
1991	2,200	65	33.0	69.2	28.10	2.2	7.3	2.7
1992	2,443	70	32.0	69.9	32.10	2.1	6.9	1.4
1993	2,382	77	31.0	69.6	39.30	2.1	6.6	1.5
1994	2,387	86	30.0	69.2	48.30	2.1	6.2	1.3
1995	2,305	81	29.0	68.9	60.50	2.0	5.9	1.1
1996	2,351	90	28.2	68.6	71.50	2.0	5.6	1.1
1997	2,360	91	27.4	68.2	82.10	1.9	5.4	0.9
1998	2,322	90	26.6	68.4	84.80	1.9	5.1	3.4

Year								
1999	2,328	90	25.8	68.6	86.90	1.9	4.8	3.0
2000	2,336	89	25.0	68.8	92.25	1.8	4.5	2.4
Viet Nam								
1985	2,186	19	43.0	62.5	1.20	4.2	10.8	n/a
1986	2,244	20	41.6	62.0	1.20	4.1	10.6	n/a
1987	2,200	19	40.2	63.4	1.20	4.0	10.3	n/a
1988	2,221	20	38.8	61.9	1.20	3.9	10.1	n/a
1989	2,233	20	37.4	63.4	1.20	3.8	9.9	n/a
1990	2,251	20	36.0	67.7	1.40	3.6	9.7	n/a
1991	2,361	24	35.2	66.7	2.00	3.4	9.4	n/a
1992	2,250	24	34.4	65.7	2.20	3.3	9.2	n/a
1993	2,389	24	33.6	65.2	3.60	3.1	9.0	n/a
1994	2,399	35	32.8	65.7	6.00	2.9	8.7	n/a
1995	2,437	36	32.0	67.1	10.50	2.7	8.5	n/a
1996	2,471	43	31.1	67.6	15.70	2.5	8.3	n/a
1997	2,484	43	30.2	68.0	17.40	2.4	8.1	n/a
1998	2,422	45	29.3	67.7	22.40	2.4	7.9	n/a
1999	2,457	44	28.5	68.0	26.70	2.3	7.7	n/a
2000	2,463	45	27.6	69.0	31.85	2.2	7.5	n/a

Source: World Bank (2004).

enced by populations. Whilst some aspects of well-being are relative (Atkinson, 1983; Kanbur, 1987; Thurow, 1980; Hirsch, 1995; Clayton and Radcliffe, 1996), a reduction in a neighbour's well-being does not impact as positively on one's own well-being as an improvement in one's own circumstances. The focus on intra-country comparisons is thus valid.

The results of the FHNI, as compared to the HDI, indicate that well-being experienced by these nine countries has increased at a greater rate than indicated by movements in the HDI, but not as much as suggested by movements in GDP per capita.

Conclusions

The approach developed in this chapter is different to previous extensions of Maslow's (1970) approach outside of the realm of management psychology. It is not an attempt to predict movements in development (Hagerty, 1999) in a similar vein to Rostow's (1971) stages of growth theory, but rather it is an approach to measuring well-being. Countries can increase their well-being without increasing economic growth or even during times of decreasing economic growth (conversely, well-being can fall despite increases in economic growth). Well-being is dependent on fulfilling a given set of hierarchical needs, and the role of the state should be to support this attainment. Therefore not only can societies aim to increase total well-being, they can also aim to achieve maximum well-being by recognizing the hierarchical structure of human needs and motivation.

Acknowledgements

The author gratefully acknowledges the work of Dr Sardar M. N. Islam and Sally Paech in previous research.

REFERENCES

Atkinson, A. (1983) *The Economics of Inequality*, Oxford: Clarendon Press.
Baster, N. (1972) "Development Indicators: An Introduction", *Journal of Development Studies* 8(3): 1–20.
Bonner, J. (1986) *The Introduction to the Theory of Social Choice*, Baltimore: Johns Hopkins University Press.
Brekke, K. (1997) *Economic Growth and the Environment*, Cheltenham: Edward Elgar.
Clayton, A. and N. Radcliffe (1996) *Sustainability: A Systems Approach*, London: Earthscan.

Clarke, M. and S. Islam (2004) *Economic Growth and Social Well-being: Operationalising Normative Social Choice Theory*, Amsterdam: North Holland.

Cochrane, W. and C. Shaw Bell (1956) *The Economics of Consumption*, New York: McGraw-Hill.

Comin, F. (2001) "Operationalizing Sen's Capability Approach", paper presented at Justice and Poverty: Examining Sen's Capability Approach, Cambridge, 5–7 June, unpublished.

Cummins, R., R. Eckersley, J. Pallant, J. Van Vugt, J. Sheeley, M. Pusey and R. Misajon (2001) "Australian Unity Wellbeing Index – Report Number 1", available at http://acqol.deakin.edu.au/index_wellbeing/index.htm.

Daly, H. (1996) *Beyond Growth*, Boston, Mass.: Beacon Press.

Dasgupta, A. and D. Pearce (1972) *Cost-benefit Analysis*, London: Macmillan.

Denison, E. (1971) *Accounting for Change*, Washington, D.C.: Brookings Institute.

Doyal, L. and I. Gough (1991) *A Theory of Need*, London: Macmillan.

Foster, C. (1966) "Social Welfare Functions in Cost-benefit Analysis", in M. Lawrence, ed., *Operational Research in the Social Services*, London: Macmillan.

Gylfason, T. (1999) *Principles of Economic Growth*, Oxford: Oxford University Press.

Hagerty, M. (1999) "Testing Maslow's Hierarchical of Needs: National Quality of Life Across Time", *Social Indicators Research* 46: 249–271.

Hirsch, F. (1995) *Social Limits to Growth*, London: Routledge.

Islam, S. and M. Clarke (2000) "Social Well-being and GDP: Can We Still Use GDP for Well-being Measurement?", seminar paper presented at the Centre for Strategic Economic Studies, Victoria University, 7 September, unpublished.

——— (2001) "Measuring Quality of Life: A New Approach Empirically Applied to Thailand", paper presented at the Centre for International Environmental Co-operation of the Russian Academy of Science, INDEX2001 Quality of Life Indicators Conference, Rome, 2–5 October, unpublished.

Kamenetsky, M. (1981) "The Economics of the Satisfaction of Needs", *Human Systems Management* 2.

Kanbur, R. (1987) "The Standard of Living: Uncertainty, Inequality and Opportunity", in G. Hawthorn, ed., *The Standard of Living*, Cambridge: Cambridge University Press.

Lovell, K., S. Richardson, P. Travers and L. Wood (1993) "Resources and Functionings: A New View of Inequality in Australia", in W. Eichhorn, ed., *Models and Measurement of Welfare and Inequality*, Berlin: Springer Verlag.

Martinetti, E. (2001) "A Multidimensional Assessment of Well-being Based on Sen's Functioning Approach", paper presented at Justice and Poverty: Examining Sen's Capability Approach, Cambridge, 5–7 June, unpublished.

Maslow, A. (1970) *The Farther Reaches of the Human Mind*, New York: Viking Press.

Max-Neef, M. (1991) *Human Scale Development*, New York: Apex Press.

McGillivray, M. (1991) "The Human Development Index: Yet Another Redundant Composite Development Indicator?", *World Development* 19(10): 1451–1460.

Morris, M. (1979) *Measuring the Condition of the World's Poor: The Physical Quality of Life Index*, New York: Pergamon.

Myers, D. (1999) "Does Economic Growth Improve Human Morale?", available at www.newdream.org/newsletter/myers.html.
Ng, Y. (2001) "From Preference to Happiness: Towards a More Complete Well-being Economics", mimeo, Faculty of Economics, Monash University, Clayton, Australia.
Nussbaum, M. (1988) "Nature, Function and Capability", *Oxford Studies in Ancient Philosophy*, Supplement 1: 145–184.
––––––– (1992) "Human Functioning and Social Justice", *Political Theory* 20(2): 202–246.
––––––– (1993) "Non-relative Values: An Aristotelian Approach", in M. Nussbaum and A. Sen, eds, *Quality of Life*, Oxford: Oxford University Press for UNU-WIDER.
––––––– (2000) *Women and Human Needs*, Oxford: Oxford University Press.
Pearce, D. and C. Nash (1981) *The Social Appraisal of Projects*, London: Macmillan.
Pusey, M. (1998) "Incomes, Standards of Living and Quality of Life", in R. Eckersley, ed., *Measuring Progress*, Melbourne: CSIRO Publishing.
Rostow, W. (1971) *The Stages of Economic Growth*, Cambridge: Cambridge University Press.
Sen, A. (1985) *Commodities and Capabilities*, Amsterdam: North Holland.
––––––– (1987a) "The Standard of Living: Lecture I, Concepts and Critiques", in G. Hawthorn, ed., *The Standard of Living*, Cambridge: Cambridge University Press.
––––––– (1987b) "The Standard of Living: Lecture II, Lives and Capabilities", in G. Hawthorn, ed., *The Standard of Living*, Cambridge: Cambridge University Press.
––––––– (1990) "Individual Freedom as a Social Commitment", *New York Review of Books* 37, 14 June: 49–54.
––––––– (1999) "The Possibility of Social Choice", *American Economic Review* 85 (June): 349–378.
Sirgy, M. (1986) "A Quality-of-life Theory Derived from Maslow's Developmental Perspective", *American Journal of Economics and Sociology* 45(3): 329–342.
Smith, G. (1993) "The Purpose of Wealth: A Historical Perspective", in H. Daly and K. Townsend, eds, *Valuing the Earth*, Cambridge, Mass.: MIT Press.
Streeten, P. (1995) *Thinking About Development*, Cambridge: Cambridge University Press.
Thurow, L. (1980) *The Zero-sum Society*, New York: Basic Books.
Theil, H. and R. Brooks (1970) "How Does the Marginal Utility of Income Change When Real Income Changes?", *European Economic Review* 2 (Winter): 218–240.
Travers, P. and S. Richardson (1993) *Living Decently*, Melbourne: Oxford University Press.
UNDP (2003) *Human Development Report*, New York: Oxford University Press.
World Bank (2001) *World Development Report 2000/2001: Attacking Poverty*, New York: Oxford University Press.
World Bank (2004) *World Development Indicators*, New York: World Bank.

12
Assessing poverty and inequality at a detailed regional level: New advances in spatial microsimulation

Ann Harding, Rachel Lloyd, Anthea Bill and Anthony King

Introduction

It has in the past been difficult for Australian policy-makers and researchers to assess the extent of poverty, wealth and income inequality at a small-area level. This chapter reports on NATSEM's (National Centre for Social and Economic Modelling) pathbreaking work to create synthetic small-area socio-demographic data and construct microsimulation models capable of predicting the regional impact of policy change on top of this synthetic base data – hereafter "spatial microsimulation".

The first section of the chapter describes the main sources of sociodemographic data currently available and the limitations of the data. The second section describes spatial microsimulation and introduces the major methods of creating synthetic microdata. The spatial microsimulation approach currently being developed by NATSEM, known as SYNAGI (Synthetic Australian Geo-demographic Information) is then described. The third section describes the policy option modelled, examines estimated national poverty rates in Australia in 2001 and looks at the change in poverty due to the policy change simulated. As an illustrative example of the capacities of the new model, the fourth section examines the likely regional distributional impact of this possible policy change and looks at the poverty profile of one postcode. The final section concludes.

Spatial microsimulation methodology

Existing individual and household data

Regional policy-makers and researchers – or national policy-makers concerned with the regional impact of their decisions – rely on the availability of detailed and current small-area data to inform their decision-making. The main source of small-area socio-demographic data in Australia is the five-yearly Census of Population and Housing conducted by the Australian Bureau of Statistics (ABS). The census is a count of the population and dwellings in Australia with details of age, sex and a variety of other characteristics (ABS, 1996). The smallest geographic area defined in the census is the census collection district (CCD), which is used for collection, processing and output of data. There are approximately 225 dwellings in each urban CCD, with fewer dwellings in rural areas. There were a total of 37,209 CCDs defined in the 2001 census.

In addition to the census the ABS conducts surveys to collect detailed information on incomes, expenditures and other individual and household characteristics, such as the Household Expenditure Survey (HES), the Survey of Income and Housing Costs (SIHC) and the National Health Survey (NHS).

Household and individual information is also collected by numerous public and private agencies in the conduct of their day-to-day activities. These administrative data can contain vast amounts of information on an individual's spending patterns, health history, travel habits and many other preferences, choices and characteristics. The results of market and attitudinal surveys are also a rich source of information and have the potential to contribute to corporate and public decision-making.

Microdata

Microdata are data that are available at the unit record level and generally consist of a list of unidentifiable individuals or households with associated characteristics obtained from a survey or census. Individual and household characteristics may include age, sex, marital status, household type, dwelling type and, possibly, a spatial indicator identifying the broad geographic location of the individual or household.

Microdata are available from the ABS from the census and many of its surveys in the form of confidentialized unit record files (CURFs). Census microdata are available as a 1 per cent household sample file of the census population, with some levels of detail collapsed for confidentiality. CURFs are also available from the HES and SIHC, again with measures taken by the ABS to ensure confidentiality. These CURFs contain unit records of all the respondents included within each survey. CURFs are a valuable source of unit record data and provide a method for analysis at the individual or household level not available from tabular output. Usage of all CURFs is strictly governed by a licensing agreement with the ABS.

Limitations of existing data

Although the census provides a comprehensive coverage of Australian households for small geographic areas, it has several major limitations. These include the following.
- The amount of information collected from each household is relatively limited. For example, only gross household income is collected and then only in broad ranges of income, and there is also no information about social security receipts, income sources, wealth or expenditure.
- Unlike many other ABS collections, the full census results are not publicly available as a unit record file. Output for the whole census file is only available as a pre-defined series of tables for each CCD, or as customized tables that can be purchased from the ABS. This means, for example, that relationships between characteristics of interest cannot be easily or fully explored (such as age by income by educational qualifications). It also means that traditional microsimulation models[1] – that are widely used by policy-makers to assess the likely impact of policy changes on certain groups in society – cannot be constructed on top of the pre-defined tables.
- To protect the confidentiality of individuals, the ABS randomizes small numbers within the census. This makes analysis of multiple characteristics for individuals or households unreliable for many small geographic areas.

Other ABS data sources, such as the HES, provide a very rich source of household information, but are not available for small geographic areas. Due to relatively small sample sizes, the need to protect the confidentiality of respondents and the limited spatial stratification of these surveys, very little information is available about the spatial variation of individual or household characteristics.

The major limitations of administrative and market survey data include their limited availability, often only partial coverage of the population, difficulty in use (most data are not collected for analytical purposes and therefore can be difficult to process, particularly geographically) and reliability.

Synthetic microdata

One solution to this lack of detailed small-area data is to merge the information-rich survey data with the geographically disaggregated census data to create *synthetic microdata* for small areas. These new data may then help to fill the deficiency in the information available to policy-makers by providing synthetic small-area unit record data – effectively by creating 225 or so synthetic households for each CCD whose characteristics match as closely as possible the characteristics of the 225 households living in that CCD as shown in the census data.

The benefits of creating synthetic microdata include:
- the creation of spatially disaggregated data from aggregated data such as national surveys
- the ability to create tables of census variables that are not available in the standard census output, such as in the basic community profiles (BCPs)
- the ability to use the many simulated characteristics of each individual or household for multivariate analysis, thereby providing a method of identifying and analysing specific socio-demographic groups at the small-area level
- the potential to use traditional microsimulation models to estimate the spatial impact of policy on particular groups within the population.

Spatial microsimulation

Spatial microsimulation is a term used to describe those techniques that create synthetic microdata for small geographic areas and allow assessment of the spatial impact of policy change (Melhuish, Blake and Day, 2002). These techniques generally rely on creating synthetic individuals or households that match the socio-demographic characteristics of the small areas of interest.

Spatial microsimulation is a technique that combines individual or household microdata, currently available only for large spatial areas, with spatially disaggregate data to create synthetic microdata estimates for small areas. (This aspect of the modelling is sometimes termed "synthetic estimation" in the international literature.) There are two possible methods by which this can be achieved: "synthetic reconstruction" or "reweighting" (Williamson, Birkin and Rees, 1998).

The synthetic reconstruction approach requires the creation of a set of synthetic individuals or households whose characteristics match aggregate characteristics for the small area, such as those in the census BCP tables. The process usually involves imputing characteristics based on the distributions within the constraining tables and building the individual or household profiles in a sequential manner.

Reweighting is achieved by altering the weights for each individual or household in the survey. As national sample surveys are based on a sample of the population, each individual or household within the survey must be weighted to represent the estimated total number of that type of household within the population (sometimes also called "grossing up"). In a similar manner, the same sample can be reweighted so that it represents the population within a small area. This can be achieved by selecting a representative set of individuals or households that, when viewed together, best fit the aggregate characteristics of the small area. One way of doing so is to select 225 or so households from the sample survey that best represent a particular CCD (this is an integer method of selection, in which all selected households have a weight of one). Alternatively, all households within the sample can be given a small fractional weight so that the sum of all weights equals the population in the selected CCD and the sum of the fractional individuals or households best matches the characteristic profile of the CCD.

The SYNAGI reweighting approach

The SYNAGI approach developed at NATSEM uses the reweighting method to blend the census and ABS sample survey data together to create a synthetic unit record file for every CCD in Australia. To date, NATSEM's efforts have focused upon the ABS HES, although efforts are currently under way to extend the methodology to enable the "regionalization" of other sample survey data. The existing model first recodes the HES and census variables to be comparable and then reweights the HES, utilizing detailed socio-demographic profiles from the census BCPs. Reweighting is undertaken using an optimization approach to generate iteratively a set of weights that "best fits" each CCD. That is, household weights are gradually changed until they produce a set of characteristics that match those of each CCD. Although a non-integer method of reweighting is used, the modelling can be seen as effectively creating 225 or so synthetic households for each CCD, with the characteristics of the synthetic households within each CCD closely matching the characteristics revealed in the census data for households in that particular CCD.

SYNAGI reweighting currently uses data from the 1996 Census of Population and Housing BCP to create target variables for each of the 34,410 CCDs in Australia.[2] The variables from the census that are chosen as targets are those that are also contained within the 1998–1999 HES. To make the variables from the HES compatible with the census, relevant HES variables are recoded so that they match the classifications and ranges that exist in the census. A total of 15 variables were used in the SYNAGI matching process for this work (see Melhuish, Blake and Day, 2002).

The matching process requires that the census and HES variables be based on the same year. This means that the target variables from the 1996 census must be updated to the year of interest. Monetary values must be inflated and the population adjusted for each CCD. The latter is done currently by using ABS demographic and building approvals data.[3] Similarly, HES income and other data are also inflated. There is no requirement to increase the population size of the HES as it is a sample and is reweighted in the SYNAGI process to match the population within each CCD.

The objective of the optimization process is to reweight the HES households in an iterative manner to create a match for the target variables in the census for each CCD. This results in a weight for each of the 6,892 household records for each of the 34,410 CCDs (although many of the weights for individual households in the HES sample for a particular CCD will be zero). The sum of these weights equals the number of households in the CCD, while applying the weights to the HES input values should create values that match the target values in the census table.

The actual optimization process consists of several linked algorithms that marginally change the values of household weights and subsequently evaluate the change in the HES variable values compared with the census targets. The evaluation measure is the sum of the absolute residuals between the reweighted HES values and the census targets. In general terms, if the change in household weights improves the fit to the census targets the weights are accepted, otherwise the change in weights is rejected. This process is undertaken many times until the reweighted HES values *converge* on the census targets. Initial evaluation of the approach suggests that it accurately reproduces the household characteristics targets for the majority of CCDs (Melhuish, Blake and Day, 2002).

The current version of the SYNAGI model is based on the 1996 census and the 1998–1999 HES, with both data sources updated for the purposes of the research presented in this study to June 2001.[4]

The addition of microsimulation

At the conclusion of the above steps a population of synthetic households has been created, with details of their household and family type, housing and labour force tenure, private income, education and so on. The next step is to impute the estimated social security and income tax liabilities of each of the synthetic households, using a microsimulation model. While information about the social security and income tax liabilities of the households is contained within the 1998–1999 HES, such variables are discarded in the modelling and replaced by new simulated receipts and tax payments. Part of the rationale for doing this is that the social security and tax systems changed substantially between 1998–1999 and 2001, so the values on the original HES file are out of date.

In previous work NATSEM created a version of its STINMOD static microsimulation model to run against the 1998–1999 HES file. The STINMOD model replicates the rules of the social security and tax system.[5] For the estimates presented in this chapter, a special version of STINMOD was created, replicating the rules of the tax and social security system as at June 2001. It must be emphasized that the results presented in this study reproduce the characteristics of populations living within small areas as shown in the 1996 census data (with some minor updating to 2001).[6] Consequently, the results reported here are preliminary and primarily designed to illustrate the potential capacities of the new spatial microsimulation techniques.

Overall impact of the policy option

A hypothetical policy change concerning income support rates of payment is used to provide an illustration of the new microsimulation capacity. An important distinction in the Australian income support system is between pensions (paid, for example, to aged people and disabled adults) and allowances (paid, for example, to people who are unemployed or temporarily incapacitated for work due to sickness). Until 1998 the base rate of assistance paid to married allowees was the same as that paid to married pensioners. However, since 1998 allowances have been indexed to movements in the consumer price index, while pensions have been indexed to movements in average male earnings. With earnings having increased more rapidly than prices, there is a growing gap between the rates of payment received by an allowee and by a pensioner. While the amount received by an allowee couple was the same as that received by a pensioner couple in 1997, by June 2001 the allowee couple received $25.40 per fortnight less (and the gap has since widened further). In June 2001 each partner within a pensioner couple received $335.50 a fortnight. In contrast, each partner within an allowee couple received only $322.80 a fortnight. A comprehensive review of poverty in Australia found a very high and rising rate of poverty amongst those who were unemployed, which suggested that those receiving unemployment allowances had fallen further behind average incomes within the community (Harding, Lloyd and Greenwell, 2001: 12).

One interesting question is therefore the impact upon poverty outcomes of restoring the relativities prevailing in 1997 between allowee and pensioner couples – and that is the policy option simulated here. This could, of course, be accomplished in two ways – by reducing pensions or by raising allowances. Given the concern with the level of unemployment allowances in relation to average community incomes, the second option is used as the illustration here. Such an option is expensive – about A$300 million – and there is no suggestion here that it would be regarded as the most desirable policy option if the government were seeking to assist the unemployed. There is continuing concern within Australia about work incentives – and there are thus questions about the extent to which the government can raise unemployment allowances without impacting upon the desirability of low-paid work. Instead, the policy option chosen here is primarily designed to provide an illustration of the spatial capacities of the new model and of the new ability to examine the spatial impacts upon poverty of possible policy changes.

In undertaking the simulation, the poverty line was set at half average disposable income, with disposable income adjusted using the detailed Henderson equivalence scale (which is an equivalence scale with a long history of use in Australia).[7] In the pre-policy-change world, the poverty line was set at $460.92 a week for a couple where the head is employed, the spouse is not in the labour force and there are two children, a boy aged between 6 and 15 years and a girl under 6 years old. The poverty line is held constant at its pre-change level when assessing the impact of the illustrative policy option.[8]

There has been intensive debate in Australia about where the poverty line should be set. A poverty line set at half the median equivalent disposable income would be $403, so one set at 60 per cent of the median, following the Eurostat standard, would be $483.60. Thus a poverty line set at 60 per cent of the median would be somewhat higher than the $461 used in this study.

The income unit used is the household, which means that poverty rates are somewhat lower than found with a more restricted definition of the income unit (Greenwell, Lloyd and Harding, 2001). The results, however, are for persons, with each person within a household being attributed the poverty status of that household.

In the world existing before the illustrative policy change, the estimated poverty rate for persons is 9.4 per cent in June 2001 (table 12.1). The rate for children is somewhat higher, at 10.7 per cent, while that for adults is lower, at 8.9 per cent. After the increase in the payment rate for allowee couples the overall poverty rate drops by 0.3 percentage points to 9.1 per cent. The illustrative policy option particularly affects child poverty, with the poverty rate among children declining to 10.2 per cent. The estimated poverty rate for adults varies only marginally, falling to 8.7 per cent.

In the pre-policy-change world the estimated number of Australians living in poverty is 1,673,000; after the policy change this falls to 1,627,000

Table 12.1 Estimated number in poverty and the poverty rate before and after the policy change, 2001

	Before policy change						After policy change					
	No. in poverty			Poverty rate			No. in poverty			Poverty rate		
	People	Adults	Children	People	Adults	Children	People	Adults	Children	People	Adults	Children
	000	000	000	%	%	%	000	000	000	%	%	%
NSW	533	371	162	8.8	8.4	10.0	518	364	154	8.6	8.2	9.6
Victoria	399	278	121	9.1	8.6	10.5	387	272	115	8.8	8.4	10.0
Queensland	334	232	102	9.9	9.3	11.4	327	228	99	9.7	9.2	10.9
South Australia	156	112	44	11.1	10.6	12.6	151	109	42	10.8	10.4	12.0
Western Australia	160	111	49	9.1	8.7	10.2	156	109	47	8.9	8.5	9.8
Tasmania	56	39	17	12.7	12.2	14.1	54	39	16	12.4	12.0	13.4
ACT	19	13	6	6.5	6.4	6.7	18	13	5	6.4	6.3	6.6
Australia	1,673	1,166	507	9.4	8.9	10.7	1,627	1,143	484	9.1	8.7	10.2

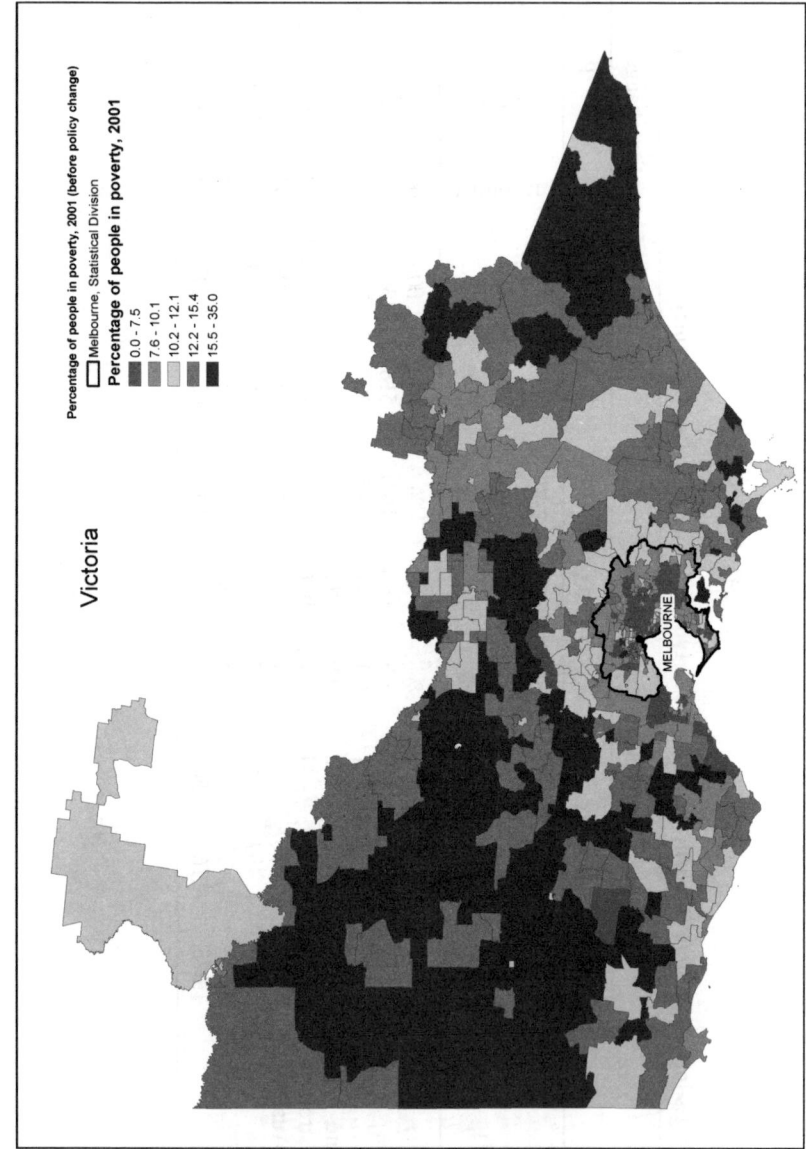

Figure 12.1 Estimated poverty rates by postcode before the policy change, Victoria and Queensland, 2001

Figure 12.1 (cont.)

– that is, by almost 50,000 people.[9] As table 12.1 shows, the fall is evenly spread between adults and children. Because the estimated number of children in poverty in Australia is lower than the estimated number of adults in poverty, this fall produces a greater reduction in the child poverty rate than the adult poverty rate.

Australia is divided into eight states and territories, of which seven are shown in table 12.1.[10] Both before and after the policy change the highest poverty rates are found in South Australia and Tasmania, while the lowest are found in the Australian Capital Territory (which contains Australia's capital, Canberra). The other states all tend to have poverty rates that are relatively close to the Australian average. It should be noted here that these poverty rates should be treated with some caution, as they have been estimated using a *national* poverty line that takes no account of the differential costs of living in the different states and territories (which is particularly important for housing costs).

To this point, the aggregate or national results are no more informative than could be achieved with a national microsimulation model (one which also contains information about which state or territory respondents live in). However, we can now look in more detail at the spatial impact of the illustrative policy change, using the capacities of the new modelling techniques.

Spatial impact of the policy option

As noted earlier, results have been calculated in this simulation for ABS postal areas (hereafter called "postcodes" for convenience).

Mapping results

The postcode poverty rates estimated with the new microsimulation capacity can be mapped so as to get a visual impression of whether poverty is much higher in particular areas of a state or territory. This is done for Victoria and Queensland (fig. 12.1). These show that that the rate of poverty tends to be lower in the capital cities of the two states than in rural and regional areas.

The new modelling also allows us to look at the *change* in the poverty rate within each postcode resulting from the policy initiative simulated. This is shown for Victoria and Queensland in figure 12.2, and suggests that the greatest falls in poverty as a result of the new policy would be in regional and remote areas rather than in the capital cities.

One problem with simply looking at the poverty rates of different areas is that an area with a very high poverty rate might contain almost no people, while an area with an average poverty rate might contain substantial numbers of people. Such an analysis might thus provide a misleading picture of where poverty is actually concentrated. In an initial attempt to address this, figure 12.3 looks at the *number* of people in poverty by postcode within Victoria and Queensland. This gives a quite different impression to figure 12.1, with poverty being more heavily concentrated in the capital cities and the coastal belt – although with some inland areas showing a high number of people in poverty. A more complex but more accurate method of assessing this issue might be to look at the number of poor people per square kilometre, which the authors intend to do in future work.

Results for individual postcodes

Spatial microsimultion allows us to examine the profile of poverty in individual postcodes both before and after the policy change. As a case study this chapter examines a postcode located in metropolitan Sydney. An estimated 3,980 people living in this postcode are in poverty before the policy change, with an estimated 1,520 of these being children and the remainder adults. The postcode is relatively large, with well over 25,000 people contained within it. The estimated poverty rate before the policy change is 14.8 per cent.

After the simulated policy change an estimated 210 people are lifted above the poverty line, reducing the poverty rate to 14.1 per cent.

This selected postcode is interesting, because it has a very different poverty profile to the average picture for Australia. As previous research has shown (Harding, Lloyd and Greenwell, 2001) and as demonstrated again in the second column in table 12.2, poverty in Australia is typically associated with such factors as not being in paid work, being dependent on government cash benefits and being a sole parent or having a large family.

The majority of those in poverty in the selected postcode live in a household where the head is of working age – between 25 and 54 years. Compared to the average, this postcode has relatively fewer households in poverty that are headed by either a young Australian aged less than 25 years or an older Australian aged 65 or more years. For example, while an estimated 10.5 per cent of all Australians in poverty live in a household headed by a person aged 65 or older, in the selected postcode the proportion is only 2.0 per cent.

A poor person in the selected postcode is three times as likely to be living in a household headed by a person employed full time compared with the national average for poor households. Thus almost one in every seven poor people in the selected postcode live in a household headed by

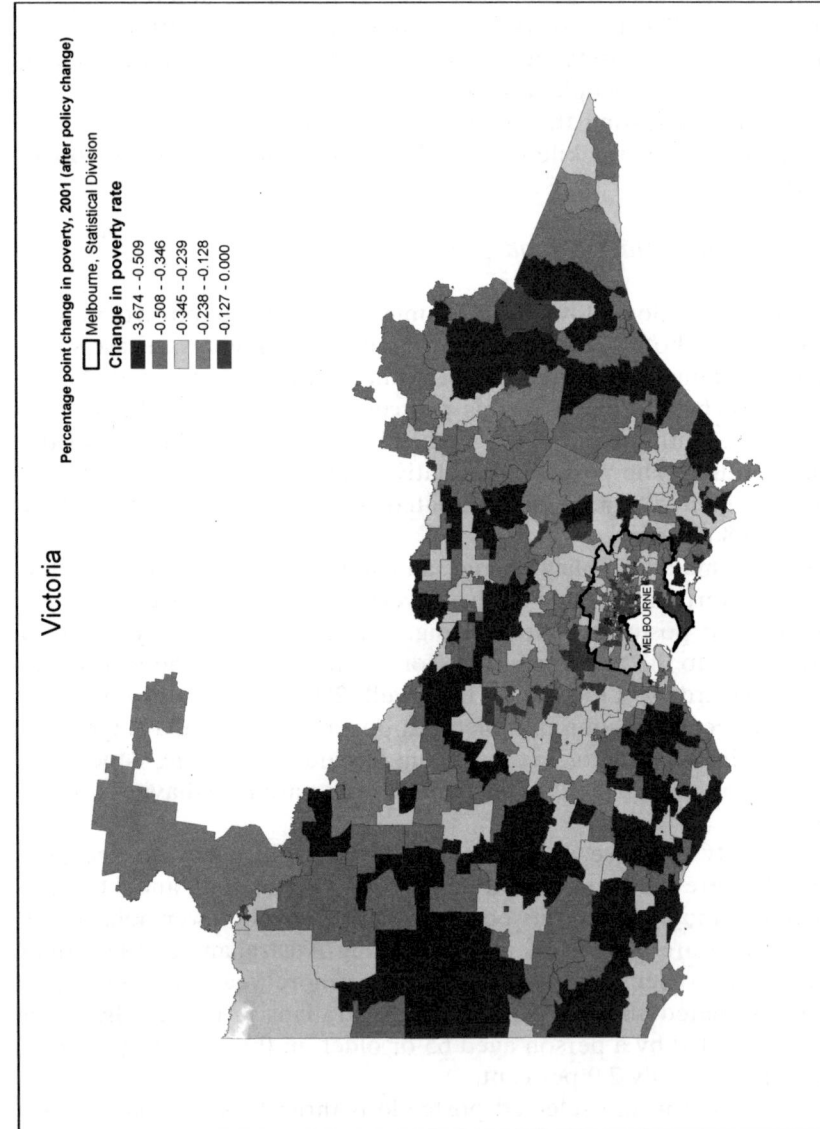

Figure 12.2 Estimated change in poverty rates by postcode as a result of the policy change, Victoria and Queensland

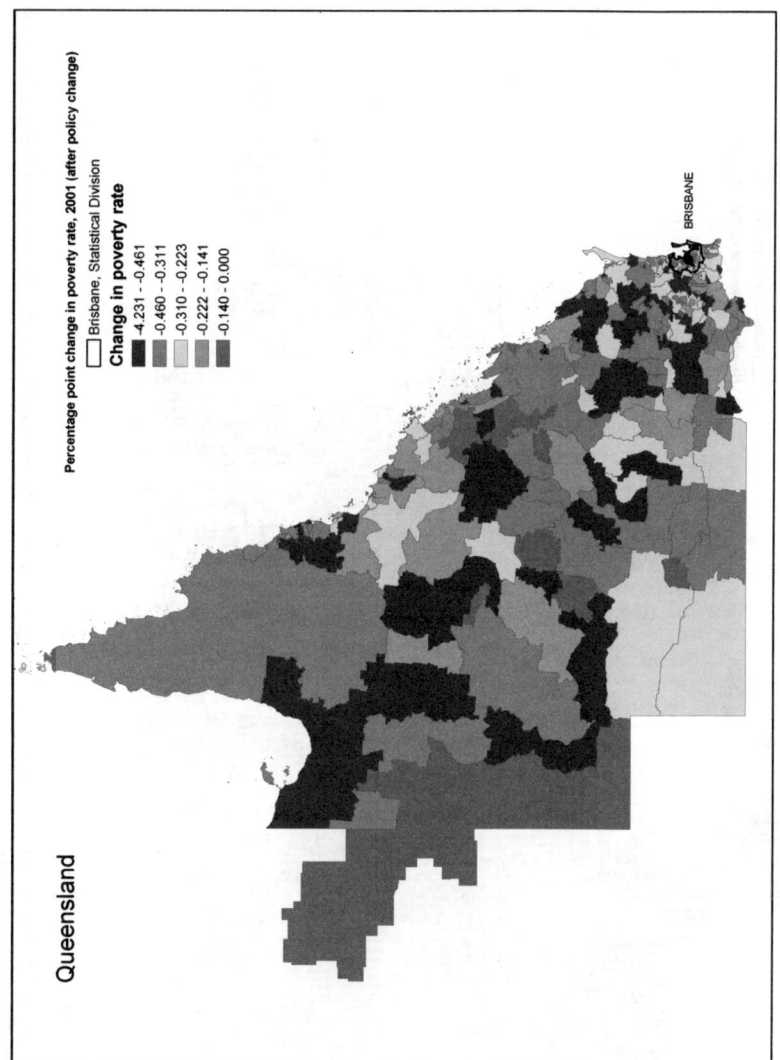

Figure 12.2 (cont.)

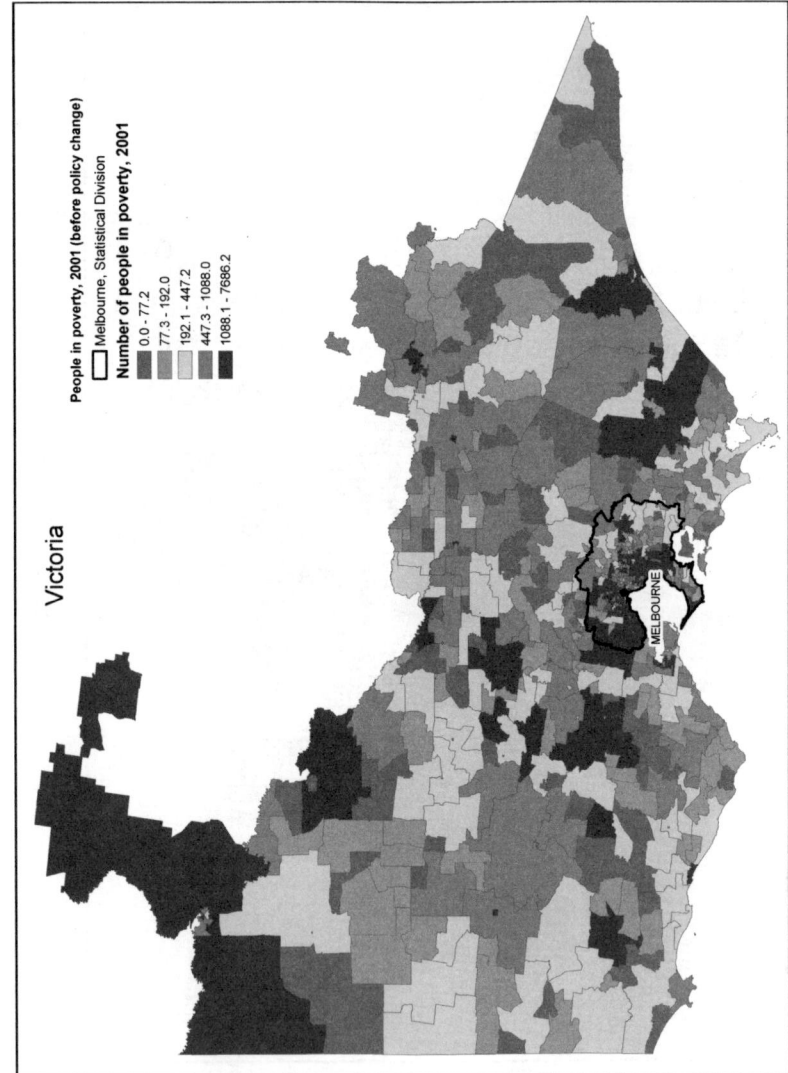

Figure 12.3 Estimated number of people in poverty by postcode before the policy change, Victoria and Queensland, 2001

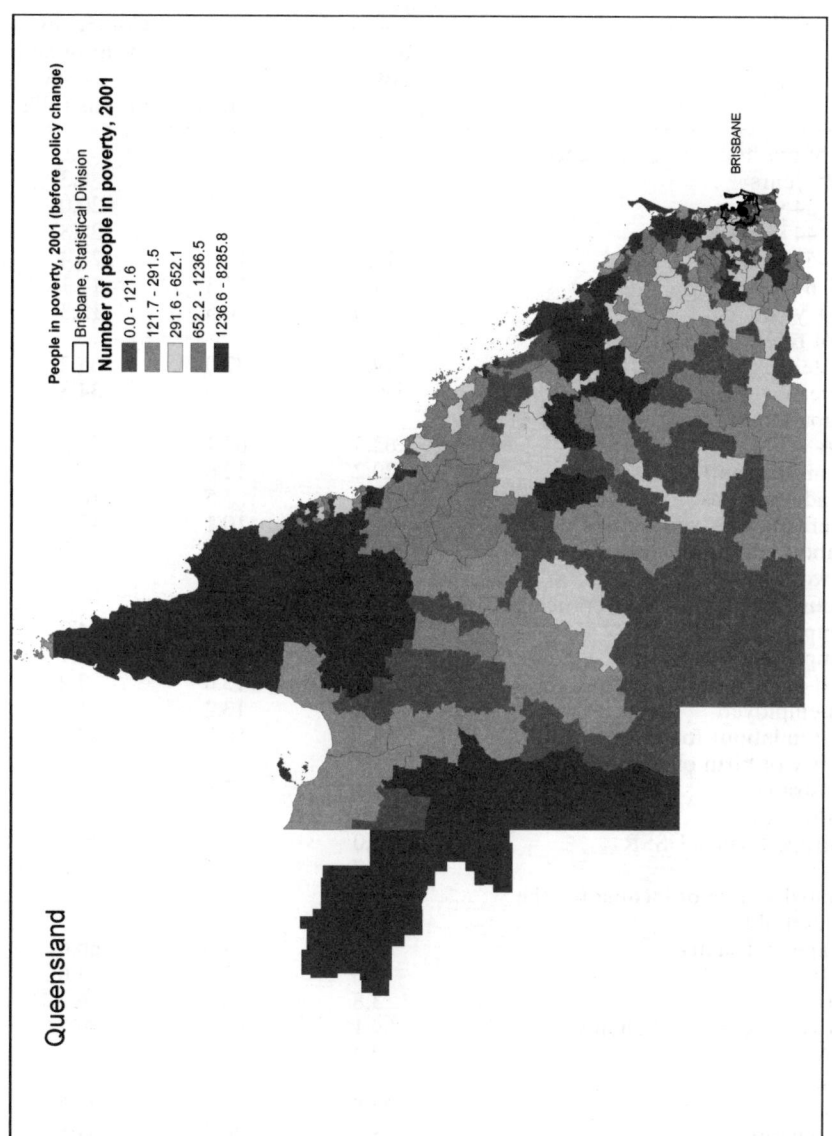

Figure 12.3 (cont.)

Table 12.2 Characteristics of residents of poor households in selected postcode in NSW compared with national profile of poor and non-poor Australians (before policy change)

	Composition of those in poverty in		Composition of those not in poverty in Australia
	Selected Sydney postcode	Australia	
Age of the household reference person			
<25 years	1.7	4.1	4.3
25–34 years	27.4	20.3	20.0
35–44 years	38.3	35.1	28.8
45–54 years	15.7	17.7	23.4
55–64 years	14.9	12.3	11.1
65+ years	2.0	10.5	12.3
Sex of reference person			
Male	49.4	37.0	65.2
Female	50.6	63.0	34.8
Occupation of reference person			
NA	62.5	64.1	28.5
Managers and professionals	20.2	12.6	34.3
Tradespersons	2.1	3.5	10.8
Clerical, sales and service	1.6	10.1	13.5
Labourers, production and transport workers	13.6	9.7	12.9
Labour force status of reference person			
Employee – FT	15.3	4.9	54.2
Employee – PT	13.2	15.9	10.1
Self-employed	9.1	15.0	7.2
Unemployed	8.2	13.2	1.2
Not in labour force	54.3	50.9	27.4
Country of birth of reference person			
Australia	21.1	67.3	69.5
Other	24.3	8.7	7.2
Europe/former USSR	12.0	14.7	16.3
Asia	42.7	9.3	7.0
Principal source of income for the household			
Wage and salary	26.6	14.6	66.0
Self-employed	8.0	7.9	7.0
Other	3.8	6.7	6.2
Government cash benefits	59.1	65.2	20.7
NA	2.4	5.5	
Tenure type			
Owner	27.5	33.5	37.2
Purchaser	28.2	26.7	34.5
Public housing	9.0	10.7	4.4
Private renter	27.7	24.2	22.0
Other, rent-free	7.6	4.8	1.9

Table 12.2 (cont.)

	Composition of those in poverty in		Composition of those not in poverty in Australia
	Selected Sydney postcode	Australia	
Marital status of reference person			
Never married	3.4	11.8	10.2
Separated/divorced/widowed	7.1	19.7	16.1
Married	89.5	68.5	73.7
Household type			
Single person	7.0	16.6	8.9
Couple only	4.8	15.8	20.1
Couple with children	68.9	46.8	45.3
Sole parent	3.6	10.6	11.6
Multiple families	15.7	10.2	14.1
Number of dependants in the household			
None	19.8	42.1	45.6
One	12.6	12.6	16.9
Two	43.1	18.7	22.0
Three	19.9	16.1	11.5
Four	3.9	7.3	3.1
Five or more	0.7	3.2	0.9

someone working full time – suggestive of a significant "working poor" representation. Conversely, a poor person living in the selected postcode is less likely than a poor person nationally to be living in a household headed by an unemployed or self-employed person.

The country of birth of the household head is also strikingly different for poor households in the selected postcode than poor households nationally. Nationally about two-thirds of all poor Australians live in a household with an Australian-born head, while in the selected postcode the comparative proportion is about one-fifth. Instead, poor households in the selected postcode are much more likely to be headed by a migrant, and particularly one born in Asia.

Poor households in the selected postcode are somewhat less likely than poor households nationally to own their own home outright, while they are also somewhat less likely to live in public housing. Further reinforcing the profile of difference, more than two-thirds of all those in poverty in the selected postcode live in "couple-with-children" households, a proportion more than 20 per cent higher than the national average for poor households. The proportion living in multiple-family households is also high, while poor sole parents, single people and couple-without-children households are underrepresented compared to the national average for poor households.

The selected postcode provides a good illustration of the capacities of the new spatial microsimulation to shed light on the reasons for poverty in different regions of Australia. Its poverty profile is very different to that of poverty within Australia generally, consisting disproportionately of migrants who are working in lowly paid jobs, are married and have children. While there are still poor people living in the selected postcode who are dependent on unemployment or sickness allowances – and who would thus be affected by the policy option modelled here – the majority of poor residents in this area would not be assisted by such a policy option. This illustrates how the new spatial microsimulation can be used to inform decisions by policy-makers about the most appropriate policy responses to poverty.

Conclusions

In recent years NATSEM has developed spatial microsimulation models which attempt to create geographically detailed unit record files of synthetic households. During the past decade NATSEM has created many microsimulation models which have allowed policy-makers to assess the immediate distributional and revenue impact of possible policy changes at the *national* level. However, in the past suitable microdata have not been available in Australia to assess the impact of existing policy or possible policy changes at a more detailed spatial level. The new techniques developed at NATSEM attempt to redress this deficiency.

This chapter has described NATSEM's first attempt to simulate the spatial impact of a possible policy change – namely, increasing the rate of social security paid to allowee couples to the same level as that paid to pensioner couples. While these two rates used to move in tandem, in recent years there has been a widening gap between them.

It must be emphasized that the results presented here are intended to illustrate the potential capacities of the new models being developed rather than to be treated as firm estimates of the extent of poverty in Australia today. There has been intense public debate in Australia about the most appropriate way to measure poverty and the accuracy of the national sample survey data that underlie most poverty estimates in Australia. In addition, and even more importantly, the findings presented here are the result of blending the 1998–1999 ABS HES unit record data with the 1996 census basic community profiles (with some minor updating of both data sources to reflect the 2001 world better). Future work will provide a more up-to-date picture of the extent of disadvantage by region by combining the HES data with 2001 census data. Finally, the results presented here have arisen from NATSEM's first attempt to simulate the spatial impact of a policy change by linking its STINMOD microsimulation model of the tax and transfer system with the synthetic household microdata. Much research remains to be done to confirm the extent to which the synthetic results match other available benchmark data (such as administrative data on the number of social security recipients by postcode). NATSEM has not yet undertaken the further research required to validate the accuracy of the social security payments simulated within STINMOD *at the regional level.*

With these caveats firmly in mind, the simulation suggested that restoring the social security rate paid to allowee couples to the same level as that paid to pensioner couples would reduce overall poverty within Australia by 0.3 per cent and child poverty by 0.5 per cent.

This mapping of estimated poverty rates by postcode suggested that poverty is not uniformly spread across the different geographic regions of Australia but shows great variation. In addition, the policy change modelled would also have disparate spatial impacts, benefiting some postcodes much more than others.

Examination of the profile of poverty before the policy change in one postcode in Sydney showed that the new spatial microsimulation model would be very useful in assisting policy-makers to understand the different characteristics of those in poverty in particular geographic areas. It would also help in exploring which policy changes would be most likely to assist those geographic regions of particular concern to policy-makers.

Acknowledgements

The current phase of work for the SYNAGI model is being jointly funded by NATSEM, the Australian Research Council (Project No. LP349152), the NSW Premier's Department, the Queensland Department of Premier and Cabinet, Queensland Treasury, the Queensland Department of Local Government and Planning, the ACT Chief Minister's Department, the Victorian Department of Sustainability and Environment and the ABS. NATSEM gratefully acknowledges the funding and enthusiasm of these research partners for the project. The authors would also like to acknowledge work on SYNAGI by Tony Melhuish, Marcus Blake and Susan Day (with the second section of this study drawing heavily upon their earlier research) as well as Otto Hellwig's significant contribution to spatial microsimulation at NATSEM. They would also like to thank Rebecca Cassells for research assistance. All views expressed in this chapter are the authors' own and not necessarily shared by the industry partners.

General caveat: NATSEM research findings are generally based on estimated characteristics of the population. Such estimates are usually derived from the application of microsimulation modelling techniques to microdata based on sample surveys. These estimates may be different from the actual characteristics of the population because of sampling and non-sampling errors in the microdata and because of the assumptions underlying the modelling techniques. The microdata do not contain any information that enables identification of the individuals or families to which they refer.

Notes

1. Microsimulation models traditionally use microdata to estimate the likely impact of social or economic policy change on individuals or households by applying a set of rules to the individuals in the microdata. They are particularly useful for the analysis of the distribution of outcomes within the population rather than just aggregate outcomes.
2. CCDs are defined for each Census of Population and Housing. Reference was made in the second section to the 37,209 CCDs defined in the 2001 census. The number of CCDs defined for the 1996 census was 34,410.
3. The method of updating census variables in the current approach is fairly crude. As SYNAGI develops, methods will be developed to improve the estimation of population change for small areas and to estimate the likely change in the characteristics of these small areas. Given the complexities of change at the small-area level, even between censuses, this task is far from trivial and would rely on ancillary data, such as labour force estimates, to inform the updating process.
4. In this chapter the postal area weights from Marketinfo2001 have been used. The "postal area" is an ABS approximation of the postcodes used by Australia Post for mail delivery. Postal areas are aggregations of CCDs and 2,379 postal areas were defined by the ABS for use with the 1996 census data.
5. For more information see the STINMOD Technical Papers Nos 1–7, available from the NATSEM website (www.natsem.canberra.edu.au).
6. The 2001 census data were released after this work was undertaken. A new version of SYNAGI has subsequently been developed based on the 2001 data.
7. See Lloyd, Harding and Greenwell (2002) for more details on the equivalence scale. Disposable income equals gross income minus income tax. This chapter has not attempted to simulate the impact of any increase in income tax to fund the increase in allowances, although this could easily be done as STINMOD also replicates the rules of the income tax system.
8. Since the poverty line is linked to average disposable incomes across the population, a more complete analysis might also incorporate the small increase in the poverty line which would stem from the increase in incomes received by allowees.
9. Note that the results presented here for the illustrative application only cover part of the impact of the policy change on poverty. The poverty "headcount" identifies where the increase in payment is enough to move someone from below to above the poverty

line. It does not identify those cases where people's incomes have been increased but they remain either above or below the poverty line.
10. The Northern Territory has been excluded here because the HES sample from which these results are derived excludes remote areas, and an estimated one-quarter of the Northern Territory population are thus not captured in the survey. Many of those excluded are indigenous Australians, among whom poverty is often very pronounced.

REFERENCES

ABS (1996) *1996 Census Dictionary*, ABS Cat. No. 2901.0, Canberra: Australian Bureau of Statistics.

Greenwell, H., R. Lloyd and A. Harding (2001) "An Introduction to Poverty Measurement Issues", Discussion Paper No. 55, National Centre for Social and Economic Modelling, Canberra.

Harding, A., R. Lloyd and H. Greenwell (2001) *Financial Disadvantage in Australia 1900 to 2000: The Persistence of Poverty in a Decade of Growth*, Camperdown, NSW: The Smith Family, available at www.smithfamily.org.au.

Lloyd, R., A. Harding and H. Greenwell (2002) "Worlds Apart: Postcodes with the Highest and Lowest Poverty Rates in Today's Australia", in A. Eardley and B. Bradbury, eds, *Refereed Proceedings of the National Social Policy Conference 2001*, SPRC Report 1/02, April, available at www.natsem.canberra.edu.au.

Melhuish, T., M. Blake and S. Day (2002) "An Evaluation of Synthetic Household Populations for Census Collection Districts Created Using Spatial Microsimulation Techniques", paper prepared for the Twenty-sixth Australia and New Zealand Regional Science Association International (ANZRSAI) Annual Conference, 29 September–2 October, Gold Coast, Queensland, Australia, available at www.natsem.canberra.edu.au.

Williamson, P., M. Birkin and P. H. Rees (1998) "The Estimation of Population Microdata by Using Data from Small Area Statistics and Samples of Anonymised Records", *Environment and Planning A*, 30: 785–816.

Part III

Well-being case studies

13

Longevity in Russia's regions: Do poverty and low public health spending kill?

Oleksiy Ivaschenko

Introduction

Poor health is a fundamental obstruction to human capital. It not only affects the length and quality of individual lives, but also undermines the future economic prospects of a country. These concerns make it very important from a policy perspective to understand the determinants of health outcomes. This chapter explores a unique regional-level dataset on life expectancy, the incidence of poverty and real per capita public health spending in Russia over the period 1994–2000 to explain the variations in longevity over time.[1]

It is by now a well-established fact that life expectancy, an aggregate measure of the population's health, declined dramatically in Russia during the first years of economic and social transition. It increased somewhat as the process of economic recovery started, but declined again in the aftermath of the 1998 financial crisis (see fig. 13.1).

Cornia and Paniccià (2000) and Cockerham (1999) discuss the causes of the mortality crisis in Russia. However, this research has several shortcomings. First, most studies are highly descriptive and concentrate on the determinants of mortality using immediate causes of death. Shkolnikov et al. (1999), Shkolnikov and Meslé (1996) and Walberg et al. (1998) identify the dominant contributors to rising mortality to be cardiovascular diseases, injuries and violence, suicide and alcohol-related disorders, such as cirrhosis of the liver and accidental alcohol poisoning. Although important for gaining insight into the nature of the mortality crisis, these

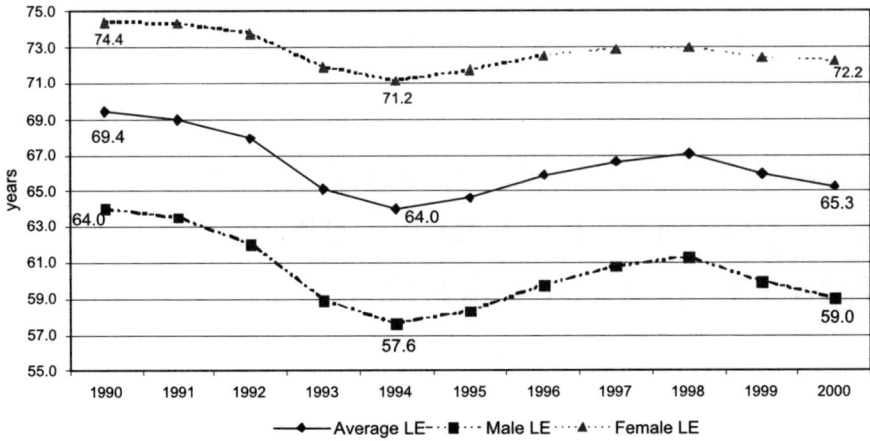

Figure 13.1 Life expectancy at birth in Russia, 1990–2000

studies do not investigate the impact of the underlying factors affecting health outcomes in Russia.

Second, although many studies recognize that changes in mortality are likely to be affected by the economic and social changes associated with the transition, the empirical evidence on the direct impact of these changes on longevity or mortality in Russia is not conclusive, as Becker and Hemley (1998), Brainerd and Varavikova (2001) and Kennedy, Kawachi and Brainerd (1998) attest.

Third, although Nell and Stewart (1994) and Zoohori et al. (1998) speculate that the health status of Russians is affected strongly by an increasing incidence of poverty and a deteriorating public health infrastructure, the impacts of these factors on longevity or other measures of health have not been adequately explored empirically.[2] Finally, most of the studies focus on explaining mortality during the initial period of economic transition before 1995, e.g. Shkolnikov et al. (1999) and Walberg et al. (1998). The trends in health outcomes after 1994, particularly in the aftermath of the 1998 financial crisis, have received little attention in the literature.

This chapter examines the direct impact of poverty and public health expenditure on life expectancy in Russia using a dataset that covers 77 regions from 1994 to 2000. Considering that most health policy decisions are made at the country level, the empirical analysis of the relationship between health outcomes and socio-economic conditions using regional data is expected to have much more policy relevance than cross-country studies. Moreover, these measures of poverty and public health spending

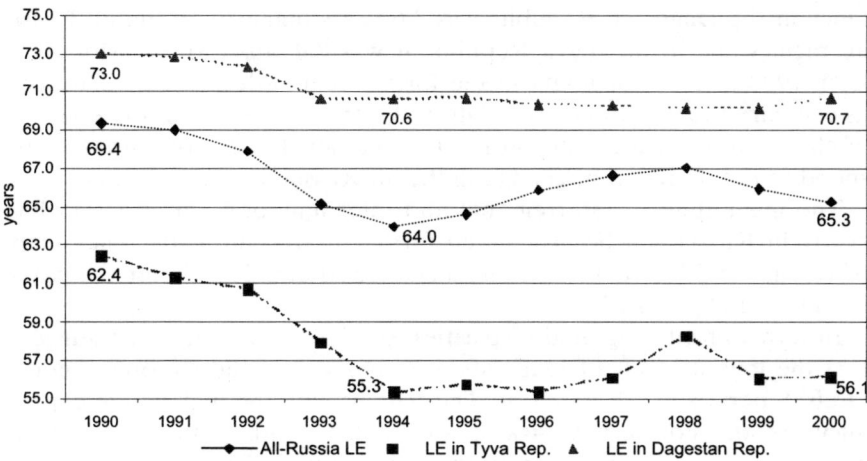

Figure 13.2 Life expectancy at birth in selected regions of Russia, 1990–2000

are better indicators of socio-economic differences and health effort than variables used in previous studies on Russia.

The remainder of the chapter is organized as follows. The second section presents the regional differences and the overall trends in life expectancy from 1990 to 2000 in Russia. This section also discusses the potential causes of the observed changes in longevity. The third section provides the theoretical underpinnings of the empirical model and discusses both the empirical specification and the estimation methodology. The fourth section describes the data used in the empirical analysis; the fifth section discusses the estimation results. The sixth section tests the robustness of the results to alternative model specifications and estimation techniques. The final section concludes by highlighting the main findings and discussing their policy implications.

Geographical patterns of life expectancy, variations over time and potential causes

Average life expectancy figures for Russia disguise considerable regional differences in the levels of, and changes in, life expectancy. The scope of these regional disparities is revealed in figure 13.2, which compares all-Russia life expectancy during the period 1990–2000 to life expectancy in regions which are the least and most successful in terms of longevity.

Figure 13.2 provides a clear indication that Russia's regions differ tremendously not only in the levels of longevity at any given period, but also in the changes in longevity over time. For instance, in 1990 life expectancy in the Dagestan Republic was 3.6 years higher than the all-Russia average, while in the Tyva Republic it was 7.0 years lower. Moreover, from 1990 to 1994 longevity in the former region declined by 2.4 years, as compared to 7.1 years in the latter. As one can see, even the *direction* of change in life expectancy at the regional level does not always correspond to the direction of change in the all-Russia life expectancy.

The magnitude of interregional and inter-temporal variations in longevity in Russia can be articulated further by the life expectancy maps of Russia for 1998 (before the financial crisis) and 2000 (after the crisis) presented in figures 13.3 and 13.4.

In terms of interregional disparities, the life expectancy map suggests that the lowest levels of longevity are observed in the European north, Urals, Siberia and the Far East. The regions with the highest life expectancy are the northern Caucasus and Volga-Vyatka. As mentioned in many studies, such regional patterns of mortality in Russia have been observed for many years (Shkolnikov et al., 1999).

In terms of the regional *trends* in longevity, it is worth noting that northern Russia, east Siberia and the Far East have witnessed the greatest declines in life expectancy. Between 1990 and 1994, the period of the largest drop in longevity across all Russian regions, life expectancy declined by 7.0 years in the northern region, 6.7 years in east Siberia, 5.8 years in western Siberia and 5.7 years in both Urals and the Far East. Notably, these regions were among those which experienced the greatest economic and social disruption, as indicated by the rates of industrial output decline, job turnover, unemployment, divorce and fertility. As recognized in the literature, declines in life expectancy were the smallest in the agricultural regions of the south and in the regions of central Russia having the most developed medical services infrastructure. However, even there the longevity declines were quite substantial. So, from 1990 to 1994, life expectancy in the north Caucasus and the Volga Basin regions declined by 3.1 and 4.1 years respectively – hence dramatic changes in longevity during the 1990s were observed in *all* regions of Russia.

Notably, the regions with the largest declines in longevity during the 1990–1994 period experienced the most noticeable improvements starting in 1995. For instance, life expectancy rose from 1994 to 1998 by an average 4.5 years in the north, 3.5 years in Siberia and 3.4 years in the Far East. However, longevity improvements after 1994 have not lasted very long. As figures 13.3 and 13.4 suggest, the financial crisis that erupted in the autumn of 1998 has led to worsening longevity in all regions. In the north, Urals and central regions life expectancy declined on average by more than two years in the period from 1998 to 2000. The smallest declines in longevity during the crisis were observed in the north Caucasus and western Siberia.

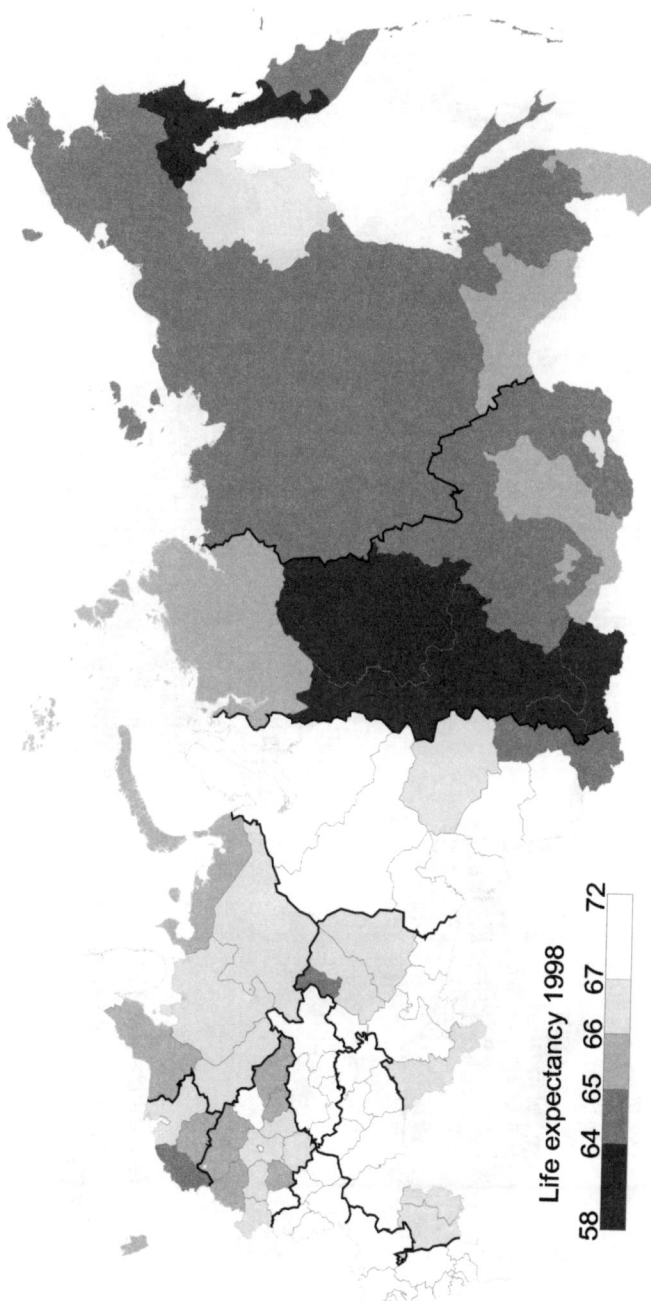

Figure 13.3 Life expectancy in Russia's regions, 1998

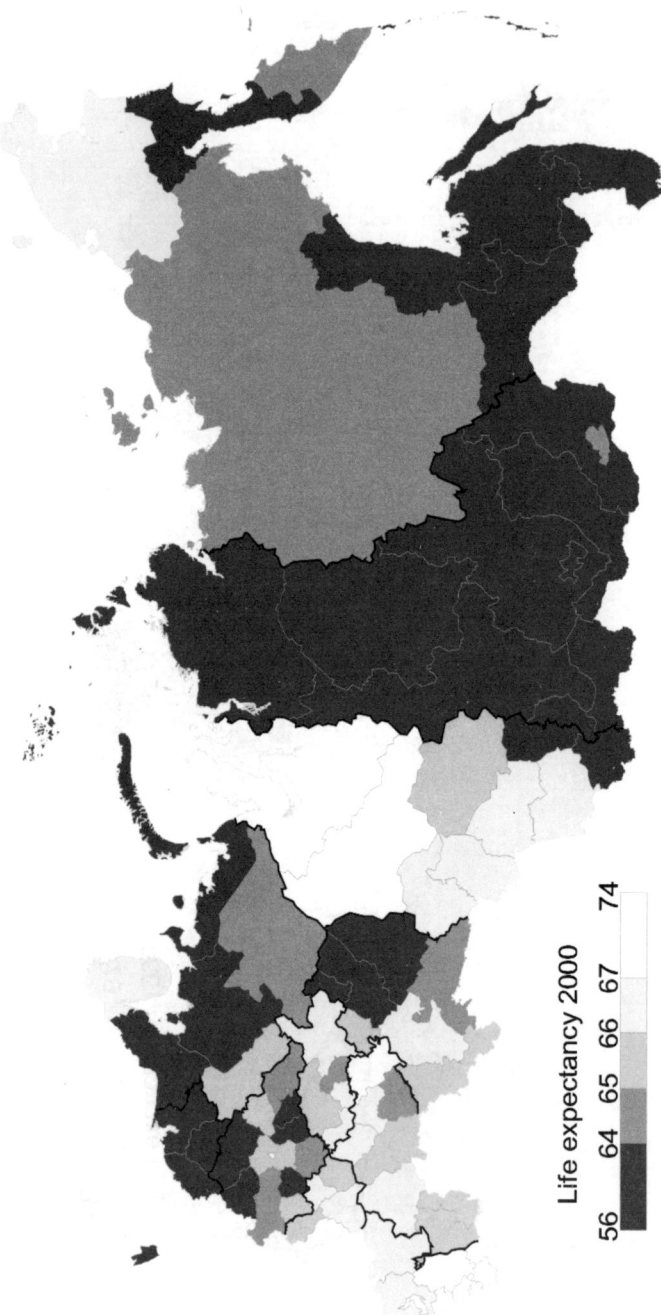

Figure 13.4 Life expectancy in Russia's regions, 2000

Empirical evidence on the direct effects of poverty and public health spending on longevity in Russia is scarce. However, the unprecedented regional disparities in these factors, as well as the variations in them over time, indicate that they are very likely determinants of the observed regional and temporal patterns of longevity. Support for this hypothesis comes from studies that find a strong impact on life expectancy in Russia of the variables closely associated with poverty and public health spending, as well as from cross-country studies on the impact of those variables. These studies are discussed below.

Zoohori et al. (1998), Stegmayr et al. (2001) and Shkolnikov et al. (1999) argue that rising mortality from cardiovascular disease, which is the dominant cause of increased mortality, is due to the high levels of stress experienced by Russians during the transition.[3] These authors recognize that rising stress levels should be regarded not as an addition to, but rather as a consequence of, economic factors such as high labour force turnover, the decline in real income and the increase in poverty.[4]

Increased mortality rates are also related to the stress associated with the break-up of old social networks and the necessity to find new ways of social interactions in the new economic conditions, as Rose (2000) and Rose and McAllister (1996) acknowledge. Individuals who are not able to reshuffle their portfolios of social networks to reflect the new reality better fare much worse in terms of income security, sufficiency of food and even personal safety, which are factors known to affect longevity.

Brainerd and Varavikova (2001) show that changes in life expectancy in Russia are related to changes in per capita income. Walberg et al. (1998) demonstrate a similar impact from income distribution. For a given poverty line, the prevalence of poverty in a region is a function of average per capita income and income inequality. Hence, these studies provide implicit support for the hypothesis that poverty matters to longevity.

Brainerd and Varavikova (2001), Kennedy, Kawachi and Brainerd (1998) and Walberg et al. (1998) find the crime rate to be a significant predictor of both male and female mortality. Notably, Kennedy, Kawachi and Brainerd (1998) find that the effects of per capita income and poverty on life expectancy vanish if the crime rate is included in the regression, hence the crime rate can be considered to be a function of economic circumstances, *ceteris paribus*.

Increased alcohol consumption during the transition is another factor contributing to the rise in mortality in Russia, as Brainerd and Varavikova (2001), Britton, McKee and Leon (1998), Leon et al. (1997), McKee (2001) and Ryan (1995) demonstrate. Moreover, these authors recognize the need to identify the underlying reasons for the observed drinking patterns. Some empirical evidence supports the notion that in Russia the increase in alcohol consumption and other behaviour deleterious to health is driven by deteriorating socio-economic conditions, as Zohoori et al. (1998) report.

Brainerd and Varavikova (2001), Paniccià (2000), Shkolnikov and Cornia (2000) and Shkolnikov and Meslé (1996) document a rapid increase in mortality due to preventable diseases that are normally associated with deteriorating medical and sanitary services, e.g. infectious and parasitic diseases. Although public spending on health as a share of GDP remained largely unchanged, the shrinking economy and the strained government budget led to a substantial drop in real public health spending across the regions, often to levels well below those necessary to cover the most basic expenditures.[5] McKee (2001) argued that the weakness of the medical care system in Russia was likely to play an increasing role during the latter part of the 1990s.

Finally, attempts to identify the effects of poverty and public health spending on longevity using cross-country data generally find that these factors matter to the health of the population, e.g. Anand and Ravallion (1993), Bidani and Ravallion (1997), Calfat (1996), Carrin and Politi (1995), Filmer and Pritchett (1999), Kakwani (1993), Lichtenberg (2002) and Rajkumar and Swaroop (2002). Nonetheless, these studies have shortcomings that may affect the results.

First, by not addressing the possible endogeneity of the explanatory variables, they risk identifying a merely associative, rather than causative, relationship between the dependent and explanatory variables. Second, the cross-sectional nature of the data does not permit accounting for country-specific or region-specific fixed effects, which may lead to biased estimates. Third, cross-sectional studies, by their nature, are constrained to leave unexplained the critical variability in health indicators over time. Fourth, the empirical models are static, with the exception of Lichtenberg (2002), so that they fail to consider the dynamic nature of health outcomes such as life expectancy. Finally, the quality of the cross-country data makes comparability problematic and, thus, the legitimacy of their use questionable.[6] Using panel data, the present study aims to address the above limitations.

Model

Theoretical grounds

This section begins by asserting that *individual* health in year t is a function of the stock of health in year $t-1$ and the private and public real per capita health expenditures in year t, so that:

$$h_{it} = f(h_{it-1}, HE\_private_{it}, HE\_public_{it}, v_r) \qquad (1)$$

where h_{it} is the health of individual i in year t, h_{it-1} is the lagged stock of health, $HE\_private_{it}$ is private investment in health by individual i in year t, HE_public_{it} is public health spending per individual i in year t and v_r are time-invariant regional factors (e.g. climate, pollution) affecting health.

Private health expenditure can be best approximated by individual income, in which case equation (1) transforms into:

$$h_{it} = f_i(h_{it-1}, y_{it}, HE\_public_{it}, v_r) \qquad (2)$$

where y_{it} is income of individual i in year t.

There is considerable empirical evidence to suggest that the relationship between income and health is non-linear; that is, increasing income improves health, but after a certain point exerts diminishing effects (Backlund, Sorlie and Johnson, 1996; Deaton, 2001). The assumed concave relationship between health and income implies that *population* health (which can be represented by a summary statistic such as life expectancy) depends not only on the mean income of the people living in a region, but also on the distribution of income around the mean.[7] At the same time, public health expenditure as a public good can be assumed to be equally available to each resident in a region. When aggregating to the regional (population) level, these assumptions allow us to express equation (2) as:

$$H_{rt} = f_r(H_{rt-1}, Y_{rt}, I_{rt}, HE\_public_{rt}, v_r) \qquad (3)$$

where H_{rt} is a measure of population health in region r in time t, H_{rt-1} is the lagged value of population health, Y_{rt} is the average income of people in a region r in time t, I_{rt} is the measure of income inequality in a region r in time t, HE_public_{rt} is real per capita public health expenditure in a region r in time t and v_r are time-invariant regional factors (e.g. climate, pollution) affecting health.

At a given regional poverty line, the mean income in a region and the distribution of incomes around the mean would define the incidence of poverty. Hence equation (3) can be alternatively presented as:

$$H_{rt} = f(H_{rt-1}, P_{rt}, HE\_public_{rt}, v_r) \qquad (4)$$

where P_{rt} is the incidence of poverty (poverty headcount index) in region r at time t, and all other variables are as defined above.[8]

Next the chapter discusses the specification of equation (4), which is to be empirically estimated.

Empirical specification and estimation technique

As the rates of poverty and public health spending are likely to have diminishing marginal effects on longevity, this empirical specification follows many other studies (e.g. Anand and Ravallion, 1993; Collins and Thomasson, 2002; Lichtenberg, 2002; Pritchett and Summers, 1997) in assuming the log-linear relationship between life expectancy, an aggregate indicator of population health on the regional level and the variables determining it. The baseline regression equation takes the following form:

$$\ln(LE_{rt}) = \alpha + \beta_1 * \ln(LE_{rt-1}) + \beta_2 * \ln(P_{rt})$$

$$+ \beta_3 * \ln(HE\_public_{rt}) + v_r + \varepsilon_{rt} \quad (5)$$

where r indexes regions, t indexes time periods, v_r are time-invariant region-specific characteristics that affect life expectancy and $\varepsilon_{rt} \sim \mathrm{iid}(0, \sigma_e^2)$ is a disturbance term.[9]

One can estimate equation (5) separately for male and female life expectancies, thereby allowing the coefficients to be gender-specific.

There is substantial debate in the literature on whether one should use the natural logarithm of life expectancy or some other transformation of this variable in the regression equation (e.g. Anand and Ravallion, 1993; Kakwani, 1993). The former study suggests a non-linear transformation of life expectancy of the form ln(*maximum achievable LE − actual LE*) as an alternative to ln(*actual LE*). Such a transformation would reflect the fact that life expectancy is bounded from above, and that it takes greater effort to increase life expectancy by the same number of years in a country where life expectancy is initially higher.[10] Therefore the robustness of the estimates will be checked by performing the regression analysis using this alternative definition of the dependent variable as well.

It can be argued that the amount of public health spending in a given period can be a reflection of the observed health situation in a region. In other words, one might expect that worsening health outcomes may induce regional (or federal) government to spend more on health. If that is indeed the case, then the estimated contemporaneous effect of public health spending on life expectancy will be biased. To deal with this issue, the lagged value of public health spending is used in the estimations. Another argument for using a lagged rather than contemporaneous value of public health spending is that the effect of this factor on longevity is likely to take time to be felt. There will also be a high correlation between simultaneous values of public health spending and poverty if higher levels of spending are geared towards poorer regions, or if poor regions spend less on public health.

The estimation of a dynamic regression model represented by equation (5) using OLS will result in biased and inconsistent estimates (Davidson and MacKinnon, 1993: 330). To overcome this problem the study uses the dynamic panel data GMM estimator derived by Arellano and Bond (1991) as the main instrument of the empirical analysis.[11]

Expressing equation (5) in the first difference form, and using the *lagged* rather than contemporaneous public health spending, gives:

$$\Delta \ln(LE_{rt}) = \gamma_0 + \gamma_1 * \Delta \ln(LE_{rt-1}) + \gamma_2 * \Delta \ln(P_{rt})$$
$$+ \gamma_3 * \Delta \ln(HE\_public_{rt-1}) + \Delta \varepsilon_{rt} \qquad (6)$$

This transformation effectively removes region-specific fixed effects v_r which are present in equation (5). The second lag of the level, $\ln(LE_{rt-2})$, as well as subsequent lags, are used as instruments for $\Delta \ln(LE_{rt-1})$.[12] Instrumenting with the lagged levels gives an advantage over instrumenting with the lagged differences in terms of gaining an additional time period (hence an additional 77 observations) in the estimation. Assuming that the poverty rate and lagged public health spending are exogenous variables, the first differences of these variables will serve as their own instruments. Nevertheless, if these variables are considered to be predetermined then they must be treated similarly to the lagged dependent variable. Estimations are performed that explore both of these assumptions, and the robustness of the findings is also checked to alternative model specifications. But before turning to the regression results, the next section discusses the data used in the empirical analysis.

The data

Any cross-country study that aims to establish the relationship between health outcomes and such factors as poverty and public health spending will inevitably face the problem of comparability of poverty and public health expenditure estimates across countries, and even over time for a given country.

The problem of the comparability of poverty data emerges because of differences in the survey instruments (e.g. living standards measurement survey, LSMS, versus household budget survey, HBS), sampling designs, definitions of variables and richness of information used in the construction of the income or consumption aggregate. As argued by Deaton

Table 13.1 Summary statistics of the poverty data, 1994–2000

Variable		Mean	Std dev.	Minimum	Maximum	Observations
hc	overall	31.998	14.538	11.500	98.595	N = 535
	between		13.002	15.230	87.399	n = 77
	within		7.859	−4.805	65.971	T = 7

hc = poverty headcount index (incidence of poverty)

(2001), the problem of data consistency can be substantially diminished by using regional-level data for a country. This is because national surveys use a uniform survey instrument and the same methodology of estimating a welfare aggregate. Hence, the errors in the estimated poverty rates remain constant across administrative regions and over time within regions, and thus the spatial and inter-temporal comparisons are not affected. The problem that often emerges with the use of regional data is that household surveys, which are nationally representative, are often not designed to be regionally representative, which precludes the possibility of making cross-region comparisons.

For this analysis a unique panel of comparable poverty estimates was compiled for the regions of Russia. The data come from the HBS conducted each year by the State Statistical Agency of Russia (Goskomstat).[13] The HBS has a sample size of around 49,000 households and is nationally and regionally representative.[14] Goskomstat poverty estimates are based on regional poverty lines (national poverty line expressed in regional prices), and use per capita money incomes (since 1992) and per capita disposable resources (since 1997) as welfare measures. *Money income* is determined as total cash income received from formal sources (such as wages and salaries, social benefits, pensions and stipends), property income, plus estimates of income obtained outside officially registered economic activity (income from self-employment, sales of agricultural products, etc.). *Disposable resources* consist of cash expenditures, monetary assessment of in-kind consumption, plus withdrawn savings and borrowed funds during the survey period.[15] This study uses the money income poverty rates (poverty headcount indexes) because these data provide a longer time-series dimension. Nevertheless, the choice of the welfare indicator (money income versus disposable resources) is not expected to affect the results when the objective is to make comparisons across regions and over time using a given measure of welfare.[16] Table 13.1 presents summary statistics of the regional incidence of money income poverty.[17]

It is worth noting that when one weights a sample by using the size of the regional population as a weight (in order to get nationally representative summary statistics), one finds that 28.6 per cent of the Russian population on average were poor during the period under consideration. This is slightly less than the sample mean of 32 per cent.[18] The poverty map of Russia clearly indicates the scope of regional disparities in the incidence of poverty (see fig. 13.5).

Figure 13.5 indicates that while in some regions less than 20 per cent of the population are located below the poverty line, in other regions the prevalence of poverty is almost universal. The picture of regional disparities appears to be similar when disposable resources are used as a welfare aggregate (see fig. 13.6).

For an indicator such as public health expenditure, any attempt at making cross-country comparisons can also introduce significant problems unless a researcher has detailed information on which entries make up the total public health spending in each country. In other words, the general term "public spending on health" can, in fact, imply concepts that vary considerably across countries. Fortunately, this problem does not apply with the region-level data. The data on regional public health expenditures in current roubles are available from the Goskomstat. Regional public health spending is defined as the expenditure from the consolidated (federal plus local) budget on health care in a given region.[19] To obtain the per capita health spending in constant 2000 roubles, one deflates (in fact, inflates) total regional health expenditures expressed in current roubles with the non-food price index and then divides them by the size of the regional population. Table 13.2 provides summary statistics of the per capita public health spending data.

The table suggests that the real value of per capita public health expenditure varies considerably not only across regions but also over time. The distribution of public health spending across Russia's regions is very unequal, as can be seen from the public health expenditure map in figure 13.7.

The public health expenditure per capita in the region with the best publicly financed health system exceeds the expenditure in the worst-funded region by as much as 19 times.

Finally, data on the dependent variable, life expectancy at birth, come from the *Statistical Yearbook of Russia 2001* publication of the Goskomstat.[20] This publication represents the most comprehensive source of socio-economic information on the administrative regions of Russia. Table 13.3 shows summary statistics of the life expectancy data used in the empirical analysis.

The comparison of *within* (over time) and *between* (across regions) standard deviations indicates that, although life expectancy variation across regions dominates life expectancy variation over time, the latter is still quite substantial.

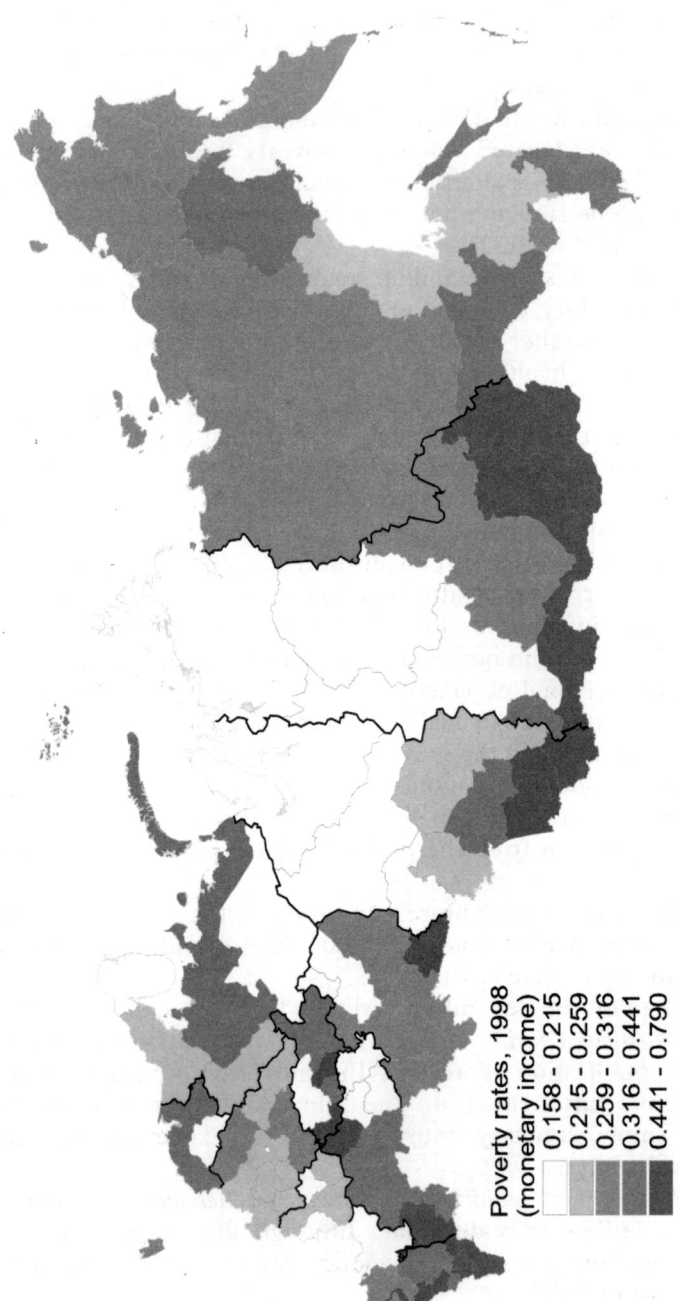

Figure 13.5 Money income poverty (headcount index) in Russia's regions, 1998

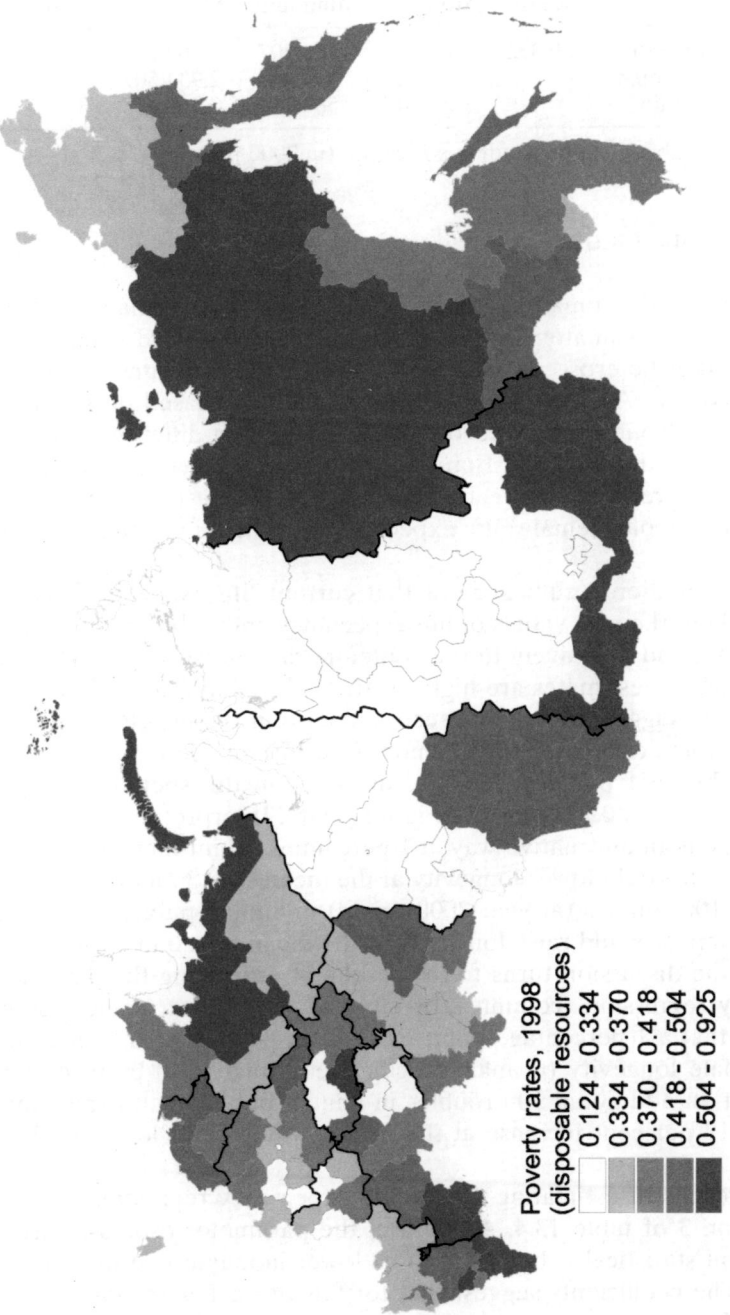

Figure 13.6 Disposable resources poverty (headcount index) in Russia's regions, 1998

Table 13.2 Summary statistics of the public health spending data, 1994–2000

Variable		Mean	Std dev.	Minimum	Maximum	Observations
hexp_pc	overall	880.322	538.388	238.707	4,502.601	N = 539
	between		442.772	412.009	2,934.507	n = 77
	within		309.841	−587.214	2,448.415	T = 7

hexp_pc = public health spending per capita (in 2000 prices)

Estimation results

The results of estimating equation (6) using the Arellano and Bond (1991) GMM estimator are given below.[21] The reported results refer to the one-step heteroscedasticity-corrected GMM estimates.[22] Since consistency of the Arellano-Bond GMM estimator is based on the assumption of no second-order autocorrelation in the first-differenced residuals, the results of the Arellano-Bond test for first- and second-order autocorrelation are reported for each regression.[23] The estimation results for overall (male plus female) life expectancy are shown in column 1 of table 13.4.

The estimation results suggest that current life expectancy is related positively to the past values of life expectancy and public health spending per capita, and negatively to the contemporaneous incidence of poverty. All parameter estimates are highly statistically significant. The estimated coefficients suggest that a 1 per cent increase in the incidence of poverty would be associated with a 0.1 month decline in life expectancy at the mean, while a 1 per cent increase in public health spending per capita would result in a 0.17 month rise in longevity. Interpreting the parameter estimates in an alternative way, a 1 percentage point increase in poverty at the mean would lower longevity at the mean by 0.3 months, and an additional 100 roubles (at year 2000 prices) in annual public health spending per capita would raise longevity at the mean by 2.0 months.[24]

Next the discussion turns to the results of estimating the male life expectancy regression (column 2 of table 13.4). The parameter estimates suggest that a 1 percentage point increase in poverty at the mean would lower male longevity (at male-specific mean longevity) by 0.44 months, and that an additional 100 roubles in annual public health spending per capita (12 per cent increase at the mean) would raise longevity by 2.24 months.

The results of estimating female life expectancy regression are shown in column 3 of table 13.4. As before, the parameter estimates are very significant statistically, but seem to be lower in magnitude than those for males. The coefficients suggest that for females a 1 percentage point in-

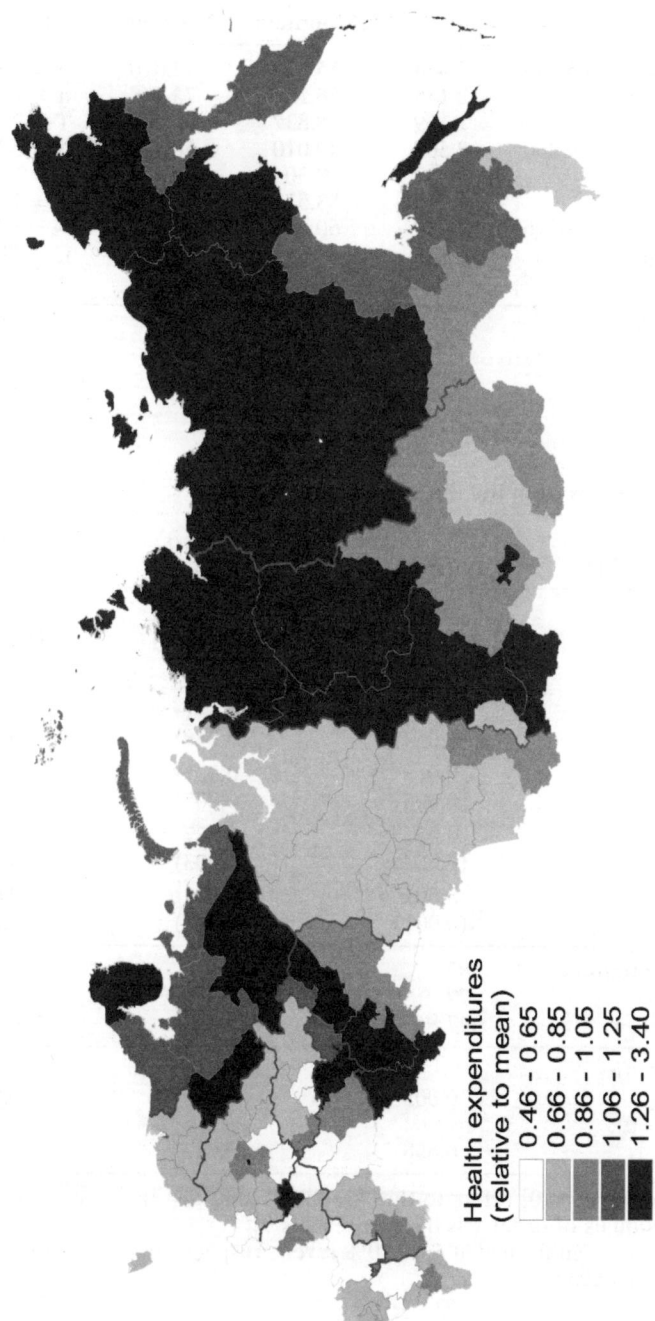

Figure 13.7 Public health spending per capita in Russia's regions, 1998

Table 13.3 Summary statistics of the life expectancy data, 1994–2000

Variable		Mean	Std dev.	Minimum	Maximum	Observations
le_all	overall	65.493	2.434	55.310	73.010	N = 537
	between		2.185	56.126	72.448	n = 77
	within		1.169	58.837	68.404	T = 7
le_m	overall	59.460	2.569	49.010	68.570	N = 537
	between		2.237	50.304	66.970	n = 77
	within		1.325	53.578	62.795	T = 7
le_f	overall	72.116	2.089	60.890	79.030	N = 537
	between		1.946	63.079	77.838	n = 77
	within		0.823	64.637	74.203	T = 7

le_all = overall LE
le_m = male LE
le_f = female LE

Table 13.4 Estimates from the life expectancy equation

Dependent variable	$Ln(LE_{rt})$	$Ln(LE_{rt})$ (male)	$Ln(LE_{rt})$ (female)
Explanatory variable	Coefficient (std error) 1	Coefficient (std error) 2	Coefficient (std error) 3
$Ln(LE_{rt-1})$	0.595*** (0.063)	0.671*** (0.048)	0.336*** (0.082)
$Ln(P_{rt})$	−0.013*** (0.005)	−0.021*** (0.005)	−0.005* (0.005)
$Ln(HE\_public_{rt-1})$	0.022*** (0.002)	0.027*** (0.003)	0.013*** (0.002)
Constant	−0.001 (0.001)	−0.001 (0.001)	0.001* (0.000)
No. of observations	382	382	382
No. of groups	77	77	77
Wald chi^2(3)	447.81	640.00	156.05
AB test ($\rho1 = 0$): Prob. > z	0.003	0.000	0.000
AB test ($\rho2 = 0$): Prob. > z	0.638	0.933	0.520

AB test ($\rho1 = 0$) [$\rho2 = 0$] refers to the Arellano-Bond test that average autocorrelation in residuals of order 1 is 0 [of order 2 is 0]
***, **, *indicate significance at 1, 5, 10% levels, respectively
Source: Author's estimates.

Table 13.5 Estimates from the life expectancy equation (with interaction term)

Dependent variable	Ln(LE$_{rt}$)	Ln(LE$_{rt}$) (male)	Ln(LE$_{rt}$) (female)
Explanatory variable	Coefficient (std error) 1	Coefficient (std error) 2	Coefficient (std error) 3
Ln(LE$_{rt-1}$)	0.625*** (0.073)	0.717*** (0.060)	0.345*** (0.088)
Ln(P$_{rt}$)	−0.012*** (0.004)	−0.020*** (0.005)	−0.004* (0.002)
Ln(HE_public$_{rt-1}$)	0.018*** (0.002)	0.022*** (0.004)	0.012*** (0.002)
Ln(HE_public$_{rt-1}$) * Ln(P$_{rt-1}$)	0.002*** (0.000)	0.002*** (0.000)	0.001** (0.000)
Constant	−0.001 (0.001)	−0.002** (0.001)	0.001 (0.001)
No. of observations	382	382	382
No. of groups	77	77	77
Wald chi^2(4)	449.21	587.26	158.26
AB test ($\rho1 = 0$): Prob. > z	0.005	0.000	0.000
AB test ($\rho2 = 0$): Prob. > z	0.900	0.368	0.519

AB test ($\rho1 = 0$) [$\rho2 = 0$] refers to the Arellano-Bond test that average autocorrelation in residuals of order 1 is 0 [of order 2 is 0]
***, **, *indicate significance at 1, 5, 10% levels, respectively
Source: Author's estimates.

crease in poverty at the mean would lower longevity by 0.12 months, and an additional 100 roubles in annual public health spending per capita would raise longevity by 1.36 months.

The next step is to test the hypothesis that the effect of public expenditure on health in the region increases with the incidence of poverty. In other words, it is expected that the impact of public spending is larger when private expenditure is not adequate for maintaining good health. This hypothesis is tested by adding the interaction term between the lagged public health spending and lagged poverty into the baseline regression equation. The regression results are presented in table 13.5.

The results support the idea that the impact of public health spending on longevity is larger for those regions experiencing a higher incidence of poverty. Taking into consideration the interaction effect, the elasticity of longevity with respect to public health spending suggests that at the mean of poverty an additional 100 roubles in annual public health spending per capita would raise life expectancy by 2.7 months for men and 1.5 months for women. For a given region, the interaction effects imply that the impact of public expenditure on health increases as more people in a region become poor.

The next step of the empirical analysis estimates the regression equation that includes time dummies among controls, to ensure that it is not simply the similar time trends in the dependent and explanatory variables driving the results. It is worth mentioning that at the very end of 1998 a financial crisis struck Russia. The consequences of the crisis, such as declining real incomes due to rapidly rising prices, were felt by the population mostly during 1999. Hence the inclusion of the time dummies for the pre-crisis, crisis (1999) and post-crisis (2000) periods should allow one, in addition simply to controlling for a time trend, to see whether the financial crisis affected longevity through mechanisms other than the rising poverty and declining real value of public health spending.[25] The estimation results from the specifications which include the period dummies (for male and female life expectancies, with and without interaction terms) are given in table 13.6.

The inclusion of a time trend in the male life expectancy regression makes only the coefficient on poverty remain statistically significant. It also reduces the magnitude of the parameter estimate on poverty. In the female life expectancy regression the parameter estimate on poverty becomes insignificant. Nevertheless, the coefficient on public health spending remains highly significant and of the same size as in the specification without time dummies.

The parameter estimates reported in column 1 of table 13.6 suggest a long-run elasticity of male longevity with respect to poverty of −0.022. This means that a *permanent* 1 per cent increase in the regional incidence of poverty would lead to a 0.022 per cent reduction in male life expectancy. Expressed alternatively, this elasticity suggests that a 1 *percentage point* increase in poverty at the mean would lower male longevity at the mean by half a month. The coefficient on health spending in column 2 (table 13.6) indicates the *long-run* elasticity of female life expectancy with respect to health expenditure of 0.02. This elasticity translates into a 1.94 months decline in longevity with a 100 roubles decline in public health spending.

One next estimates the specification of the equation that includes an interaction term between poverty and health spending along with period dummies. The estimates from these regressions are reported in columns 3 and 4 of table 13.6. The levels of poverty and public health spending remain significant determinants of longevity for men and women, respec-

Table 13.6 Estimates from the life expectancy equation (with a time trend)

Dependent variable	Ln(LE$_{rt}$) (male)	Ln(LE$_{rt}$) (female)	Ln(LE$_{rt}$) (male)	Ln(LE$_{rt}$) (female)
Explanatory variable	Coefficient (std error) 1	Coefficient (std error) 2	Coefficient (std error) 3	Coefficient (std error) 4
Ln(LE$_{rt-1}$)	0.462*** (0.058)	0.375*** (0.104)	0.457*** (0.065)	0.367*** (0.100)
Ln(P$_{rt}$)	−0.012** (0.005)	−0.001 (0.004)	−0.016*** (0.005)	−0.002 (0.003)
Ln(HE_public$_{rt-1}$)	−0.007 (0.008)	0.012*** (0.002)	−0.012 (0.008)	0.011*** (0.002)
Ln(HE_public$_{rt-1}$) * Ln(P$_{rt-1}$)	–	–	0.002** (0.001)	0.001 (0.001)
Pre-crisis year (dummy)	0.038*** (0.009)	0.019** (0.008)	0.038*** (0.009)	0.018*** (0.004)
Crisis year (dummy)	ref.	ref.	ref.	ref.
Post-crisis year (dummy)	−0.013*** (0.003)	−0.002 (0.003)	−0.016*** (0.003)	−0.003 (0.002)
Constant	0.008*** (0.002)	0.004** (0.002)	0.003** (0.001)	0.002** (0.001)
No. of observations	382	382	382	382
No. of groups	77	77	77	77
Wald chi^2	1001.63	267.22	931.61	199.69
AB test ($\rho1 = 0$): Prob. > z	0.000	0.000	0.000	0.000
AB test ($\rho2 = 0$): Prob. > z	0.483	0.970	0.879	0.957

AB test ($\rho1 = 0$) [$\rho2 = 0$] refers to the Arellano-Bond test that average autocorrelation in residuals of order 1 is 0 [of order 2 is 0]
***, **, *indicate significance at 1, 5, 10% levels, respectively
Source: Author's estimates.

tively. Nevertheless, the interaction term is found to be significant for men only.[26]

It is worth mentioning that the coefficients on the time dummies clearly suggest that the financial crisis in Russia had severe demographic costs beyond those associated with rising poverty and reduced public health spending triggered by the crisis. Such "indirect" costs could be related, for instance, to an increased level of stress induced by the crisis. The period dummies indicate that, controlling for the poverty and health spending effects, life expectancy in 1999 was 3.9 per cent and 1.9 per cent lower than in the pre-crisis years for men and women, respectively. It continued to decline for the former group during 2000.[27]

Robustness of results

This section investigates the robustness of the estimates to alternative specifications and the treatment of explanatory variables as predetermined rather than strictly exogenous. It starts from the discussion of the choice of a functional form. A number of studies (Anand and Ravallion, 1993; Kakwani, 1993; Pritchett and Summers, 1997) argue that the double-log functional form for the life expectancy regression may not provide the best fit for the data since it imposes a constant elasticity. In fact, life expectancy is effectively bounded from above, which suggests a growing effort to achieve the same absolute gain in life expectancy for a country where life expectancy is initially higher. Clearly, if regions had fairly similar levels of life expectancy, the choice of the functional form would not be expected to affect the results significantly. However, the sheer diversity in longevity across the Russian regions is likely to render the functional form important.

To address a possible non-linearity in the relationship between longevity and its determinants, this study alternatively uses in the estimations a non-linear transformation of life expectancy of the form proposed by Anand and Ravallion (1993). When one considers that in the sample the maximum life expectancy at birth equals 68.1 years for men and 78.6 years for women, the choice of a bound that equals respectively 70 and 80 years appears to be quite natural. The estimation results for the regressions that use ln(*bound-actual LE*) as a dependent variable are presented below. Note that since a dependent variable effectively measures a *shortfall of life expectancy* from the achievable maximum, a negative sign of the coefficient should be interpreted as a positive effect (life expectancy increases), while a positive sign should be considered as indicative of a negative effect (life expectancy declines). To make the exposition shorter, only the estimates obtained from the specifications that include time dummies are discussed, since these specifications deliver more conservative estimates. The model which does not include an interaction term between poverty and public health spending is estimated first. The regression for men is estimated using 70 and 80 years as alternative values of the upper bound for the dependent variable in order to check the robustness of the results to the choice of the maximum level of longevity, while the regression for women uses only the dependent variable with 80 years as the upper bound. The parameter estimates from

Table 13.7 Estimates from the life expectancy equation (with a time trend and alternative dependent variable)

Dependent variable	$Ln(max\text{-}LE_{rt})$ (male, max = 70)	$Ln(max\text{-}LE_{rt})$ (male, max = 80)	$Ln(max\text{-}LE_{rt})$ (female, max = 80)
Explanatory variable	Coefficient (std error) 1	Coefficient (std error) 2	Coefficient (std error) 3
$Ln(max\text{-}LE_{rt-1})$	0.666*** (0.102)	0.511*** (0.063)	0.362** (0.068)
$Ln(P_{rt})$	0.071** (0.029)	0.035** (0.014)	0.020 (0.036)
$Ln(HE\_public_{rt-1})$	−0.004 (0.061)	0.013 (0.024)	−0.115*** (0.018)
Pre-crisis year (dummy)	−0.183*** (0.064)	−0.106*** (0.024)	−0.081 (0.078)
Crisis year (dummy)	ref.	ref.	ref.
Post-crisis year (dummy)	0.017 (0.030)	0.030*** (0.010)	−0.007 (0.020)
Constant	−0.024 (0.016)	−0.020*** (0.005)	−0.017 (0.014)
No. of observations	382	382	382
No. of groups	77	77	77
Wald chi^2(6)	1,067.46	1,082.28	230.91
AB test ($\rho 1 = 0$): Prob. > z	0.002	0.001	0.001
AB test ($\rho 2 = 0$): Prob. > z	0.769	0.922	0.133

AB test ($\rho 1 = 0$) [$\rho 2 = 0$] refers to the Arellano-Bond test that average autocorrelation in residuals of order 1 is 0 [of order 2 is 0]
***, **, *indicate significance at 1, 5, 10% levels, respectively
Source: Author's estimates.

these alternative longevity (in fact, a shortfall from the maximum longevity) equations are shown in table 13.7.

The regression results indicate that the coefficients on poverty for men and health spending for women are very significant statistically and much larger in magnitude compared to their predecessors in the specification that uses ln(LE) as a dependent variable. The parameter estimate on poverty reported in column 1 of table 13.7 implies a *long-run* poverty elasticity of male life expectancy of 0.21. This elasticity suggests that at the mean of male life expectancy a permanent 10 per cent increase in the incidence of poverty in a region would lead to a 15.2 months decline in male longevity.

The results of the estimations that use ln(80-LE) instead of ln(70-LE) as a dependent variable for men are reported in column 2 of table 13.7. As before, poverty is found to have an impact on life expectancy. However, a change of the upper bound for longevity from 70 to 80 years halved the magnitude of the coefficient. The lower magnitude of the parameter estimate may reflect the fact that the choice of 80 years as the maximum achievable level of longevity for men is probably not very appropriate; male life expectancy in Russia did not exceed 70 years anywhere in the country during the period under consideration.

The estimation of the similar specification for women produces the results reported in column 3 of table 13.7. The regression results for women indicate, as before, that only public health spending appears to affect longevity.[28] The parameter estimate suggests a *long-run* elasticity of female life expectancy with respect to health spending of -0.19. At the mean longevity for women this elasticity indicates that a 10 per cent increase in per capita public health expenditure would lead to almost 1.5 years increase in life expectancy. Noteworthy in these specifications is the fact that the "crisis" effect is statistically significant only for men.

When the interaction term between the lagged value of the poverty headcount index and lagged public health spending is added to the specifications reported in table 13.7, the interaction effect is found to be significant for men only.[29] As before, the sign of the interaction term indicates that public health spending has a greater (positive) effect on longevity at high levels of poverty.

The next estimate is the model treating poverty and public health spending as predetermined rather than exogenous variables. This is a more relaxed assumption because the feedback effects from the lagged dependent variable (or lagged errors) to current and future values of the explanatory variables are not ruled out. Hence, with this assumption one effectively allows, for instance, that individual incentives for generating incomes (and related to these regional poverty rates) could be affected by past observations of longevity. The regression results for male and female longevity, with and without interaction terms, are shown in table 13.8.

In the life expectancy equations for men the parameter estimates on poverty are highly significant, and notably larger than their counterparts from the specification that considers poverty as strictly exogenous rather than predetermined (see table 13.7). The coefficient on poverty shown in column 1 of table 13.8 implies a *long-run* poverty elasticity of 0.47. It is worth noting that treating poverty as predetermined makes it significant for also explaining female longevity (see column 3 of table 13.8). The es-

Table 13.8 Estimates from the life expectancy equation (treating explanatory variables as predetermined)

Dependent variable	Ln(max-LE$_{rt}$) (male, max = 70)	Ln(max-LE$_{rt}$) (male, max = 80)	Ln(max-LE$_{rt}$) (female, max = 80)
Explanatory variable	Coefficient (std error) 1	Coefficient (std error) 2	Coefficient (std error) 3
Ln(max-LE$_{rt-1}$)	0.620*** (0.097)	0.493*** (0.058)	0.413*** (0.083)
Ln(P$_{rt}$) *(predetermined)*	0.180*** (0.055)	0.075*** (0.021)	0.128** (0.050)
Ln(HE_public$_{rt-1}$) *(predetermined)*	0.007 (0.104)	0.031 (0.041)	−0.103*** (0.021)
Pre-crisis year *(dummy)*	−0.157 (0.109)	−0.108*** (0.041)	−0.087 (0.160)
Crisis year *(dummy)*	ref.	ref.	ref.
Post-crisis year *(dummy)*	0.053*** (0.026)	0.042*** (0.010)	0.010 (0.017)
Constant	−0.029 (0.020)	−0.023*** (0.007)	−0.007* (0.004)
No. of observations	382	382	382
No. of groups	77	77	77
Wald chi^2	830.01	956.44	234.32
AB test ($\rho 1 = 0$): Prob. > z	0.000	0.000	0.000
AB test ($\rho 2 = 0$): Prob. > z	0.249	0.392	0.085

AB test ($\rho 1 = 0$) [$\rho 2 = 0$] refers to the Arellano-Bond test that average autocorrelation in residuals of order 1 is 0 [of order 2 is 0]
***, **, *indicate significance at 1, 5, 10% levels, respectively
Source: Author's estimates.

timated long-term poverty elasticity for women indicates that a 1 percentage point increase in poverty at the mean would reduce longevity at the mean by 2.9 months. Although still significant at a 1 per cent level, the coefficient on health spending for women is somewhat lower than its predecessor in the specification that treats this variable as strictly exogenous. Nevertheless, the estimation results for women reported in table 13.8 have to be treated with some degree of caution, since in this case a zero hypothesis of no second-order autocorrelation in the residuals cannot be rejected at a 10 per cent level.[30]

To sum up, the regression results reported in this section of the chapter support the finding that changes in poverty and public health spending have considerable impact on changes in life expectancy. Treating longevity as bounded from above, and relaxing the assumption of strict exogeneity of the explanatory variables, increases the estimated impacts of poverty and inequality on life expectancy.

Conclusions

This chapter aims to establish the causal impact of poverty and public health spending on life expectancy using unique panel data covering 77 Russian regions over the period 1994–2000. The use of regional-level data from a single country overcomes the problem of data comparability which is often faced in studies that rely on cross-country data. The determination of longevity is modelled as a dynamic process. The estimation of the model is performed using the Arellano-Bond (1991) GMM estimator. The study takes advantage of the panel nature of the data in addressing the issue of endogeneity of the lagged dependent, as well as of the other explanatory variables, and controlling for the region-specific fixed effects that result in the omitted variable bias when the cross-section data are used. The robustness of the empirical results to several alternative model specifications and estimation assumptions is tested.

The results presented in this chapter suggest that a reduction in the regional incidence of absolute poverty and an increase in regional public investments in health generally have positive impacts on longevity. Nevertheless, the magnitudes of the estimated effects vary substantially depending on the model specification, and whether poverty and public health spending are treated as strictly exogenous or predetermined variables.

In accordance with the findings of several other studies (e.g. Brainerd and Varavikova, 2001; Shkolnikov and Cornia, 2000), the results of this chapter indicate that the incidence of poverty in a region has a greater effect on the life expectancy of men. The coefficient on poverty is always significant (at a 1 per cent level) for men, but the estimated short-term poverty elasticity of life expectancy varies from -0.01 to -0.18 depending on the model specification. The parameter estimate on poverty is insignificant in most of the specifications for women, and when significant varies from -0.01 (significant at a 10 per cent level) to -0.12 (significant at a 5 per cent level).[31] Therefore the estimated poverty elasticity of life expectancy is generally in the range of estimates reported by other studies, which vary from -0.04 in Carrin and Politi (1995) to -0.21 in Anand and Ravallion (1993) and Calfat (1996).

In contrast to the effect of poverty, the impact of public health spending is found to be stronger for women. The parameter estimate on health spending in the estimations for men is insignificant in most cases and when significant varies from 0.02 to 0.03 (both significant at a 10 per cent level). The parameter estimate on health spending is always significant (at a 1 per cent level) for women, and the estimated short-term elasticity of life expectancy with respect to public health spending varies from 0.01 to 0.12 depending on specification. This is generally within the range found in some other studies that use longitudinal data – from 0.04 in Lichtenberg (2002) to 0.13 in Bidani and Ravallion (1997) – but lower than the 0.3 reported in cross-country studies by Anand and Ravallion (1993). That the present estimates are lower than those based on cross-section data is probably due to the fact that this study is able to deal better with the endogeneity of the explanatory variables and the estimator used in the study does not employ the cross-sectional variation in data.

The estimation results of this chapter support the idea that the impact of public health spending on longevity is greater in those regions experiencing a higher incidence of poverty. In other words, the importance of publicly provided healthcare increases when the private resources that can be allocated to healthcare become scarcer. This confirms the finding of the study by Bidani and Ravallion (1997), which is based on cross-country data.

The finding of the substantial *long-run* effects of poverty and public health spending on longevity suggests that a permanent negative shock to the incidence of poverty and/or the amount of publicly provided healthcare in a region results in enduring consequences for the health of the population. The study also found a noticeable adverse impact of the financial crisis that erupted in Russia at the end of 1998 on the life expectancy of the country's population, even after controlling for the close association of the crisis with changes in poverty and the real value of public health spending.

The findings presented in this chapter are significant from a policy perspective since they emphasize the need for stimulating regional economic development and enhancing healthcare provision in Russia. Importantly, the results indicate that measures aimed at the reduction in the incidence of regional poverty can be effective for the improvement of population health, especially under conditions when public provision of health services cannot be easily extended.

Acknowledgements

The author is grateful to Arne Bigsten, Christopher Barrett, Peter Glick, Bjorn Gustafsson, Per Lundborg and seminar participants at Gothenburg University and Cornell University for their insightful comments on an earlier draft of this study. The efforts of Uwe Deichmann in producing the life expectancy, health expenditure and poverty maps of Russia are very much appreciated. The author would also like to thank Ruslan Yemtsov for providing the regional data on poverty and Stepan Titov for providing the regional data on public health spending.

The findings and interpretation of this chapter are those of the author and should not be attributed to the World Bank Group or any affiliated organizations.

Notes

1. In contrast to the crude death rates data, life expectancy data allow an abstraction from the age structure of the population and hence give a more accurate picture of differences in excess mortality across regions and over time (Nell and Stewart, 1994). The quality of Russian demographic data is widely regarded to be comparable to that for the United States (e.g. Becker and Hemley, 1998).
2. Brainerd and Varavikova (2000) and Cockerham (1999) make attempts to do so.
3. Increased stress may also lead to an increased consumption of tobacco and alcohol, as well as to other unhealthy behaviour.
4. Malnutrition is not considered to be a major cause of health problems in transition economies. Although in many countries of the FSU diets have undoubtedly deteriorated, the average calorie intake remains quite high. However, poor people may have substantial nutritional deficiencies, as Shkolnikov and Meslé (1996) argue for Russia. Hence the poverty rate may be a better indicator than average calorie intake of the possible incidence of malnutrition among the population.
5. Among those government expenditures that went to the health sector, the dominant share was allocated to salaries of health sector employees so that resources for medicine and medical equipment were lacking. As a result of shortages, numerous reports of doctors performing surgery with razors and reusing disposable equipment are documented in Davis (1993). Davis (1993) and Rozenfeld (1996) provide detailed accounts of the crisis in the Russian healthcare system.
6. However, it is recognized that using subnational data for a country as large and diverse as Russia is also problematic. First, the quality of the data is likely to vary across regions at any given point in time, which does not pose a problem because this analysis is focused mostly on inter-temporal variation. Second, the data quality over time has remained high in major urban areas, but deteriorated in economically depressed areas, especially in the north Caucasus. Hence, the sensitivity of the regression results was tested to the exclusion of observations for the north Caucasus. Third, the lack of subregional, i.e. urban/rural, and rayon data prevented accounting for the substantial heterogeneity within individual regions of Russia.
7. Several hypotheses have been presented as to why average income and income distribution should affect the health of the population. A useful review of these is provided in Wagstaff and van Doorslaer (2000). In the same study one can find evidence that population health is a function of mean income and income inequality. Note that the authors also show that the assumption of the absolute income hypothesis (AIH) suggested by equation (2) is not critical in getting this relationship.
8. It would be reasonable to expect that the impact of public health spending depends not only on its size but also on the possibilities in the region for people to procure adequate

health services through private means. In other words, public health expenditure is likely to be of more consequence in the poorer regions. This hypothesis will be tested later in the chapter.
9. To check the robustness of the results, the study also introduces the time-specific effects in the estimations to capture the unobserved factors influencing life expectancy in a given period.
10. This may be seen from the fact that if life expectancy increases by the *same* number of years in countries A and B, the percentage decline in the $\ln(max - LE_{rt})$ index will be larger for a country with a higher initial life expectancy.
11. The consistency of this estimator hinges on the assumption of no second-order autocorrelation in the first-differenced idiosyncratic errors (the validity of this assumption is tested in the sixth section of this chapter).
12. The full set of moment conditions is given by: $E[y_{i,t-s}(\Delta y_{i,t} - \alpha \Delta y_{i,t-1})] = 0$, for $t = 3, \ldots, T$ and $s = 2, \ldots, (t-1)$. In this case y_i would denote life expectancy for region i, and $T = 7$.
13. Another survey instrument available for Russia, the Russian Longitudinal Monitoring Survey (RLMS), has a small sample size and, in contrast to the HBS, does *not* generate representative data at the regional level.
14. The sample size and regional representativeness of the HBS make it very similar to the US Current Population Survey that covers 50,000 households and generates state-representative data.
15. For a more detailed discussion of the welfare indicators used in Russia see Yemtsov (2002).
16. With regard to the sensitivity of a region's poverty ranking to the choice of welfare indicator, the analysis of the data suggests that the list of the richest and poorest regions is practically unaffected by the choice of measuring poverty in terms of per capita money income or in terms of per capita disposable resources.
17. The overall and within (over time) standard deviations are calculated for all 535 observations. The between (across regions) standard deviation is calculated over the means ($\bar{x}_i$) for 77 regions. Note that the *within* component can be negative since it is defined as $(x_{it} - \bar{x}_i + \bar{\bar{x}})$, where the global mean $\bar{\bar{x}}$ is added back to make results comparable.
18. In weighting a sample using regional population size, one takes into account the fact that the *number* of people affected by poverty differs in each region.
19. In principle, public health spending also includes expenditure from the (non-budgetary) Health Insurance Fund. This expenditure (which constitutes on average about 18 per cent of the total) is not included in this study's measure of public health spending (which accounts for only budgetary expenses on health) due to the lack of region-disaggregated data.
20. It is worth mentioning that even health outcome data cannot always be consistently compared across countries. In Russia until only recently, for instance, the child mortality rate was measured differently from the standard Western method.
21. Note that a number of studies have investigated the small sample properties of the dynamic panel data estimators (e.g. Arellano and Bond, 1991; Kiviet, 1995; Judson and Owen, 1999). While finding a (negative) bias on the autoregressive parameter, these studies indicate that GMM is virtually unbiased as far as the β vector of parameters is concerned.
22. This study has also used the two-step estimator, but since two-step standard errors tend to be downward biased in small samples, it follows Arellano and Bond (1991) in using one-step results for inference on the coefficients.
23. Note that even if the residuals in the levels model (equation 5) are not autocorrelated, expressing the model in first differences is likely to induce AR(1) processes. The study

has also tested the validity of the over-identifying restrictions using the two-step Sargan test (Sargan, 1958). The results of the Sargan test are not shown here since they lead to the same conclusions in all cases as the Arellano-Bond test of autocorrelation.
24. Note that 100 Russian roubles at year 2000 prices are equal to about US$4.
25. The model was also estimated with time dummies for separate years, but since the coefficients on the dummies for the pre-1999 years were found *not* to be statistically different, the year effects are considered to be the same prior to 1999 and the chapter reports the results in a more convenient form for interpretation.
26. The insignificance of the interaction term for women could be due to its high correlation with the current period's poverty ($\rho = 0.61$), and with the lagged value of public health spending ($\rho = 0.38$), which enters the interaction term.
27. Note that the results of the Arellano-Bond test of second-order autocorrelation in the first-differenced residuals for all specifications considered above indicate that the model is well specified (i.e. the over-identifying restrictions are valid).
28. It is worth noting that the observed differential impact of poverty for men and women confirms the results of other studies for Russia (e.g. Brainerd and Varavikova, 2001; Shkolnikov and Cornia, 2000).
29. These results are not shown here for the sake of brevity, but are available from the author on request.
30. The study also estimated the static specification of the model using the random-effects GLS estimator, which represents a weighted average of the *between* and *within* estimators, and thus takes into account the variation in life expectancy across regions and over time (the estimation procedure also allowed the disturbance term to be first-order autoregressive). The estimation results (not shown here for brevity, but available from the author on request) indicate that both poverty and public health spending are statistically significant (at a 1 per cent level) determinants of longevity for men, while only the latter factor is a significant (also at a 1 per cent level) determinant of longevity for women. The interaction term between poverty and health spending is found to be significant (at a 1 per cent level), and to have an expected sign, for both samples. The magnitude of the coefficients reported in the static specification cannot be compared directly to those reported in the main body of the study since the lagged dependent variable in this case does not enter the regression equation.
31. The results of the estimates that consider life expectancy as a bounded variable should perhaps be considered as the most plausible.

REFERENCES

Anand, S. and M. Ravallion (1993) "Human Development in Poor Countries: On the Role of Private Incomes and Public Services", *Journal of Economic Perspectives* 7(1): 133–150.

Arellano, M. and S. Bond (1991) "Some Tests of Specification for Panel Data: Monte Carlo Evidence and an Application to Employment Equations", *Review of Economic Studies* 58: 277–297.

Backlund, D., P. D. Sorlie and N. J. Johnson (1996) "The Shape of the Relationship between Income and Mortality in the United States: Evidence from the National Longitudinal Mortality Study", *Annals of Epidemiology* 6: 12–23.

Becker, C. and D. Hemley (1998) "Demographic Change in the Former Soviet Union during the Transition Period", *World Development* 26(11): 1957–1975.

Bidani, B. and M. Ravallion (1997) "Decomposing Social Indicators Using Distributional Data", *Journal of Econometrics* 77: 125–139.
Brainerd, E. and E. Varavikova (2001) "Death and the Market", paper prepared for the WHO Commission on Macroeconomics and Health, unpublished.
Britton, A., M. McKee and D. A. Leon (1998) "Cardiovascular Disease and Heavy Drinking: A Systematic Review", Public Health and Policy Departmental Publications No. 28, London School of Hygiene and Tropical Medicine, London.
Calfat, G. (1996) "Explaining the Expansion of Human Capabilities in Developing Countries", Center for Development Studies Publication No. 19, UFSIA, Antwerp.
Carrin, G. and C. Politi (1995) "Exploring the Health Impact of Economic Growth, Poverty Reduction and Public Health Expenditure", *Tijdschrift voor Economie en Management* 15(3/4): 227–246.
Cockerham, W. C. (1999) *Health and Social Change in Russia and Eastern Europe*, London: Routledge.
Collins, W. J. and M. A. Thomasson (2002) "Exploring the Racial Gap in Infant Mortality Rates, 1920–1970", Working Paper No. 8836, National Bureau of Economic Research, Cambridge, Mass.
Cornia, G. A. and R. Paniccià, eds (2000) *The Mortality Crisis in Transitional Economies*, Oxford: Oxford University Press for UNU-WIDER.
Davidson, R. and J. G. MacKinnon (1993) *Estimation and Inference in Econometrics*, Oxford: Oxford University Press.
Davis, M. C. (1993) "The Health Sector in the Soviet and Russian Economies: From Reform to Fragmentation to Transition", in R. F. Kaufman and J. P. Hardt, eds, *The Former Soviet Union in Transition*, report prepared for the Joint Economic Committee, Congress of the United States.
Deaton, A. (2001) "Health, Inequality, and Economic Development", Working Paper No. 8318, National Bureau of Economic Research, Cambridge, Mass.
Filmer, D. and L. Pritchett (1999) "The Impact of Public Spending on Health: Does Money Matter?", *Social Science and Medicine* 49: 1309–1323.
Goskomstat (2001) *Statistical Yearbook of Russia 2001*, Moscow: Goskomstat.
Judson, R. A. and A. L. Owen (1999) "Estimating Dynamic Panel Data Models: A Guide for Macroeconomists", *Economic Letters* 65: 9–15.
Kakwani, N. (1993) "Performance in Living Standards", *Journal of Development Economics* 41: 307–336.
Kennedy, B. P., I. Kawachi and E. Brainerd (1998) "The Role of Social Capital in the Russian Mortality Crisis", *World Development* 26(11): 2029–2043.
Kiviet, J. F. (1995) "On Bias, Inconsistency, and Efficiency of Various Estimators in Dynamic Panel Data Models", *Journal of Econometrics* 68: 53–78.
Leon, D. A., L. Chenet, V. M. Shkolnikov, S. Zakharov, J. Shapiro, G. Rakhmanova, S. Vassin and M. McKee (1997) "Huge Variation in Russian Mortality Rates 1984–94: Artefact, Alcohol, or What?", *The Lancet* 350: 383–388.
Lichtenberg, F. R. (2002) "Sources of US Longevity Increase, 1960–1997", Working Paper No. 8755, National Bureau of Economic Research, Cambridge, Mass.

McKee, M. (2001) "The Health Consequences of the Collapse of the Soviet Union", in D. A. Leon and G. Walt, eds, *Poverty, Inequality, and Health: An International Perspective*, Oxford: Oxford University Press.

Nell, J. and K. Stewart (1994) "Death in Transition: The Rise in the Death Rate in Russia since 1992", Innocenti Occasional Papers Economic Policy Series No. 45, UNICEF, Florence.

Paniccià, R. (2000) "Transition, Impoverishment, and Mortality: How Large an Impact?", in G. A. Cornia and R. Paniccià, eds, *The Mortality Crisis in Transitional Economies*, Oxford: Oxford University Press for UNU-WIDER.

Pritchett, L. and L. H. Summers (1997) "Wealthier is Healthier", *Journal of Human Resources* 31(4): 841–868.

Rajkumar, A. S. and V. Swaroop (2002) "Public Spending and Outcomes: Does Governance Matter?", Development Research Group Working Paper, World Bank, Washington, D.C.

Rose, R. (2000) "Uses of Social Capital in Russia: Modern, Pre-Modern and Anti-Modern", *Post-Soviet Affairs* 16(1): 33–57.

Rose, R. and I. McAllister (1996) "Is Money the Measure of Welfare in Russia?", *Review of Income and Wealth* 42(1): 75–90.

Rozenfeld, B. (1996) "The Crisis of Russian Health Care and Attempts at Reform", in J. DaVanzo and G. Farnsworth, eds, *Russia's Demographic Crisis*, Los Angeles, Calif.: RAND Corporation.

Ryan, M. (1995) "Alcoholism and Rising Mortality in the Russian Federation", *British Medical Journal* 310: 646–648.

Sargan, J. D. (1958) "The Estimation of Economic Relations Using Instrumental Variables", *Econometrica* 26: 393–415.

Shkolnikov, V. and G. A. Cornia (2000) "Population Crisis and Rising Mortality in Transitional Russia", in G. A. Cornia and R. Paniccià, eds, *The Mortality Crisis in Transitional Economies*, Oxford: Oxford University Press for UNU-WIDER.

Shkolnikov, V. and F. Meslé (1996) "The Russian Epidemiological Crisis as Mirrored by Mortality Trends", in J. DaVanzo and G. Farnsworth, eds, *Russia's Demographic Crisis*, Los Angeles, Calif.: RAND Corporation.

Shkolnikov, V., G. A. Cornia, D. A. Leon and F. Meslé (1999) "Causes of the Russian Mortality Crisis: Evidence and Interpretations", *World Development* 26(11): 1995–2011.

Stegmayr, B., T. Vinogradova, S. Malyutina, M. Peltonen, Y. Nikitin and K. Asplund (2001) "Widening Gap of Stroke Between East and West: Eight-year Trends in Occurrence and Risk Factors in Russia and Sweden", *Stroke* January: 2–8.

Wagstaff, A. and E. van Doorslaer (2000) "Income Inequality and Health: What Does the Literature Tell Us?", *Annual Review of Public Health* 21: 543–567.

Walberg, P., M. McKee, V. Shkolnikov, L. Chenet and D. A. Leon (1998) "Economic Change, Crime, and Mortality Crisis in Russia: A Regional Analysis", *British Medical Journal* 317: 312–318.

Yemtsov, R. (2002) "*Quo Vadis*: Inequality and Poverty Dynamics Across Russian Regions in 1992–2000", paper presented at the Cornell–LSE–UNU-

WIDER Conference on Spatial Poverty and Inequality, London School of Economics, 28–30 June; revised version published in R. Kanbur and A. J. Venables, eds (2004) *Spatial Inequality and Development*, Oxford: Oxford University Press for UNU-WIDER.

Zohoori, N., T. A. Mroz, B. Popkin, E. Glinskaya, M. Lokshin, D. Mancini, P. Kozyreva, M. Kosolapov and M. Swafford (1998) "Monitoring the Economic Transition in the Russian Federation and its Implications for the Demographic Crisis – The Russian Longitudinal Monitoring Survey", *World Development* 26(11): 1977–1993.

14

The medium- and long-term effects of an expansion of education on poverty in Côte d'Ivoire: A dynamic microsimulation study

Michael Grimm

Introduction

It is widely recognized today that human capital, in particular that acquired through schooling, is a key factor of development. The link is clearly established at the microeconomic level. Individuals with more education receive on average more income (for example Mincer, 1974; Schultz, 1994, 1999). This implies that a more egalitarian distribution of education may constitute an efficient means for reducing inequality of income distribution. At the macroeconomic level the "new growth theory", pioneered by Lucas (1988) and Romer (1990), suggests that the accumulation of human capital may have externalities which drive the economy on a continuous path of growth. Empirically, however, the link seems less clear. Whereas Krueger and Lindahl (2000) find that faster growth of the human capital stock also leads to faster growth of per capita income, other authors are more sceptical. Pritchett (2001), for instance, claims that a rise in education can only play the "engine of growth" role if that rise is accompanied by a higher demand for education, if education satisfies a certain quality standard and if education is not allocated to socially inefficient tasks. Education is thus viewed as a necessary but not sufficient condition, or, as Pritchett writes, "Education is no magic bullet". Benhabib and Spiegel (1994), and more recently Bils and Klenow (2000), even completely deny this link, putting forward the argument of inverse causality; that is, that economic growth accelerates human capital investments and not the other way around.

In any case, besides the link from education to income one attributes numerous positive external effects to education, in particular to women's education: fewer (albeit healthier and better-educated) children, higher autonomy of women and increased labour supply outside the household (e.g. Jejeebhoy, 1995). Some authors even argue that an improvement of women's circumstances may be a source of economic growth (e.g. Klasen, 1999). Likewise, in the Millennium Development Goals education is seen as a powerful instrument not only "for reducing poverty and inequality", but also "for improving health and social well-being, laying the basis for sustained economic growth and being essential for building democratic societies and dynamic, globally competitive economies" (UNDP, 2003).

Whereas East and South-East Asia as well as Latin America have experienced significant progress in terms of education over the last decades, sub-Saharan Africa is still far behind. This region has the lowest enrolment ratios at each level, and the average African adult has acquired less than three years of schooling (World Bank, 2001). This fact raises several important questions. Why are enrolment rates at this low level? What kind of policies may be appropriate to increase them? Should policies focus more on the demand side, more on the supply side, or consider both? What are the effects on growth and the distribution of income once enrolment rates do really rise? This chapter focuses on the last question. More precisely, it analyses the effects in the medium and long term of a significant expansion of education in sub-Saharan Africa on income distribution and poverty. What would be the magnitude of the direct effects between education and income? What would be the role of the different transmission channels, such as fertility, age at marriage, formation and composition of households and labour supply? An attempt will be made to answer these questions for the case of Côte d'Ivoire using a dynamic microsimulation model. The simulations consider policies which are in force or subject to debate in this country. Their impact on household incomes and their distribution are examined from 1998 until 2015 under several assumptions concerning the evolution of labour demand and returns to education.[1]

The second section provides a brief summary of education policies and the evolution of the distribution of education in Côte d'Ivoire. The third section presents the microsimulation model used and the main transmission channels between education and income distribution. The fourth section outlines the policy experiments that are simulated, and the fifth section analyses the simulation results. The final section concludes.

Education in Côte d'Ivoire

Education system and education policy since independence

The education system in Côte d'Ivoire is based on the model inherited from the French colonial era. School normally starts at the age of five, but many children enter later. Children stay in primary school for a total of six years, then move to junior secondary school (four years) and upper secondary school (three years). Entrance to junior secondary school is permitted upon success in the Certificat d'Etudes Primaires et Elementaire (CEPE) examination and access to upper secondary school is controlled by the Brevet d'Etudes du Premier Cycle (BEPC). At the end of secondary school each student has to pass the *baccalauréate* examination before going to university. Professional training and technical education are situated mainly at the secondary level.

After independence, Côte d'Ivoire allocated approximately 40 per cent of public expenditures to education, more than twice the share allocated in Burkina Faso or Senegal. However, with the onset of an economic crisis in the beginning of the 1980s this share decreased progressively, preventing an improvement of the efficiency of the school system – which was already judged as unsatisfactory. A large part of education expenditure has been used for salaries. The primary school sector has been systematically neglected. This explains to some extent why a large part of the population, in particular rural and female, has received no education. Furthermore, repetition rates of 30 per cent are frequent and only about 35 per cent pass the BEPC successfully (Cogneau and Mesplé-Somps, 2003).

Enrolment ratios and education level

The following descriptive statistics are based on two household surveys, the Enquête Prioritaire of 1993 and the Enquête de Niveau de Vie of 1998 (called EP 1993 and ENV 1998 hereafter), both carried out by the Institut National de la Statistique de la Côte d'Ivoire (INS) and the World Bank.

Table 14.1 shows that a large part of the Ivorian population is still unable to read and write. Illiteracy is particularly high in rural areas and among women. However, the evolution between 1993 and 1998 shows that illiteracy is decreasing. The enrolment ratios (table 14.2) also show a significant inequality between cities and rural areas. One can also see an abrupt fall of enrolment ratios after primary school and a strong difference between gross and net enrolment ratios.[2] This difference can be explained by delayed entries in the schooling system, frequent schooling

Table 14.1 Illiteracy rates (population 15 years and older)

	Abidjan		Other urban		Rural	
	1993	1998	1993	1998	1993	1998
Men	0.28	0.25	0.43	0.37	0.63	0.58
Women	0.48	0.42	0.63	0.57	0.83	0.80
All	0.38	0.33	0.53	0.47	0.73	0.69

Source: EP 1993, ENV 1998; computations by the author.

Table 14.2 Enrolment ratios

	Abidjan		Other urban		Rural	
	1993	1998	1993	1998	1993	1998
GERP	1.04	1.05	0.79	0.99	0.49	0.67
NERP	0.69	0.69	0.52	0.63	0.32	0.45
Girls ratio	0.47	0.49	0.47	0.45	0.37	0.41
GERJS	0.46	0.60	0.43	0.61	0.13	0.17
NERPJS	0.14	0.24	0.12	0.21	0.04	0.04
Girls ratio	0.41	0.44	0.37	0.39	0.22	0.28
GERUS	0.25	0.47	0.25	0.23	0.08	0.08
NERUS	0.05	0.10	0.04	0.05	0.01	0.02
Girls ratio	0.36	0.39	0.30	0.32	0.12	0.30
GERHE	0.03	0.09	0.01	0.02	0.01	0.01
NERHE	0.02	0.07	0.01	0.01	0.00	0.00
Girls ratio	0.18	0.36	0.14	0.45	0.13	0.17

Source: EP 1993, ENV 1998; computations by the author.
GERP/NERP = gross/net enrolment ratio in primary school.
GERJS/NERJS = gross/net enrolment ratio in junior secondary school.
GERUS/NERUS = gross/net enrolment ratio in upper secondary school.
GERHE/NERHE = gross/net enrolment ratio in higher education.

interruptions and high repetition rates, in particular during the last two years of primary schooling. Girls are strongly underrepresented in secondary school and university. Enrolment ratios, however, increase at all schooling levels.[3]

Current education programmes

The current education policy of Côte d'Ivoire focuses principally on three objectives (INS, 2001):[4] first, to achieve almost universal primary school enrolment, according to the aim fixed at the World Conference on Education for All, held in Jomtien, Thailand, in 1990; second, to reduce gender inequality in terms of education; and third, to make the adult population literate. The means by which the Ivorian authorities want to achieve these objectives are mainly orientated to the supply side. They include, among other things, construction of primary schools and education centres for adults, reorganization of education management, pre-service and in-service training of teachers, larger distribution of schooling materials such as textbooks and revision of curriculum content and implementation. These measures are supported by several World Bank programmes (see World Bank, 2002a, 2002b).

Model structure

Key characteristics of the model

A dynamic microsimulation model is used, designed to simulate, at the individual level, the most important demographic and economic events through time. The microsimulation approach allows us to take individual heterogeneity into account, in particular regarding the capacity of accumulating human capital and earning income. Furthermore, it allows the analysis of policy outcomes in terms of inequality and poverty, and not only in terms of growth, as does an aggregated model. The dynamic approach is important to account for the time it takes to accumulate human capital and the occurring interactions with other economic and demographic variables during this period. The applied model is similar to simulation models used in industrialized countries to analyse pension reforms, the distribution of life-cycle incomes or the accumulation of wealth. The base unit is the individual, but each individual belongs in each period to a specific household. The model is a discrete time model. Each period corresponds to one year. A fixed order is assumed concerning the different events: marriage, household formation, school enrolment, fertility, mortality, international immigration, reallocation of land, occupational choices, generation of individual earnings and household income. The population of departure is constructed using the EP 1993. This survey contains information about the socio-demographic characteristics of households and its members: their housing, education, employment, agricultural and non-agricultural enterprises, earnings, expenditures and assets. From March to June 1992 1,680 households in Abidjan (economic capital of Côte d'Ivoire), and from June to November 1993 7,920 households in the rest of the country (among them 3,360 in other Ivorian towns), were interviewed. The total sample covers 58,014 individuals. The sample was calibrated on 1 January 1993. Other data sources used are census data, UN demographic projections, a demographic and health survey, a migration survey and another household income survey conducted in 1998. The following subsections briefly present the modelling of schooling, occupational choices and earnings, which constitute the central building blocks of the model. The modelling of the other demographic behaviours, i.e. marriage, household formation, fertility, mortality and immigration, follow similar principles and are for lack of space not presented here. However, for more details regarding the data used, estimation techniques and estimation results, the interested reader can refer to Grimm (2002). Due to a lack of longitudinal data, most regressions used are based on information derived from cross-section data. When using these regressions to simulate dynamic behaviour, one must of course make the strong assumption that individuals behave over time as individuals of different ages observed in the base year. The most critical reason for doing this is that with cross-section data one cannot separate age, period and cohort effects.

Modelling of schooling decisions

The information on current enrolment and enrolment in the previous year in the EP 1993 and the ENV 1998 is used to estimate transition rates into and out of schooling. The models are estimated separately for boys and girls aged 5 to 25 years old, using age, household composition, Ivorian citizenship, educational level already attained, matrimonial status, relation to the household head, land owned by the household, region of residence and educational attainment of the father and the mother as explicative variables. Unfortunately, the dataset used contains no information on the quality of the school, the distance to the school or the cost of schooling. The estimated coefficients of the corresponding probit models, as well as a comparison of observed and simulated enrolment ratios for 1998 figure, are given in tables 14.3 and 14.4. They show that the probability of school entry depends strongly, as one can expect, upon age. It is higher for children with educated parents (notably for girls), and lower for children in non-Ivorian households. Furthermore, the probability of entry is higher if the child has already acquired some education in the past. The probability of staying in school depends positively on the educational level already attained, negatively on marriage and the quantity of land owned by the household, and is higher in urban areas, especially Abidjan. During the simulation, enrolment status is updated in each period for all children from 5 to 25 years old using the estimated coefficients and either a Monte Carlo lottery[5] or fixed progression rates imposed according to the performed policy experiment. In the latter case the estimated parameters are used to select the children with the highest empirical probability of experiencing the respective transition. As mentioned above, repetition of classes is very frequent in Côte

Table 14.3 Probit estimations of the probability of being enrolled in t conditional on the state in $t-1$ (children aged between 5 and 25 years)

	Children not enrolled in $t-1$	
Variables	Boys	Girls
Age	1.352* (0.135)	0.932* (0.108)
Age^2/100	−12.872* (1.286)	−9.304* (0.993)
Age^3/1,000	3.048* (0.312)	2.287* (0.239)
No diploma (ref.)		
Attained primary schooling	1.584* (0.271)	0.873* (0.252)
Attained junior secondary[a] schooling	2.214* (0.436)	1.542* (0.326)
Attained upper secondary schooling	2.011* (0.570)	
Married		
Non-Ivorian	−0.394* (0.063)	−0.291* (0.066)
Not child of household head	0.299* (0.063)	0.209* (0.067)
Father illiterate (ref.)		
Father can read and write	0.327* (0.085)	0.305* (0.092)
Father attained primary schooling	0.481* (0.080)	0.647* (0.081)
Father attained junior secondary schooling	0.788* (0.110)	0.652* (0.110)
Father attained upper secondary or more	0.986* (0.178)	1.193* (0.179)
Mother illiterate (ref.)		
Mother can read and write	0.242* (0.096)	0.429* (0.096)
Mother attained primary schooling	0.390* (0.103)	0.416* (0.108)
Mother attained junior secondary schooling	0.242 (0.202)	0.774* (0.186)
Mother attained upper secondary or more	1.815* (0.576)	0.700* (0.275)
Household head male		−0.124 (0.104)
No. of household members ≥ 60 years	−0.086 (0.048)	
Household size		0.014* (0.005)
Abidjan (ref.)		
Other urban	−0.310* (0.071)	−0.311* (0.068)
East Forest	−0.608* (0.089)	−0.668* (0.087)
West Forest	−0.636* (0.090)	−0.536* (0.089)
Savannah	−0.608* (0.086)	−0.659* (0.085)
ENV 1998	0.319* (0.051)	0.430* (0.051)
Constant	−4.833* (0.401)	−3.810* (0.348)
Number of observations	11,861	14,680
Log likelihood	−2048	−1793
Age	0.062* (0.030)	−0.043* (0.012)
Age^2/100	−0.424* (0.106)	
No diploma (ref.)		
Attained primary schooling	−0.005 (0.075)	−0.022 (0.087)
Attained junior secondary schooling	0.372* (0.126)	0.517* (0.165)
Attained upper secondary schooling	0.499* (0.197)	0.232 (0.287)
Married	−0.980* (0.179)	−0.884* (0.161)

Table 14.3 (cont.)

	Children enrolled in $t-1$	
Variables	Boys	Girls
Not child of household head		−0.155* (0.071)
Mother illiterate (ref.)		
Mother can read and write		0.242 (0.132)
Mother attained primary schooling		−0.119 (0.133)
Mother attained junior secondary schooling		0.324 (0.244)
Mother attained upper secondary or more		0.659 (0.400)
No. of household members ≥ 60 years		−0.105 (0.057)
Household size	0.023* (0.008)	
Household without land (ref.)		
0 ha < lands. < 1 ha	−0.068 (0.126)	0.364* (0.148)
1 ha ≤ lands. < 2 ha	−0.307* (0.117)	−0.432* (0.145)
2 ha ≤ lands. < 5 ha	−0.371* (0.114)	−0.216 (0.120)
5 ha ≤ lands. < 10 ha	−0.228* (0.126)	−0.060 (0.133)
10 ha ≤ lands.	0.032 (0.135)	0.096 (0.136)
Abidjan (ref.)		
Other urban	−0.267* (0.081)	−0.262* (0.085)
East Forest	−0.520* (0.127)	−0.519* (0.135)
West Forest	−0.448* (0.129)	−0.366* (0.150)
Savannah	−0.193 (0.142)	−0.243 (0.155)
ENV 1998	0.574* (0.064)	0.588* (0.074)
Constant	1.388* (0.201)	2.111* (0.132)
Number of observations	8,535	5,835
Log likelihood	−2146	−1471

Source: EP 1993, ENV 1998; estimations by author.
Notes
[a] The categories "junior secondary" and "upper secondary" have been aggregated for girls non-enrolled in $t-1$.
* significant at 5 per cent.
Standard errors in parentheses. Standard errors have been corrected for clustering within the household. During the simulations the dummy for the 1998 survey (ENV 1998) comes successively into play by multiplying its coefficient in each period by $t/5$ so that the coefficient has no effect in 1993 and an effect of 100 per cent in 1998. From 1998 on this dummy variable is fixed to one.

d'Ivoire, especially before entry to junior secondary school. To account for this phenomenon the repetition rates were fixed at 20 per cent for the fifth year of primary school, at 50 per cent for the sixth year of primary school and at 10 per cent for all other classes. However, when the school policy reforms took effect in 1998 it is assumed that these repetition rates are zero (see below).

Table 14.4 Observed and simulated enrolment ratios in 1998

	Obs.	Sim.		Obs.	Sim.
GERP	0.81	0.84	GERUS	0.21	0.15
NERP	0.53	0.51	NERUS	0.05	0.02
Girls ratio	0.44	0.43	Girls ratio	0.35	0.27
GERJS	0.39	0.39	GERHE	0.03	0.01
NERJS	0.13	0.08	NERHE	0.02	0.01
Girls ratio	0.38	0.40	Girls ratio	0.35	0.08

Source: ENV 1998; computations and simulations by author.
GERP/NERP = gross/net enrolment ratio in primary school.
GERJS/NERJS = gross/net enrolment ratio in junior secondary school.
GERUS/NERUS = gross/net enrolment ratio in upper secondary school.
GERHE/NERHE = gross/net enrolment ratio in higher education.

Modelling of occupational choices and earnings

The labour income model draws from Roy's model (1951) as formalized by Heckman and Sedlacek (1985). It is competitive in the sense that no segmentation or job rationing prevails, but only slightly, because labour mobility across sectors does not equalize returns to observed and unobserved individual characteristics. The model is estimated using the EP 1993. It is assumed that each individual older than 11 years and out of school faces three kinds of work opportunities: family work, self-employment or wage work. Family work includes all kinds of activities under the supervision of the household head; that is, family help in agricultural or informal activities, but also domestic work, non-market labour and various forms of declared "inactivity". Self-employment corresponds to informal independent activities. In agricultural households (households where some independent agricultural activity is carried out) the household head may be considered as a self-employed worker bound to the available land or cattle. Wage work concerns dependent employment principally in the formal public and private sectors.

To both non-agricultural self-employment and wage work, individual potential earnings functions are associated, which only depend on individual characteristics and task prices:

$$\ln w_{1i} = \ln p_1 + X_{1i}\beta_1 + t_{1i} \qquad (1)$$

$$\ln w_{2i} = \ln p_2 + X_{2i}\beta_2 + t_{2i} \qquad (2)$$

where for each individual i and for each labour market segment $j = 1, 2$, w_{ji} are individual potential earnings, X_{ji} are observable individual characteristics (human capital, place of dwelling, sex, nationality), t_{ji} are sector-specific unobservable individual productive abilities and p_j is the price paid for each efficiency unit of labour.

For family work an unobserved individual value is associated, which also depends on household characteristics and other members' labour supply decisions:

$$\ln w_{0i} = (X_{0i}, Z_{0h})\beta_0 + t_{0i} \qquad (3)$$

where for each individual i pertaining to household h, Z_{0h} summarizes invariant household characteristics and other members' decisions which influence labour market participation.

For agricultural households a reduced farm profit function derived from a Cobb-Douglas technology is associated:

$$\ln \Pi_{0h} = \ln p_0 + \alpha \ln L_h + Z_h\theta + u_{0h} \qquad (4)$$

where Π_{0h} is the farm profit of household h (including self-consumption and minus hired labour), p_0 is the price of the agricultural good, L_h the total amount of labour available for agricultural activity, Z_h other household characteristics like arable land and u_{0h} stands for unobservable idiosyncratic factors' global productivity.

Then, when the household head is a farmer, secondary members may participate in farm work and therefore w_{0i} is assumed to depend on the "individual's contribution" to farm profits. This contribution is evaluated while holding other members' decisions as fixed and the global factor productivity of the farm u_{0h}:

$$\ln \Delta\Pi_{0i} = \ln p_0 + \ln(L_{h+i}^{\alpha} - L_{h-i}^{\alpha}) + Z_h\theta + u_{0h} \qquad (5)$$

where $L_{h+i} = L_h$ and $L_{h-1} = L_h - 1$ if i is actually working on the farm in h, and $L_{h+i} = L_h + 1$ and $L_{h-1} = L_h$ alternatively.

This means that the labour decision model is hierarchical between the household head and secondary members, and simultaneous à la Nash among secondary members (secondary members do not take into account the consequences of their activity choice on that of other secondary members). In the case of agricultural households, one may then rewrite the family work value as follows:

$$\ln w_{0i} = (X_{0i}, Z_{0h})\beta_0 + \gamma[\ln p_0 + \ln(L_{h+i}^{\alpha} - L_{h-i}^{\alpha}) + Z_h\theta] + t_{0i} \qquad (6)$$

where γ stands for the (non-unitary) elasticity of the value of family work in agricultural households to the price of agricultural products. For non-agricultural household members, w_0 may be seen as a pure reservation wage, where the household head's earnings and other non-labour income of the household are introduced in order to account for an income effect on participation in the labour market.

Comparing the respective values attributed to the three labour opportunities, workers allocate their labour force according to their individual comparative advantage:

$$i \text{ chooses family work iff } w_{0i} > w_{1i} \text{ and } w_{0i} > w_{2i} \qquad (7)$$

$$i \text{ chooses self-employment iff } w_{1i} > w_{0i} \text{ and } w_{1i} > w_{2i} \qquad (8)$$

$$i \text{ chooses wage work iff } w_{2i} > w_{0i} \text{ and } w_{2i} > w_{1i} \qquad (9)$$

The following estimation strategy is adopted. For non-agricultural households the occupational choice/labour income model represented by equations (1)–(3) and the series of selection conditions (7)–(9) are estimated simultaneously by maximum likelihood techniques; one obtains a bivariate tobit, like in Magnac (1991). For agricultural households a limited-information approach is followed: in a first step, the reduced farm profit function (4) is estimated, then an estimate for the individual potential contribution to farm production (5) is derived; in a second step, the reservation wage equation (6) is estimated and the individual potential contribution included and, because of the small sample of rural wage workers, the wage functions (1) and (2) estimated for non-agricultural households are retained. Using this set of equations, occupational choices and earnings are simulated in each period for each individual and household. The residual terms t_{1i}, t_{2i}, t_{0i} and u_{0h} are first estimated for each individual/household and then kept constant over the whole simulation horizon. For individuals joining the sample by birth or migration, these error terms are drawn according to the estimated variance of these residuals and the correlation between them.

As one can see in table 14.5, education plays a crucial role in the occupational choices and earnings model. The estimated parameters linked to the education variable reveal that the return to education is the highest in the wage sector with a 17 per cent increase for each additional year, and the lowest in the informal sector with only 7 per cent increase for each additional year. The impact of education on the reservation wage lies in between, with a return of 10 per cent. The reservation wage of household members other than the household head depends positively on the household head's income. The estimated agricultural profit function implies that a doubling of the number of involved family members

Table 14.5 Activity choice and labour income model (dependent variable log monthly earnings; bivariate tobit estimation, i.e. all three equations are estimated simultaneously)

Variables	Non-farm self-employed		Wage earner		Reservation wage	
Non-agricultural households						
Schooling	0.069*	(0.004)	0.171*	(0.004)	0.101*	(0.005)
Experience	0.078*	(0.005)	0.080*	(0.005)	−0.011*	(0.006)
Experience^2/100	−0.074*	(0.007)	−0.094*	(0.008)	0.059*	(0.008)
Abidjan	0.348*	(0.047)	0.529*	(0.042)	0.358*	(0.056)
Other urban	0.300*	(0.043)	0.257*	(0.038)	0.100*	(0.052)
Woman	0.042	(0.038)	−0.830*	(0.035)	−0.217*	(0.045)
Non-Ivorian	−0.030	(0.032)	−0.261*	(0.030)	−0.215*	(0.036)
No. childr. aged 0–1 in hh.					0.038	(0.024)
No. childr. aged 1–3 in hh.					−0.018	(0.018)
No. childr. aged 3–9 in hh.					−0.035*	(0.017)
No. childr. aged 9–12 in hh.					0.028*	(0.013)
No. men aged > 11 in hh.[1]					0.026*	(0.007)
No. women aged > 11 in hh.[1]					−0.002	(0.007)
Household head					−1.177*	(0.040)
Spouse of household head					−0.168*	(0.033)
Child of household head					0.189*	(0.036)
Other hh. member (ref.)						
Income of hh. head/ 1,000,000					0.009	(0.006)
Intercept	8.472*	(0.109)	8.600*	(0.100)	10.586*	(0.115)
Number of observations			14,369			
Log likelihood			−87881			
Agricultural households						
Schooling	0.069	(−)	0.171	(−)	0.026	(0.020)
Experience	0.078	(−)	0.080	(−)	−0.005	(0.016)
Experience^2/100	−0.074	(−)	−0.094	(−)	0.033	(0.022)
Abidjan	0.348	(−)	0.529	(−)	−0.241	(0.259)
Other urban	0.300	(−)	0.257	(−)	−0.576*	(0.155)
Woman	0.042	(−)	−0.830	(−)	−0.764*	(0.108)
Non-Ivorian	−0.030	(−)	−0.261	(−)	−0.513*	(0.095)
No. childr. aged 0–1 in hh.					0.067	(0.056)

Table 14.5 (cont.)

Variables	Non-farm self-employed		Wage earner		Reservation wage	
No. childr. aged 1–3 in hh.					−0.050	(0.040)
No. childr. aged 3–9 in hh.					−0.003	(0.047)
No. childr. aged 9–12 in hh.					0.036	(0.037)
No. men aged > 11 in hh.[1]					0.056*	(0.022)
No. women aged > 11 in hh.[1]					−0.018	(0.018)
Spouse of household head					−0.002	(0.074)
Child of household head					0.022	(0.077)
Other hh. member (ref.)						
ln $\Delta\Pi_{0i}$					0.316*	(0.095)
Intercept	8.472	(−)	8.600	(−)	9.095*	(0.905)
Number of observations			9,884			
Log likelihood			−7660			

Source: EP 1993; estimations by author.
Notes
The estimates of the corresponding variance and correlation parameters can be obtained on request from the author.
* significant at 5 per cent.
(−) coefficient constrained.
[1] without accounting for the individual itself.

leads to an approximately 50 per cent increase in agricultural profits. The amount of arable land also comes out with a decreasing marginal productivity. The above-defined potential individual contribution to the agricultural profit increases the propensity to work on the farm with a reasonable elasticity of +0.3 (table 14.6).

Land is, of course, a key variable in the generation of agricultural income. Land is attributed in each household to the household head. If the household head leaves the household to marry, for instance, land is attributed to the new household head. If the first-born boy of a household leaves to marry, he receives 50 per cent of the household's land. The land of households which disappear, due to the demise of all the members, is reallocated within each stratum among the households without land in equal parts and so that the proportions of households owning land remain constant with respect to 1993. At the end of each period the quantity of land is increased for each household by 3 per cent, which is

Table 14.6 Agricultural profit function (dependent variable log profit last 12 months; OLS estimation)

Variables		
Log of no. of household members involved in farm work	0.531*	(0.026)
Land: none or less than 1 ha (ref.)		
Land: 1–2 ha	0.349*	(0.043)
Land: 2–5 ha	0.553*	(0.042)
Land: 5–10 ha	0.897*	(0.047)
Land: more than 10 ha	0.964*	(0.052)
Experience	0.012*	(0.004)
Experience^2/100	−0.022*	(0.005)
Woman	−0.136*	(0.042)
Savannah (ref.)		
Urban	−0.554*	(0.038)
East Forest	−0.329*	(0.035)
West Forest	−0.230*	(0.035)
Intercept	12.304*	(0.089)
Number of observations		4,204
Adj. R^2		0.319

Source: EP 1993; estimations by author.
Notes
*significant at 5 per cent.
Standard errors in parentheses.

the approximate natural population growth rate in the model. Households switch to the agricultural sector – that is, become agricultural households – if the land they own exceeds a certain threshold level, which is fixed at 0.1 ha; conversely, they exit the agricultural sector – that is, become non-agricultural households – if land size falls under this threshold (in the base sample 45.6 per cent of the households are involved in independent agricultural activity, 18.3 per cent urban and 81.7 per cent rural, and 54.4 per cent are not, 86.9 per cent urban and 13.1 per cent rural).

Transmission channels between education and income distribution in the model

As a key determinant of wages and non-farm profits, education has, of course, direct effects on household income. Then education determines, besides other individual and household characteristics, activity choices of individuals who compare their potential remunerations in the two market activities with their reservation wage. Given that wage work offers the highest return to education, this activity becomes more and more lucrative as education increases. Furthermore, education influences negatively on fertility. Fertility is a key variable of the reservation wage and modifies the number of consumption units in the household and, in the long term, the quantity of labour supply available in the household. Finally, parental education influences schooling choices of the children and therefore also modifies the income and demographic behaviour of the children's generation. However, the model does not account for direct effects of education on mortality, and especially of the mother's education on child mortality.

Policy experiments

A number of education policies (including variants) plus one reference case have been simulated. These experiments are in line with the education programmes debated or already in effect in Côte d'Ivoire. They are summarized in table 14.7 and explained in detail in what follows. The simulations start in 1993 and end in 2015. They are identical for all experiments until 1998.

REFSIM, the reference simulation or baseline, consists of maintaining the enrolment ratios at the different schooling levels at levels which Côte d'Ivoire would experience if the observed conditions in 1998 persisted; that is 50 per cent of all children having achieved no schooling or less than six years, 22 per cent having achieved primary education, 20 per cent having achieved junior secondary education, 6 per cent having achieved upper secondary education and a little less than 2 per cent having achieved at least one year of university education. These proportions imply progression rates between the different schooling levels of 40 per cent, 30 per cent and 30 per cent. The simulation works as follows. In 1998 50 per cent of all six-year-old children enter primary school and stay for six years until they obtain the CEPE. Those children with the highest empirical probability to be enrolled are selected. This probability is calculated using the estimated equation linking enrolment status to individual and household characteristics (see table 14.3). Then 40 per cent are selected out of those having achieved primary school, likewise according to their empirical probability to be enrolled. They will complete junior secondary school. Then the simulation continues in the same way for the following schooling levels. Furthermore, in the reference case as well as in all other simulations, the repetition rates are set at zero from 1998 on.

PRIMED simulates the case of an almost universal primary school education by assuming an entry rate of 90 per cent for the generation of six-year-olds and younger in 1998. The desired net enrolment ratio is attained in 2003 when the sixth cohort enters primary school. The selection of children and the simulation process resemble the reference case.

Table 14.7 Summary of the policy experiments, in percentages

Simulation	Schooling level	Progress rate from 1998 on	1998 GER	1998 NER	2005 GER	2005 NER	2010 GER	2010 NER
REFSIM	Primary	50	77	41	59	50	50	50
	Junior secondary	40	33	7	34	25	20	20
	Upper secondary	30	14	2	10	5	6	6
	University	30	2	2	2	2	2	2
PRIMED	Primary	90	77	41	100	90	90	90
	Junior secondary	22	33	7	23	20	20	20
	Upper secondary	30	14	2	5	3	6	6
	University	30	2	2	2	2	1	1
HIGHED	Primary	90	77	41	100	90	90	90
	Junior secondary	60	33	7	61	47	54	54
	Upper secondary	60	14	2	27	12	34	34
	University	30	2	2	3	3	7	7
ALPH—	HIGHED+							
	From 1998 on, in each period 10 per cent of men and 20 per cent of women between 15 and 40 years old and illiterate are selected. Duration of programme: three years, then the years of schooling are set to two (literate).							
—CR	Constant return to education.							
—DR	Decreasing return to education: elasticity between the return to education in each sector and the share of the workforce having more than five years of schooling of −1/3.							
—IR	Increasing return to education: elasticity between the return to education in each sector and the share of the workforce having more than five years of schooling of +1/3.							
—SM	Maintenance of the share of the workforce employed in the (formal) wage-earner sector at the share simulated for 1997, which is 11.34 per cent.							

GER/NER = gross/net enrolment ratio.

HIGHED assumes, in addition to the 90 per cent entry rate to primary school, progression rates between the following schooling levels of 60 per cent, 60 per cent and 30 per cent instead of 40 per cent, 30 per cent and 30 per cent.

ALPH completes the former simulation with an adult literacy programme. From 1998 on, in each period 10 per cent of men and 20 per cent of women between 15 and 40 years old and having less than two years of schooling are randomly selected. The literacy programme is supposed to last three years. Then the years of schooling of all participants are set to two. It is assumed that participants are able to work full time while following the programme. To reduce gender inequality, more women are selected than men. This last experiment is performed under four different assumptions, three concerning the evolution of the return to education and one concerning the evolution of labour demand in the (formal) wage earner sector.

First, one may think, according to neo-classical theory, that the entry of more and more educated individuals into the labour market reduces the return to education. Bils and Klenow (2000), for instance, find that countries with higher education levels experience lower returns. For example, as years of schooling go from 2 to 6 to 10, the implied income growth for 1 additional year of schooling falls from 21.6 per cent to 11.4 per cent to 8.5 per cent. In contrast, one may assume that the return to education increases if the expansion of education is accompanied by an increased demand for education, due to technological progress or international trade, for instance. This last hypothesis was put forward by Katz and Murphy (1992) in the case of the United States. Finally, one may assume that the return to education remains constant (Card, 1995). For the decreasing-return scenario, ALPHDR, an elasticity was set between the return to education in each sector and the share of the workforce (20 years and older) having more than five years of schooling to be minus one-third. That means if that share increases by 1 per cent, the return to education decreases by 0.33 per cent. In the case of increasing returns, ALPHIR, the elasticity is supposed to be plus one-third. The share of the workforce having more than five years of schooling increases in the simulation ALPH by approximately 3 per cent per year. This implies that the return to education between 1998 and 2015 in the wage-earner sector, for instance, increases from 17.1 per cent to 20.5 per cent under the hypothesis of increasing returns and decreases from 17.1 per cent to 14.3 per cent under the hypothesis of decreasing returns. ALPHCR indicates the constant-return scenario.

Another variant, ALPHSM, simulates the case of a segmented labour market. As mentioned in the previous section (see also table 14.5), more education renders wage work more and more lucrative compared to work in other sectors. However, in the Ivorian context it is less likely that labour demand in the wage-earner sector, principally formal, increases without limit. The simulation consists in maintaining the share of the workforce employed in the wage-earner sector at the level simulated for 1997, which is 11.34 per cent. The individuals who are rationed are, according to the efficiency wage theory (Bulow and Summers, 1986), those where the difference between their potential wage (given their individual characteristics) and their opportunity cost, which is $\ln(w_{\text{wage}}) - \max[\ln(w_{\text{self-empl.}}), \ln(w_{\text{reserv.wage}})]$, is the lowest. The persons who are not selected are employed in the non-agricultural self-employment sector, if $\ln(w_{\text{self-empl.}}) > \ln(w_{\text{reserv.wage}})$, or they remain inactive or work on the family farm if $\ln(w_{\text{self-empl.}}) < \ln(w_{\text{reserv.wage}})$. In this variant the return to education decreases because of rationing in the

Table 14.8 Illiteracy rate and average years of schooling (simulations 1993–2015)

	1998	2005	2010	2015	Growth per annum 1997–2015
Illiteracy rate: men, 15 years and older					
REFSIM	0.46	0.43	0.43	0.44	−0.003
PRIMED	0.46	0.44	0.39	0.35	−0.016
HIGHED	0.46	0.44	0.39	0.34	−0.017
ALPHCR	0.46	0.35	0.25	0.17	−0.054
Illiteracy rate: women, 15 years and older					
REFSIM	0.64	0.60	0.59	0.59	−0.006
PRIMED	0.64	0.60	0.53	0.47	−0.017
HIGHED	0.64	0.60	0.53	0.48	−0.017
ALPHCR	0.64	0.39	0.23	0.15	−0.078
Average years of schooling: men, 20–25 years old					
REFSIM	5.50	4.81	5.05	5.18	−0.001
PRIMED	5.51	4.30	4.45	6.69	0.013
HIGHED	5.52	5.53	6.05	9.41	0.032
ALPHCR	5.57	5.85	6.36	9.22	0.031
Average years of schooling: women, 20–25 years old					
REFSIM	3.29	3.85	4.01	3.59	0.004
PRIMED	3.29	3.62	3.48	5.90	0.032
HIGHED	3.27	4.27	4.42	7.56	0.047
ALPHCR	3.30	4.61	5.04	7.78	0.048

Source: Simulations by the author.
Note: During the simulations it is assumed that individuals with less than two years of schooling are illiterate.

wage-earner sector, the sector offering the highest return to education. The assumptions of this scenario correspond thus to another model than that implied by the simulations ALPHDR/IR.

Results

Evolution of the level and distribution of education

Table 14.8 shows that a persistence of the conditions in the education system from 1998 (REFSIM) until 2015 leads to a decrease of the illiteracy rate by 2 percentage points for men and 5 points for women. This is due to the disappearance of older, less-educated generations and the emergence of younger, better-educated generations. If primary education becomes almost universal (PRIMED), then these rates will even decline to 35 per cent and 47 per cent. However, only a huge adult literacy programme with a particular attention to women will reduce the illiteracy

Table 14.9 Average years of schooling by birth cohort simulated for Côte d'Ivoire for 2015 and observed for some other countries and regions in the 1990s

	1940	1950	1960	1970	1980	1990	1995
Simulation for Côte d'Ivoire							
REFSIM			2.8	3.6	4.4	4.5	4.0
PRIMED			3.0	3.5	4.3	4.7	6.4
HIGHED			3.0	3.5	4.8	6.2	8.7
ALPHCR			3.3	4.3	5.6	6.6	8.9
Observation for some other countries and regions							
Brazil	3.6	5.2	6.2	6.7			
Mexico	4.2	6.7	8.2	9.3			
Chile	7.1	8.9	10.1	11.1			
Latin America (average)	5.3	6.9	8.2	8.8			
South Korea	7.7	9.5	11.0	12.0			
Taiwan	5.8	8.9	11.0	12.3			

Source: For Côte d'Ivoire, simulations by the author; data for other countries and regions are taken from Behrman, Duryea and Székely (1999).
Note: For the simulations, five-year birth cohorts are considered, 1958–1962, 1968–1972...

rate below 20 per cent in the considered time scale (ALPHCR). The increase of enrolment ratios at all schooling levels (HIGHED) increases significantly the average years of schooling and reduces the gender gap in particular.

Table 14.9 shows the policy outcome by generation. The experiment HIGHED conducts the generation born in 1995, being thus 20 years old in 2015, to an average schooling level of 8.7 years, which approximately corresponds to the average in Latin America for the generation born in 1970. The progress made by the Ivorian generations born between 1960 and 1990 under the assumption HIGHED is similar to that made by the Brazilian generations born between 1940 and 1970. However, to attain the level of Chile, South Korea or Taiwan a much longer time scale would be necessary.

Impact on growth and the distribution of income

The reader should note that even in the reference simulation, income, inequality and poverty are changing due to shifts in the population structure. All scenarios draw a rather optimistic picture of the evolution of the Ivorian economy, but given the difficulty in predicting the long-run evolution of the economy and the structure of economic growth, the results should be interpreted principally in relation to the reference scenario and not in absolute terms. Over the period 1992–2015 the growth gain per capita of the most optimistic policy (ALPH) relative to the persistence of the *status quo* (REFSIM) is about 0.3 points per year if the return to education remains constant (ALPHCR), −0.9 points per year if the return to education decreases (ALPHDR) and 1.8 points per year if the return increases (ALPHIR) (see table 14.10). As emphasized in the preceding section, the empirical evidence concerning the relation between the stock of education and returns to education is very controversial. In consequence the uncertainty of the possible results is very high. However, if the share of the workforce employed in the (formal) wage sector remains rationed to that of 1997 (ALPHSM), which seems a rather likely scenario, no growth gain will be generated at all. The simulations show also that a policy which is limited to universal primary education (PRIMED) does not contribute to further poverty reduction relative to the reference case. This is mainly because in the early stages the rise in schooling reduces the workforce. The average household income per capita starts rising faster only after 2005, when the first better-educated cohorts enter the labour market. Furthermore the return to education for up to six years of schooling is not sufficient to achieve significantly higher income. Purely universal primary education may foster growth only in the very long run, when a large part of the population has benefited from it.

With the exception of the experiment where the return to education rises (ALPHIR), the increase in inequality of the income distribution remains rather moderate. The policy HIGHED produces a slightly more unequal distribution than the reference case. However, if HIGHED is complemented with adult literacy programmes, this difference disappears. Figure 14.1 shows the evolution of income and that of the Gini index for the three return scenarios. Decreasing returns produce an inverse U-shaped evolution of inequality in the spirit of Kuznets (1955). Constant returns lead to a stabilization of income inequality from 2004 on and to an expected decrease in inequality in the long term. Finally, increasing returns produce an ever-increasing Gini index. The Kuznets effect is usually considered in relation to the passage of workers from rural and poor areas to urban and richer areas. Kuznets (1955) concentrates only on the composition effect; that is, the fact that an increased offer of skilled individuals raises, at least for a certain time and if the initial share of unskilled is not already too high, the inequality of income distribution. The simulations show, however, that a contraction of the returns to education accelerates the arrival of the phase of decreasing inequalities.

Figure 14.2 shows the relative changes with respect to REFSIM of mean household income per capita for each percentile of the distribution in 2015. ALPHCR leads to an improvement beyond the 25th percentile. Increasing returns have a clear positive effect over the total distribution,

Table 14.10 Income, inequality and poverty (simulations 1993–2015): REFSIM in levels, other levels in percentage deviations from REFSIM and for growth rate in absolute deviations

	1998	2005	2010	2015	% growth per annum, 1997–2015
Mean household income					
REFSIM	1,465	1,664	1,752	1,852	1.42
PRIMED	−0.1%	−1.0%	−1.0%	−1.8%	−0.10
HIGHED	0.5%	−1.7%	−0.4%	0.5%	0.03
ALPHCR	−1.4%	−0.8%	0.8%	4.1%	0.23
ALPHDR	−2.0%	−9.7%	−11.7%	−15.8%	−0.96
ALPHIR	−1.1%	8.1%	18.7%	37.9%	1.83
ALPHSM	−0.6%	−2.3%	−2.4%	−1.8%	−0.10
Mean household income per capita					
REFSIM	351	457	498	546	2.61
PRIMED	−0.3%	−0.7%	−0.6%	−2.6%	−0.15
HIGHED	2.0%	−2.2%	−0.6%	−0.5%	−0.02
ALPHCR	−0.3%	−2.0%	1.4%	5.3%	0.30
ALPHDR	−2.6%	−10.5%	−11.4%	−15.0%	−0.92
ALPHIR	−1.1%	5.3%	17.9%	36.8%	1.80
ALPHSM	0.0%	−4.2%	0.6%	0.9%	0.06
Gini index of income per capita (households)					
REFSIM	0.598	0.609	0.609	0.609	0.18
PRIMED	−0.2%	−0.8%	−0.7%	−1.0%	−0.06
HIGHED	−0.8%	0.2%	1.0%	1.3%	0.07
ALPHCR	0.0%	0.0%	0.2%	0.2%	0.00
ALPHDR	−0.7%	−3.1%	−2.6%	−4.8%	−0.28
ALPHIR	−0.3%	2.5%	3.9%	6.9%	0.37
ALPHSM	−0.3%	−0.8%	0.2%	0.0%	0.00
Headcount ratio (US$1 PPP) for income per capita (households)					
REFSIM	0.348	0.300	0.271	0.254	−1.75
PRIMED	0.0%	−2.0%	−2.2%	0.0%	−0.01
HIGHED	−0.3%	−0.7%	4.8%	4.3%	0.22
ALPHCR	1.7%	−1.0%	−0.7%	−0.8%	−0.05
ALPHDR	0.6%	3.3%	7.0%	5.1%	0.27
ALPHIR	0.0%	−3.0%	−5.5%	−10.6%	−0.62
ALPHSM	0.6%	0.7%	2.2%	2.4%	0.12
Headcount ratio (US$1 PPP) for income per capita (individuals)					
REFSIM	0.411	0.384	0.362	0.345	−1.02
PRIMED	1.3%	1.1%	0.6%	2.5%	0.14
HIGHED	1.8%	2.4%	5.1%	6.6%	0.35
ALPHCR	1.8%	1.6%	−1.2%	1.7%	0.09
ALPHDR	2.0%	5.7%	6.9%	7.7%	0.41
ALPHIR	2.6%	−2.6%	−6.2%	−7.9%	−0.45
ALPHSM	2.5%	1.4%	3.3%	4.0%	0.21

Source: Simulations by the author.
Note: Income in 1,000 CFA francs 1998 – Abidjan.

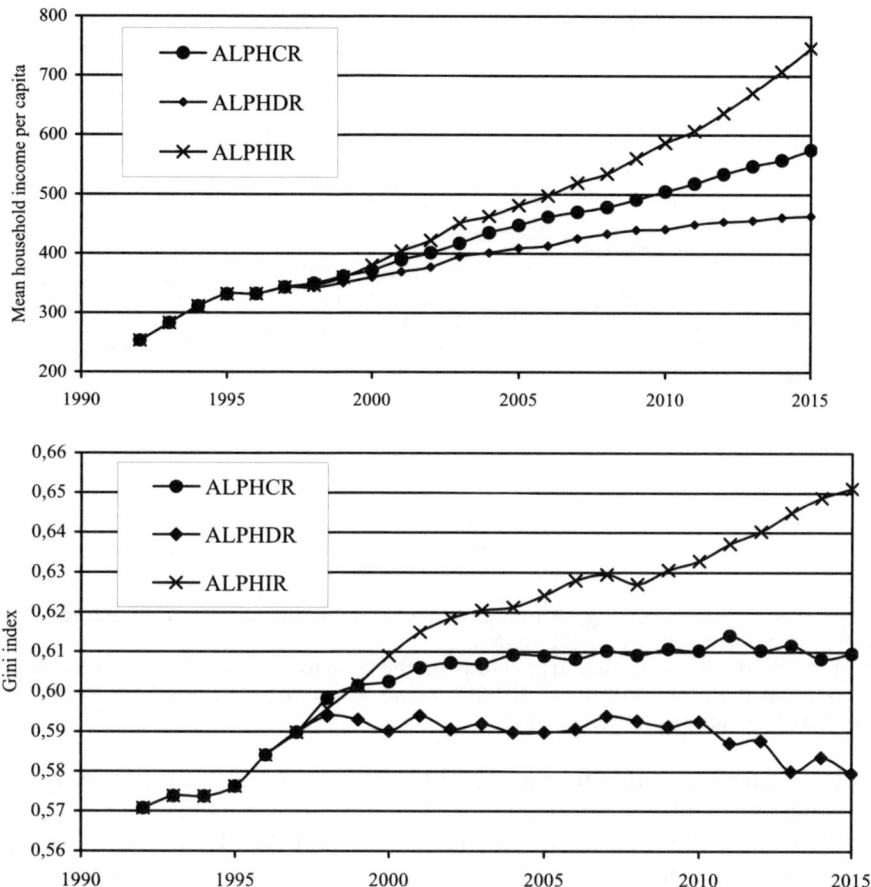

Figure 14.1 Level and inequality of household income per capita
Source: Simulations by the author.

with huge relative income changes at the top of the distribution. In contrast, decreasing returns lead to income losses relative to the reference scenario over the entire distribution. For the experiment ALPHSM, the potential gains stemming from the education expansion are overcompensated until the 60th percentile through the rationing of (formal) wage work, only above incomes exceeding those of the reference case.

Indirect effects through the different transmission channels

Inactivity decreases in all policy experiments, but this decrease is the more pronounced the more individuals have acquired education, the

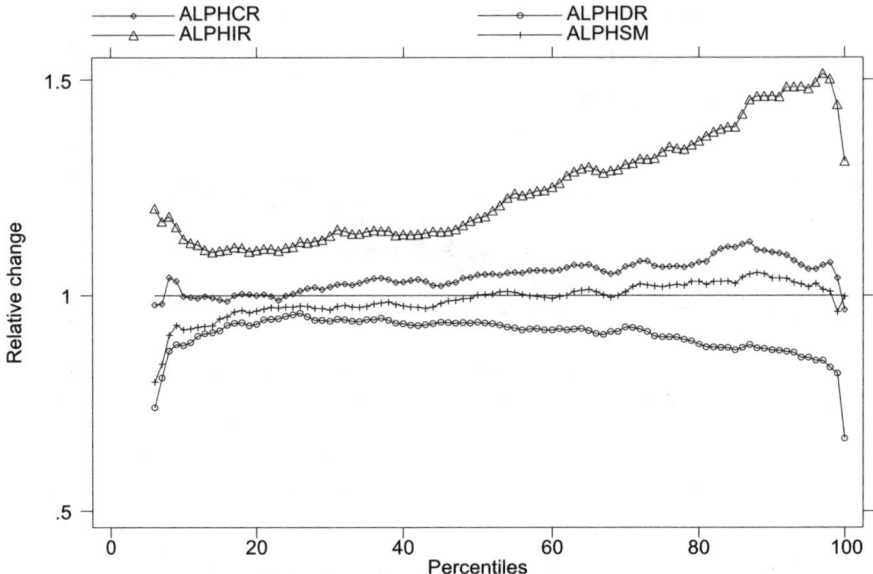

Figure 14.2 Relative changes of mean household income per capita by percentiles (income in 2015 relative to REFSIM)
Note: The distributions are truncated for the first five percentiles, because zero incomes at the bottom of the distribution lead to very erratic relative changes.
Source: Simulations by the author.

better education is remunerated and the easier (formal) wage work is accessible. Particularly interesting is the difference between the policies PRIMED, on the one hand, and HIGHED and ALPHCR on the other hand: an expansion of education up to primary school does not render entry into the labour market sufficiently attractive. This is in particular the case for women. According to the used labour supply model, an "average" woman living in a non-agricultural household has to achieve at least upper secondary school for her potential earnings drawn from wage work to compensate her reservation wage. This result is in line with those of other studies. Lam and Duryea (1999) show, for instance, that in Brazil the increase in domestic productivity following an expansion of education is sufficiently high to compensate for the increase of potential earnings on the labour market corresponding to eight years of schooling. Likewise, Behrman et al. (1999) find in the case of India positive and high returns to education for women in domestic activity.

The decrease of inactivity results principally in an increase of wage work and non-farm self-employment. Wage work is more attractive the higher the return to education. For the experiment ALPHIR, the share of wage earners grows from 11.3 to 16.4 per cent between 1997 and

2015, reducing inactivity and domestic work (including work on the family farm). In contrast, the rationing of wage work to 11.3 per cent of the total workforce (ALPHSM) increases the inactivity rate particularly, and to a smaller extent the share of non-farm self-employment.

Concerning the demographic transmission channels, one can see a decrease of the total fertility rate (TFR) from 5.0 to 4.3 children per woman between 1997 and 2015. Given that women's education is a key determinant in the fertility model used, this decrease is stronger the higher the schooling level of women. In the long term the difference of 0.33 children between the experiments REFSIM and ALPHCR will increase, because the cohort of six-year-olds in 1998 reaches the age of only 24 in 2015 and is therefore still at the beginning of its fertility cycle.

Furthermore, in the model it is assumed that the preferences regarding fertility are constant, which is less likely to happen in reality. A significant expansion of education will probably change fertility behaviour in general, by diffusion of knowledge and contraception technologies for instance, and incite couples, independently of their own education, to limit the number of children. The mean household size decreases by about 0.75 persons between 1992 and 2015 for every scenario considered. In contrast, the dependency ratio decreases strongly, but differently for the considered experiments. As already mentioned, the expansion of education has two effects: an increase of enrolment rates reduces the workforce in the early stages, but raises, once the cohorts attain the age of activity, their propensity to work on the labour market because of the positive return to education. This can explain why the dependency ratio decreases the most under ALPHIR and the least under ALPHDR and ALPHSM.

To sum up, in the medium and long term more education decreases fertility and increases participation rates on the labour market, in particular for women, if the educational expansion is sufficiently strong. This results in a contraction of the dependency ratio, which finally raises mean household income per capita. These are the indirect effects which complete the increase of income due to higher schooling, holding participation behaviour and demographic behaviour constant.

Conclusion

If the most optimistic policy considered in this study were to be put into effect, the cohorts born in 1995 and thereafter would achieve an education level by the time they enter the labour market which would correspond to the Latin American average of cohorts born in 1970. The effect of such an expansion of education in terms of income growth, inequality and poverty in the coming 15 years depends very crucially on the assumptions made for the evolution of returns to education and labour demand. Over the period 1992–2015, the growth gain per capita relative to the persistence of the 1998 age-schooling pattern is about 0.3 points per year if returns to education remain constant, about −0.9 point per year if returns decrease by about 20 per cent and about 1.8 points per year if returns increase by about 20 per cent. If the labour demand in the (formal) wage-earner sector remains rationed to the share of the total workforce observed in 1997 (11.34 per cent), no growth gain at all will be generated. A much quicker poverty reduction relative to the reference scenario may only be possible with rising returns to education and an increasing demand for skilled work. Otherwise the expansion of education will have only a minor effect, at least in the considered time scale, on the headcount index, among other things, because the poor population is only marginally concerned by higher enrolment rates in secondary and higher education.[6] In other words, the simulations show that a policy which is limited to universal primary education is not sufficient to eradicate poverty. These results thus suggest that an expansion of education has to be accompanied by a policy attracting investment and creating demand for skilled labour. To achieve increasing returns to education, it is necessary that other production factors complementary to education, such as physical capital and technological progress, increase simultaneously. Furthermore, expanding school enrolment may lead to a decline in school quality, since new teachers must be hired and teacher-training standards may have to be lowered to find enough teachers.[7] Therefore measures have to be undertaken to ensure a certain quality standard of schooling so that returns to education do not fall. The fact that education is not a sufficient condition for poverty alleviation does not lessen its importance, but rather raises the importance of undertaking complementary reforms that will lead to education paying off. Furthermore, as emphasized in the introduction, education induces many other beneficial effects, such as lower child mortality.

The picture drawn by this study may have been even more pessimistic if it had taken into account possible general equilibrium effects and the negative effects of financing the considered policies. Future work should also investigate what precise type of policy may be adapted in the case of Côte d'Ivoire to achieve the expansion of education simulated in this study.

Acknowledgements

The author thanks Denis Cogneau for his extremely useful comments and discussions. The study also benefited from comments made at the International Conference on Staying Poor: Chronic Poverty and Development

Policy, held in April 2003 in Manchester, as well as at the UNU-WIDER Conference on Inequality, Poverty and Human Well-Being, held in May 2003 in Helsinki. The labour supply and earnings model used in this study was constructed jointly with Denis Cogneau. It is also used in a paper studying the distributional impact of AIDS in Côte d'Ivoire.

Notes

1. The purpose of this study is similar to that of Ferreira and Leite (2002), who analyse the case of the Ceará region (Brazil). However, they work with a constant population structure. Among the demographic variables such as fertility, mortality, migration and marriage, only the distribution of education and the size of the households are taken into account. Furthermore, their analysis uses a comparative static framework; therefore it does not allow reproducing the trajectory between the point of departure and arrival of individuals and households.
2. The gross enrolment ratio is the ratio of total enrolment, regardless of age, to the population of the age group that officially corresponds to the level of education shown. The net enrolment ratio is the ratio of the number of children of official school age (as defined by the education system) enrolled in school to the number of children of official school age in the population.
3. A part of the increase may be due to measurement errors. In contrast to the ENV 1998, the EP 1993 was carried out in rural areas and in cities other than Abidjan during the summer holidays. It is thus possible that some children have been declared not enrolled even when enrolment for the following schooling year was envisaged; in other cases, parents perhaps may have not decided.
4. The increase of educational attainment is not only an auto-declared objective of the Ivorian authorities; the criteria of the Highly Indebted Poor Countries Initiative also stipulate a rise in the budget allocated to education.
5. Monte Carlo lotteries within a microsimulation model consist of assigning to each individual i in the current period a certain probability for the occurrence of a given event, say a birth. This probability is drawn from a uniform law comprised between zero and one. The empirical probability that a woman experiences a birth during this period is calculated using a formerly estimated (econometrically, for instance) function, where her individual characteristics enter as arguments. If the randomly drawn number is lower than the empirical probability, then a birth is simulated. If the number of women is sufficiently high, the aggregated number of births should be equal or very close to the sum of the individual empirical probabilities.
6. This is in line with the evidence presented in Li, Steele and Glewwe (1999). They found in a study based on relatively large sample of developing countries that the share of the richest income quintile in public spending on education (28 per cent) was more than double that of the poorest income quintile (13 per cent).
7. This may pose a problem especially in Côte d'Ivoire, given that this country is severely burdened with the AIDS epidemic.

REFERENCES

Behrman, J. R., S. Duryea and M. Székely (1999) "Schooling Investments and Aggregate Conditions: A Household-Survey Based Approach for Latin

America and the Caribbean", GDN Global Research Project Paper, University of Pennsylvania, Philadelphia.

Behrman, J. R., A. D. Foster, M. R. Rosenzweig and P. Vashishtha (1999) "Women's Schooling, Home Teaching, and Economic Growth", *Journal of Political Economy* 107(4): 682–714.

Benhabib, J. and M. Spiegel (1994) "Role of Human Capital in Economic Development: Evidence from Aggregate Cross-country Data", *Journal of Monetary Economics* 34: 143–173.

Bils, M. and P. J. Klenow (2000) "Does Schooling Cause Growth?", *American Economic Review* 90(5): 1160–1183.

Bulow, J. I. and L. H. Summers (1986) "A Theory of Dual Labor Markets with Application to Industrial Policy, Discrimination, and Keynesian Unemployment", *Journal of Labor Economics* 4(3): 376–414.

Card, D. (1995) "Earnings, Schooling, and Ability Revisited", in S. W. Polachek, ed., *Research in Labor Economics*, 14, Greenwich, Conn. and London: JAI Press, pp. 23–48.

Cogneau, D. and S. Mesplé-Somps (2003) *La Côte d'Ivoire peut-elle devenir un pays émergent?*, Paris: Karthala and OECD.

Ferreira, F. H. G. and P. G. Leite (2002) "Educational Expansion and Income Distribution. A Micro-simulation for Ceará", PUC-RIO Texto para discussão No. 456, Departamento de Economica, PUC-RIO, Rio de Janeiro.

Grimm, M. (2002) "Demo-economic Behaviour, Income Distribution, and Development. Dynamic Micro-simulations Applied to Côte d'Ivoire", PhD thesis, Institut d'Etudes Politiques de Paris, Paris, unpublished.

Heckman, J. and G. Sedlacek (1985) "Heterogeneity, Aggregation, and Market Wages Functions: An Empirical Model of Self-selection in the Labor Market", *Journal of Political Economy* 93: 1077–1125.

INS (2001) *Recensement Général de la Population et de l'Habitation de 1998. Rapport d'analyse. Thème 6: Alphabétisation, niveau d'instruction et fréquentation scolaire*, Abidjan: Institut National de la Statistique, République de Côte d'Ivoire.

Jejeebhoy, S. J. (1995) *Women's Education, Autonomy, and Reproductive Behaviour: Experience from Developing Countries*, Oxford: Clarendon Press.

Katz, L. and K. Murphy (1992) "Changes in the Wage Structure 1963–87: Supply and Demand Factors", *Quarterly Journal of Economics* 107: 35–78.

Klasen, S. (1999) "Does Gender Inequality Reduce Growth and Development: Evidence from Cross-country Regressions", Gender and Development Working Paper Series No. 7, World Bank, Washington, D.C.

Krueger, A. B. and M. Lindahl (2000) "Education for Growth: Why and For Whom?", Working Paper No. 7591, National Bureau of Economic Research, Cambridge, Mass.

Kuznets, S. (1955) "Economic Growth and Income Inequality", *American Economic Review* 45: 1–28.

Lam, D. and S. Duryea (1999) "Effects of Schooling on Fertility, Labour Supply, and Investment in Children, with Evidence from Brazil", *Journal of Human Resources* 34(1): 160–192.

Li, G., D. Steele and P. Glewwe (1999) "The Distribution of Government Education Expenditure in Developing Countries", Development Research Group, World Bank, Washington, D.C., mimeo.

Lucas, R. E. Jr (1988) "On the Mechanics of Economic Development", *Journal of Monetary Economics* 22: 3–42.

Magnac, T. (1991) "Segmented or Competitive Labor Markets?", *Econometrica* 59(1): 165–187.

Mincer, J. (1974) *Schooling, Experience and Earnings*, New York: Columbia University Press.

Pritchett, L. (2001) "Where Has All the Education Gone?", *World Bank Economic Review* 15(3): 367–391.

Romer, P. (1990) "Endogenous Technical Change", *Journal of Political Economy* 94(5): S71–S102.

Roy, A. (1951) "Some Thoughts on the Distribution of Earnings", *Oxford Economic Papers* 3: 135–146.

Schultz, T. P. (1994) "Human Capital and Economic Development", Center Discussion Paper 711, Economic Growth Center, Yale University, New Haven, CT.

——— (1999) "Health and Schooling Investments in Africa, *Journal of Economic Perspectives* 13(3): 67–88.

UNDP (2003) *The Human Development Report 2003: Millennium Development Goals: A Compact among Nations to End Human Poverty*, New York: Oxford University Press for UNDP.

World Bank (2001) "A Chance to Learn. Knowledge and Finance for Education in Sub-Saharan Africa", Africa Region Human Development Series, World Bank, Washington, D.C.

——— (2002a) *Pilot Literacy Project*, Washington, D.C.: World Bank.

——— (2002b) *Education and Training Support Project*, Washington, D.C.: World Bank.

15
Dynamics of poverty in Ethiopia

Arne Bigsten and Abebe Shimeles

Introduction

Standard measures of poverty such as the headcount ratio do not account for the type of poverty being experienced or the heterogeneity of the poor. For instance, the headcount ratio in a given period is an aggregation of individuals with different experiences of movements into and out of poverty. Some have already spent a long time in poverty at the time of interview, while others found themselves in poverty only at the time of the interview and still others found themselves out of poverty but with a high probability of falling back into it. The first category represent the chronically poor, the second the transitory poor and the third the vulnerable. The distinction between these different types of poverty, along with time-varying and individual-specific determinants, is very important for policy purposes.

The current literature[1] on the dynamics of poverty focuses on the mobility of individuals or households across a given income threshold or poverty line, and attempts to distinguish chronic poverty from transient poverty. A household's consumption level in a specific year will depend on its assets, returns on those assets, shocks and the ability of the household to translate incomes into consumption. If the household is credit constrained it will find it hard to cope with negative shocks and smooth consumption. The chronic component of poverty will depend on the household's lack of assets or its limited ability to translate assets into incomes. Incomes change over time by asset accumulation, and in returns driven by savings behaviour or exogenous shocks.[2] Household income will depend on the schooling, gender and other characteristics of its members, the size of the household and the characteristics of the labour market. Part of the exercise in poverty dynamics is to investigate how these factors influence the persistence of poverty.

For policy purposes, but also for understanding of the processes involved, it is useful to make a distinction between chronic and transient poverty.[3] Chronic poverty has generally been assessed in two ways: the spells approach, focusing on transitions into and out of poverty, and the components approach, which tries to isolate the permanent component of poverty from transitory poverty (Hulme and Shepherd, 2003). The latter can take, as is done here, the average consumption level over several periods as the indicator of chronic poverty. The spells approach is a powerful tool for understanding how the transient poor can emerge from poverty if the analysis can clearly identify the factors that underlie transitions. To understand chronic poverty one needs to analyse social structures and mobility within them.

The discussion of transient poverty also leads on, quite naturally, to the discussion of vulnerability. This is not necessarily captured by current income estimates. What one would need to know is the extent to which households have assets that can serve as buffers against shocks. The shocks can be of several kinds: there may be droughts affecting agricultural output, but they may also come in the form of illness or even death of senior members of the household. Particularly access to liquid assets can help protect households. These could include monetary assets or livestock (although in a general crisis the prices of livestock may collapse). Households may also incur debt, sell other assets than livestock or pull children out of school. They may also draw on their social networks or in the end rely on government support or support from other institutions.

Empirical studies that focus on the dynamics of poverty have been relatively rare in the development literature. Bane and Ellwood (1986: 2–4) looked into approaches that were used early on to analyse the dynamics of poverty. They classified the methods into statistical methods which model the level of some variable such as income, allowing for complex lag or error structures, and methods using spell durations and exit probabilities and tabulations of the event (poverty) over some fixed time frame. More recently McKay and Lawson (2003) have reviewed the evidence on chronic and transient poverty and note that many studies conclude that transient poverty seems to be much more important than chronic poverty.

This chapter examines the dynamics of poverty, chronic poverty and vulnerability using a relatively richer panel dataset that covers approximately four years with a minimum of three interviews at intervals of about 1.3 years. To the authors' knowledge such empirical work, notably work that is based on the spells approach, is rare in the developing country context and non-existent for Africa. This chapter thus fills some of the gaps in the empirical literature.

The rest of the chapter is organized as follows. The second section outlines the methodology to capture poverty transitions, chronic poverty and vulnerability. The third section describes the data and reports exit and re-entry probabilities out of or into poverty states for different household types. Measures of poverty transition are constructed based on specific processes characterizing the income-generating potential of households; the transitory component of poverty is separated from the chronic one, which is essential for the discussion of policy options to fight poverty. This section also analyses household vulnerability to poverty and compares it with the determinants of chronic poverty, and discusses the policy implications of the results. The final section is the summary and conclusions.

Approaches to the analysis of poverty dynamics

This analysis of poverty dynamics in Ethiopia uses both the spells approach and the components approach. First it employs the spells approach, since it is interesting to understand the underlying processes which push people into and out of poverty over a given time span. Second, for policy purposes, it is important to be able to distinguish the chronically poor from the temporarily poor, which can be achieved with the components approach. This naturally also leads to the analysis of vulnerability.

Duration analysis

The common practice for capturing the poverty spell is to compute the probabilities of falling into poverty given the condition of the household and its other characteristics (e.g. Stevens, 1995). The elements of interest in this exercise are the estimation of entry and exit probabilities for the condition of being poor or in poverty, which can be considered as random variables with known probability distributions (see Antolin, Dang and Axley, 1999). More specifically, let X be a random variable indicating the duration of a spell in poverty or the length of time the corresponding individual has been in poverty. Let the distribution function of duration X be $F(x) = \text{prob}(x < X)$ for $x > 0$ and let the density function be $f(x) = \text{d}F/\text{d}x$. The corresponding hazard or conditional probability is:

$$\theta(x) = pr(x \leq X/X \geq x) = \frac{f(x)}{1 - F(x)} \tag{1}$$

Assuming that θ follows a logistic structure, we have:

$$\theta(x) = \frac{\exp(x)}{1 + \exp(x)} \tag{2}$$

Length of the poverty spell can be expressed as a function of a set of variables, Z, which vary across spells and time. It includes individual characteristics and other factors that influence the flow of resources to a household or individual. Thus,

$$x_{idt} = \alpha_{id} + \beta Z_{it} \tag{3}$$

where subscript i indexes individuals, t indexes time and d indexes number of years in poverty. The probability of exiting poverty in year x for an individual i with a current duration in poverty of d years is given by the following hazard function:

$$\theta_{idt} = \frac{\exp(\alpha_{id} + \beta_{it} Z_{it})}{1 + \exp(\alpha_{id} + \beta_{it} Z_{it})} \tag{4}$$

Thus exit probabilities are functions of duration effects, α_{id} and other variables, Z, which vary across people and time. Equation (4) is estimated by maximizing the relevant log-likelihood function for all observations. The likelihood function is the product of spells of observed duration, d and of right-censored observations (that is, observations that are included at the beginning of the spell, but not at the ending date).[4]

This approach does not provide an analytical model of poverty dynamics. It does not explain why households or individuals move into or out of poverty over the course of a fixed time period. The model proposed by Burgess and Propper (1998) goes a step further. In their approach, the state in which households find themselves is endogenous to their decisions. In future work the authors intend to extend the analysis in this direction.[5]

Measuring vulnerability to poverty and chronic poverty

The idea of vulnerability to poverty is increasingly recognized as being an integral part of poverty analysis. In addition to offering insights into other poverty dimensions, it determines and predicts future poverty (Duclos, 2002). There is a close interconnection between vulnerability, risk, insecurity and poverty traps and, if well analysed, it can be very useful for public policy (see for example Dercon, 2000).

Vulnerability to poverty captures the risk of a household falling into poverty at least once over the next few years (Pritchett, Suryahadi and Sumarto, 2000). The measures of vulnerability may be regarded as probability distributions with respect to variability in the welfare indicator. Formally, one can express this definition for a typical household as follows:

$$R(n, Z) = 1 - [(1 - P(y_{t+1}^h < z) * \cdots * (1 - P(y_{t+n}^h < z)]$$

where $R(\ )$ defines the vulnerability of a household over n periods, Z is the poverty line and y is total consumption expenditure by household h in each period t. The above expression essentially defines vulnerability as one minus the joint probability of not being in poverty throughout the n periods. Operationalizing this measure requires a few assumptions on the distribution of consumption variability and threshold on the probability of being vulnerable. Pritchett, Suryahadi and Sumarto (2000) assume that the vulnerability of a typical household is the function of the probability threshold p, the poverty line Z and the number of periods under consideration. Thus:

$$V_i^h(p, n, Z) = I[(R_i^h(n, Z) > p)]$$

where I is an indicator function. The threshold probability level assumed in Pritchett, Suryahadi and Sumarto (2000) is 0.5. The necessary other assumption is to specify the distribution on consumption variability. Once one has these, quantitative estimates of vulnerability are possible.

This chapter follows Pritchett, Suryahadi and Sumarto (2000) and McCulloch and Calandrino (2003) for estimating vulnerability and estimates the probability of being poor at any point in time. Pritchett, Suryahadi and Sumarto define vulnerability as the probability of being below the poverty line in a given year, that is:

$$V_h = P(y_{ht} < z)$$

where V_h is vulnerability, y_{ht} is per capita consumption of household h in year t and z is the poverty line. To compute the probability of a household being poor at any given time, one assumes the distribution of its consumption expenditures is normal, while variance and means are allowed to vary between households. One computes the mean consumption expenditure of the household y^* and the inter-temporal standard deviation of consumption for each household. The probability of consumption falling below the poverty line can then be written as:

$$V_h = P\left(\frac{y_{ht} - \mu_h}{\sigma_h} < \frac{z - y_h^*}{s_h}\right)$$

where y_h^* is the mean consumption expenditure of a household and s_h is the intertemporal standard deviation of household consumption. This is thus the probability that the standard normal variate will fall below the poverty line normalized by subtracting inter-temporal mean consumption and dividing by the inter-temporal standard deviation.

Chronic poverty, the condition of persistent poverty, has been measured in recent literature by two different methods. As an indication of chronic poverty, some analysts take the number of times an individual has been in poverty (for example, McCulloch and Calandrino, 2003), while others use the income expected over a certain period of time (Jalan and Ravallion, 2000; Haddad and Ahmed, 2003).

This indicator mainly decomposes the extent of poverty experienced, P_i, into a transient component T_i and a chronic component C_i, where each is defined over a stream of income, y_{it} for the ith individual within D time period, as follows:

$$P_i = P(y_{i1}, y_{i2}, \ldots y_{iD})$$

$$C_i = P(Ey_i, Ey_i, \ldots Ey_i)$$

and

$$T_i = P_i = P(y_{i1}, y_{i2}, \ldots y_{iD}) - C_i = P(Ey_i, Ey_i, \ldots, Ey_i).$$

This chapter reports both types of chronic poverty for rural as well as urban households. In addition, it compares the measures of vulnerability with chronic poverty to understand poverty persistence.

The persistence of poverty

The data for this study come from a panel dataset collected by the Department of Economics, Addis Ababa University, in collaboration with the University of Oxford and Göteborg University. The data consist of 3,000 urban and rural households, equally divided, covering household

Table 15.1 Definition of variables used in the study

Variable definition	Explanation
Rural households	
Household characteristics	
Hhsize	Household size
Agehhh	Age of head of the household
agehhh2	Squared age of the head of the household
Meanage	Mean age of the household
Meanage2	Squared mean age of the household
Dependrat	Dependency ratio (ratio of employed to dependants)
Hhhfem	Female-headed households
Hhhprime	Dummy for household head completing primary school
Wifeprime	Dummy for a wife completing primary school
Household assets	
Landsz	Land size
Assetval	Value of household assets (durables)
Cropsale	Value of crops sold
Cultivat	Size of cultivated land
Oxen	Number of oxen owned
Types of crops planted	
Teff	Dummy if major crop grown is teff
Coffee	Dummy if major crop grown is coffee
Chat	Dummy if major crop grown is chat
Enset	Dummy if major crop grown is enset
Other means of income	
Offfarm	Off-farm income
Regional variables	
Market	Access to local market
North	Dummy if the village is located in the north
Urban households	
Household characteristics	
Hhsize	Household size
Agehhh	Age of head of household
agehhh2	Squared age of head of household
Meanage	Mean age in the household
Meanage2	Squared mean age in the household
Dependrat	Dependency ratio
Hhhfem	Dummy if household head is female
Hhhprime	Dummy if household head completed primary school
Wifeprime	Dummy if wife completed primary school
Occupation	
Privbuss	Household head is in private business
Ownaccnt	Household head is own account worker
Civilserv	Household head is civil servant
Publicen	Household head is employed by public enterprise
Privempl	Household head is private sector employed
Casualwor	Household head is casual worker
Unemp	Household head is unemployed
Regional variable	
North	The town is located in the north

Table 15.2 Percentage of households by poverty status, 1994–1997

Poverty status	Rural	Urban
Always poor	12	22
Sometimes poor	55	37
Never poor	33	41

living conditions, income, expenditure, occupation, demographic aspects, health and education status, occupation, production activities, asset ownership and several other important aspects of the household economy.

The data were collected in four waves for rural households and three waves for urban households. A stratified sampling technique was used to take into account the diverse agro-ecological factors of the rural areas as well as the diverse conditions of the major towns in the urban survey. Table 15.1 lists the variables used in the analysis, particularly in reporting the regression tables.

The estimates of household consumption are adjusted for household size by computing per capita consumption. They are also adjusted for price changes over time and location and converted to the 1994 price level, based on price data collected in connection with the surveys.

Table 15.2 shows the percentage distribution of households according to poverty persistence. A surprisingly small percentage of households are always poor, and it is also noteworthy that persistent poverty is more widespread in urban rather than in rural areas. This may be due to the fact that there is greater variability in incomes in rural areas because of the reliance of agricultural incomes on weather and fluctuating output prices. Alternatively, larger consumption fluctuations in rural areas may be caused by the lack of ability to smooth consumption.

It is interesting to note that the percentages of households consistently non-poor and poor are much higher in urban areas than rural areas, indicating that poverty is more chronic in the former.

In an effort to present some of the socio-economic characteristics of households according to their poverty status during the sample period, table 15.3 reports the trends for rural households. It gives an interesting picture that is consistent with what one would expect with regard to poverty correlations. In almost all attributes there is a clear pattern underpinning the spell of poverty experienced by households; household size, age, education of household head and physical assets play a significant role in the wealth of rural households. Compared to households that have never been poor, one notes that persistently poor households have had, on average, two extra household members; household heads are relatively older, or female; a significantly lower proportion of family

Table 15.3 Descriptive statistics for selected variables according to the number of years in poverty, rural households

Variable	Never poor	Poor, once	Poor, twice	Always poor
Household size (numbers)	5.7	6.4	7.0	8.0
Age of head of household (years)	46	49	48	50
Female-headed households (%)	20	23	21	27
Household head with primary education (%)	12	9	8	2
Wife completed primary school (%)	3	2	0.6	0.1
Land size (hectare)	1.69	1.4	1.2	0.98
Crop sale (Birr)	429	280	186	174
Asset value (Birr)	280	192	128	111
Off-farm employment (%)	30	35	42	36
No. of oxen	1.6	1.3	1.0	0.8

Table 15.4 Descriptive statistics for selected variables according to the number of years in poverty, urban households

Variable	Never poor	Poor, once	Poor, twice	Always poor
Household size (numbers)	5.6	6.0	6.3	7.2
Age of head of household (years)	46	50	49	49
Female-headed households (%)	30	40	43	38
Household head with primary education (%)	59	37	27	24
Wife with primary education (%)	32	20	13	9
Private business (%)	3	1	0.1	0.0
Own account employee (%)	20	20	13	16
Civil servant (%)	22	13	8	10
Public sector employee (%)	10	7	4	6
Private sector employee (%)	6	4	4	2
Casual worker (%)	3	6	11	12
Unemployed (%)	3	4	7	7
Resides in the capital (%)	75	84	80	86

members had completed primary school; they survived on a small size of land; owned, at most, a single ox or none; and were engaged mainly in off-farm activities. As a result, the value of crops sold and average wealth were significantly lower than in households experiencing no poverty during the sample period.

Similarly, in table 15.4, average values for a number of variables follow a clear pattern related to the poverty status of the household. In urban areas, too, size of the household, age/gender and occupation of the household head play a significant role in affecting the status of the household. Typically, the most-chronically poor households have large house-

Table 15.5 Percentage of rural households based on permanent income[1] and current income[2] by region

Region	Headcount (CI-1994)	Headcount (CI-1995)	Headcount (CI-1997)	Headcount (PI-1994–97)
Haresaw	70.51	32.05	37.18	31.25
Geblen	89.06	45.31	39.06	53.13
Dinki	65.06	61.45	50.60	50.60
Debre Berhan	15.61	30.06	10.40	6.94
Yetmen	18.97	31.03	17.24	13.56
Shumsheha	19.55	6.77	31.58	5.84
Sirbana Godeti	8.51	15.96	27.66	7.37
Adele Keke	9.68	10.75	15.05	6.38
Korodegaga	85.00	38.72	76.64	61.68
Turufe Kechma	24.24	32.32	41.41	26.00
Imdibir	67.69	80.00	38.46	69.23
Aze Deboba	25.68	44.59	24.32	17.57
Adado	48.78	66.67	29.27	42.28
Gara Godo	76.60	61.70	65.96	69.47
Dommaa	47.69	32.31	43.08	30.30
Total	42.00	37.70	35.50	30.00

[1] Permanent income is average per capita consumption expenditure for each household in the panel between 1994 and 1997.
[2] Current income is per capita consumption expenditure.

hold size, older household heads; they are mainly casual labourers, unemployed, own-account workers or government employed. Household heads with their own private business were not in the group experiencing poverty during the sample period.

One looks next at the geographic dimension of poverty, which may be useful in identifying geographic poverty traps. Tables 15.5 and 15.6 provide estimates of poverty based on current income in the three rounds plus an estimate based on permanent income, which in this study is the average level of consumption over the three rounds. One notes that that there are instances where the headcount ratio using the permanent income is fairly low, while at the same time it can be extremely high for an individual year. This suggests that the scope for consumption smoothing is very limited, particularly in the rural areas, where hardly any formal credit markets exist for rural households.

A simple correlation coefficient between the headcount, as measured by the inter-temporal consumption expenditure and current consumption expenditure for the three years, shows[6] that the problem of consumption smoothing is not prevalent only in certain rural regions but is evident in nearly all regions, albeit not to the same degree. This makes a case for reducing consumption variability to fight poverty in rural areas.

Table 15.6 Percentage of urban households based on permanent income[1] and current income[2] by town

Region	Headcount (CI-1994)	Headcount (CI-1995)	Headcount (CI-1997)	Headcount (PI-1994–97)
Addis Ababa	46.81	42.86	35.84	37.37
Awasa	40.00	35.00	28.33	33.33
Bahri Dar	25.37	28.36	26.87	39.40
Dessie	35.00	37.50	36.25	32.50
Dire Dawa	15.63	27.08	35.42	20.83
Jimma	33.33	24.64	36.23	26.09
Mekele	38.46	36.54	32.69	28.95
Total	41.00	39.00	35.00	34.00

[1] Permanent income is average per capita consumption expenditure for each household in the panel 1994–1997.
[2] Current income is per capita consumption expenditure.

Table 15.7 Transition probabilities by poverty status

Poverty status for rural households	Poor	Non-poor	Total
Poor	47.40	52.60	100
Non-poor	29.41	70.59	100
Total	36.56	63.44	100
Poverty status for urban households	Poor	Non-poor	Total
Poor	64.14	35.86	100
Non-poor	18.71	81.29	100
Total	36.80	63.20	100

Looking at urban areas one notes a similar trend as for rural households, i.e. the headcount ratio based on inter-temporal consumption expenditure is much lower than the headcount ratio based on current income.

Transition probabilities

A first step in the analysis of movement into and out of poverty is to tabulate transition probabilities, i.e. probabilities of a change in the categorical variables of being poor and non-poor over time. For instance, in rural areas the probabilities of remaining poor or escaping poverty are 47 and 53 per cent, respectively, for the sample period. For urban households the corresponding figures are 64 and 36 per cent, respectively. Thus in table 15.7 one sees again that mobility into and out of poverty is much

Table 15.8 Transition probabilities by expenditure decile for rural households

Decile	1	2	3	4	5	6	7	8	9	10
1	22.41	15.72	12.04	11.04	8.36	10.70	5.02	6.02	5.02	3.68
2	14.24	17.55	11.92	9.93	8.61	9.93	9.60	7.28	5.63	5.30
3	15.63	14.24	9.03	12.85	12.85	7.29	7.64	4.51	9.72	6.25
4	9.71	10.43	12.23	12.95	10.43	10.43	8.27	6.47	6.47	10.79
5	9.49	10.95	9.49	9.85	9.49	10.58	11.31	12.04	9.49	7.30
6	7.25	9.06	10.87	8.70	13.41	9.42	10.14	9.42	9.78	11.96
7	4.26	7.45	8.87	8.87	9.93	10.64	9.93	14.54	11.35	14.18
8	6.15	5.38	10.00	8.08	6.92	11.54	12.69	10.38	12.31	16.54
9	4.42	3.06	8.16	7.14	9.52	8.84	11.56	12.93	19.05	15.31
10	4.74	6.72	7.51	7.11	9.09	7.91	17.79	10.28	15.42	13.44

Table 15.9 Transition probabilities by expenditure decile for urban households

Decile	1	2	3	4	5	6	7	8	9	10
1	37.08	21.25	17.50	9.17	5.00	3.75	2.08	2.92	0.42	0.83
2	18.50	23.23	17.32	13.78	10.24	5.51	6.30	2.36	1.57	1.18
3	21.62	15.32	14.86	9.91	12.16	6.76	7.21	4.95	5.86	1.35
4	8.63	12.94	15.29	14.90	13.73	11.37	9.41	6.67	2.75	4.31
5	4.12	8.23	9.05	16.87	17.70	12.76	10.29	9.05	7.00	4.94
6	5.56	7.26	8.55	6.84	15.61	18.80	11.54	10.26	10.68	4.70
7	2.08	3.75	7.92	12.50	8.33	16.67	17.92	12.92	11.67	6.25
8	3.27	4.49	2.86	8.57	7.35	10.61	15.92	18.78	19.59	8.57
9	1.22	1.22	1.22	6.53	4.08	8.16	13.88	16.73	24.90	22.04
10	0.42	1.26	1.26	3.78	3.78	6.30	5.88	15.55	16.81	44.95

more extensive in the rural areas and rural households experience larger swings in consumption than urban households. Urban poverty is, to a greater degree, more chronic. The urban poor appear to have little chance of breaking out of poverty. Tables 15.8 and 15.9 provide a more detailed breakdown of transition probabilities by decile, but the picture is essentially the same.

When one reviews the probabilities in general terms (without poverty status), probabilities of being poor and non-poor are similar for households in rural and urban areas. This is a crude indicator, again alerting one to the fact that poverty in Ethiopia is not only a rural phenomenon; urban areas are just as susceptible to poverty.

Duration analysis

This section extends the mobility discussion by taking into consideration the length of time a household struggles with poverty. A start for the du-

Table 15.10 Exit and re-entry hazard ratios conditional on duration

	Exit[1]	Re-entry[2]
Rural households	0.50	0.50
Urban households	0.34	0.25

[1] Exit rates are ratios of individuals who moved out of poverty after one year of being in poverty to the individuals who were poor in 1994.
[2] Re-entry rates are ratios of individuals who were non-poor for at least one year and became poor to individuals who were poor in 1994.

Table 15.11 Odds ratios for the probability of exiting poverty, rural households

Exit	Odds ratio	Std err.	z	P > |z|	(95% conf. interval)	
hhsize	0.927	0.025	−2.83	0.005	0.879	0.977
agrozone	1.692	0.715	1.25	0.213	0.739	3.874
hhhfem	0.982	0.161	−0.11	0.914	0.713	1.354
hhhprime	0.750	0.180	−1.20	0.230	0.468	1.201
wifeprim	0.676	0.369	−0.72	0.473	0.232	1.969
landsz	1.117	0.043	2.85	0.004	1.035	1.206
meanage	0.955	0.026	−1.69	0.092	0.905	1.007
agehhh	1.036	0.024	1.50	0.133	0.989	1.084
assetval	1.000	0.000	−0.24	0.814	0.999	1.000
haresaw	0.676	0.266	−0.99	0.320	0.312	1.463
geblen	1.105	0.399	0.28	0.781	0.545	2.242
dinki	1.189	0.418	0.49	0.622	0.597	2.367
debreber	0.944	0.284	−0.19	0.848	0.524	1.701
shumsheh	0.155	0.074	−3.92	0.000	0.061	0.394
sirbana	0.540	0.202	−1.65	0.100	0.259	1.124
adele	0.187	0.100	−3.15	0.002	0.066	0.531
korodega	0.421	0.154	−2.36	0.018	0.205	0.864
imdibir	4.060	1.689	3.37	0.001	1.796	9.176
azedeboa	2.760	1.147	2.44	0.015	1.222	6.232
adado	3.226	1.330	2.84	0.004	1.438	7.236
garagodo	1.705	0.699	1.30	0.193	0.763	3.809
market	1.000	0.000	−1.30	0.193	1.000	1.000
agehhh2	1.000	0.000	−0.99	0.322	0.999	1.000
meanage2	1.000	0.000	0.72	0.474	1.000	1.001
depndrat	1.377	0.584	0.75	0.451	0.599	3.164
offfarm	1.014	0.143	0.10	0.920	0.770	1.336
teff	0.725	0.149	−1.56	0.118	0.485	1.085
coffee	0.905	0.230	−0.39	0.693	0.549	1.489
chat	0.946	0.266	−0.20	0.843	0.545	1.641
oxen	1.077	0.054	1.49	0.135	0.977	1.188

Table 15.12 Odds ratios of logit estimates for entering poverty, rural households

Logit estimates					No. of observations	= 4,197
					LR chi^2(30)	= 163.22
					Prob > chi^2	= 0.000
Log likelihood = −986.041					Pseudo R^2	= 0.076

exit	Odds ratio	Std err.	z	P > |z|	[95% conf. interval]	
hhsize	0.823	0.026	−6.18	0.000	0.774	0.876
lagrozone3	0.409	0.187	−1.95	0.051	0.167	1.002
hhhfem	0.779	0.129	−1.51	0.131	0.563	1.077
hhhprime	1.337	0.330	1.18	0.239	0.824	2.170
wifeprim	0.950	0.415	−0.12	0.906	0.403	2.237
landsz	1.149	0.046	3.44	0.001	1.062	1.244
meanage	0.961	0.033	−1.16	0.245	0.898	1.028
agehhh	1.050	0.028	1.86	0.063	0.997	1.106
assetval	1.000	0.000	−0.01	0.989	1.000	1.000
haresaw	2.398	1.080	1.94	0.052	0.992	5.796
geblen	1.948	0.841	1.54	0.122	0.836	4.540
dinki	1.986	0.889	1.53	0.125	0.826	4.774
debreber	0.217	0.078	−4.25	0.000	0.107	0.438
shumsheh	2.262	0.932	1.98	0.048	1.008	5.074
sirbana	1.203	0.378	0.59	0.556	0.650	2.229
adele	0.931	0.461	−0.14	0.886	0.353	2.456
korodega	2.800	0.831	3.47	0.001	1.565	5.010
imdibir	0.446	0.279	−1.29	0.197	0.131	1.520
azedeboa	0.890	0.437	−0.24	0.812	0.340	2.332
adado	0.395	0.216	−1.70	0.090	0.135	1.155
garagodo	1.244	0.445	0.61	0.541	0.617	2.509
market	1.000	0.000	2.00	0.045	1.000	1.000
meanage2	1.000	0.001	−0.25	0.801	0.999	1.001
agehhh2	1.000	0.000	−0.82	0.415	0.999	1.000
depndrat	0.790	0.358	−0.52	0.604	0.325	1.922
offfarm	1.207	0.175	1.30	0.195	0.908	1.605
teff	0.915	0.175	−0.46	0.642	0.629	1.331
coffee	0.682	0.278	−0.94	0.348	0.306	1.517
chat	0.490	0.247	−1.42	0.157	0.182	1.315
oxen	1.129	0.056	2.46	0.014	1.025	1.243

ration analysis is to estimate the hazard ratios for urban and rural households, so that exit rates are the ratio of individuals moving out of poverty after one year to those individuals who were at risk of being poor in 1994 (see Antolin, Dang and Axley, 1999 for such a definition of exit or entry hazards). This is a crude measure of the probability of exiting or entering poverty, given the initial risk of being in poverty. Re-entry rates constitute the ratio of individuals who were non-poor for at least one year but became impoverished compared to those individuals who were poor in

Table 15.13 Odds ratios of exiting poverty, urban households

Logit estimates					No. of observations	= 3,624
					LR chi^2(21)	= 38.10
					Prob > chi^2	= 0.013
Log likelihood = −667.022					Pseudo R^2	= 0.028

Exit	Odds ratio	Std err.	z	P > |z|	[95% conf. interval]	
hhsz	1.016657	0.0356095	0.47	0.637	0.9492057	1.088902
meanage	1.013343	0.0342576	0.39	0.695	0.9483756	1.082761
femhhh	0.9376821	0.1910814	−0.32	0.752	0.6289227	1.398022
agehhh	1.006725	0.0253745	0.27	0.790	0.9582003	1.057707
hhhprime	0.8084067	0.170153	−1.01	0.312	0.5351425	1.22121
wifprime	1.057313	0.2449382	0.24	0.810	0.6714491	1.664921
privbuss	0.2437612	0.2481388	−1.39	0.166	0.0331495	1.792473
ownaccnt	1.044463	0.2313181	0.20	0.844	0.6766692	1.612164
civilser	0.5256135	0.1673967	−2.02	0.043	0.2815638	0.9811967
publicen	0.4128531	0.1839765	−1.99	0.047	0.1723778	0.9888031
privempl	0.8341955	0.3502907	−0.43	0.666	0.3662992	1.899764
casualwo	0.9309434	0.2933669	−0.23	0.820	0.5019787	1.726479
depenrat	2.259731	1.000046	1.84	0.065	0.9491974	5.379684
north	2.24515	1.40865	1.29	0.197	0.6564253	7.679014
meanage2	0.999997	0.0004004	−0.01	0.994	0.9992126	1.000782
agehhh2	0.9999218	0.000261	−0.30	0.765	0.9994103	1.000434
addis	2.953991	1.533778	2.09	0.037	1.067693	8.172819
awasa	2.810675	1.763224	1.65	0.099	0.8219124	9.611601
bahrdar	1.150949	0.5823888	0.28	0.781	0.426915	3.102919
dessie	0.9060722	0.447511	−0.20	0.842	0.3441538	2.385465
diredawa	0.8846076	0.6043851	−0.18	0.858	0.2318406	3.375296

1994. It is important to mention that the maximum number of poverty spells allowed by this sample is one period or "year"[7] before a household exits, or in the case of entry, the maximum number of spells of not being impoverished is one period.

The probability of leaving poverty is higher for a rural household than for an urban one, but the chances of falling back into poverty are also higher in the rural sector than in the urban one. The cyclical nature of consumption expenditure is pronounced for rural households (table 15.10). It may be also useful to recall the main events of the period 1994–1997, as these could have seriously affected rural livelihoods. In 1994 Ethiopia experienced a drought that reduced agricultural output considerably (real growth in agriculture was −3.7 per cent), but in 1995 the sector recovered and registering a growth rate of 3.5 per cent, plus a bumper harvest in 1996 with a 14 per cent increase. This continued throughout 1997, when agriculture grew by 3.4 per cent (World Bank, 2002).

Table 15.14 Odds ratios for entering poverty, urban households

Logit estimates				No. of observations		= 3,624
				LR chi^2(21)		= 20.80
				Prob > chi^2		= 0.471
Log likelihood = −526.615				Pseudo R^2		= 0.019

Exit	Odds ratio	Std err.	z	P > |z|	[95% conf. interval]	
hhsz	1.008	0.042	0.18	0.857	0.929	1.093
meanage	1.007	0.048	0.14	0.890	0.917	1.105
femhhh	1.089	0.260	0.36	0.721	0.682	1.737
agehhh	1.050	0.045	1.14	0.254	0.966	1.141
hhhprime	0.701	0.176	−1.41	0.158	0.428	1.148
wifprime	0.788	0.228	−0.83	0.409	0.447	1.388
privbuss	0.921	0.682	−0.11	0.912	0.216	3.932
ownaccnt	0.830	0.237	−0.65	0.514	0.474	1.452
civilser	0.841	0.287	−0.51	0.611	0.431	1.640
publicen	1.029	0.408	0.07	0.942	0.473	2.238
privempl	1.228	0.571	0.44	0.659	0.494	3.053
casualwo	1.203	0.432	0.51	0.607	0.595	2.433
depenrat	2.144	1.144	1.43	0.153	0.754	6.099
north	0.520	0.272	−1.25	0.211	0.186	1.449
meanage2	1.000	0.001	−0.35	0.727	0.999	1.000
agehhh2	1.000	0.000	−1.07	0.287	0.999	1.000
addis	0.502	0.168	−2.07	0.039	0.261	0.965
awasa	0.420	0.250	−1.46	0.145	0.131	1.350
bahrdar	1.187	0.668	0.30	0.761	0.394	3.574
dessie	1.266	0.694	0.43	0.667	0.432	3.706
diredawa	0.776	0.329	−0.60	0.549	0.338	1.780

Next a set of logit regressions were conducted, as described in equations (1)–(4) above, including dummies to control for community-level effects. The rural regressions show that only the marginal coefficients associated with household size, agricultural zone[8] and size of land are significant. Factors contributing positively to the probability of exiting poverty were the size of land and ownership of oxen. If the odds ratios are taken as a guide for the probability of exiting poverty (see tables 15.11–15.14), households in the cereal-growing areas generally tend to have smaller chances of exiting poverty as compared to those in enset-growing areas. Coffee growers had a better chance of exiting poverty. The effect of chat[9] growing was not significant here, although it did play an important role in keeping people from re-entering poverty (see table 15.12). Household size and being a teff grower erode the chances of exiting poverty.

Similarly, tables 15.15–15.16 describe the marginal effect of a house-

Table 15.15 Marginal effects for the probability of exiting poverty for rural households

Variable	dy/dx	P > |z|
Household characteristics		
Household size	−0.004	0.004
Household head is female*	−0.001	0.995
Household head completed primary*	−0.015	0.950
Wife completed primary*	−0.019	0.972
Land size (hectares)	0.006	0.004
Mean age in household	−0.003	0.091
Age of head of household	0.002	0.132
Cash value of durables	−0.000	0.814
Access to market	−0.000	0.192
Age of hh2	−0.000	0.321
Meanage2	0.000	0.474
Dependency ratio	0.019	0.451
Household head engaged in off-farm*	0.001	0.995
Number of oxen owned	0.004	0.134
Village characteristics		
Farming system (cereal-growing area = 0)	0.031	0.213
Haresaw village*	−0.020	0.960
Geblen village*	0.006	0.987
Dinki village*	0.011	0.976
Debreberhan village*	−0.003	0.991
Shumsha village	−0.061	0.898
Sirbana Godeti village*	−0.029	0.939
Adele village*	−0.055	0.918
Korodega village*	−0.037	0.920
Imdibir village*	0.142	0.732
Azedeboa village*	0.088	0.832
Adado village*	0.105	0.799
Garagodo village*	0.038	0.926
Major crop is teff*	−0.018	0.930
Major crop is coffee*	−0.006	0.982
Major crop is chat*	−0.003	0.991

*dy/dx is for discrete change of dummy variable from 0 to 1.

hold entering poverty after being categorized as non-poor for a year. The significant coefficients are household size, land size, age of the household head, proximity to nearest market and ownership of oxen. Most coefficients have the expected signs, except for household size and size of land (which reduce the odds of re-entering poverty). But other variables (age of the head of the household, off-farm activity, teff production) increase the odds of re-entering poverty. In addition, as can be seen from table 15.13, if one takes into account the odds ratios and the measure of statistical significance associated with the respective variables, one also

Table 15.16 Marginal effects for the probability of re-entering poverty for rural households

Variable	dy/dx	P > |z|
Household characteristics		
Household size	−0.010	0.000
Household head is female*	−0.012	0.943
Household head completed primary*	0.016	0.947
Wife completed primary*	−0.003	0.995
Land size owned	0.007	0.001
Mean age in household	−0.002	0.245
Age of head of household	0.002	0.062
Cash value of durables	−0.000	0.989
meanage2	−0.000	0.801
agehhh2	−0.000	0.415
depndrat	−0.012	0.604
offfarm*	0.010	0.946
oxen	0.006	0.014
Village characteristics		
Farming system	0.054	0.910
Haresaw village*	0.063	0.889
Geblen village*	0.044	0.918
Dinki village*	0.046	0.919
Debreber village*	−0.049	0.891
Shumsheh village*	0.056	0.892
Sirbana village*	0.010	0.975
Adele village*	−0.004	0.994
Korodega village*	0.078	0.794
Imdibir village*	−0.030	0.962
Azedeboa village*	−0.006	0.991
Adado village*	−0.034	0.950
Garagodo village*	0.012	0.973
Market village	0.000	0.045
meanage2	−0.000	0.801
agehhh2	−0.000	0.415
depndrat	−0.012	0.604
offfarm*	0.010	0.946
teff*	−0.004	0.981
coffee*	−0.017	0.966
chat*	−0.028	0.956

* dy/dx is for discrete change of dummy variable from 0 to 1.

has some community-level dummies that are significant in affecting the odds of entering into poverty.

For urban households there are hardly any significant estimates, except that having a civil service job reduces the likelihood of becoming impoverished (see also the odds ratios reported in tables 15.13 and 15.14). Government jobs thus seem to be a good insurance against income losses.

Table 15.17 Odds ratio: Marginal effects for the probability of exiting poverty for urban households

$y = \Pr(\text{exit})$ (predict)
$= 0.0414$

Variable	dy/dx	P > |z|
hhsz	−0.128	0.000
meanage	0.011	0.330
femhhh*	0.150	0.770
agehhh	−0.004	0.439
hhhprime*	0.434	0.033
wifprime*	0.247	0.316
privbuss*	0.587	0.430
ownaccnt*	0.146	0.567
civilser*	0.397	0.141
publicen*	−0.599	0.181
privempl*	0.110	0.980
casualwo*	−0.192	0.481
depenrat	−0.026	0.064
north*	0.042	0.947
meanage2	−0.000	0.994
agehhh2	−0.000	0.764
addis*	0.039	0.941
awasa*	0.064	0.919
bahrdar*	0.006	0.991
dessie*	−0.004	0.994
diredawa*	−0.005	0.995

*dy/dx is for discrete change of dummy variable from 0 to 1.

As far as urban households are concerned, employment in the public sector or civil service seems to reduce the probability of re-entry. The major finding of this section is that there was little mobility among urban households with respect to poverty (tables 15.17 and 15.18), and that expanding opportunities would offer the best options for fighting poverty in this area.

Vulnerability and its determinants

Vulnerability is here defined as a probability function from a standard normal distribution, where the distance from the poverty line to the per capita income of each household is computed and normalized by standard deviation. Summarizing this with respect to income decile and quintile, the results show that there is a great deal of vulnerability among lower-income deciles in Ethiopia. In the bottom four deciles, vulnerabil-

Table 15.18 Marginal effects of the probability of re-entry into poverty for urban households

$y = \Pr(\text{entry}) (\text{predict})$
$= 0.031$

Variable	dy/dx	P > |z|
hhsz	0.257	0.000
meanage	−0.007	0.409
femhhh*	0.197	0.990
agehhh	−0.006	0.480
hhhprime*	−1.160	0.000
wifprime*	−0.486	0.061
privbuss*	−2.117	0.006
ownaccnt*	−0.723	0.011
civilser*	−0.648	0.047
publicen*	−0.065	0.854
privempl*	−0.710	0.107
casualwo*	−0.003	0.993
depenrat	0.032	0.064
north*	−0.016	0.975
meanage2	−0.000	0.727
agehhh2	−0.000	0.284
addis*	−0.023	0.944
awasa*	−0.019	0.975
bahrdar*	0.006	0.992
dessie*	0.008	0.989
diredawa*	−0.007	0.987

* dy/dx is for discrete change of dummy variable from 0 to 1.

ity is higher in urban areas than in rural areas, but further up the income scale vulnerability is more extensive in the rural sector. High-income earners in urban areas have a more secure position than those in rural settings. Also the better-off rural households are sensitive to swings reflecting weather or market conditions.

Tables 15.19 and 15.20 present some simple regressions to identify the determinants or correlates of rural and urban vulnerability. The results show that larger households are much more vulnerable, and particularly so in the rural areas. Education also seems to reduce vulnerability in both environments, but much more strongly so in the urban setting. In rural areas, vulnerability is reduced when crop sales are high (note the high significance of chat sales) and when the household owns oxen and other assets. It is noteworthy that good access to markets also reduces vulnerability. In the urban setting, it is particularly the access to various forms of wage employment that reduces vulnerability; see tables 15.21–15.23.

Table 15.19 Determinants of vulnerability in rural Ethiopia

No. of observations = 4,199
F (18, 4180) = 120.66
Prob > F = 0.000
R^2 = 0.291
Root MSE = 0.258

Regression with robust standard errors

zvulneb	Coef.	Robust Std err.	t	P > |t|	[95% conf. interval]	
hhsize	0.028	0.002	18.11	0.000	0.025	0.031
meanage	0.001	0.002	0.45	0.652	−0.003	0.004
agehhh	0.004	0.001	3.26	0.001	0.002	0.007
agehhh2	−0.000	0.000	−1.66	0.097	−0.000	0.000
eanage2	−0.000	0.000	−3.53	0.000	−0.000	−0.000
hhprime	−0.046	0.015	−3.14	0.002	−0.074	−0.017
wifeprim	−0.040	0.028	−1.42	0.156	−0.096	0.015
depndrat	0.104	0.028	3.71	0.000	0.049	0.158
cultivat	−0.015	0.002	−6.18	0.000	−0.020	−0.010
landsz	(dropped)					
cropsale	−0.000	0.000	−11.59	0.000	−0.000	−0.000
oxen	−0.022	0.003	−7.49	0.000	−0.028	−0.016
assetval	−0.000	0.000	−10.31	0.000	−0.000	−0.000
market	−0.000	0.000	−10.04	0.000	−0.000	−0.000
offfarm	0.041	0.009	4.67	0.000	0.024	0.058
teff	0.014	0.010	1.43	0.153	−0.005	0.034
coffee	0.001	0.014	0.05	0.956	−0.027	0.029
chat	−0.220	0.016	−14.12	0.000	−0.251	−0.190
north	−0.105	0.011	−9.30	0.000	−0.128	−0.083
_cons	0.278	0.038	7.31	0.000	0.203	0.352

Determinants of chronic poverty

To complement the analysis of transitory poverty, a regression on chronic poverty was also conducted. Also here education significantly reduces poverty. The likelihood of chronic poverty is reduced, as is to be expected, by variables such as crop sales and ownership of assets. Market access appears to reduce chronic poverty significantly. Interestingly, off-farm activity is associated with higher chronic poverty, suggesting that off-farm income activity is a survival strategy rather than a sign of a household moving up the income scale. The production of chat is again a very reliable way out of poverty.

Figures 15.1 and 15.2 map the measure of vulnerability against the measure of chronic poverty. As can be noted, the degree of vulnerability is extensive also among households that are well below the poverty line.

Table 15.20 Determinants of vulnerability in urban Ethiopia

Regression with robust standard errors

No. of observations = 3,624
$F (17, 3606)$ = 99.47
Prob > F = 0.000
R^2 = 0.259
Root MSE = 0.300

zvulneb	Coef	Robust Std err.	t	P > |t|	[95% conf. interval]	
hhsz	0.022	0.002	9.97	0.000	0.018	0.026
meanage	−0.010	0.003	−3.82	0.000	−0.015	−0.005
femhhh	−0.038	0.013	−3.04	0.002	−0.063	−0.014
agehhh	0.005	0.002	3.64	0.000	0.003	0.008
hhhprime	−0.142	0.013	−10.79	0.000	−0.168	−0.116
wifprime	−0.138	0.013	−10.34	0.000	−0.164	−0.112
privbuss	−0.324	0.026	−12.54	0.000	−0.375	−0.277
ownaccnt	−0.167	0.015	−10.99	0.000	−0.197	−0.137
civilser	−0.135	0.016	−8.55	0.000	−0.166	−0.104
publicen	−0.131	0.021	−6.39	0.000	−0.172	−0.091
privempl	−0.189	0.025	−7.57	0.000	−0.238	−0.140
casualwo	0.036	0.022	1.65	0.098	−0.007	0.080
depenrat	0.272	0.029	9.27	0.000	0.215	0.330
north	−0.056	0.014	−3.87	0.000	−0.084	−0.027
capitalc	0.062	0.013	4.70	0.000	0.036	0.087
meanage2	0.000	0.000	2.69	0.007	0.000	0.000
agehhh2	−0.000	0.000	−3.48	0.001	−0.000	−0.000
_cons	0.377	0.060	6.31	0.000	0.260	0.494

Thus these two measures do not measure exactly the same thing, but complement each other; see also table 15.24.

Concluding remarks

These results show that poverty in Ethiopia is more persistent in urban areas than in rural areas. The proportion of people who remained poor throughout the sample period in urban areas was twice that of rural areas. This suggests the need for different approaches to fight poverty in these areas. Security issues tend to be more important in rural areas, while expanding opportunities seems to be appropriate in urban areas.

In addition, the proportion of people in poverty declined considerably in rural as well as urban areas over the period covered. The measure of vulnerability indicates that, on average, the probability of a household being poor at any point in time during this period was about 40 per cent,

Table 15.21 Vulnerability by inter-temporal consumption expenditure decile

Inter-temporal mean consumption decile	Urban households	Rural households
1	0.99	0.98
2	0.89	0.83
3	0.72	0.64
4	0.46	0.43
5	0.26	0.30
6	0.18	0.22
7	0.14	0.18
8	0.12	0.17
9	0.09	0.16
10	0.07	0.15

Table 15.22 Vulnerability by inter-temporal consumption expenditure decile

Inter-temporal mean consumption decile	Urban households	Rural households
1	0.94	0.90
2	0.59	0.54
3	0.22	0.26
4	0.13	0.17
5	0.08	0.16

Table 15.23 Measures of vulnerability for rural and urban households by the status of chronic poverty

Households	Vulnerability to poverty	Frequency (no. of households)
Rural households		
Non-poor	0.23 (0.13)	973
Poor	0.81 (0.17)	430
All households	0.41 (0.30)	1,403
Urban households		
Non-poor	0.17 (0.14)	803
Poor	0.83 (0.17)	405
All households	0.39 (0.35)	1,208

Source: Authors' calculation.

DYNAMICS OF POVERTY IN ETHIOPIA 349

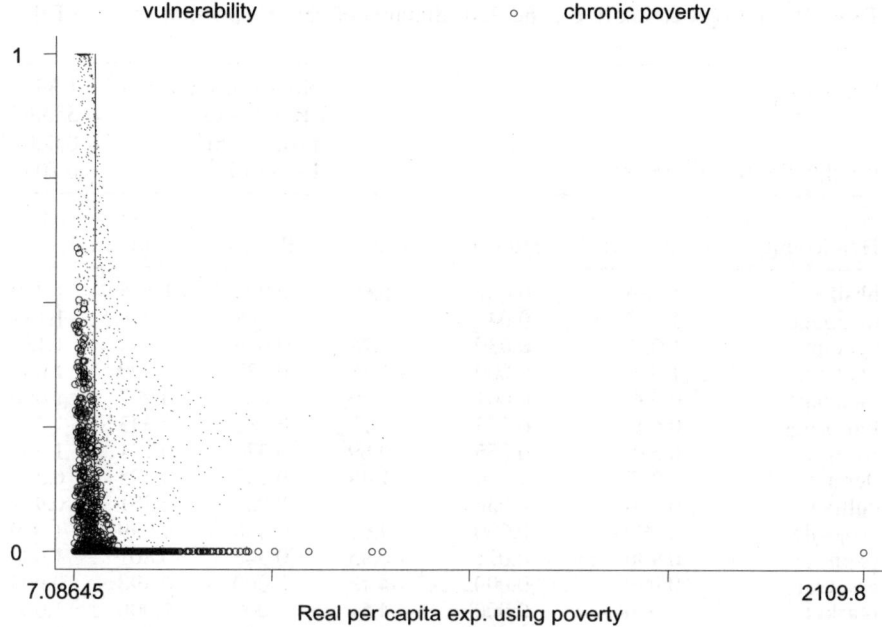

Figure 15.1 Vulnerability and chronic poverty in rural Ethiopia

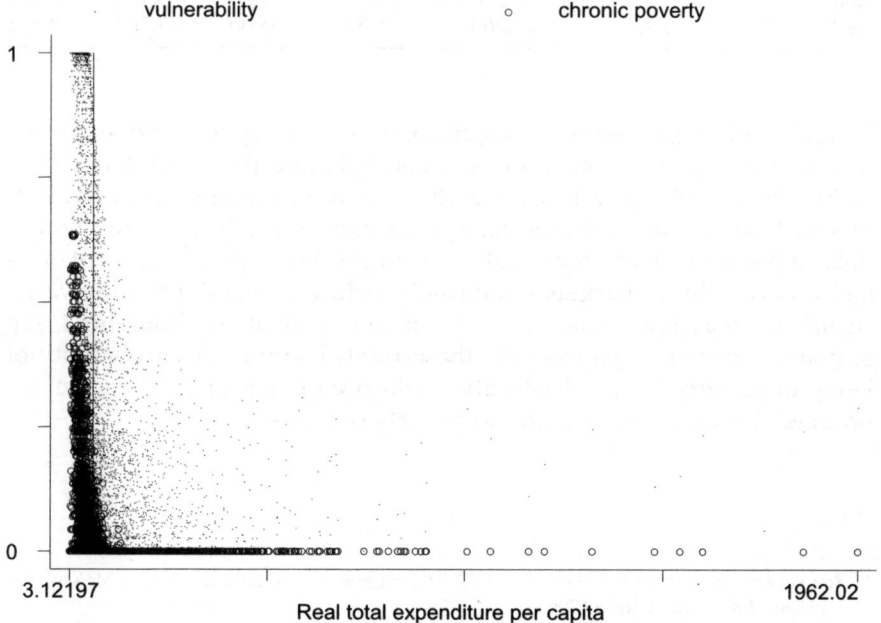

Figure 15.2 Vulnerability and chronic poverty for urban Ethiopia

Table 15.24 Logit estimate for the determinants of chronic poverty in rural Ethiopia

Logit estimates						
Log likelihood = −685.498				No. of observations = 1,399 LR chi² (18) = 353.67 Prob > chi² = 0.000 Pseudo R² = 0.205		
Headcount	Odds ratio	Std err.	z	P > |z|	[95% conf. interval]	
hhsize	1.196	0.032	6.69	0.000	1.135	1.260
meanage	1.027	0.047	0.57	0.568	0.938	1.124
agehhh	1.051	0.030	1.78	0.076	0.995	1.111
agehhh2	1.000	0.000	−1.18	0.237	0.999	1.000
meanage2	0.999	0.001	−1.70	0.088	0.997	1.000
hhhprime	0.605	0.175	−1.74	0.082	0.343	1.066
wifeprim	0.575	0.356	−0.89	0.371	0.171	1.936
depndrat	2.257	1.230	1.49	0.135	0.775	6.570
cultivat	0.850	0.036	−3.80	0.000	0.781	0.924
cropsale	0.999	0.000	−4.67	0.000	0.999	1.000
oxen	0.930	0.071	−0.95	0.343	0.801	1.080
assetval	0.999	0.000	−4.13	0.000	0.998	0.999
market	1.000	0.000	−4.51	0.000	1.000	1.000
offfarm	1.450	0.205	2.62	0.009	1.098	1.914
teff	0.924	0.149	−0.49	0.624	0.674	1.267
coffee	0.962	0.203	−0.18	0.854	0.636	1.454
chat	0.281	0.086	−4.13	0.000	0.154	0.513
north	0.375	0.066	−5.53	0.000	0.265	0.531

indicating the high degree of insecurity in the society. In rural areas factors such as age of the head of the household and the dependency ratio within the household greatly affect the odds of moving into poverty. Factors such as size of cultivated land, education of the head of the household, education of the wife, value of crop sales, type of crops planted and access to local markets significantly reduce vulnerability to poverty. In urban areas household size, age of the head of the household and region of residence (particularly the capital) increase the probability of being in poverty. A good education and occupation of the head of the household reduce vulnerability to poverty significantly.

Notes

1. See surveys in Baulch and Hoddinott (2000), Hulme and Shepherd (2003), McKay and Lawson (2003) and Yaqub (2003).
2. Gunning et al. (2000) investigated the income dynamics in the resettlement areas of Zim-

babwe. They had data on asset accumulation over time, and combined these with estimates of changes in asset returns in an interesting analysis of a process of income convergence. There is little evidence in the literature on the cumulative income of shocks to households.
3. The households that remain poor over a given period constitute the chronically poor (see e.g. Jalan and Ravallion 1998). Jalan and Ravallion (2000) give two conditions for a household to experience transient poverty. First, the household must be observed to be poor for at least one date in some period of time for which data are available. Second, the household's standard of living must vary over time within the time period. They then propose a decomposition of total poverty into chronic poverty and transient poverty. A slightly different approach was suggested by Rodgers and Rodgers (1991), where permanent income, instead of current consumption, is used to measure persistent or chronic poverty.
4. See Stevens (1995) for a discussion of estimating multiple spells (that is, including individuals that exit and re-enter the poverty zone in the duration period, d) and the problem of heterogeneity in the spell of exit and entry across individuals.
5. This approach enables one to explore the following aspects of the dynamics of poverty. One can compute the poverty transition rates, which are state-dependent. This allows the persistence of poverty to differ depending on the current state across different groups. The framework also allows one to address the unconditional probability of being poor by integrating across subgroups. It helps to compare predicted poverty rates with actual poverty rates and test the robustness of the method. One can also estimate the implications of behavioural change on the time path of poverty.
6. Starting from 1994, respectively the figure is 0.91, 0.822 and 0.79.
7. The period covered by the data is 1994–1997, with no information on 1996. Thus the length of time in poverty after 1995 can be interpreted as a period, instead of years.
8. This variable identifies whether a household is in the cereal-growing area(s) or the enset-growing area(s). Enset is a rootcrop derived from false banana.
9. Chat is a stimulant (mild drug) that is widespread in eastern Africa, mainly in Ethiopia, Somalia and Djibouti. It is lucrative crop that has had a marked impact on poverty in Ethiopia.

REFERENCES

Antolin, P., Thai-Thanh Dang and H. Axley (1999) "Poverty Dynamics in Four OECD Countries", Economics Department Working Papers 212, ECO/WKP (99) 4, OECD, Paris.

Bane, M. J. and D. T. Ellwood (1986) "Slipping Into and Out of Poverty. The Dynamics of Spells", *Journal of Human Resources* 21: 1–23.

Baulch, B. and J. Hoddinott (2000) "Economic Mobility and Poverty Dynamics in Developing Countries", *Journal of Development Studies* 36(6): 1–24.

Burgess, S. M. and C. Propper (1998) "An Economic Model of Household Income Dynamics, with an Application to Poverty Dynamics among American Women", Paper CASE/9, Centre for Analysis of Social Exclusion, London School of Economics, London.

Dercon, S. (2000) "Income Risk, Coping Strategies and Safety Nets", Background Paper for *World Development Report 2000*, World Bank, Washington, D.C.

Duclos, J.-Y. (2002) "Vulnerability and Poverty Measurement Issues for Public Policy", Social Protection Discussion Paper Series 0230, World Bank, Washington, D.C.

Gunning, J., J. Hoddinott, B. Kinsey and T. Owens (2000) "Revisiting Forever Gained: Income Dynamics in the Resettlement Areas of Zimbabwe, 1983–1996", *Journal of Development Studies* 36(6): 131–154.

Haddad, L. and A. Ahmed (2003) "Chronic and Transitory Poverty: Evidence from Egypt, 1997–99", *World Development* 31(1): 71–85.

Hulme, D. and A. Shepherd (2003) "Conceptualizing Chronic Poverty", *World Development* 31(3): 403–424.

Jalan, J. and M. Ravallion (1998) "Transient Poverty in Rural China", *Journal of Comparative Economics* 26(2): 338–357.

—— (2000) "Is Transient Poverty Different? Evidence from Rural China", *Journal of Development Studies* 36(6): 82–99.

McCulloch, N. and M. Calandrino (2003) "Vulnerability and Chronic Poverty in Rural Sichuan", *World Development* 31(3): 611–628.

McKay, A. and D. Lawson (2003) "Assessing the Extent and Nature of Chronic Poverty in Low-income Countries: Issues and Evidence", *World Development* 31(3): 425–439.

Pritchett, L., A. Suryahadi and S. Sumarto (2000) "Quantifying Vulnerability to Poverty: A Proposed Measure, with Application to Indonesia", Working Paper, SMERU Research Institute, Jakarta.

Rodgers, J. and J. Rodgers (1991) "Measuring the Intensity of Poverty among Sub-populations: Applications to the US", *Journal of Human Resources* 21(2): 338–359.

Stevens, A. H. (1995) "Climbing Out of Poverty, Falling Back In: Measuring the Persistence of Poverty over Multiple Spells", Working Paper 5390, National Bureau of Economic Research, Cambridge, Mass.

Yaqub, S. (2003) "Chronic Poverty. Scrutinizing Patterns, Correlates and Explorations", CPRC Working Paper 21, University of Manchester, Manchester.

World Bank (2002) *World Bank Africa Database 2002*, Washington, D.C.: World Bank.

16

Prospects for "pro-poor" growth in Africa

Arne Bigsten and Abebe Shimeles

Introduction

In recent decades Africa has been the worst-performing region of the world in terms of poverty reduction (Chen and Ravallion, 2004). Between 1984 and 2001 poverty incidence remained at 46 per cent, while the number of poor people increased from 198 million to 313 million. Per capita incomes in sub-Saharan Africa (SSA) fell by 20 per cent from a peak in 1974 to a low in 1994 (World Bank, 2002). The 1990s saw some recovery in SSA in terms of improved macroeconomic management, growth and poverty reduction in certain countries (Christiaensen, Demery and Paternostro, 2002), and there was a modest 4 per cent increase in per capita incomes between 1994 and 2000. But the question still remains as to whether African economies can in general achieve the goals of poverty reduction and improvements in human development set out in the poverty reduction strategy papers (PRSPs) and Millennium Development Goals (MDGs).

The 1990s witnessed diverse and interesting experiences across Africa in terms of growth and poverty reduction. There is a growing policy and research interest in the scope for poverty reduction through pro-poor growth. This chapter is a contribution to this literature and is organized as follows. The second section looks at the state of income distribution and poverty in Africa, while the third section reviews pro-poor growth indices. The fourth section presents measures of estimates of pro-poor growth for selected African countries and looks at the implications for

Table 16.1 Median values of Gini coefficient by region

Region	1960s	1970s	1980s	1990s
Eastern Europe	22.76	21.77	24.93	28.60
South Asia	31.67	32.32	32.22	31.59
OECD and high-income countries	32.86	33.04	32.20	33.20
East Asia and the Pacific	34.57	34.40	34.42	34.80
Middle East and North Africa	41.88	43.63	40.80	39.72
Sub-Saharan Africa	49.90	48.50	39.63	42.30
Latin America	53.00	49.86	51.00	50.00

Source: Deininger and Squire (1998: 263).

poverty reduction in the cases of Ethiopia, Uganda, Mozambique and South Africa. The fifth section discusses some policy challenges for pro-poor growth in Africa, and the sixth section summarizes and concludes the discussion.

Trends in income distribution and poverty in Africa

The Deininger-Squire[1] dataset on income distribution shows that Africa is one of the most unequal regions in the world, second only to South America (table 16.1). In addition, the Gini coefficient has varied considerably within short periods of time for many African countries. To some extent this is due to data problems (Deaton, 2003), but there are also real factors that make incomes and income distributions unstable in Africa. Income distribution is strongly affected, for example, by the weather, political changes or policy shocks (Easterly, 2000).

Figure 16.1 shows that the Gini coefficients in Africa are concentrated in the range of 40–55 per cent.[2] Out of the sample of 37 countries, close to half have had a Gini coefficient greater than 50 per cent, at least once in the past. This indicates that income distribution is a serious concern in Africa and that it needs to be understood to facilitate growth strategies that benefit the poor.

Tables 16.2 and 16.3 report changes, mainly covering the 1990s, in per capita income and income distribution for 17 African countries. One sees a decline in the income share of the poorest quintile in only 6 cases, while the share of the poorest quintile increased in 11 cases. There is thus no clear trend in inequality in this African dataset. The poorest quintiles actually did rather well in maintaining or even improving their income shares, but, of course, in absolute terms they still did not do well. The absolute income of the poorest quintile increased in only four cases. In spite of Africa's growth performance being erratic and often negative, its im-

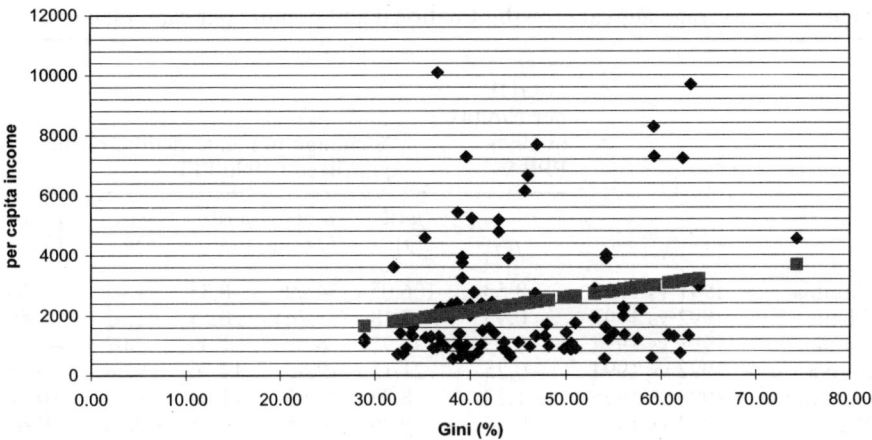

Figure 16.1 Per capita income and the Gini coefficient for selected African countries
Source: UNU-WIDER WIID (2000).

Table 16.2 Average annual percentage change of quintile income shares and the Gini coefficient

Country	Year	Quintiles					Gini coefficient
		Poorest	2nd	3rd	4th	Richest	
Gambia	1991 vs 1992	113.59	39.10	12.31	−0.92	−10.47	−15.10
Ghana	1992 vs 1997	1.23	0.33	−0.38	0.09	−0.24	−0.56
Guinea	1991 vs 1994	28.73	7.81	0.45	−3.92	−2.03	−4.82
Kenya	1992 vs 1994	21.45	20.14	15.04	9.85	−9.90	−11.82
Mauritania	1993 vs 1995	9.62	12.19	12.31	10.58	−9.81	−11.57
Niger	1992 vs 1995	0.00	0.00	0.00	0.00	0.00	0.00
Nigeria	1991 vs 1997	1.45	−1.44	−2.32	−3.15	2.04	2.01
Senegal	1991 vs 1994	22.48	14.00	7.65	2.13	−6.32	−8.63
Tanzania	1991 vs 1993	66.94	38.55	20.90	7.47	−14.88	−19.38
Uganda	1992 vs 1993	−2.65	5.72	5.85	4.31	−4.43	−4.32
Zambia	1991 vs 1997	−5.49	−3.06	−2.00	−0.85	1.93	2.67
Ethiopia	1981 vs 1995	−1.33	−1.07	−0.86	−0.45	1.03	1.51
Lesotho	1986 vs 1993	−1.35	−2.12	−1.40	0.01	0.51	0.49
Madagascar	1980 vs 1993	1.28	0.84	0.44	0.00	−0.40	−0.60
Mali	1989 vs 1994	−8.13	−6.72	−5.46	−2.50	5.03	6.78
Rwanda	1983 vs 1984	0.00	0.84	−0.90	−0.18	0.21	0.17
Tunisia	1965 vs 1971	−2.16	−8.94	−6.33	−5.72	4.80	5.35

Source: Authors' computations.

Table 16.3 Average annual growth of national and quintile per capita income

		% change in GDP per capita in 1996 PPP $	% change in mean income of the quintiles in 1996 PPP $				
		μ	μ of Q1	μ of Q2	μ of Q3	μ of Q4	μ of Q5
Gambia	1991 vs 1992	−3.53	106.05	34.19	8.35	−4.42	−13.63
Ghana	1992 vs 1997	0.93	2.18	1.26	0.55	1.02	0.69
Guinea	1991 vs 1994	0.93	29.93	8.81	1.39	−3.02	−1.12
Kenya	1992 vs 1994	−0.25	21.15	19.85	14.76	9.58	−10.12
Mauritania	1993 vs 1995	−1.12	8.38	10.93	11.04	9.34	−10.82
Niger	1992 vs 1995	−0.86	−0.86	−0.86	−0.86	−0.86	−0.86
Nigeria	1991 vs 1997	−0.38	1.06	−1.81	−2.69	−3.52	1.65
Senegal	1991 vs 1994	−2.11	19.89	11.59	5.38	−0.03	−8.29
Tanzania	1991 vs 1993	−1.76	64.00	36.11	18.77	5.58	−16.38
Uganda	1992 vs 1993	3.96	1.20	9.91	10.04	8.44	−0.64
Zambia	1991 vs 1997	−4.62	−9.86	−7.55	−6.53	−5.44	−2.78
Ethiopia	1981 vs 1995	−1.29	−2.60	−2.34	−2.14	−1.74	−0.27
Lesotho	1986 vs 1993	−0.10	−1.45	−2.22	−1.51	−0.09	0.41
Madagascar	1980 vs 1993	−2.93	−1.69	−2.11	−2.50	−2.93	−3.32
Mali	1989 vs 1994	−1.90	−9.88	−8.50	−7.26	−4.36	3.03
Rwanda	1983 vs 1984	−9.70	−9.70	−8.94	−10.51	−9.87	−9.51
Tunisia	1965 vs 1971	2.84	0.62	−6.36	−3.66	−3.04	7.77

Source: Authors' computations.

pact on the well-being of the poor has not been dramatic; rather, distributional changes have cushioned the impact. This finding is consistent with recent work on the dynamics of poverty in Africa (Christiaensen, Demery and Paternostro, 2002). Still, there is little to suggest that Africa is on track towards the MDGs in terms of poverty reduction.

Against this background it seems clear that it will not be possible to achieve substantial and sustained reductions in poverty without economic growth. The debate beyond this has come to focus on whether it is possible to bring about a pattern of growth that is particularly beneficial for the poor, and this is the focus of the chapter.

Measures of "pro-poor" growth

In the 1970s the importance of the pattern of growth for poverty reduction was discussed under the label "redistribution with growth" (Chenery et al., 1974). The resurgence of interest in this issue is largely due to the failure to achieve poverty reduction in Africa under the structural adjustment programmes. There has been an outpouring of empirical research on the link between growth and poverty (see, among others, Demery and Squire, 1996; Ali, 1996; Ravallion and Chen, 1997, 2000; Fields, 1998; Collier and Dollar, 2000; Easterly, 2000; Dollar and Kraay, 2000; World Bank, 2000; Geda, Shimeles and Weeks, 2002). The advent of the MDGs and the PRSPs has underlined the need to explore the interconnection between growth, poverty and income distribution.

The recent discussion of pro-poor growth started with a focus on evaluating the percentage change in the income of "poor" people in the course of economic growth (Dollar and Kraay, 2000; Eastwood and Lipton, 2001). Statistical exercises to evaluate the elasticities that connect poverty changes with growth are sensitive to functional specification as well as to the data sources used.[3] Besides, one needs some degree of conceptualization of what it means when a growth process is pro-poor. Recent literature has suggested different ways of measuring pro-poor growth.

White and Anderson (2000) suggest three measures on pro-poor growth using incremental income shares of the poor normalized by their base-year share, population share or some international norm. The first measure implies that the income share of the poor population must increase if the growth pattern is to be regarded as pro-poor.[4] Or equivalently, the rate of growth of the mean income of the poor should be greater than the rate of growth of the mean income for the whole population. According to the second measure, the share of the poor in the income increase should be greater than the headcount ratio itself. This implies that the poor should get a share of the income increase that is at least as large as their population share if the process is to be characterized as pro-poor. This is an extremely stringent condition and therefore not very useful as a guide for policy-makers who are intent in monitoring the progress of pro-poor growth.

The third measure says that the incremental income share of the poor should be measured against some international norm, such as the median income shares of the bottom 20 or 40 per cent.[5] Pro-poor growth in this case means that the share of the poorest quintile in the growing income equals at least that of the median of share of the poorest quintile around the world.

What one notes from these measures is that the focus is on the relative change in the income of the poor, not on what happens to poverty as a result. That is, it does not matter whether poor people escape poverty or not as a result of growth.

There are other pro-poor growth measures that have a closer connection with poverty measures and satisfy desirable axioms. For example,

Kakwani and Pernia (2000) propose a measure of pro-poor growth that is derived from poverty elasticities. They use the ratio of poverty elasticities with respect to actual growth and distributional neutral growth, and define a pro-poor growth index as:

$$\phi = \frac{\eta}{\eta_g} \qquad (1)$$

where ϕ is their index of pro-poor growth and η is the elasticity of poverty with respect to per capita income (gross elasticity), and ηg is the elasticity of poverty with respect to per capita income, assuming no change in income distribution. If $\phi > 1$, the growth process is considered to be pro-poor. If $0 < \phi < 1$, economic growth reduces poverty but the "inequality effect" of economic growth is negative, so that the poor benefit proportionately less from economic growth than the non-poor. This is characterized as trickle-down growth. In the case of an economic recession, the pro-poor index is inverted to be $\eta g/\eta$. The recession will be pro-poor if $\eta < \eta g$. Kakwani and Pernia (2000) also show how equation (1) can be decomposed into growth and inequality effects. A growth episode is called pro-poor only if inequality declines or remains unchanged. Growth episodes accompanied by even the slightest increase in income inequality are considered anti-poor.

Ravallion and Chen (2000) are concerned about this feature and propose a pro-poor measure which focuses mainly on the changes in the income of the poor in a growth episode. In addition, their measure is linked to a specific poverty index, Watt's index of poverty,[6] which satisfies several desirable axioms. The Ravallion and Chen measure of pro-poor growth essentially cumulates the rate of change in the income of the population identified as poor before growth occurs and takes the average using the number of the poor population. This is different from the rate of change in the mean income of the poor. The two coincide if each poor person's income grows at an equal rate.[7]

The broad distinction in the debate is between measures that look at the relative growth rate of the incomes of the poor and those that look at absolute income changes of the poor. In the latter type of definition even very unequal growth can increase the real incomes of the poor and improve their welfare.

To see some empirical implications of the choice of pro-poor growth indices, some estimates of pro-poor growth as they apply to selected African countries are reported in table 16.4. The picture which emerges is that more growth or recession episodes are characterized as pro-poor under the first White and Anderson (2000) measure than under the Kakwani and Pernia (2000) measure. The first measure classifies 57 per cent

Table 16.4 Pro-poor growth measure for selected African countries

Country	Year	Measure of pro-poor growth		Growth of GDP per capita: 1996 PPP	Growth in the Gini index
		White and Anderson	Kakwani and Pernia (ϕ)		
Côte d'Ivoire	1985 v 1993	2.72	4.063	−2.34	−1.37
Côte d'Ivoire	1986 v 1993	0.08	1.687	−2.85	−0.64
Côte d'Ivoire	1987 v 1993	1.42	2.274	−2.90	−1.34
Côte d'Ivoire	1988 v 1993	0.78	1.326	−2.68	0.01
Côte d'Ivoire	1985 v 1988	6.02	−0.735	−1.77	−3.62
Côte d'Ivoire	1986 v 1988	−1.65	1.814	−3.27	−2.27
Ethiopia	1981 v 1995	−1.33	1.085	−1.29	1.51
Gambia	1991 v 1992	113.59	−0.206	−3.53	−14.83
Ghana	1987 v 1997	1.88	0.458	1.11	−0.78
Ghana	1988 v 1997	2.14	0.606	1.04	−1.03
Ghana	1989 v 1997	2.36	0.975	1.05	−1.45
Ghana	1992 v 1997	1.23	0.295	0.93	−0.72
Ghana	1993 v 1997	1.39	0.437	0.72	−0.82
Ghana	1987 v 1993	2.22	0.724	1.37	−0.75
Ghana	1988 v 1993	2.75	0.387	1.30	−1.20
Ghana	1989 v 1993	3.34	1.171	1.37	−2.07
Ghana	1992 v 1993	0.63	−0.027	1.78	−0.32
Ghana	1987 v 1992	2.54	0.40	1.29	−0.83
Ghana	1988 v 1992	3.29	0.856	1.18	−1.42
Ghana	1989 v 1992	4.26	1.738	1.24	−2.65
Guinea	1991 v 1994	28.73	22.81	0.93	0.00
Kenya	1992 v 1994	21.45	−0.014	−0.25	2.82
Lesotho	1986 v 1993	−1.35	0.064	−0.10	0.48
Lesotho	1987 v 1993	−1.57	0.206	−0.45	0.56
Madagascar	1960 v 1993	1.24	−12.0	−2.34	−0.60
Madagascar	1980 v 1993	1.28	−11.52	−2.93	−0.58
Mali	1989 v 1994	−8.13	0.382	−1.90	6.70
Mauritania	1988 v 1995	8.38	6.845	−0.03	−1.27
Mauritania	1993 v 1995	9.62	−10.98	−1.12	−11.84
Mauritania	1988 v 1993	7.89	−11.18	0.41	3.31
Niger	1960 v 1995	−0.11	0.096	−1.73	1.14
Niger	1992 v 1995	0.00	0.09	−0.86	11.84
Niger	1960 v 1992	−0.12	0.096	−1.81	0.19
Nigeria	1959 v 1997	−1.24	2.12	0.47	−0.02
Nigeria	1985 v 1997	−2.65	−3.857	0.42	2.26
Nigeria	1986 v 1997	−4.16	−10.33	0.22	2.87
Nigeria	1991 v 1997	1.45	6.253	−0.38	1.96
Nigeria	1992 v 1997	−7.96	−3.055	0.88	4.20
Nigeria	1993 v 1997	2.24	−0.95	3.37	7.78
Nigeria	1959 v 1993	−1.64	12.66	0.13	−0.90
Nigeria	1985 v 1993	−5.01	0.791	−1.02	−0.40
Nigeria	1986 v 1993	−7.64	0.554	−1.53	0.17
Nigeria	1991 v 1993	−0.13	0.117	−7.48	−8.75

Table 16.4 (cont.)

Country	Year	Measure of pro-poor growth		Growth of GDP per capita: 1996 PPP	Growth in the Gini index
		White and Anderson	Kakwani and Pernia (ϕ)		
Nigeria	1959 v 1992	−0.18	5.139	0.40	−0.65
Nigeria	1985 v 1992	1.32	−6.323	0.10	0.89
Nigeria	1986 v 1992	−0.88	7.953	−0.32	1.78
Nigeria	1985 v 1991	−6.59	−1.212	1.24	2.55
Nigeria	1986 v 1991	−10.49	−3.894	0.96	3.98
Rwanda	1983 v 1984	0.00	0.072	−9.70	0.00
Senegal	1960 v 1994	2.27	−1.176	−0.81	−0.89
Senegal	1991 v 1994	22.48	−5.416	−2.11	−8.63
Senegal	1960 v 1991	0.50	−0.134	−0.68	−0.11
Tanzania	1964 v 1993	1.21	15.04	0.09	−1.19
Tanzania	1991 v 1993	66.94	−14.05	−1.76	−19.54
Tanzania	1964 v 1991	−2.47	12.66	0.23	0.33
Uganda	1989 v 1993	−6.18	−0.678	2.21	4.40
Uganda	1992 v 1993	−2.65	1.604	3.96	−3.87
Uganda	1989 v 1992	−7.33	−2.235	1.64	7.31
Zambia	1959 v 1996	−1.09	0.032	−1.76	0.10
Zambia	1976 v 1996	0.64	0.082	−3.37	−0.12
Zambia	1991 v 1996	−5.49	0.535	−4.62	2.74
Zambia	1993 v 1996	2.50	0.863	−2.84	2.53
Zambia	1959 v 1993	−1.40	−0.02	−1.66	−0.11
Zambia	1976 v 1993	0.31	−0.018	−3.46	−0.58
Zambia	1991 v 1993	−16.32	0.522	−7.24	3.04
Zambia	1959 v 1991	−0.38	−0.144	−1.30	−0.31
Zambia	1976 v 1991	2.76	−2.517	−2.94	−1.05

of the growth and recession episodes as being pro-poor, while the second index classifies only 40 per cent of them as pro-poor. The two measures come up with similar classifications in only 45 per cent of the cases. In the Kakwani-Pernia case the pro-poor index is problematic in situations where recession leads to a reduction in poverty due to a decline in income inequality. An example is given in table 16.5, where recessions that led to significant reduction in poverty could not be classified unambiguously. In fact, if one follows the definitions provided in Kakwani and Pernia (2000), a value exceeding one is considered pro-poor, and pro-rich otherwise. According to this definition, thus, the recession episodes in table 16.5 are pro-rich, which clearly is not the case.

One conclusion emerges from the estimates: even in times of economic decline, there are several cases where the poor did not suffer very severely (this is also reported in Christiaensen, Demery and Paternostro, 2002). That is, poverty did not increase as a consequence of economic

Table 16.5 Ambiguity in the Kakwani-Pernia measure of pro-poor growth

Country	Period	Growth in per capita GDP (%)	Change in the headcount (%)	Kakwani-Pernia index
Côte d'Ivoire	1985–1988	−1.77	−3.99	−0.735
Senegal	1991–1994	−2.11	−9.60	−0.185
Tanzania	1991–1993	−1.76	−14.35	−0.071

Source: Authors' calculations.

decline (e.g. in Côte d'Ivoire, Gambia, Kenya, Madagascar, Mauritania, Nigeria, Senegal and Zambia). Still, as far as poverty reduction and pro-poor strategy are concerned, distributional changes and growth both have a vital role to play. The next two sections deal with these issues.

The equity-growth trade-off

At the heart of the above discussion on the measurement of pro-poor growth lies the issue of income distribution change as an essential component of poverty reduction in such regions as Africa. At the analytical level any poverty measure can be defined over per capita income and a measure of income inequality (Kakwani, 1991; Ravallion, 1992). That is:

$$P = P(z, \mu, G) \qquad (2)$$

According to equation (2), if one knows the level of the poverty line, z, mean per capita income, μ, and the distribution underlying that per capita income, G,[8] it is possible to obtain a measure of poverty that is consistent with standard axioms.[9] Poverty rises with the poverty line and the Gini coefficient, and declines with per capita income. It is homogeneous of degree zero with respect to z and μ. Using these properties of the poverty index, from (2) one can generate a set of per capita income and Gini coefficients that give rise to a given level of poverty; that is, iso-poverty curves as depicted in figure 16.2. This relationship has been innovatively utilized by Bourguignon (2002) and Ashan and Oberi (2002) to establish the link between economic growth and poverty reduction in a consistent and analytically appealing manner. Assuming that the poverty lines remain constant over time, one can link per capita income and the Gini to generate a locus of points for a given level of poverty as shown in figure 16.2. The slope of the iso-poverty curve is the issue of concern here. Figure 16.2 assumes convex iso-poverty curves, where the second-order condition depends on the second derivatives of the poverty function with

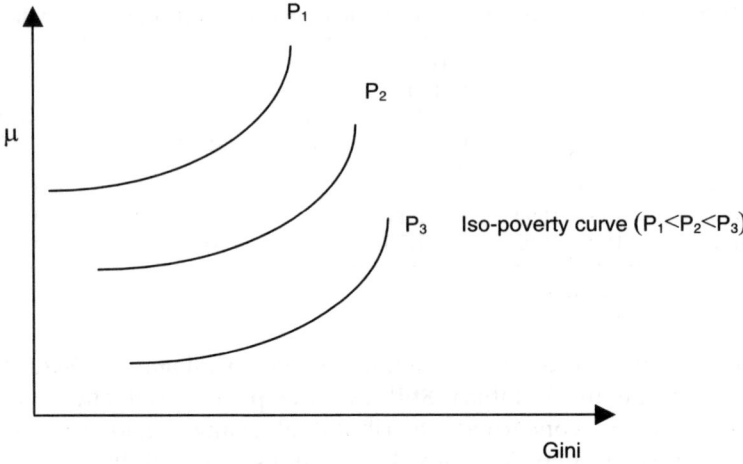

Figure 16.2 Per capita income-inequality trade-off

respect to μ and G and the interactions between μ and G. If one follows Kakwani, Khandker and Son (2003), one tends to get this convex shape for the iso-poverty curves.[10] Bourguignon (2002) used the decomposition that follows from the definition of poverty (à la Kakwani, 1991 and Datt and Ravallion, 1992) to estimate the elasticity of poverty with respect to economic growth, taking the impact of distributional changes fully into account. This leads to a specification of an econometric model that can be used to estimate the connection between growth, poverty and income inequality.

If there is any theoretically or empirically motivated structural relationship between income inequality and per capita income, there is an opportunity to superimpose this on the definition-driven iso-poverty curve and work out possible growth paths for a given country. Here the interest is to get an idea of what it takes in terms of growth and distributional change to keep abreast of a given level of poverty, since there is a trade-off between inequality and growth.

Regarding the trade-off, one can get some idea by looking at the slope of the iso-poverty curves. One can derive the magnitudes involved by totally differentiating (2) and setting changes in poverty equal to zero. Thus:

$$\frac{d\mu}{dG}\frac{G}{\mu} = -\frac{\dfrac{\partial P}{\partial G}\dfrac{G}{P}}{\dfrac{\partial P}{\partial \mu}\dfrac{\mu}{P}} \qquad (3)$$

Table 16.6 Equity-growth "trade-off" for selected African countries

Country	Year	V₁	V₂	Gini coefficient	Per capita income (in 1996 PPP)
Burundi	1992	1.54	0.268	33.33	926
Burkina Faso	1994	1.67	0.325	48.20	971
Botswana	1986	–	0.510	54.21	3,895
CAR	1993	–	0.789	61.33	1,306
Côte d'Ivoire	1993	–	1.700	36.91	1,970
Ethiopia	1995	0.60	−0.213	40.00	583
Gabon	1960	7.14	3.056	64.00	2,966
Ghana	1997	2.54	0.940	32.70	1,416
Guinea	1994	6.28	2.742	46.80	2,732
Gambia	1992	2.71	0.797	47.80	1,312
Kenya	1994	2.34	0.669	57.50	1,215
Lesotho	1993	5.06	2.022	57.94	2,215
Morocco	1984	–	3.439	39.19	3,242
Madagascar	1993	1.43	0.216	43.44	888
Mali	1994	1.35	0.172	50.50	854
Mozambique	1996	1.75	0.371	39.61	1,003
Mauritania	1995	2.83	0.914	38.90	1,399
Namibia	1993	11.46	–	74.30	4,541
Niger	1995	0.61	0.205	50.50	880
Nigeria	1997	1.93	0.467	50.56	1,072
Rwanda	1984	–	0.518	28.90	1,108
Senegal	1994	3.10	1.050	41.28	1,498
Tunisia	1971	–	2.949	53.00	2882
Tanzania	1993	0.51	−0.240	38.20	553
Uganda	1993	1.16	0.083	39.20	788
South Africa	1993	–	8.924	62.30	7,289
Zambia	1996	1.40	0.205	49.80	876
Zimbabwe	1990	–	3.031	56.83	2,948

Source: Authors' computation.

and one can rewrite equation (3) as:

$$v = -\frac{\theta}{\varepsilon} \quad (4)$$

where v is elasticity of per capita income with respect to the Gini, θ is elasticity of poverty with respect to Gini and ε is elasticity of poverty with respect to mean income. If v is small (say <1), the effectiveness of redistribution as a tool for poverty reduction would tend to be small. When the elasticity is high, on the other hand, the payoff for a strategy of redistribution would be substantial. This elasticity has been computed for 28 countries in Africa, as reported in table 16.6, using headcount ratio as the measure of poverty.

To retain the same level of poverty, the extent of trade-off between growth and income distribution depends on the slope of the iso-poverty curve. Suppose a country wishes to remain on one iso-poverty curve (see, for example, Ali and Elbadawi, 1999), then it may have a choice between a policy that increases mean incomes and increases inequality and another one that lowers per capita incomes but reduces inequality. The extent of the trade-off depends on the ratio of the elasticity of poverty with respect to income distribution and per capita income, as shown in table 16.6.

For most African countries this ratio is quite small, suggesting that there is little to gain in terms of poverty reduction from a redistribution policy. For countries with high initial inequality, such as Gabon, South Africa and Zimbabwe, the inequality-growth trade-off is high. In those cases there will be a significant poverty reduction impact from small reductions in inequality. It is important to notice that the elasticity varies considerably at the point where the poverty line is located and the slope of the Lorenz curve at that point. Nevertheless, table 16.6 gives an illustration of the trade-off between growth and redistribution in Africa. One has to be cautious in interpreting these elasticities since they are essentially mechanical, non-behavioural relations.

In table 16.6 two different poverty lines are applied to compute the slope of the iso-poverty curve. These are the US$1 and US$2 a day per person amounts that are often used in cross-country poverty comparisons. Had the data been available, it would have been more sensible to use national poverty lines to evaluate the elasticity ratios to determine how a movement along an iso-poverty curve behaves with changes in either income inequality or per capita income. The relevant elasticities could not be computed for some countries, particularly for the relatively high-income countries when the poverty line was set at US$1 a day per person. It was too low to compute poverty estimates.[11] Nevertheless, one can observe at least three factors from table 16.6.

One is that high-inequality and relatively high-income countries (for example, Namibia, South Africa, Senegal, Gabon and Zimbabwe) had higher elasticity of the iso-poverty curve, indicating that redistribution policies may be effective tools in dealing with poverty in those countries. For instance, if one takes South Africa, at the poverty line close to US$750 per person a year, a 1 per cent decline in the measure of income inequality needs about 9 per cent decline in per capita income to remain on the same poverty level. This means that any reduction in per capita income less than 9 per cent, following a 1 per cent decline in the Gini, would lead to a reduction in poverty. It takes a large reduction in per capita income following a 1 per cent reduction in the Gini for poverty not to decline. On the other hand, any increase in income inequality, beyond its current level, requires a large per capita income growth to keep abreast with the existing level of poverty.

The second point to note is that for low-income countries, such as Burundi, Burkina Faso, Niger, Ethiopia, Tanzania and Zambia, the room for poverty reduction via redistribution is very limited. A 1 per cent reduction in income inequality would need a small change in per capita income just to stay on the same level of poverty. The iso-poverty curves for these countries are flatter. Likewise, the effect of rising income inequality on poverty would be offset by a low rate of growth in per capita income. An increase in inequality may not be a significant poverty threat if there is a high rate of growth in these countries.

Finally, one notes that the elasticity is considerably higher at the lower poverty line. This would seem to suggest that redistribution policies are relatively more beneficial for the very poor. What it shows, when one uses the headcount index as the measure of poverty, is that there are more people just below the poverty line of US$1 than immediately below the poverty line of US$2.

The main message of this section is, thus, that the trade-off between redistribution and growth as tools of a poverty policy varies quite a lot by country. Depending on the order of magnitude involved in the trade-off, the best choice of a pro-poor growth path varies. One should add, however, that these estimates are based entirely on the definition of poverty, with no inherent functional relationship between growth and income inequality. If there is a structural relationship between the two, as there is, then the choices that a country has may be restricted. The much harder question to analyse is how different pro-poor policies affect the growth rate of the economy. This requires such analytical tools as economy-wide equilibrium models, which would take us beyond the simple analysis of this chapter.

Still, to extend this simple analysis somewhat, one can look at the poverty outcomes of two growth scenarios for four countries. One scenario is that income inequality remains unchanged (or distribution-neutral growth, DNG) and the other scenario is that additional income is equally distributed; that is, growth follows an equally distributed growth (EDG) path. This is the second measure of White and Anderson (2000) discussed above. The latter is, of course, an extreme definition of pro-poor growth, but it is included to illustrate the sensitivity of poverty to distributional changes. The chapter looks at three countries considered by African standards to be success cases; namely Ethiopia, Mozambique and Uganda. It then also adds one high-inequality, high-average-income country – South Africa. In all cases it also compares the outcomes of the simulations with actual changes in poverty.

Table 16.7 reports the impact of the two types of growth patterns men-

Table 16.7 Simulation of the impact of pattern of growth on poverty in Ethiopia

Year	Real per capita GDP in PPP (1996 prices)	Headcount (DNG)	Gini (DNG)	Headcount (EDG)	Gini (EDG)
1995	583	42.0	41.0	42.0	41.0
1996	600	40.0	41.0	36.0	39.0
1997	618	38.0	41.0	33.0	38.0
1998	637	37.0	41.0	29.0	37.0
1999	656	34.0	41.0	26.0	36.0
2000	675	32.0	41.0	20.0	35.0

Source: Authors' calculation.

tioned above on Ethiopia based on GDP in PPP from Penn World Tables using a poverty line of US$1 per day. The average growth rate in real per capita GDP that prevailed in 1993–2000, which was 3 per cent, was taken as the measure of the long-term growth that can be sustained by the economy.[12] One type of growth pattern is a situation where the Gini coefficient remains unchanged (DNG) throughout the growth episode. The other is an EDG pattern, where all additional income is divided equally across the population. It can be seen that even under a DNG, poverty in Ethiopia would have declined by 10 percentage points over the period 1995–2000, a very significant reduction.

In the second – utopian – scenario, where additional income is equally distributed, Ethiopia could have halved poverty by 2000! It would have required a reduction in the Gini coefficient of 6 percentage points and a 3 per cent per capita growth in this period. What, in actual fact, would a reduction of such order mean in the Gini coefficient? In this case it means that the income of the richest quintile would grow only by 8 per cent in this period, while the income of the poorest quintile would grow by nearly 50 per cent!

Bigsten et al. (2003) showed that poverty in Ethiopia (using consumption-based estimates) declined by 5 percentage points between 1994 and 1997, while the Gini coefficient increased by 4 percentage points. This suggests that the impact of growth on poverty in Ethiopia was less than what it would have been under the DNG scenario. One might in this case argue that this increase was hard to avoid. During the period considered, Ethiopia was in transition from conflict. During conflict episodes it is particularly the transaction-intensive sectors that decline, while subsistence activities, on which the poorest depend, decline less. When peace is restored the transaction-intensive sectors are bound to bounce back, and it is thus natural to expect an increase in inequality. This effect of a return to normalcy is not to be deplored. However, over

Table 16.8 Simulation of pattern of growth on poverty in Mozambique

Year	Per capita GDP in PPP (1996 prices)	Headcount (under DNG)	Gini (under DNG)	Headcount (under EDG)	Gini (under EDG)
1996	1,003	48	40	48	40
1997	1,034	46	40	43	39
1998	1,066	44	40	42	38
1999	1,133	42	40	40	37
2000	1,168	40	40	35	35
2001	1,204	39	40	32	34
2002	1,241	37	40	29	34
2003	1,280	35	40	23	32

Source: Authors' calculation.

Table 16.9 Simulation of pattern of growth on poverty in Uganda

Year	Per capita GDP in PPP	Headcount (under DNG)	Gini (under DNG)	Headcount (under EDG)	Gini (under EDG)
1993	788	62	40.0	62	40.0
1994	814	60	40.0	59	38.0
1995	841	58	40.0	57	37.0
1996	868	56	40.0	54	36.6
1997	897	54	40.0	51	34.5
1998	926	52	40.0	49	34.0
1999	957	50	40.0	45	32.0
2000	989	48	40.0	42	31.0
2001	1,021	46	40.0	38	29.6
2002	1,055	44	40.0	34	29.0
2003	1,090	42	40.0	29	28.0

Source: Authors' calculation.

the longer term it is important for Ethiopia to be aware of the distributional consequences of policy choices.

The study also looks at the poverty impact of growth patterns in Mozambique and Uganda. Here poverty was computed based on GDP estimates in PPP from Penn World Tables and using a poverty line of US$2 a day per person. Tables 16.8 and 16.9 report the DNG and EDG patterns for Mozambique and Uganda, which were among the fastest-growing African economies in the 1990s. Mozambique's per capita GDP grew at a rate of 3.1 per cent between 1990 and 2000, while that of Uganda grew at a rate of 3.3 per cent during the same period.

It can be seen that Mozambique could have reduced poverty by about 13 percentage points between 1996 and 2003 if growth remained distribu-

Table 16.10 Simulation of growth pattern on poverty in South Africa

Year	Headcount (DNG)	Gini (DNG)	Headcount (EDG)	Gini (EDG)
1993	22.0	62	22.0	62.0
1994	21.5	62	20.0	61.5
1995	21.7	62	19.7	61.2
1996	21.6	62	19.6	61.2
1997	21.3	62	19.5	61.1
1998	20.7	62	16.8	59.0
1999	20.6	62	16.7	58.6
2000	20.5	62	16.5	58.2
2001	20.4	62	11.2	57.2

Source: Authors' computations at a poverty line of US$3 per day per person in PPP.

tion neutral. But the actual growth scenario of Mozambique did not translate into a poverty reduction of that magnitude, although the country did manage to reduce poverty by 9 percentage points during the 1990s (ECA, 2003). The growth pattern of Mozambique was thus similar to that of Ethiopia, with a strong recovery in the modern sector. Again, one could argue that the role of pro-poor growth should increase once the economy gets richer and returns to normalcy. To maintain the existing level of inequality the government would probably have to introduce deliberate egalitarian policy measures.

Uganda managed to reduce poverty during the period 1992–2000 by 22 percentage points, according to the consumption poverty estimates by Appleton (2001). The positive distributional outcome for Uganda was largely driven by the recovery in cash-crop agriculture. The recent dramatic decline in coffee prices may partly have reversed the positive picture evident until 2000. Still, the simulations show that the poverty impact of growth that is distribution neutral is very significant. If Uganda could achieve at least a similar pattern of growth and maintain the GDP growth rate, the country would certainly meet the MDG of poverty reduction well before 2015.

Finally, the study simulates the development in a high-inequality country, namely South Africa (table 16.10). Per capita income in South Africa has hardly increased over the last decade. The average growth in real per capita GDP between 1993 and 2000 was about 0.5 per cent. Taking this as a proxy for long-term growth (though one may hope for a growth recovery after the transition in South Africa), one sees that such growth does not have much impact on poverty. The slow growth in per capita GDP and the very high level of income inequality provide a case for policy measures focusing on redistribution. The impact of such redistribution on incentive structures, productivity and growth is uncertain, but some forms of transfers might actually even speed up the process of growth. The results of the simulation of the radically egalitarian growth pattern show that in a high-income country even slow growth generates large resources that can potentially be used to fight poverty.

In short, the preceding discussion illustrates the potential poverty impact of policies that target both distribution and growth. The big challenge, however, is to identify policy instruments that address in the context of Africa both growth and distributional issues. The next section looks briefly at some of the challenges of addressing distributional issues in the African context.

The challenges of pro-poor growth strategies

It has been observed that average incomes in Africa are very low while inequality is quite high. Hence there are two problems for policy-makers to worry about, namely how to increase aggregate growth and how to improve the distribution of the proceeds of this growth. There has been a very extensive debate about the growth failure of African countries, referred to as "Africa's growth tragedy" by Easterly and Levine (1997). This chapter will not enter into this general debate. It may suffice to note that growth tends to be high in environments that have the characteristics of macroeconomic stability and a realistic exchange rate, competitive domestic markets, a stable financial system, an abundance of human capital, an effective physical infrastructure, unbiased institutions, good governance, political maturity, a broad-based development pattern, limited aid dependence and a controlled level of foreign debt.

The discussion here is confined to policies that can improve the poverty reduction impact of growth and thus make it pro-poor. Again, this is not an easy analytical task. To understand the determinants of income distribution, one needs to understand the process that generates the income pattern. The income distribution of a country is the outcome of the entire economic process, where factor prices are determined within an interdependent system. To analyse changes in income distribution properly it would thus be very useful to use an economy-wide computable general equilibrium model, where it is possible to identify the variables that drive both economic growth and income distribution in a given setting. Without such information, it is difficult for policy-makers to implement pro-poor growth policies.

The importance of the pattern of growth for poverty reduction was discussed in the 1970s under the label "redistribution with growth" (Chenery et al., 1974). The issue was out of favour during the 1980s, when policy debate centred on macroeconomic stabilization and structural adjustment. The *World Development Report* of 1990 (World Bank, 1990) reflected a renewed focus on poverty and argued for a three-pronged pro-poor development strategy. The three pillars of the strategy were that it should increase demand for the assets of the poor, it should help build up the assets of the poor and there should also be a safety net for those that could not earn money in the market. During the 1990s poverty gained in importance in the policy debate. At present the base for development lending and strategy is the PRSPs and the poverty reduction growth facilities. Stern (2003) notes that there are two main components in a strategy for pro-poor growth. First, it should create a good investment climate and thus generate aggregate growth; and second, there should be empowerment and investment in poor people so that they can participate in the growth.

The first point to note is that the sector focus of development efforts may have a strong bearing on the poverty impact. Growth patterns where agriculture and other rural activities figure prominently generally have a good distributional profile. There are also significant regional or urban versus rural differences in incomes (Bigsten, 1980; Bigsten et al., 2003). In general, inequality tends to be higher in urban areas than in rural areas in most parts of Africa. Similarly, within urban and rural areas inequality tends to vary across agro-climatic zones and economic sectors (such as formal versus informal, service versus manufacturing).

Standard explanations of income inequality relate to the underlying asset distribution. Several studies have shown land distribution in particular to be important in the determination of income inequality. However, in terms of the Gini coefficient for land distribution, SSA is the least-unequal region (Deininger and Squire, 1998). Physical and human capital, however, are especially scarce in Africa and their distribution is highly skewed. This certainly contributes very significantly to the extent of inequality. Still, a policy of redistribution is politically difficult and asset redistribution may have costs in terms of lost growth. These could arise from efficiency and output losses from one-off redistribution, or through the impact on investment incentives.

Widespread poverty is often accompanied by several forms of market imperfections: indivisibility of investment and strategic complementarities among economic agents can have a dampening effect on economic growth (see Lustig, Arias and Rigolini, 2002, for a review of the literature). Credit rationing in these economies makes it very difficult for poor people to break out of the poverty trap. The strategic complementarities introduce the issue of coordination failures, where incentives for the expropriation of other people's wealth dominate the strategy of individual economic agents. Poverty itself generates a high degree of risk aversion and reduces the incentive for investment. One policy implication is for governments to invest in the basic infrastructures (namely physical and financial) that reduce transaction costs to individuals. Redistribution of assets, such as land, can also ease the credit constraint faced by the poor.

Another aspect highly correlated with poverty is the low level of human development, which in itself affects subsequent growth. The literature has indicated that better education and health are very important for economic growth, and thus for poverty reduction. Analyses of poverty profiles confirm that the poor have relatively low levels of education and health. One reason for this is the very fact that they are poor. The opportunity cost for poor households of sending children to school is higher than in better-off households. Against this background it is clear that the efficiency and composition of public expenditures are critical determinants of growth and poverty. This is an area where African countries face extremely serious problems. The countries are generally good at producing well-written strategy papers and PRSPs, but they have immense problems in getting the day-to-day work of the administration to function, with civil servants who are underpaid, badly trained and poorly motivated. Provision of public services is constrained by low levels of public revenue, which could, in principle, be solved by higher levels of taxation. However, in some countries rapidly increased taxation might pose a severe constraint on private investment, and thus might impact negatively on future growth and hence on revenue collection as well.

The *World Development Report 2000/2001* (World Bank, 2000) extended the concept of poverty beyond income and consumption plus education and health, to include risk and vulnerability as well as voicelessness and powerlessness. Poor households are susceptible to a wide range of risks, some which are idiosyncratic, such as illness, while others are common, such as natural disasters. As a result, poor households may adopt production plans or employment strategies to reduce their exposure to risk, even if this entails lower average income. Poor households may also try to smooth consumption by creating buffer stocks, withdrawing children from school and developing credit and insurance arrangements. Social networks also help provide informal insurance. Nevertheless, there are limits to the usefulness of networks that do not extend outside the local community. This makes them very vulnerable to natural disasters and economic shocks, since geographically defined networks provide little protection against shocks of this type. In such instances the government needs to intervene with *targeted measures*. It is very hard for African governments to target the poor, since the required information is often lacking. The government therefore has to devise other methods of reaching the poor, such as indicator targeting or self-targeting.

Finally, along with these factors are the ill-feeling and social unrest that widespread poverty instils among members of society. Poverty undermines stability, well-functioning institutions and good governance. Many African countries have gone through destructive civil wars, conflicts and social upheavals in the recent past. A major cause of such instability is poverty itself. The challenge for Africa, therefore, is to ensure a growth process that benefits a larger segment of the poor population.

Conclusion

Countries that have been successful in terms of aggregate economic growth have generally been successful in reducing poverty. How strong a poverty-reducing effect growth has depends on what happens to income distribution. This chapter has investigated some dimensions of income distribution in Africa. The focus has been on the link between changes in average per capita income and the incomes of the poor. Different pro-poor growth indices have been estimated. The results suggest that, in several cases, economic declines have affected the poor surprisingly little. On the other hand, there were also cases where the poor did not benefit from economic growth, a fact which led to rising poverty.

Using the definition of income poverty as a function of income distribution and per capita income, this chapter has attempted to show the implied trade-off between the two that exists to maintain a given level of poverty. Such trade-offs illustrate the choices open to different countries between growth and redistribution depending on their level of inequality and per capita income. High-inequality and high-income countries were found to have a higher value of the elasticity of the iso-poverty curve, indicating that redistribution policies for poverty reduction may be more effective there. For most of these countries, if inequality were to increase further, the rate of growth in per capita income needed just to keep abreast with existing levels of poverty is very substantial. Thus policies that lead to a further rise in income inequality must have a very strong growth effect for the poor to benefit. On the other hand, low-income countries tended to have had on average flatter iso-poverty curves, implying that a 1 per cent increase in income inequality needs a much lower rise in per capita income just to stay at the same level of income inequality. Here growth strategies leading to inequality are more acceptable from a poverty point of view, provided that they generate sufficient growth.

There may be a conflict between short-term distributional measures and immediate poverty reduction on the one hand, and long-term growth-supporting measures and long-term poverty reduction on the other. But there may also be win-win situations, where a policy for equity has a beneficial effect on growth. Typically, such policies have built up the assets of the poor and helped to increase the demand for those assets.

This has meant, for example, expansion of education (building up assets) and measures that increase the relative prices of agricultural commodities and the wages of unskilled labour (increasing demand). Along with measures to secure the long-term growth of the incomes of the poor, there is a need for transfer schemes that help households to cope with risk, which is high for many poor groups.

The main point is that without growth in per capita incomes, poverty will persist. Governments intent on poverty reduction must therefore create an environment that is conducive to growth. For the efforts to be effective, the government must develop good institutions and provide good governance. The way in which the interaction between civil society and government is played out will have major implications for the growth outcome. Understanding the nature of domestic politics is thus a key to successful economic reform.

Poverty can generally be reduced if there is sufficient economic growth, and it can be reduced faster if it has a pro-poor pattern. Growth can be substantial if the policy and institutional environment is right, but some aspects of the environment are hard to change and some politicians may be unwilling to change them. This environment also determines the distribution of the proceeds of growth. It is therefore largely in the social and political arenas where the scope for poverty reduction will be determined. It is important to complement the analysis of growth policy with the analysis of its distributional consequences. It has to be put on the political agenda in order to increase the chances of achieving rapid poverty reduction.

Notes

1. See Deininger and Squire (1998) for details on the construction of the income distribution datasets.
2. The solid points represent a linear regression fit.
3. The elasticity estimates may be affected by variations in the sources of underlying variables. Some use distribution data from household surveys and growth data from national accounts, e.g. Ballad, 2002; Karshenas, 2001; Sala-i-Martin, 2002.
4. Let the income share of the poor at time t and $t-1$ respectively be φ_t and φ_{t-1}. Then growth is pro-poor if $\varphi_t/\varphi_{t-1} > 1$. If the LHS is less than 1 growth is said to be anti-poor. Or, in other words, this is a requirement that the rate of growth in the share of the income of the poor be greater than zero:

$$\frac{\varphi_t - \varphi_{t-1}}{\varphi_{t-1}} > 0.$$

5. According to White and Anderson (2000), the median income share of the bottom 20 and 40 per cent is 5.6 per cent and 16.7 per cent, respectively.

6. Watt's index can be written as:

$$W_t = \int_0^h (\ln z - \ln y_t)\, dp$$

where z is the poverty line, y income and h the number of poor.
7. Kakwani, Khandker and Son (2003) suggest a measure of pro-poor growth which is a generalization of the Ravallion and Chen measure and can be applied to well-known measures of poverty.
8. Bourguignon (2002: fig. 3) uses G on the vertical axis and z/μ on the horizontal axis to depict an iso-poverty curve which is downward sloping for a given poverty line. His main concern is to address the heterogeneity often reported in the elasticity of poverty with respect to economic growth.
9. These axioms mainly are axioms of focus, monotonicity, transfer, subgroup consistency and decomposability. See Hagenaars (1987) for an interesting in-depth discussion of the properties of poverty indices.
10. If one follows the common practice in the empirical literature (e.g. Besely and Burgess, 2002; Fosu, 2002; Ali, 1996), where log of poverty is regressed over log of income inequality and per capita income, to obtain elasticity values one can think of a Cobb-Douglas specification for the poverty function and determine the shape of the poverty function on the basis of the elasticity values.
11. The POVCAL program by Ravallion, Chen and Datt of the World Bank has been used. This program returns no results (or run-time error) if the poverty line, compared to the mean, is set either too low or too high.
12. See World Bank (2002) for the per capita growth figures. In addition, the Ministry of Economic Development and Finance (2002) believes that Ethiopia would achieve a 3 per cent per capita growth easily in the coming decades.

REFERENCES

Ali, A. G. A. (1996) "Dealing with Poverty and Income Distribution Issues in Developing Countries: Cross Regional Experiences", paper presented at the Bi-annual Workshop of the African Economic Research Consortium. Nairobi, unpublished.

Ali, A. G. A. and E. Elbadawi (1999) "Inequality and the Dynamics of Poverty and Growth", CID Working Papers Series No. 32, Harvard University, Cambridge, Mass.

Appleton, S. (2001) "Education, Incomes and Poverty in Uganda in the 1990s", Research Paper 01/22, Centre for Research in Economic Development and Trade, University of Nottingham, Nottingham.

Ashan, S. M. and J. Oberi (2002) "Inequality, Well-being and Institutions in Latin America and the Caribbean", Working Paper No. 846, CESifo, Munich.

Ballad, S. (2002) "Imagine There Is No Country: Poverty, Inequality and Growth in the Era of Globalization", Institute for International Economics, Washington, D.C.

Besely, T. and R. Burgess (2002) "Halving Global Poverty", Department of Economics, London School of Economics, mimeo.

Bigsten, A. (1980) *Regional Inequality and Development: The Case of Kenya*, Farnborough: Gower.
Bigsten, A., B. Kebede, A. Shimeles and M. Taddesse (2003) "Growth and Poverty Reduction in Ethiopia: Evidence from Household Surveys", *World Development* 31(1): 87–107.
Bourguignon, F. (2002) "The Growth Elasticity of Poverty Reduction: Explaining Heterogeneity across Countries and Time Periods", in T. Eichler and S. Turnovsky, eds, *Growth and Inequality*, Cambridge, Mass.: MIT Press.
Chen, S. and M. Ravallion (2004) "How Have the World's Poorest Fared since the Early 1980s?", *World Bank Research Observer* 19(2): 141–169.
Chenery, H. B., M. Ahluwalia, C. Bell, J. Duloy and R. Jolly (1974) *Redistribution with Growth: Policies to Improve Income Distribution in Developing Countries in the Context of Economic Growth*, Oxford: Oxford University Press.
Christiaensen, L., L. Demery and S. Paternostro (2002) "Growth, Distribution and Poverty in Africa. Messages from the 1990s", Working Paper, World Bank, Washington, D.C.
Collier, P. and D. Dollar (2000) "Can the World Cut Poverty by Half?", World Bank, mimeo.
Datt, G. and M. Ravallion (1992) "Growth and Redistribution Components of Changes in Poverty Measures: Decomposition with Applications to Brazil and India in the 1980s", *Journal of Development Economics* 38: 275–295.
Deaton, A. (2003) "How to Monitor Poverty for the Millennium Development Goals", Princeton University, mimeo.
Deininger, K. and L. Squire (1996) "A New Data Set Measuring Income Inequality", *World Bank Economic Review* 10: 565–591.
—— (1998) "New Ways of Looking at Old Issues: Inequality and Growth", *Journal of Development Economics* 57: 259–287.
Demery, L. and L. Squire (1996) "Macroeconomic Adjustment and Poverty in Africa: An Emerging Trend", *World Bank Research Observer* 11(1): 24–39.
Dollar, D. and A. Kraay (2000) "Growth Is Good for the Poor", World Bank, draft; reproduced in A. Shorrocks and R. van der Hoeven, eds (2004) *Growth, Inequality, and Poverty: Prospects for Pro-poor Economic Development*, Oxford: Oxford University Press for UNU-WIDER.
Easterly, W. (2000) "The Effect of International Monetary Fund and World Bank Programs on Poverty", Working Paper Series 2517, World Bank, Washington, D.C.
Easterly, W. and R. Levine (1997) "Africa's Growth Tragedy: Politics and Ethnic Divisions", *Quarterly Journal of Economics* 112: 1230–1250.
Eastwood, R. and M. Lipton (2001) "Pro-poor Growth and Pro-growth Poverty", Asia and Pacific Forum on Poverty, mimeo.
ECA (2003) *Africa Economic Report*, UN Economic Commission for Africa, draft.
Fields, G. (1998) "Poverty, Inequality and Economic Well-being: African Economic Growth in Comparative Perspective", paper presented to the African Research Consortium, Nairobi, unpublished.
Fosu, A. (2002) "Inequality and the Growth-Poverty Nexus: Evidence from Sub-

Saharan Africa", paper presented at the CSAE Conference on Understanding Poverty and Growth in SSA, Oxford, unpublished.

Geda, A., A. Shimeles and J. Weeks (2002) "Prospect for Pro-poor Growth Strategies in Ethiopia", Ministry of Economic Development and Finance of Ethiopia, mimeo.

Hagenaars, A. (1987) "A Class of Poverty Indices", *International Economic Review* 28(3): 583–607.

Kakwani, N. (1991) "Poverty and Economic Growth, with an Application to Côte d'Ivoire", *Review of Income and Wealth* 39: 121–139.

Kakwani, N. and E. M. Pernia (2000) "What Is Pro-poor Growth?", *Asian Development Review* 18(1): 1–16.

Kakwani, N., S. Khandker and H. H. Son (2003) "Poverty-equivalent Growth Rate: With Application to Korea and Thailand", World Bank, mimeo.

Karshenas, M. (2001) "Global Poverty: New National Accounts Consistent and Internationally Comparable Poverty Estimates", Working Paper, Department of Economics, SOAS, University of London.

Lustig, N., O. Arias and J. Rigolini (2002) "Poverty Reduction and Economic Growth: A Two-way Causality", Sustainable Development Department Technical Paper Series No. POV-111, Inter-American Development Bank, Washington, D.C.

Ministry of Economic Development and Finance (2002) *Ethiopia: Sustainable Development and Poverty Reduction Programmes*, Addis Ababa: MEDF.

Ravallion, M. (1992) "Poverty: A Guide to Concepts and Methods", LSMS Working Paper 88, World Bank, Washington, D.C.

Ravallion, M. and S. Chen (1997) "What Can New Survey Data Tell Us about Recent Changes in Distribution and Poverty?", *World Bank Economic Review* 11(2): 357–382.

—— (2000) "How Did the World's Poorest Fare in the 1990s?", Working Paper, World Bank, Washington, D.C.

Sala-i-Martin, X. (2002) "The Disturbing 'Rise' of Global Income Inequality", Working Paper No. 8904, National Bureau of Economic Research, Cambridge, Mass.

Stern, N. (2003) "Growth and Poverty Reduction", *CESifo Economic Studies* 49(1): 5–25.

White, H. and E. Anderson (2000) "Growth vs Redistribution: Does the Pattern of Growth Matter?", Institute of Development Studies, University of Sussex, mimeo.

World Bank (1990) *World Development Report*, New York: Oxford University Press.

—— (2000) *World Development Report 2000/2001: Attacking Poverty*, Washington, D.C.: World Bank.

—— (2002) *World Bank Africa Database 2002*, Washington, D.C.: World Bank.

Index

Adjustment programmes
  social impacts 58
Africa. *see also* Cote d'Ivoire; Ethiopia
  income distribution and poverty,
    trends 354–356
    average annual growth and national
      and quintile per capita income 356
    average annual percentage change of
      quintile income shares and Gini
      coefficient, table 355
    per capita income and Gini coefficient,
      table 355
  prospects for pro-poor growth in
    353–376
    challenges of pro-poor growth
      strategies 369–372
    distribution of proceeds of growth 369
    equity-growth trade-off 361–369
      equity-growth trade-off, table 363
      growth scenarios 365
      high-inequality high-income
        countries 364–365
      income distribution change 361
      iso-poverty curves 362
      low-income countries 365
      per capita income-inequality trade-
        off, table 362
      simulation of impact of growth in
        Ethiopia, table 366
      simulation of pattern of growth in
        Mozambique, table 367
      simulation of pattern of growth in
        South Africa, table 367
      simulation of pattern of growth in
        Uganda, table 367
    growing interest in 353–354
    human development 371
    increasing growth 369
    land distribution 370
    market imperfections 370–371
    measures of pro-poor growth 356–361
      ambiguity in Kakwani-Pernia
        measure, table 361
      empirical implications of choice of
        indices 358–360
      incremental income shares 357
      poverty elasticities 358
      pro-poor growth measure,
        table 359–360
    median values of Gini coefficient by
      region, table 354
    risks 371
    sector focus of development 370
    social unrest 371–372
Agency
  definition 106
  incorporating in development
    indicators 108–111

Agency (cont.)
  inequality, and 106–108
  language of 112
Aggregation
  measuring poverty, and 28–29
    capability approach 33–34
    monetary approach 28–29
Alcohol consumption
  Russian life expectancy, and 271–272
Allardt's "Dimensions of Welfare" 87
Appreciation of life 78
  measures of 93–94
    contents 93–94
    limitations 94
  ordering concepts, and 81–82

Basic needs approach 121
Benchmarking
  sustainable development. see Sustainable development
Brock's classification 83

Capability approach 119–138
  advancement of humanity, and 119
  freedom, emphasis on 119–120
  fuzzy-set approach. see Fuzzy-set theory
  inequality, and. see Inequality
  measuring poverty. see Poverty
  well-being and human development and 120–122
    basic needs approach 121
    concept of utility 120–121
    criticisms 121
    UNDP human development index 121–122
Cardiovascular disease
  life expectancy in Russia, and 271
Composite indicators
  commonly used, table 67
Composite measures
  well-being, of. see Human well-being
Cote d'Ivoire
  education in 300–302
    current programmes 301–302
    education level 300–301
    education system 300
    enrolment ratios 300–301
    enrolment ratios, table 301
    illiteracy rates, table 301
    policy 300

effects of education on poverty,
  study 298–325
dynamic microsimulation study
  298–325
effect of expansion 321–322
illiteracy rate and average years of
  schooling, table 315
link between 298
model structure 302–312
  activity choice and labour income
    model, table 309–310
  agricultural profit function, table 311
  enrolment rations 1998, table 306
  key characteristics 302–303
  modelling of occupational choices
    and earnings 306–311
  modelling of schooling
    decisions 303–306
  probit estimations of probability of
    being enrolled, table 304–305
  transmission channels 311–312
policy experiments 312–315
positive effects of education 299
results 315–321
  average years of schooling by birth
    cohort, table 316
  evolution of level and distribution of
    education 315–316
  impact on growth and distribution of
    income 316–319
  income, inequality and poverty,
    table 318
  indirect effects 319–321
  level and inequality of household
    income, table 319
  relative changes of mean household
    income, table 320
sub-Saharan Africa, in 299
summary of policy experiments,
  table 313
Cummins's Comprehensive Quality of Life
  Scale 86

Development indicators
  incorporating agency and inequalities
    in 108–111
Domains of life
  subjective well-being, and. see Subjective
    well-being
Duration analysis
  poverty, of 328–329

Dynamic microsimulation
  Cote d'Ivoire study. *see* Cote d'Ivoire

Ecological footprint (1996-1998) 149
Economic well-being 54–73
  measures of well-being 61–64
    commonly used economic measures,
      table 61
    commonly used indicators 61
    differential experiences 62–63
    disadvantages of 62
    dominance of 62
    GDP per capita 62
    headcount ratios 63
    income poverty lines 63
    purchasing power parity (PPP) 63
  non-economic measures 64–67
  perception of 194
    subjective well-being, and 194
Education
  effect on poverty, study. *see* Cote d'Ivoire
Empowerment indicators
  measures of well-being 65
Environment
  liveability of 77
    aspects of 79
    contents 89–90
    limitations 90–91
    measures of 89–91
Environmental sustainability index
    (2002) 148–149
Ethiopia
  dynamics of poverty in 326–352
    approaches to analysis of 328–331
      duration analysis 328–329
      measuring vulnerability 329–331
    chronic poverty, determinants of 346
    chronic and transient poverty,
      distinction 327
    data for study 331–333
    definition of variables, table 332
    descriptive statistics for selected
      variables, rural households,
      table 334
    descriptive statistics for selected
      variables, urban households,
      table 334
    determinants of vulnerability, rural,
      table 346
    determinants of vulnerability, urban,
      table 347

duration analysis 337–344
exit and re-entry hazard ratios,
  table 338
geographic dimension 335
literature on 326–327
logit estimate for determinants of
  chronic poverty, table 350
marginal effects for probability of
  entering poverty, urban
  households, table 344
marginal effects for probability of
  exiting poverty, rural households,
  table 342
marginal effects of probability of
  exiting poverty for urban
  households, table 344
marginal effects for probability
  of re-entering poverty,
  rural households, table
  343
marginal effects of probability of
  re-entry into poverty for urban
  households, table 345
measures of vulnerability, table 348
odds ratios for probability of entering
  poverty, rural households,
  table 339
odds ratios for probability of exiting
  poverty, rural households,
  table 338
odds ratios of entering poverty, urban
  households, table 341
odds ratios of exiting poverty, urban
  households, table 340
percentage of households by poverty
  status, table 333
percentage of rural households based
  on income, table 335
percentage of urban households based
  on income, table 336
persistence of poverty 331–347
transition probabilities 336–337
transition probabilities by expenditure
  decile for rural households,
  table 337
transition probabilities by expenditure
  decile for urban households,
  table 337
transition probabilities by poverty
  status, table 336
type of poverty 326

Ethiopia (cont.)
  vulnerability 327
    its determinants, and 344–345
  vulnerability by inter-temporal
    consumption expenditure decile,
    table 348
  vulnerability and chronic poverty,
    rural, table 349
  vulnerability and chronic poverty,
    urban, table 349
  simulation of impact of growth in,
    table 366

Fuzzy-set theory 122–135
  computation of well-being
    subindices 127–134
  composite index and country ranking,
    table 130
  degrees of membership, table 132–133
  freedom dimensions 131
  genuine progress index 127
  information and communication
    technology index 131
  inter-country ranking 134
  UNDP and fuzzy-set-based indices,
    table 128–129
  HDI computation, for 122–127
    application to economic issues 123
    degrees of membership 124
    education, and 125
    "freedom to choose" 123
    fuzzy membership function 124
    macroeconomic data 123
    parameters for computing degrees of
      membership, table 126
    ranking of countries 125
    "social indicator" 122–123

GDP per capita
  poverty indicators 62
Gender empowerment measure (GEM) 67,
  169–170. see also Gender inequality
  agency and equality, and 109
Gender inequality 103, 169–181
  adjusting well-being indices for 169–181
  coefficients of statistical association
    between PPP GDP, HDI, GDI
    and GEM, table 179
  coefficients of statistical association
    between PPP GDP, HDI and
    GDI, table 176

coefficients of statistical association
  between PPP GDP, HDI and
  GEM, table 178
coefficients of statistical association
  between PPP GDP and HDI,
  table 175
data 174–175
gender-related development index
  169
results 175–177
social indicators 169
statistical methods 174–175
GDI and GEM 170–174
  GDI, definition 172–173
  GEM, definition 173
  HDI, design 170–171
Genuine progress index 127

Happiness 96
  significance 97–98
Headcount ratios 63
Hierarchical needs 217–238
  four levels 218
  fulfilment of hierarchical needs
    index 223–236
    aggregation 225–226
    analysis 226–236
      comparison of FHNI, table 226
      comparison of GDP per capita,
        table 227
      comparison of HDI, table 229
      data, table 230–235
      FHNI and GDP per capita 227–228
      FHNI and HDI 228–236
    operationalizing 223–226
    weights 223–224
  fulfilment of 220–223
    choice of indicators 222
    hindrances constructed by society 221
    limitations of indicators 223
    literature on 222
    well-being outcomes and indicators,
      table 221
  Maslow's hierarchical framework
    218–220
    basic needs 219
    belonging needs 220
    concept of hierarchy 220
    human motivation, and 219
    improving life outcomes 219
    safety needs 219–220

self-esteem needs 220
measures of well-being 217
satisfaction of 218
Human development index
fulfilment of hierarchical needs index, and 228–236
international inequality, and. see International inequality
UNDP's 88
Human Development Report (2001) 146–148
Human rights
measurement of poverty, and 59–60
Human well-being
adjusting indices for gender disparity. see Gender inequality
assessing using hierarchical needs. see Hierarchical needs
composite measures of 67–68
gender empowerment measure 67
QOL indicators 67
conceptualization of 3–4
defining 3
economic measures of. see Economic well-being
fuzzy-set based indices. see Fuzzy-set theory
gender, and 5
income as measure of 4
inequality, and, 102–106. see also Inequality
meaning and measurement of 56–61
adjustment programmes 58
basic freedoms 58–59
choosing indicators 69
data availability 68–69
"development" 57
economic growth 57
enlarging people's choices 58
evolution of indicators 60–61
evolution of, table 56
human rights, and 59–60
objective and subjective measures 59
PPAs 60
non-economic measures of 64–67
advantages of 65
commonly used composite indicators, table 67
empowerment indicators 65
limitations 65
most commonly used, table 64

nature of characteristics 66
participation indicators 65
subjective 4–5. see also Subjective well-being
sustainability measures, and 5
well-being indicators 55–56

Income
measures of human-well being 4
subjective well-being, and 189–190
Income poverty lines 63
Index of sustainable development 139–140
India
literacy levels 46
measuring poverty in 45
Inequality 101–116
agency, and 106–108
adapting attitudes 108
agency, definition 106
agent and patient contrasted 107
decision-making 107
women's roles 108
assessing at regional level. see Spatial microsimulation
capabilities approach, and 101–102
analysing inequalities 101
development indicators 108–111
degree of functioning 111
gender empowerment measure (GEM) 109
incorporating agency and inequalities in 108–111
individual assessments 111
normative assumptions 110
socio-economic position 110–111
international. see International inequality
well-being, and 102–106
assessments 103
"being able to appear in public without shame" 105
frame of reference 102
gender-based 103
"having adequate income" 104–105
individual based measures 103–104
individual versus societal 102–103
mental states 106
relational factors 104
socio-economic distribution 104
Information and communication technology index 131

International inequality 207–216
  concept and measures 208–210
    indices 208
    ordering principle 209
    types of income inequality 208
  human development, in 207–216
    correlations between HDI and component variables, table 214
    data 210–214
    estimates of 207–208
    human development index 207
    international inequality in human development dimensions, table 211, 213
    limitations 210
    per capita GDP results 212
    results 210–214
    variables 210

Life chances
  two kinds of 77
Life expectancy
  Russia, in. *see* Russia
Life results
  two kinds of 78
Life-ability of person 77–78
  kinds of 79–80
  measures of 91–92
    contents 91
    limitations 92
Lifetime poverty 24

McCall's classification 83
Maslow's hierarchical framework 218–220
Material needs' satisfaction
  perception of 194–195
    subjective well-being, and 194–195
Medical quality-of-life index 85–86
Meta-index
  sustainable development, of. *see* Sustainable development
Monetary approach
  measuring poverty 24–29. *see also* Poverty
    monetary poverty line 26–27
Multidimensionality
  defining poverty 23
  social exclusion 36

Nations
  measure of quality in 88–89

Normative assumptions
  inequality, and 110

Ordering concepts 79–84
  difference with other classifications 82–84
    Brock's classification, fit with, table 83
    McCall's classification, fit with, table 83
  meanings within quality quadrants 79–82
    appreciation of life 81–82
    aspects of liveability 79
    criteria for utility of life 80–81
    kinds of life-ability 79–80

Participation indicators
  measures of well-being 65
Participatory poverty assessments (PPAs) 38–40, 60
Participatory rural appraisal (PRAs) 38
Perceptions
  subjective well-being, and. *see* Subjective well-being
Performance indices 139–140
Poverty 19–53
  approaches to measuring 24–40
    causes of deprivation, and 48
    comparative overview 40–44
    comparison of four approaches, table 42–43
    "construction" 48
    targeting and policy 48–49
  assessing at regional level. *see* Spatial microsimulation
  capability approach 30–35
    aggregation 33–34
    commodities 31
    defining basic capabilities 31–32
    functionings 30
    measurement of capabilities 32–33
    monetary resources, and 30
    operational issues 31
    poverty line 33
    realization of human potential 30
    rejection of utilitarianism 30
    "valued" life 30
  characteristics of 55–56
  chronic and transient, distinction 327
  dynamics of in Ethiopia. *see* Ethiopia
  effect of education on. *see* Cote d'Ivoire

elimination of 19
empirical evidence on approaches to measuring 44–47
　estimating social exclusion 47
　lack of overlaps between monetary and CA poverty, table 46
　monetary and capability poverty compared, table 45
meaning and measurement of 56–61
monetary approach 24–29
　aggregation issues 28–29
　individuals versus households 27–28
　meaning 24
　minimum-rights approach 25
　monetary poverty line 26–27
　utility-maximising behaviour assumption 24–25
　validity of 25
　value judgments 29
　welfare indicator 25–26
participatory poverty assessments (PPAs) 38–40
　challenges in operationalizing 39–40
　methods 38–39
　tools 38–39
　types of 38
perception 193–194
　subjective well-being, and 193–194
policy formulation 19–20
problems defining and measuring 20–24
　absolute needs 22
　lifetime poverty 24
　multidimensionality 23
　objective or subjective, whether 21
　poverty lines 21
　spheres of concerns 20
　threshold between poor and non-poor 22
　time horizon 23–24
　unit 22–23
　universiality of definition 21
social exclusion 35–38
　application 36–37
　concept of 35
　definition 35
　dynamic focus 35–36
　main characteristics 35
　multidimensionality 36
　socially defined 36
subjective well-being, and. *see* Subjective well-being

Preventable diseases
　Russian life expectancy, and 272
Pro-poor growth
　prospects for in Africa. *see* Africa
Psychological well-being scale 86–87
Public services
　access to 190–191
　　subjective-well being, and 190–191
Purchasing power parity (PPP) 63
Purpose of life
　subjective well-being, and. *see* Subjective well-being

Qualities of life 74–100
　appreciation of life, measures of 93–94
　　contents 93–94
　　limitations 94
　connotation of inclusiveness 74
　elusive utilities 97
　four qualities of life 77–78
　　appreciation of life 78
　　life-ability of person 77–78
　　liveability of environment 77
　　table 77
　　two kinds of life chances 77
　　two kinds of life results 78
　　utility of life 78
　grouping 75–78
　　chances and outcomes 76
　　fourfold classification of welfare concepts 75
　　objective and subjective distinction 75
　　outer and inner qualities 76–77
　happiness 74
　inclusive measures of 94–96
　　cross-quadrant sum scores 95
　　happiness 96
　　inclusive measures, table 94
　life-ability, measures of 91–92
　　contents 91
　　limitations 92
　liveability, measures of 89–91
　　contents 89–90
　　limitations 90–91
　meanings in measures of 84–89
　　Allardt's "Dimensions of Welfare" 87
　　Cummins's Comprehensive Quality of Life Scale, table 86
　　measure of quality in nations 88–89
　　medical quality-of-life index 85–86

Qualities of life (cont.)
  psychological well-being scale 86–87
  sociological measure of individual quality of life 87–88
  UNDP's human development index 88
  Ware's SF-36 Health Survey, table 85
  measures for specific 89–94
  ordering concepts. *see* Ordering concepts
  ordering measures 84–94
  significance of happiness 97–98
  terms, meanings 74
  utility of life, measures for 92–93
  welfare 74
Quality of life (QOL) indicators 67

Russia 265–297
  geographical patterns of life expectancy 267–272
    alcohol consumption 271–272
    cardiovascular disease 271
    life expectancy in Russia's regions 1998, map 269
    life expectancy in Russia's regions 2000, map 270
    magnitude of variations 268
    noticeable improvements in 268
    per capita income 271
    poverty, and 271
    preventable diseases 272
    regional trends 268
    shortcomings in studies of 272
    variations over time 267–272
  life expectancy at birth in selected regions, table 267
  life expectancy at birth, table 266
  mortality crisis, causes 265
    research on 265
  study of life expectancy
    Arellano and Bond GMM estimator 280
    coefficient on poverty 290
    data 275–280
    disposable resources poverty, map 279
    empirical specification 274–275
    estimates from life expectancy equation, table 282
    estimates from life expectancy equation (treating explanatory variables as predetermined), table 289
    estimates from life expectancy equation (with interaction term), table 283
    estimates from life expectancy equation (with time trend and alternative dependent variable), table 287
    estimates from life expectancy equation (with time trend), table 285
    estimation results 280–286
    estimation technique 274–275
    impact of public health spending 290–291
    long-run effects 291
    model 272–275
    money income poverty, map 278
    public health spending per capita, map 281
    regression equation 284
    robustness of results 286–290
    summary statistics of life expectancy data, table 282
    summary statistics of poverty data, table 276
    summary statistics of public health spending data, table 280
    theoretical grounds 272–274
    time trend 284

Sen, Amartya, 119–138. *see also* Capability approach
Social exclusion. *see also* Poverty
  problems in estimating 47
Socio-economic position
  subjective well-being, and 190
Sociological measure
  individual quality of life, of 87–88
Spatial microsimulation 239–261
  impact of policy option 245–250
    Australian income support 245
    estimated number in poverty and poverty rate, table 247
    estimated poverty rates by postcode, map 248–249
    poverty line 246
  methodology 240–245
    addition of microsimulation 244–245
    existing data 240
    limitations of existing data 241
    microdata 240–241

spatial microsimulation, and 242–243
SYNAGI reweighting approach
    243–244
synthetic microdata 241–242
NATSEM 258
spatial impact of policy option 250–258
    characteristics of residents of poor
        households, table 256–257
    estimated change in poverty by
        postcode, map 252–253
    estimated number of people in poverty
        by postcode, map 254–255
    mapping results 250–251
    results for individual postcodes
        251–258
Subindices
    human-well being. *see* Fuzzy set theory
Subjective well-being (SWB) 182–206
    domains of life, and 195–198
        correlation coefficients, table 197
        life domains and SWB 196–197
        satisfaction in 196
        satisfaction in, table 196
        socio-economic indicators, and
            197–198
        socio-economic indicators and domain
            satisfaction regression coefficient,
            table 197
        taxonomy 195–196
    domains-of-life literature 183
    life purposes 183
    literature on 183–186
        approach, on the 183–185
        inferential approach 184
        inherently 185
        transdisciplinary approach 185
        well-being of a person 184
    measurement of 185–186
        main findings in literature 185–186
    perceptions, and 183, 192–195
        personal expenditure, and 193–195
        economic well-being 194
        material needs' satisfaction
            194–195
        poverty perception, and 193
    personal expenditure and economic
        well-being, table 194
    personal expenditure and poverty
        perception, table 193
    personal expenditure and satisfaction
        of material needs, table 194

socio-economic indicators, and 195
purpose of life, and 198–200
    conceptual referent for happiness
        sample distribution, table 199
    conceptual referent theory study
        198–200
    socio-economic indicators, and 200
    subjective well-being by conceptual
        referent for happiness, table 200
    SWb by conceptual referent 200
socio-economic indicators, and 189–192
    access to public services 190–191
    correlation analysis 191–192
    correlation matrix, table 191
    income 189–190
    regression analysis 192
    regression analysis, table 192
    socio-economic position 190
    subjective well-being and access to
        public services, table 191
    subjective well-being and socio-
        economic position, table 190
survey of 186–192
    database 186–187
    poverty and 187–188
    sample distribution across national
        deciles of income, table 188
    sample inference 187–188
    subjective well-being distribution,
        table 188
    subjective well-being and household
        income, table 189
    subjective well-being in 188–189
Sustainable development
    benchmarking 139–168
        application 139–140
        benchmarking, meaning 139
        index of sustainable development
            139–140
        operational indicators, choice of 140
        performance indices 139–140
        standard indicators 140
    definition 163–164
    index of, survey of existing 145–149
        ecological footprint (1996-1998) 149
        environmental sustainability index
            (2002) 148–149
        Human Development Report
            (2001) 146–148
        summary of, table 147
        well-being of nations (2001) 148

Sustainable development (cont.)
World Health report (2001) 149
meta-index of 140–145
benefit-of-doubt weighting 142
bound specifications 151
challenge in constructing 141
cluster-level analysis 156–157
correlation analysis 161–163
country rankings 151–156
cross-section of 141–142
cumulative distribution functions, graph 160
developed versus developing countries, table 157
discriminatory power 159–161
empirical results 150–159
extreme scenarios 144
methodological restrictions 144–145
MISD ranking, lower-middle-income countries, table 154
MISD ranking, upper-middle-income countries, table 153
MISD rankings, high income countries, table 152
MISD rankings, low-income countries, table 155
MISD-ISD correlation matrix, table 162
model specification 150–151
objective function 142–143
a priori restrictions 143–144
summary statistics, table 156, 160
summary statistics of weights, table 159
supplementary weight bounds 144
weight bounds motivations 145
weights 157–158

UNDP
human development index 88
capability approach, and 121–122
fuzzy-set approach. *see* Fuzzy-set theory
Utilitarianism
rejection of 30
measure of poverty, as 30
Utility of life 78
criteria for 80–81
measures for 92–93

Vulnerability
poverty, to, measuring 329–331

Ware's SF-36 Health Survey 85
Welfare concepts
fourfold classification of 75
Welfare indicator
measuring poverty, and 25–26
Well-being of nations (2001) 148
World Health Report (2001) 149